Scaling Networks v6
Labs & Study Guide

Allan Johnson

Cisco Press

800 East 96th Street

Indianapolis, Indiana 46240 USA

Scaling Networks v6, Labs & Study Guide

Allan Johnson

Copyright© 2018 Cisco Systems, Inc.

Cisco Press logo is a trademark of Cisco Systems, Inc.

Published by:
Cisco Press
800 East 96th Street
Indianapolis, IN 46240 USA

Printed in the United States of America

1   17

Library of Congress Control Number: 2017937630

ISBN-13 978-158713-433-3
ISBN-10: 1-58713-433-0

Editor-In-Chief
Mark Taub

Product Line Manager
Brett Bartow

Business Operation Manager, Cisco Press
Ronald Fligge

Executive Editor
Mary Beth Ray

Production Manager
Sandra Schroeder

Development Editor
Ellie Bru

Project Editor
Mandie Frank

Copy Editor
Geneil Breeze

Technical Editor
Tony Chen

Editorial Assistant
Vanessa Evans

Designer
Chuti Prasertsith

Composition
Tricia Bronkella

Proofreader
Debbie Williams

This book is part of the Cisco Networking Academy® series from Cisco Press. The products in this series support and complement the Cisco Networking Academy curriculum. If you are using this book outside the Networking Academy, then you are not preparing with a Cisco trained and authorized Networking Academy provider.

For more information on the Cisco Networking Academy or to locate a Networking Academy, please visit www.cisco.com/edu.

ılıılı
CISCO.

Warning and Disclaimer

This book is designed to provide information about networking. Every effort has been made to make this book as complete and as accurate as possible, but no warranty or fitness is implied.

The information is provided on an "as is" basis. The authors, Cisco Press, and Cisco Systems, Inc., shall have neither liability nor responsibility to any person or entity with respect to any loss or damages arising from the information contained in this book or from the use of the discs or programs that may accompany it.

The opinions expressed in this book belong to the author and are not necessarily those of Cisco Systems, Inc.

Trademark Acknowledgments

All terms mentioned in this book that are known to be trademarks or service marks have been appropriately capitalized. Cisco Press or Cisco Systems, Inc., cannot attest to the accuracy of this information. Use of a term in this book should not be regarded as affecting the validity of any trademark or service mark.

Special Sales

For information about buying this title in bulk quantities, or for special sales opportunities (which may include electronic versions; custom cover designs; and content particular to your business, training goals, marketing focus, or branding interests), please contact our corporate sales department at corpsales@pearsoned.com or (800) 382-3419.

For government sales inquiries, please contact governmentsales@pearsoned.com.

For questions about sales outside the U.S., please contact intlcs@pearson.com.

Feedback Information

At Cisco Press, our goal is to create in-depth technical books of the highest quality and value. Each book is crafted with care and precision, undergoing rigorous development that involves the unique expertise of members from the professional technical community.

Readers' feedback is a natural continuation of this process. If you have any comments regarding how we could improve the quality of this book, or otherwise alter it to better suit your needs, you can contact us through email at feedback@ciscopress.com. Please make sure to include the book title and ISBN in your message.

We greatly appreciate your assistance.

··|··|··
CISCO.

Americas Headquarters
Cisco Systems, Inc.
San Jose, CA

Asia Pacific Headquarters
Cisco Systems (USA) Pte. Ltd.
Singapore

Europe Headquarters
Cisco Systems International BV Amsterdam,
The Netherlands

Cisco has more than 200 offices worldwide. Addresses, phone numbers, and fax numbers are listed on the Cisco Website at **www.cisco.com/go/offices.**

Cisco and the Cisco logo are trademarks or registered trademarks of Cisco and/or its affiliates in the U.S. and other countries. To view a list of Cisco trademarks, go to this URL: www.cisco.com/go/trademarks. Third party trademarks mentioned are the property of their respective owners. The use of the word partner does not imply a partnership relationship between Cisco and any other company. (1110R)

About the Author

Allan Johnson entered the academic world in 1999 after 10 years as a business owner/operator to dedicate his efforts to his passion for teaching. He holds both an MBA and an M.Ed in occupational training and development. He taught a variety of technology courses to high school students and is an adjunct instructor at Del Mar College in Corpus Christi, Texas. Since 2006, Allan has worked full time for Cisco Networking Academy in several roles. He is currently engaged as Curriculum Lead.

About the Technical Reviewer

Tony Chen is a Cisco Certified Academy Instructor (CCAI) and has taught at College of DuPage at Glen Ellyn, Illinois, for more than 15 years. He holds CCNA certification for Routing and Switching. His other certifications include MCSA for Microsoft Server 2012 and CompTIA A+ and Server+. Tony has an understanding wife, Joanne, and two children, Kylie and Ryan.

Dedication

For my wife, Becky. What a year! I couldn't ask for a better partner in life.

Acknowledgments

The Cisco Network Academy authors for the online curriculum and series of Companion Guides take the reader deeper, past the CCENT and CCNA exam topics, with the ultimate goal of not only preparing the student for certification, but also for more advanced college-level technology courses and degrees. Thank you to the entire Curriculum and Assessment Engineering team.

Tony Chen, technical editor, did the arduous review work necessary to make sure that you get a book that is both technically accurate and unambiguous. I am grateful for his conscientious attention to detail.

Mary Beth Rey, executive editor, you amaze me with your ability to juggle multiple projects at once, steering each from beginning to end. I can always count on you to make the tough decisions.

Development editor Ellie Bru's dedication to perfection pays dividends in countless, unseen ways. Thank you again, Ellie, for providing me with much-needed guidance and support. This book could not be a reality without your persistence.

Contents at a Glance

Introduction   xxviii

Chapter 1   LAN Design   1

Chapter 2   Scaling VLANs   19

Chapter 3   STP   67

Chapter 4   EtherChannel and HSRP   111

Chapter 5   Dynamic Routing   161

Chapter 6   EIGRP   185

Chapter 7   EIGRP Tuning and Troubleshooting   233

Chapter 8   Single-Area OSPF   285

Chapter 9   Multiarea OSPF   345

Chapter 10   OSPF Tuning and Troubleshooting   379

Contents

Introduction   xxviii

Chapter 1   **LAN Design   1**

Study Guide   2

Campus Wired LAN Designs   2

Hierarchical Network Design   2

Identify Scalability Terminology   3

Selecting Network Devices   3

Selecting Switch Hardware   4

Selecting Router Hardware   4

Managing Devices   5

Basic Router Configuration Review   5

Basic Router Verification Review   6

Basic Switch Configuration Review   6

Basic Switch Verification Review   7

Packet Tracer Exercise 1-1: Basic Device Configuration   8

Labs and Activities   9

Command Reference   9

1.0.1.2 Class Activity–Network by Design   10

Objective   10

Scenario   10

Resources   10

Directions   10

1.2.1.7 Packet Tracer–Compare 2960 and 3560 Switches   11

Topology   11

Objective   11

Background   11

Part 1: Compare Layer 2 and Layer 3 Switches   11

Part 2: Compare a Layer 3 Switch and a Router   12

Suggested Scoring Rubric   13

1.3.1.1 Class Activity–Layered Network Design Simulation   14

Objectives   14

Scenario   14

Resources   14

Directions   14

1.3.1.3 Packet Tracer–Skills Integration Challenge   15

Topology   15

Addressing Table   15

VLANs and Port Assignments Table   16

Scenario   16

Documentation   16

Implementation   16

Verification   17

Troubleshooting Documentation   18

Suggested Scoring Rubric   18

Chapter 2   **Scaling VLANs   19**

Study Guide   20

VTP, Extended VLANs, and DTP   20

VTP Concepts and Operation   20

VTP Modes   20

VTP Advertisements   21

Default VTP Configuration   21

VTP Caveats   21

VTP Configuration   22

Packet Tracer Exercise 2-1: VTP Configuration   24

Extended VLANs   25

DTP   25

Troubleshoot Multi-VLAN Issues   26

Layer 3 Switching   28

Layer 3 Switching Operation   28

Layer 3 Switching Troubleshooting Scenarios   29

Labs and Activities   31

Command Reference   31

2.1.4.4 Packet Tracer–Configure VLANs, VTP, and DTP   32

Topology   32

Addressing Table   32

Objectives   32

Background/Scenario   32

Part 1: Configure and Verify DTP   33

Part 2: Configure and Verify VTP   34

2.1.4.5 Lab–Configure Extended VLANs, VTP, and DTP   39

Topology   39

Addressing Table   39

Objectives   39

Background/Scenario   39

Required Resources   40

Part 1: Configure VTP   40

Part 2: Configure DTP   41

Part 3: Add VLANs and Assign Ports   43

Part 4: Configure Extended VLAN   45

Reflection   47

Router Interface Summary Table   47

2.2.2.4 Packet Tracer–Troubleshooting Inter-VLAN Routing   48

Topology   48

Addressing Table   48

Objectives   48

Scenario   48

Part 1: Locate the Network Problems   48

Documentation Table   49

Part 2: Implement the Solutions   49

Part 3: Verify Network Connectivity   49

Suggested Scoring Rubric   49

2.2.2.5 Lab–Troubleshooting Inter-VLAN Routing   50

Topology   50

Addressing Table   50

Switch Port Assignment Specifications   51

Objectives   51

Background/Scenario   51

Required Resources   51

Part 1: Build the Network and Load Device Configurations   52

Part 2: Troubleshoot the Inter-VLAN Routing Configuration   54

Part 3: Verify VLAN Configuration, Port Assignment, and Trunking   54

Part 4: Test Layer 3 Connectivity   56

Reflection   57

Router Interface Summary Table   58

2.2.3.3 Packet Tracer–Troubleshoot VTP and DTP   59

Topology   59

Addressing Table   59

Objectives   59

Background/Scenario   59

Part 1: Troubleshoot DTP   60

Part 2: Troubleshoot VTP   60

2.3.1.5 Packet Tracer–Configure Layer 3 Switching and Inter-VLAN Routing   63

Topology   63

Addressing Table   63

Objectives   63

Background/Scenario   64

Part 1: Configure Layer 3 Switching   64

Part 2: Configure Inter-VLAN Routing   64

Chapter 3   **STP   67**

Study Guide   68

Spanning Tree Concepts   68

Draw a Redundant Topology   68

Purpose of Spanning Tree   68

Spanning Tree Operation   69

Identify the 802.1D Port Roles   71

Varieties of Spanning Tree Protocols   72

Comparing the STP Varieties   72

PVST+ Operation   74

Rapid PVST+ Operation   75

Spanning Tree Configuration   75

PVST+ and Rapid PVST+ Configuration   76

Packet Tracer Exercise 3-1: STP Configuration   78

Labs and Activities   79

Command Reference   79

3.0.1.2 Class Activity–Stormy Traffic   80

Objective   80

Scenario   80

Resources   80

Reflection   80

3.1.1.5 Packet Tracer–Examining a Redundant Design   82

Topology   82

Objectives   82

Background   82

Part 1: Check for STP Convergence   82

Part 2: Examine the ARP Process   83

Part 3: Test Redundancy in a Switched Network   83

Suggested Scoring Rubric   84

3.1.2.12 Lab–Building a Switched Network with Redundant Links   85

Topology   85

Addressing Table   85

Objectives   85

Background/Scenario   85

Required Resources   86

Part 1: Build the Network and Configure Basic Device Settings   86

Part 2: Determine the Root Bridge   86

Part 3: Observe STP Port Selection Based on Port Cost   89

Part 4: Observe STP Port Selection Based on Port Priority   91

Reflection   93

3.3.1.5 Packet Tracer–Configuring PVST+   94

Topology   94

Addressing Table   94

Switch Port Assignment Specifications   94

Objectives   94

Background   95

Part 1: Configure VLANs   95

Part 2: Configure Spanning Tree PVST+ and Load Balancing   95

Part 3: Configure PortFast and BPDU Guard   96

3.3.2.2 Packet Tracer–Configuring Rapid PVST+   97

Topology   97

Addressing Table   97

Switch Port Assignment Specifications   97

Objectives   97

Background   98

Part 1: Configure VLANs   98

Part 2: Configure Rapid Spanning Tree PVST+ Load Balancing   99

Part 3: Configure PortFast and BPDU Guard   99

3.3.2.3 Lab–Configuring Rapid PVST+, PortFast, and BPDU Guard   100

Topology   100

Addressing Table   100

VLAN Assignments   100

Objectives   100

Background/Scenario   101

Required Resources   101

Part 1: Build the Network and Configure Basic Device Settings   101

Part 2: Configure VLANs, Native VLAN, and Trunks   102

Part 3: Configure the Root Bridge and Examine PVST+ Convergence   103

Part 4: Configure Rapid PVST+, PortFast, BPDU Guard, and Examine Convergence   105

Reflection   107

Appendix A – Switch Configuration Commands   107

Switch S1   107

Switch S2   108

Switch S3   108

3.4.1.1 Class Activity–Documentation Tree   109

Objective   109

Scenario   109

Resources   109

Directions   109

Chapter 4   **EtherChannel and HSRP   111**

Study Guide   112

Link Aggregation Concepts   112

EtherChannel Advantages   112

EtherChannel Operation   112

Link Aggregation Configuration   113

Configuring EtherChannel   114

Verifying and Troubleshooting EtherChannel   115

First Hop Redundancy Protocols   119

Identify FHRP Terminology   119

Identify the Type of FHRP   120

Identify the HSRP Version   120

Determine the HSRP State   120

HSRP Implementation   121

HSRP Verification   122

HSRP Troubleshooting   122

Packet Tracer Exercise 4-1: EtherChannel and HSRP Configuration   123

Labs and Activities   124

Command Reference   124

4.0.1.2 Class Activity–Imagine This   125

Objective   125

Scenario   125

Required Resources   125

4.2.1.3 Packet Tracer–Configuring EtherChannel   126

Topology   126

Objectives   126

Background   126

Part 1: Configure Basic Switch Settings   126

Part 2: Configure an EtherChannel with Cisco PAgP   127

Part 3: Configure an 802.3ad LACP EtherChannel   127

Part 4: Configure a Redundant EtherChannel Link   128

4.2.1.4 Lab–Configuring EtherChannel   129

Topology   129

Addressing Table   129

Objectives   129

Background/Scenario   129

Required Resources   130

Part 1: Configure Basic Switch Settings   130

Part 2: Configure PAgP   131

Part 3: Configure LACP   134

Reflection   135

4.2.2.3 Packet Tracer–Troubleshooting EtherChannel   136

Topology   136

Objectives   136

Background   136

Part 1: Examine the Physical Layer and Correct Switch Port Mode
Issues   136

Part 2: Identify and Correct Port Channel Assignment Issues   137

Part 3: Identify and Correct Port Channel Protocol Issues   137

4.2.2.4 Lab–Troubleshooting EtherChannel   138

Topology   138

Addressing Table   138

VLAN Assignments   138

Objectives   138

Background/Scenario   139

Required Resources   139

Part 1: Build the Network and Load Device Configurations   139

Part 2: Troubleshoot EtherChannel   142

4.3.3.4 Lab–Configuring HSRP   145

Topology   145

Addressing Table   145

Objectives   146

Background/Scenario   146

Required Resources   146

Part 1: Build the Network and Verify Connectivity   146

Part 2: Configure First Hop Redundancy Using HSRP   148

Reflection   151

Router Interface Summary Table   151

4.3.4.4 Packet Tracer–Troubleshoot HSRP   152

Topology   152

Addressing Table   152

Objective   152

Background/Scenario   152

Troubleshooting Process   153

Running Scripts   154

PC0 and Laptop1   154

R1 Configuration   154

R2 Configuration   154

4.4.1.1 Class Activity–Linking Up   155

Objective   155

Scenario   155

Resources   155

Directions   155

4.4.1.2 Packet Tracer–Skills Integration Challenge   157

Topology   157

Addressing Table   157

Scenario   158

Requirements   158

Chapter 5   Dynamic Routing   161

Study Guide   162

Dynamic Routing Protocols   162

Dynamic Routing Protocols Classification Chart   162

Routing Protocols Characteristics   162

Comparing Routing Protocol Characteristics   163

Dynamic Routing Protocol Operation   163

Distance Vector Dynamic Routing   164

From Cold Start to Convergence   164

Distance Vector Operation and Terminology   166

Comparing RIP and EIGRP   167

Link-State Dynamic Routing   167

Link-State Routing Protocol Operation   168

Building the Link-State Database   170

Using Link-State Routing Protocols   174

Labs and Activities   175

Command Reference   175

5.0.1.2 Class Activity–How Much Does This Cost?   176

Objectives   176

Scenario   176

Activity 1   176

Activity 2   176

Required Resources   177

Scenario – Part 2 Recording Matrix   177

Reflection Questions   177

5.2.1.6 Packet Tracer–Investigating Convergence   179

Topology   179

Addressing Table   179

Objectives   179

Background   179

Part 1: View the Routing Table of a Converged Network   180

Part 2: Add a New LAN to the Topology   180

Part 3: Watch the Network Converge   181

Suggested Scoring Rubric   181

5.2.3.4 Packet Tracer–Comparing RIP and EIGRP Path Selection   182

Topology   182

Objectives   182

Scenario   182

Part 1: Predict the Path   182

Part 2: Trace the Route   183

Part 3: Reflection Questions   184

Suggested Scoring Rubric   184

Chapter 6   EIGRP   185

Study Guide   186

EIGRP Characteristics   186

Describe Basic EIGRP Features   186

Identify and Describe EIGRP Packet Types   186

Identify Elements of the EIGRP Message Formats   187

Configuring EIGRP for IPv4   190

Configuring EIGRP with IPv4   190

Verifying EIGRP with IPv4   193

EIGRP Operation   195

EIGRP Metric Concepts   195

DUAL Concepts Exercise   196

DUAL FSM Completion Exercise   199

Configuring EIGRP for IPv6   200

Comparing EIGRP for IPv4 and EIGRP for IPv6   200

Configuring and Verifying EIGRP for IPv6   200

Packet Tracer Exercise 6-1: Implement Dual Stack EIGRP   202

Labs and Activities   203

Command Reference   203

6.0.1.2 Class Activity–Classless EIGRP   204

Objectives   204

Scenario   204

Resources   204

Reflection   204

6.2.2.4 Packet Tracer–Configuring Basic EIGRP with IPv4   206

Topology   206

Addressing Table   206

Objectives   206

Background   206

Part 1: Configure EIGRP 207

Part 2: Verify EIGRP Routing 207

Suggested Scoring Rubric 208

6.2.2.5 Lab–Configuring Basic EIGRP for IPv4 209

Topology 209

Addressing Table 209

Objectives 210

Background/Scenario 210

Required Resources 210

Part 1: Build the Network and Verify Connectivity 210

Part 2: Configure EIGRP Routing 211

Part 3: Verify EIGRP Routing 211

Part 4: Configure Bandwidth and Passive Interfaces 213

Reflection 217

Router Interface Summary Table 217

6.3.4.4 Packet Tracer–Investigating DUAL FSM 218

Topology 218

Addressing Table 218

Objectives 218

Background 218

Part 1: Verify EIGRP Configuration 219

Part 2: Observe the EIGRP DUAL FSM 219

Suggested Scoring Rubric 220

6.4.3.4 Packet Tracer–Configuring Basic EIGRP with IPv6 221

Topology 221

Addressing Table 221

Objectives 221

Scenario 222

Part 1: Configure EIGRP for IPv6 Routing 222

Part 2: Verify EIGRP for IPv6 Routing 222

6.4.3.5 Lab–Configuring Basic EIGRP for IPv6 223

Topology 223

Addressing Table 223

Objectives 224

Background/Scenario 224

Required Resources 224

Part 1: Build the Network and Verify Connectivity 225

Part 2: Configure EIGRP for IPv6 Routing 225

Part 3: Verify EIGRP for IPv6 Routing 226

Part 4: Configure and Verify Passive Interfaces 228

Reflection   230

Router Interface Summary Table   230

6.5.1.1 Class Activity–Portfolio RIP and EIGRP   231

Objectives   231

Scenario   231

Resources   231

Directions   231

Reflection   232

Chapter 7   EIGRP Tuning and Troubleshooting   233

Study Guide   234

Advanced EIGRP Configurations   234

Automatic Summarization   234

Default Route Propagation   236

Fine-Tuning EIGRP Interfaces   239

Packet Tracer Exercise 7-1: Fine-Tuning EIGRP   241

Troubleshoot EIGRP   242

Commands for Troubleshooting EIGRP   242

Troubleshoot EIGRP Connectivity Issues   242

Labs and Activities   246

Command Reference   246

7.0.1.2 Class Activity–EIGRP–Back to the Future   247

Objectives   247

Scenario   247

Resources   247

7.1.2.4 Packet Tracer–Propagating a Default Route in EIGRP for IPv4 and IPv6   248

Topology   248

Addressing Table   248

Objectives   248

Scenario   249

Part 1: Propagate a Default Route in EIGRP for IPv4   249

Part 2: Propagate a Default Route in EIGRP for IPv6   249

Part 3: Verify Connectivity to Outside Hosts   249

7.1.3.6 Lab–Configuring Advanced EIGRP for IPv4 Features   250

Topology   250

Addressing Table   250

Objectives   251

Background/Scenario   251

Required Resources   252

Part 1: Build the Network and Configure Basic Device Settings   252

Part 2: Configure EIGRP and Verify Connectivity   252

Part 3: Configure EIGRP for Automatic Summarization   253

Part 4: Configure and Propagate a Default Static Route   254

Part 5: Fine-Tune EIGRP   255

Reflection   256

Router Interface Summary Table   257

Appendix A: Configuration Commands   257

Router R1   257

Router R2   258

Router R3   258

7.2.3.5 Packet Tracer–Troubleshooting EIGRP for IPv4   259

Topology   259

Addressing Table   259

Scenario   259

Troubleshooting Process   259

Documentation Table   260

7.2.3.6 Lab–Troubleshooting Basic EIGRP for IPv4 and IPv6   261

Topology   261

Addressing Table   261

Objectives   262

Background/Scenario   262

Required Resources   263

Part 1: Build the Network and Load Device Configurations   263

Part 2: Troubleshoot Layer 3 Connectivity   266

Part 3: Troubleshoot EIGRP for IPv4   268

Part 4: Troubleshoot EIGRP for IPv6   269

Reflection   271

Router Interface Summary Table   271

7.2.3.7 Lab–Troubleshooting Advanced EIGRP   272

Topology   272

Addressing Table   272

Objectives   273

Background/Scenario   273

Required Resources   273

Part 1: Build the Network and Load Device Configurations   274

Part 2: Troubleshoot EIGRP   277

Reflection   279

Router Interface Summary Table   279

7.3.1.1 Class Activity–Tuning EIGRP   280

Objectives   280

Scenario   280

Resources   280

Directions   280

7.3.1.2 Packet Tracer–Skills Integration Challenge   282

Topology   282

Addressing Table   282

Scenario   283

Requirements   283

Suggested Scoring Rubric   283

Chapter 8   Single-Area OSPF   285

Study Guide   286

Characteristics of OSPF   286

OSPF Terminology   286

OSPF Concepts   287

OSPF Operation   288

Configuring Single-Area OSPFv2   291

The Router ID   291

Single-Area OSPFv2 Basic Configuration Scenario   292

Adjusting OSPF Cost   295

Verify the OSPF Configuration   296

Configure Single-Area OSPFv3   297

Comparing OSPFv2 and OSPFv3   297

Configuring OSPFv3   298

Verifying OSPFv3   299

Packet Tracer Exercise 8-1: Implement Dual-Stacked OSPF   299

Labs and Activities   301

Command Reference   301

8.0.1.2 Class Activity–Can Submarines Swim?   302

Objectives   302

Scenario   302

Resources   302

Reflection   302

8.2.2.7 Packet Tracer–Configuring OSPFv2 in a Single Area   304

Topology   304

Addressing Table   304

Objectives   304

Background   304

Part 1: Configure OSPFv2 Routing   305

Part 2: Verify the Configurations   305

8.2.4.5 Lab–Configuring Basic Single-Area OSPFv2   306

Topology   306

Addressing Table   306

Objectives   306

Background/Scenario   307

Required Resources   307

Part 1: Build the Network and Configure Basic Device Settings   307

Part 2: Configure and Verify OSPF Routing   308

Part 3: Change Router ID Assignments   312

Part 4: Configure OSPF Passive Interfaces   314

Part 5: Change OSPF Metrics   318

Reflection   326

Router Interface Summary Table   327

8.3.3.5 Packet Tracer–Configuring Basic OSPFv3 in a Single Area   328

Topology   328

Addressing Table   328

Objectives   328

Background   329

Part 1: Configure OSPFv3 Routing   329

Part 2: Verify Connectivity   329

8.3.3.6 Lab–Configuring Basic Single-Area OSPFv3   330

Topology   330

Addressing Table   330

Objectives   331

Background/Scenario   331

Required Resources   331

Part 1: Build the Network and Configure Basic Device Settings   331

Part 2: Configure OSPFv3 Routing   332

Part 3: Configure OSPFv3 Passive Interfaces   336

Reflection   339

Router Interface Summary Table   339

8.4.1.1 Class Activity–Stepping Through OSPFv3   340

Objectives   340

Scenario   340

Resources   340

Directions   340

Reflection   341

8.4.1.2 Packet Tracer–Skills Integration Challenge   342

Topology   342

Addressing Table   342

Background   342

Requirements   343

Chapter 9   Multiarea OSPF   345

Study Guide   346

Multiarea OSPF Operation   346

Multiarea OSPF Terminology and Concepts   346

Multiarea OSPF LSA Operation   347

OSPF Routing Table and Types of Routes   348

Configuring Multiarea OSPF   349

Configuring Multiarea OSPF   349

Verifying Multiarea OSPF   352

Packet Tracer Exercise 9-1: Implement Dual-Stacked Multiarea
  OSPF   352

Labs and Activities   354

Command Reference   354

9.0.1.2 Class Activity–Leaving on a Jet Plane   355

Objective   355

Scenario   355

Required Resources   355

Directions   356

Summary   356

Reflection   356

9.2.2.6 Packet Tracer–Configuring Multiarea OSPFv2   358

Topology   358

Addressing Table   358

Objectives   358

Background   358

Part 1: Configure OSPFv2   359

Part 2: Verify and Examine Multiarea OSPFv2   359

Reflection Questions   359

Suggested Scoring Rubric   360

9.2.2.7 Packet Tracer–Configuring Multiarea OSPFv3   361

Topology   361

Addressing Table   361

Objectives   361

Background   362

Part 1: Configure OSPFv3   362

Part 2: Verify Multiarea OSPFv3 Operations   362

9.2.2.8 Lab–Configuring Multiarea OSPFv2 363

Topology 363

Addressing Table 363

Objectives 363

Background/Scenario 363

Required Resources 364

Part 1: Build the Network and Configure Basic Device Settings 364

Part 2: Configure a Multiarea OSPFv2 Network 365

Reflection 368

Router Interface Summary Table 368

9.2.2.9 Lab–Configuring Multiarea OSPFv3 369

Topology 369

Addressing Table 369

Objectives 370

Background/Scenario 370

Required Resources 370

Part 1: Build the Network and Configure Basic Device Settings 370

Part 2: Configure Multiarea OSPFv3 Routing 371

Reflection 376

Router Interface Summary Table 376

9.3.1.1 Class Activity–Digital Trolleys 377

Objective 377

Scenario 377

Required Resources 377

Directions 377

Chapter 10   OSPF Tuning and Troubleshooting 379

Study Guide 380

Advanced Single-Area OSPF Configurations 380

Identify Network Types 380

OSPF and Multiaccess Networks 381

OSPF and Multiaccess Networks Completion Exercise 381

DR/BDR Election Exercise 383

Redistributing an OSPF Default Route Exercise 384

Fine-Tuning OSPF Interfaces 386

Packet Tracer Exercise 10-1: Fine-Tune Dual-Stacked OSPF 387

Troubleshooting Single-Area OSPF Implementations 388

OSPF Adjacency Issues 388

Identify OSPFv2 Troubleshooting Commands 388

Identify OSPFv3 Troubleshooting Commands   391

Labs and Activities   393

Command Reference   393

10.0.1.2 Class Activity–DR and BDR Elections   394

Objectives   394

Scenario   394

Required Resources   394

Directions   394

10.1.1.12 Packet Tracer–Determining the DR and BDR   396

Topology   396

Addressing Table   396

Objectives   396

Scenario   396

Part 1: Examine DR and BDR Changing Roles   396

Part 2: Modify OSPF Priority and Force Elections   398

Suggested Scoring Rubric   398

10.1.1.13 Lab–Configuring OSPFv2 on a Multiaccess Network   399

Topology   399

Addressing Table   399

Objectives   399

Background/Scenario   399

Required Resources   400

Part 1: Build the Network and Configure Basic Device Settings   400

Part 2: Configure and Verify OSPFv2 on the DR, BDR, and
DROther   401

Part 3: Configure OSPFv2 Interface Priority to Determine the DR and
BDR   402

Reflection   404

Router Interface Summary Table   404

10.1.2.5 Packet Tracer–Propagating a Default Route in OSPFv2   405

Topology   405

Addressing Table   405

Objectives   405

Background   405

Part 1: Propagate a Default Route   406

Part 2: Verify Connectivity   406

10.1.3.4 Packet Tracer–Configuring OSPFv2 Advanced Features   407

Topology   407

Addressing Table   407

Objectives   407

Scenario   408

Part 1: Modify OSPF Default Settings   408

Part 2: Verify Connectivity   408

10.1.3.5 Lab—Configuring OSFPv2 Advanced Features   409

Topology   409

Addressing Table   409

Objectives   409

Background/Scenario   410

Required Resources   410

Part 1: Build the Network and Configure Basic Device Settings   410

Part 2: Configure and Verify OSPF Routing   411

Part 3: Change OSPF Metrics   411

Part 4: Configure and Propagate a Static Default Route   413

Reflection   415

Router Interface Summary Table   415

10.2.2.3 Packet Tracer—Troubleshooting Single-Area OSPFv2   416

Topology   416

Addressing Table   416

Scenario   416

Troubleshooting Process   417

Documentation Table   417

10.2.3.3 Lab—Troubleshooting Basic Single-Area OSPFv2 and OSPFv3   418

Topology   418

Addressing Table   418

Objectives   419

Background/Scenario   419

Required Resources   420

Part 1: Build the Network and Load Device Configurations   420

Part 2: Troubleshoot Layer 3 Connectivity   422

Part 3: Troubleshoot OSPFv2   424

Part 4: Troubleshoot OSPFv3   426

Reflection   430

Router Interface Summary Table   430

10.2.3.4 Lab—Troubleshooting Advanced Single-Area OSPFv2   431

Topology   431

Addressing Table   431

Objectives   431

Background/Scenario   432

Required Resources   432

Part 1: Build the Network and Load Device Configurations   432

Part 2: Troubleshoot OSPF   435

Reflection   436

Router Interface Summary Table   436

10.2.4.3 Packet Tracer–Troubleshooting Multiarea OSPFv2   437

Topology   437

Addressing Table   437

Objectives   438

Background/Scenario   438

Part 1: Use Show Commands to Troubleshoot OSPFv2 Area 1   438

10.2.4.4 Packet Tracer–Troubleshooting Multiarea OSPFv3   441

Topology   441

Addressing Table   441

Objectives   442

Background/Scenario   442

Part 1: Use Show Commands to Troubleshoot OSPFv3 Area 1   442

10.2.4.5 Lab–Troubleshooting Multiarea OSPFv2 and OSPFv3   445

Topology   445

Addressing Table   445

Objectives   446

Background/Scenario   446

Required Resources   447

Part 1: Build the Network and Load Device Configurations   447

Part 2: Troubleshoot Layer 3 Connectivity   450

Part 3: Troubleshoot OSPFv2   450

Part 4: Troubleshoot OSPFv3   452

Reflection   455

Router Interface Summary Table   455

10.3.1.1 Class Activity–OSPF Troubleshooting Mastery   456

Objective   456

Scenario   456

Required Resources   456

Topology Diagram   456

Directions   457

10.3.1.2 Packet Tracer–Skills Integration Challenge   458

Topology   458

Addressing Table   458

Scenario   458

Requirements   458

Icons Used in This Book

Router   Bridge   Hub   DSU/CSU

Catalyst Switch   Multilayer Switch   ATM Switch   ISDN/Frame Relay Switch

Communication Server   Gateway   Access Server

Command Syntax Conventions

The conventions used to present command syntax in this book are the same conventions used in the IOS Command Reference. The Command Reference describes these conventions as follows:

- **Boldface** indicates commands and keywords that are entered literally as shown. In actual configuration examples and output (not general command syntax), boldface indicates commands that are manually input by the user (such as a **show** command).

- *Italics* indicate arguments for which you supply actual values.

- Vertical bars (|) separate alternative, mutually exclusive elements.

- Square brackets [ ] indicate optional elements.

- Braces { } indicate a required choice.

- Braces within brackets [{ }] indicate a required choice within an optional element.

Introduction

This book supports instructors and students in Cisco Networking Academy, an IT skills and career building program for learning institutions and individuals worldwide. Cisco Networking Academy provides a variety of curricula choices including the popular CCNA curriculum. It includes four courses oriented around the topics of the Cisco Certified Entry Networking Technician (CCENT) and Cisco Certified Network Associate (CCNA) certifications.

Scaling Networks v6.0 Labs & Study Guide is a supplement to your classroom and laboratory experience with the Cisco Networking Academy. To be successful on the exam and achieve your CCNA certification, you should do everything in your power to arm yourself with a variety of tools and training materials to support your learning efforts. This Labs & Study Guide is just such a collection of tools. Used to its fullest extent, it will help you gain the knowledge as well as practice the skills associated with the content area of the *Scaling Networks v6.0* course. Specifically, this book will help you work on these main areas:

- Describe the operations and benefits of the Spanning Tree Protocol (STP).

- Configure and troubleshoot STP operations.

- Describe the operations and benefits of link aggregation and Cisco VLAN Trunk Protocol (VTP).

- Configure and troubleshoot VTP, STP, DTP, and RSTP.

- Configure and troubleshoot inter-VLAN routing.

- Configure and troubleshoot EtherChannel and HSRP.

- Configure and troubleshoot basic operations of routers in a complex routed network for IPv4 and IPv6.

- Configure and troubleshoot advanced operations of routers and implement OSPF and EIGRP routing protocols for IPv4 and IPv6.

Labs & Study Guides similar to this one are also available for the other three courses: *Introduction to Networks v6 Labs &Study Guide*; *Routing and Switching Essentials v6 Labs &Study Guide*; and *Connecting Networks v6 Labs &Study Guide.*

Goals and Methods

The most important goal of this book is to help you pass the 200-105 Interconnecting Cisco Networking Devices Part 2 (ICND2) exam, which is the second exam for the Cisco Certified Network Associate (CCNA) certification. Passing the ICND2 exam means that you have the knowledge and skills required to manage a small, enterprise network. You can view the detailed ICND2 exam topics any time at http://learningnetwork.cisco.com. They are divided into five broad categories:

- LAN Switching Technologies

- Routing Technologies

- WAN Technologies

- Infrastructure Services

- Infrastructure Maintenance

Each chapter of this book is divided into a Study Guide section followed by a Lab section.

The Study Guide section offers exercises that help you learn the concepts, configurations, and troubleshooting skills crucial to your success as a CCNA exam candidate. Each chapter is slightly different and includes some or all of the following types of exercises:

- Vocabulary Matching Exercises

- Concept Questions Exercises

- Skill-Building Activities and Scenarios

- Configuration Scenarios

- Packet Tracer Exercises

- Troubleshooting Scenarios

The Labs and Activities section includes all the online course labs and Packet Tracer activity instructions. If applicable, this section begins with a Command Reference that you will complete to highlight all the commands introduced in the chapter.

Packet Tracer and Companion Website

This book includes the instructions for all the Packet Tracer activities in the online course. You need to be enrolled in the *Scaling Networks v6.0* course to access the Packet Tracer files.

However, there are nine Packet Tracer activities created exclusively for this book. You can access these unique Packet Tracer files at this book's companion website.

To get your copy of Packet Tracer software and the nine unique files for this book, please go to the companion website for instructions. To access this companion website, follow these steps:

1. Go to www.ciscopress.com/register and log in or create a new account.

2. Enter the ISBN: 9781587134333.

3. Answer the challenge question as proof of purchase.

4. Click on the Access Bonus Content link in the Registered Products section of your account page to be taken to the page where your downloadable content is available.

Audience for This Book

This book's main audience is anyone taking the Scaling Networks course of the Cisco Networking Academy curriculum. Many Academies use this Labs & Study Guide as a required tool in the course, whereas other Academies recommend the Labs & Study Guide as an additional resource to prepare for class exams and the CCNA certification.

The secondary audiences for this book include people taking CCNA-related classes from professional training organizations and students in college- and university-level networking courses, as well as anyone wanting to gain a detailed understanding of routing. However, the reader should know that the content of this book tightly aligns with the Cisco Networking Academy course. It may not be possible to complete some of the Study Guide sections and Labs without access to the online course. Fortunately, you can purchase the *Scaling Networks v6 Companion Guide* (ISBN: 9781587134340).

How This Book Is Organized

Because the content of the *Scaling Networks v6 Companion Guide* and the online curriculum is sequential, you should work through this *Labs & Study Guide* in order beginning with Chapter 1.

The book covers the major topic headings in the same sequence as the online curriculum. This book has 10 chapters, with the same names as the online course chapters.

- **Chapter 1, "LAN Design":** This chapter provides vocabulary and concept exercises to reinforce your understanding of hierarchical network design and selecting hardware. You also practice basic router and switch configuration and verification.

- **Chapter 2, "Scaling VLANs":** Focuses on the configuration, verification, and troubleshooting of static routes for IPv4 and IPv6, including default routes, floating static routes, and static host routes.

- **Chapter 3, "STP":** The exercises in this chapter cover the concepts, operations, configuration, and verification of all the current varieties of STP.

- **Chapter 4, "EtherChannel and HSRP":** This chapter's exercises are devoted to the concepts, configuration, verification, and troubleshooting of EtherChannel and HSRP.

- **Chapter 5, "Dynamic Routing":** To route dynamically, a router needs a routing protocol. The exercises in this chapter are devoted to all the basic routing protocol concepts, including protocol operation and characteristics, how a router learns about networks, and deep dives into distance vector and link-state routing protocols.

- **Chapter 6, "EIGRP":** The exercises in this chapter are devoted to the basic concepts and configuration of Cisco's routing protocol, EIGRP for IPv4 and IPv6.

- **Chapter 7, "EIGRP Tuning and Troubleshooting":** This chapter focuses on advanced EIGRP concepts, configuration, verification, and troubleshooting.

- **Chapter 8, "Single-Area OSPF":** This chapter introduces OSPF with exercises for reinforcing your understanding of OSPF operations. In addition, activities allow you to practice configuration and troubleshooting for both single-area OSPFv2 and OSPFv3.

- **Chapter 9, "Multiarea OSPF":** The CCNA exam now includes multiarea OSPF. So, this chapter includes exercises covering multiarea OSPF concepts and configuration, verification, and troubleshooting.

- **Chapter 10, "OSPF Tuning and Troubleshooting":** This chapter focuses on advanced OSPF concepts, configuration, verification, and troubleshooting.

CHAPTER 1

LAN Design

As a business grows, so does its networking requirements. To keep pace with a business's expansion and new emerging technologies, a network must be designed to scale. A network that scales well is not only one that can handle growing traffic demands, but also one designed to expand as needed. This short chapter sets the stage for the rest of the course. This chapter covers the campus wired LAN designs and appropriate device selections that you can use to systematically design a highly functional network.

Study Guide

Campus Wired LAN Designs

An enterprise network must be designed to support the exchange of various types of network traffic, including data files, email, IP telephony, and video applications for multiple business units.

Hierarchical Network Design

Enterprise networks are large multilocation networks that often span the globe. They must be able to support a variety of critical applications, converge different network traffic types, address diverse business needs, and provide centralized management control. The basic building block for enterprise networks is the LAN. The LAN is the networking infrastructure that provides access to network services for end users. LANs can be wired or wireless. Over a small geographic area, an enterprise interconnects these LANs into a campus network.

The campus wired LAN uses a hierarchical design model to break up the design into three layers. Designing a network using the three-layer hierarchical design model helps optimize the network. In Figure 1-1, label the three layers of the hierarchical design model.

Figure 1-1   Hierarchical Design Model

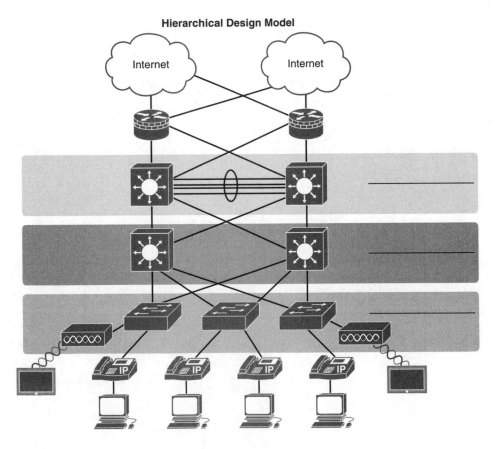

Briefly describe each layer of the hierarchical design model.

_____

_____

_____

_____

Identify Scalability Terminology

Match the definition on the left with the term on the right. This is a one-to-one matching exercise.

Definition

___ Isolates routing updates and minimizes the size of routing tables

___ Cisco proprietary distance vector routing protocol

___ Allows for redundant paths by eliminating switching loops

___ Technique for aggregating multiple links between equipment to increase bandwidth

___ Minimizes the possibility of a single point of failure

___ Supports new features and devices without requiring major equipment upgrades

___ Link-state routing protocol with a two-layer hierarchical design

___ Increases flexibility, reduces costs, and provides mobility to users

Terms

a. Modular equipment

b. OSPF

c. EIGRP

d. Wireless LANs

e. Redundancy

f. Spanning Tree Protocol

g. Scalable Routing Protocol

h. EtherChannel

Selecting Network Devices

When designing a network, it is important to select the proper hardware to meet current network requirements and to allow for network growth. Within an enterprise network, both switches and routers play a critical role in network communication.

Selecting Switch Hardware

Match the business consideration on the left with the switch feature on the right. This is a one-to-one matching exercise.

Business Consideration

___ Should provide continuous access to the network

___ Daisy-chain switches with high-bandwidth throughput

___ Refers to a switch's ability to support the appropriate number of devices on the network

___ Ability to adjust to growth of network users

___ How fast the interfaces will process network data

___ Important consideration in a network where there may be congested ports to servers or other areas of the network

___ Provides electrical current to other device and supports redundant power supplies

___ Switches with preset features or options

___ Depends on the number and speed of the interfaces, supported features, and expansion capability

___ Switches with insertable switching line/port cards

Switch Feature

a. Reliability

b. Modular

c. Uninterruptible power supply

d. Stackable

e. Frame buffers

f. Cost

g. Fixed configuration

h. Scalability

i. Port speed

j. Port density

Selecting Router Hardware

In Table 1-1, select the router category that applies to each description.

Table 1-1   Identify Router Category Features

Router Description	Branch Routers	Network Edge Routers	Service Provider Routers
Fast performance with high security for data centers, campus, and branch networks			
Simple network configuration and management for LANs and WANs			
Optimizes services on a single platform			
End-to-end delivery of subscriber services			
Delivers next-generation Internet experiences across all devices and locations			
High capacity and scalability with hierarchical quality of service			
Maximizes local services and ensures 24/7/365 uptime			
Unites campus, data center, and branch networks			

Managing Devices

A basic router or switch configuration includes the hostname for identification, passwords for security, and assignment of IP addresses to interfaces for connectivity and management. A router configuration also includes basic routing.

In addition to configuration commands, router and switch verification commands are used to verify the operational status of the router or switch and related network functionality. Use the address scheme in Table 1-2 in the following exercises that review the most common router and switch configuration and verification commands.

Table 1-2   Router and Switch Addressing Table

Device	Interface	IPv4 Address	Subnet Mask	Default Gateway
R1	G0/0	192.168.1.1	255.255.255.0	N/A
	S0/0/0	172.16.3.1	255.255.255.252	N/A
	S0/0/1	192.168.10.5	255.255.255.252	N/A
S1	VLAN 1	192.168.1.5	255.255.255.0	192.168.1.1

Basic Router Configuration Review

Using Table 1-2 and the following requirements, record the commands, including the router prompt, to implement a basic router configuration:

- Hostname is **R1**.
- Console and Telnet line's password is **cisco**.
- Privileged EXEC password is **class**.
- Banner message-of-the-day.
- Interface addressing.
- RIPv2 routing.
- Save the configuration.

```
Router(config)# _____
```

_____

_____

_____

_____

_____

_____

_____

_____

_____

_____

_____

_____

_____

_____

_____

_____

_____

_____

_____

_____

_____

_____

_____

_____

_____

_____

_____

_____

_____

Basic Router Verification Review

In Table 1-3, record the verification command that will generate the described output.

Table 1-3   Router Verification Commands

Command	Command Output
	Displays the routing table for known networks, including administrative distance, metric, and outbound interface
	Displays information about routing protocols, including process ID, router ID, and neighbors
	Displays information about directly connected Cisco devices
	Displays all interfaces in an abbreviated format, including IP address and status
	Displays one or all interfaces, including status, bandwidth, and duplex type

Basic Switch Configuration Review

Using Table 1-2 and the following requirements, record the commands, including the switch prompt, to implement a basic switch configuration:

- Hostname is **S1**.

- Console and Telnet line's password is **cisco**.

- Privileged EXEC password is **class**.
- Banner message-of-the-day.
- VLAN 1 interface addressing.
- Save the configuration.

```
Switch(config)#
```

_____

_____

_____

_____

_____

_____

_____

_____

_____

_____

_____

_____

_____

_____

_____

_____

Basic Switch Verification Review

In Table 1-4, record the verification command that will generate the described output.

Table 1-4   Switch Verification Commands

Command	Command Output
	Displays information about directly connected Cisco devices
	Displays all secure MAC addresses
	Displays a table of learned MAC addresses, including the port number and VLAN assigned to the port
	Displays one or all interfaces, including status, bandwidth, and duplex type
	Displays information about maximum MAC addresses allowed, current counts, security violation count, and action to be taken

Packet Tracer Exercise 1-1: Basic Device Configuration

Now you are ready to use Packet Tracer to apply your documented configuration. Download and open the file LSG03-0101.pka found at the companion website for this book. Refer to the Introduction of this book for specifics on accessing files.

Note: The following instructions are also contained within the Packet Tracer Exercise.

In this Packet Tracer activity, you will configure a router and a switch with basic settings and verify connectivity. Use the commands you documented in the section "Managing Devices." You will then verify that other routers can ping PC1.

Requirements

Configure the routers with the following settings:

- Name the router **R1** and the switch **S1**.
- The privileged EXEC password is **class**.
- The line password is **cisco**.
- All plaintext passwords should be encrypted.
- Users must login to the console and vty lines.
- The message-of-the-day is **Authorized Access Only!**
- Configure and activate all interfaces according to Table 1-2.
- Save the configurations.
- Verify connectivity from R2 and R3 to PC1.

Your completion percentage should be 100%. All the connectivity tests should show a status of "successful." If not, click **Check Results** to see which required components are not yet completed.

Labs and Activities

Command Reference

In Table 1-5, record the command, including the correct router or switch prompt, that fits the description. Fill in any blanks with the appropriate missing information.

Table 1-5   Commands for Chapter 1, LAN Design

Command	Description
	Enter privileged EXEC mode.
	Exit privileged EXEC mode.
	Enter global configuration mode.
	Configure R1 as the hostname for the router.
	Enter line configuration mode for the console.
	Configure the console password to be "cisco123".
	Require a password for user EXEC mode.
	Configure "Authorized Access Only" as the message of the day. Use $ as the delimiting character.
	Enter interface configuration mode for g0/0.
	Configure the IPv4 address 172.16.1.1 255.255.255.0 on interface g0/0.
	Activate the interface.
	Enter router configuration mode for RIP.
	Configure RIP version 2.
	Configure RIP to advertise 172.16.0.0.
	On switch S1, enter interface configuration mode for VLAN 1.
	Configure interface VLAN 1 with the IP address 172.16.1.5/24.
	Configure S1 with the default gateway address 172.16.1.1.

1.0.1.2 Class Activity–Network by Design

Objective

Explain the need to design a hierarchical network that is scalable.

Scenario

Your employer is opening a new branch office.

You have been reassigned to the site as the network administrator where your job will be to design and maintain the new branch network.

The network administrators at the other branches used the Cisco, three-layer, hierarchical approach when designing their networks. You decide to use the same approach.

To get an idea of what using the hierarchical model can do to enhance the design process, you research the topic.

Resources

- Internet access
- Word processing software

Directions

Step 1.   Use the Internet to find information and take notes about the Cisco, three-layered hierarchical model. The site should include information about the:

    a.   Access layer

    b.   Distribution layer

    c.   Core layer

Step 2.   In your research, make sure to include:

    a.   A simple definition of each hierarchical layer

    b.   Three concise facts about each layer

    c.   Network device capabilities needed at each layer

    d.   A detailed graphic that shows a full, three-layer hierarchical model design

Step 3.   Create a simple table to organize and share your research with another student, group, the class, or instructor.

1.2.1.7 Packet Tracer–Compare 2960 and 3560 Switches

Topology

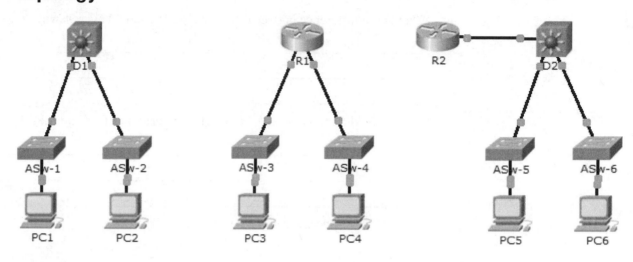

Objective

Part 1: Compare Layer 2 and Layer 3 Switches

Part 2: Compare a Layer 3 Switch and a Router

Background

In this activity, you will use various commands to examine three different switching topologies and compare the similarities and differences between the 2960 and 3560 switches. You will also compare the routing table of a 1941 router with a 3560 switch.

Part 1: Compare Layer 2 and Layer 3 Switches

a. Examine the physical aspects of **D1** and **ASw-1**.

Each individual switch has how many physical interfaces? _____

How many Fast Ethernet and Gigabit Ethernet interfaces does each switch have?

_____

List the transmission speed of the Fast Ethernet and Gigabit Ethernet interfaces on each switch.

_____

Are either of the two switches modular in design? _____

b. The interface of a 3560 switch can be configured as a Layer 3 interface by entering the **no switchport** command in interface configuration mode. This allows technicians to assign an IP address and subnet mask to the interface the same way it is configured on a router's interface.

What is the difference between a Layer 2 switch and a Layer 3 switch?

_____

_____

_____

What is the difference between a switch's physical interface and the VLAN interface?

_____

_____

_____

On which layers do 2960 and 3560 switches operate?

_____

Issue the **show run** command to examine the configurations of the **D1** and **ASw-1** switches. Do you notice any differences between them?

_____

_____

Display the routing table on both switches using the **show ip route** command. Why do you think the command does not work on **ASW-1**, but works on **D1**?

_____

_____

_____

Part 2: Compare a Layer 3 Switch and a Router

a. Up until recently, switches and routers have been separate and distinct devices. The term switch was set aside for hardware devices that function at Layer 2. Routers, on the other hand, are devices that make forwarding decisions based on Layer 3 information. They use routing protocols to share routing information and to communicate with other routers. Layer 3 switches, such as the 3560, can be configured to forward Layer 3 packets. Entering the **ip routing** command in global configuration mode allows Layer 3 switches to be configured with routing protocols, thereby possessing some of the same capabilities as a router. Although similar in some forms, switches are different in many other aspects.

Open the Physical tab on D1 and R1. Do you notice any similarities between the two? Do you notice any differences between the two?

_____

_____

_____

Issue the **show run** command and examine the configurations of R1 and D1. What differences do you see between the two?

_____

_____

Which command allows D1 to configure an IP address on one of its physical interfaces?

_____

Use the **show ip route** command on both devices. Do you see any similarities or differences between the two tables?

_____

_____

_____

Now, analyze the routing table of R2 and D2. What is evident now that was not in the configuration of R1 and D1?

_____

_____

b. Verify that each topology has full connectivity by completing the following tests.

- Ping from **PC1** to **PC2**

- Ping from **PC3** to **PC4**

- Ping from **PC5** to **PC6**

In all three examples, each PC is on a different network. Which device is used to provide communication between networks?

_____

Why were we able to ping across networks without there being a router?

_____

_____

_____

Suggested Scoring Rubric

Activity Section	Question Location	Possible Points	Earned Points
Part 1: Compare Layer 2 and Layer 3 Switches	a	20	
	b	40	
	Part 1 Total	60	
Part 2: Compare a Layer 3 Switch and a Router	a	30	
	b	10	
	Part 2 Total	40	
	Total Score	100	

1.3.1.1 Class Activity–Layered Network Design Simulation

Objectives

Explain the need to design a hierarchical network that is scalable.

Scenario

As the network administrator for a very small network, you want to prepare a simulated-network presentation for your branch manager to explain how the network currently operates.

The small network includes the following equipment:

- One Cisco 2911 series router
- One Cisco 3560 switch
- One Cisco 2960 switch
- Four user workstations (PCs or laptops)
- One printer

Resources

- Packet Tracer software

Directions

Step 1.   Create a simple network topology using Packet Tracer software. Place the devices at the appropriate levels of the Cisco three-layer hierarchical model design, including:

    a.   One Cisco 2911 series router

    b.   One Cisco 3560 switch

    c.   One Cisco 2960 switch

    d.   Four user workstations (PCs or laptops)

    e.   One printer

Step 2.   Using Packet Tracer's drawing tool, indicate the hierarchical layers with different color coding and labels:

    a.   Access layer

    b.   Distribution layer

    c.   Core layer

Step 3.   Configure the network and user devices. Check for end-to-end connectivity.

Step 4.   Share your configuration and hierarchical network design Packet Tracer file with another student, group, the class, or the instructor.

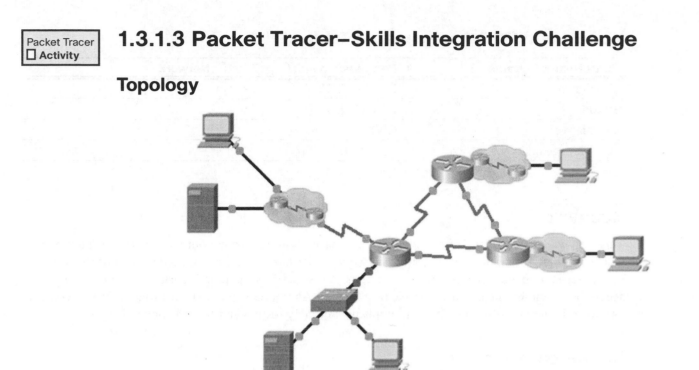

Packet Tracer
☐ **Activity**

1.3.1.3 Packet Tracer–Skills Integration Challenge

Topology

Addressing Table

Device	Interface	IP Address	Subnet Mask	Default Gateway
[[R1Name]]	G0/0.15	[[R1G0sub15Add]]	[[R1G0sub15SM]]	N/A
	G0/0.30	[[R1G0sub30Add]]	[[R1G0sub30SM]]	N/A
	G0/0.45	[[R1G0sub45Add]]	[[R1G0sub45SM]]	N/A
	G0/0.60	[[R1G0sub60Add]]	[[R1G0sub60SM]]	N/A
	S0/0/0	[[R1S000Add]]	255.255.255.252	N/A
	S0/0/1	[[R1S001Add]]	255.255.255.252	N/A
	S0/1/0	[[R1S010Add]]	255.255.255.252	N/A
[[R2Name]]	G0/0	[[R2G00Add]]	[[R2R3LanSM]]	N/A
	S0/0/0	[[R2S000Add]]	255.255.255.252	N/A
	S0/0/1	[[R2S001Add]]	255.255.255.252	N/A
[[R3Name]]	G0/0	[[R3G00Add]]	[[R2R3LanSM]]	N/A
	S0/0/0	[[R3S000Add]]	255.255.255.252	N/A
	S0/0/1	[[R3S001Add]]	255.255.255.252	N/A
[[S1Name]]	VLAN 60	[[S1VLAN60Add]]		
[[PC1Name]]	NIC	DHCP Assigned	DHCP Assigned	DHCP Assigned

VLANs and Port Assignments Table

VLAN Number - Name	Port assignment	Network
15 - Servers	F0/11 - F0/20	
30 - PCs	F0/1 - F0/10	
45 - Native	G0/1	
60 - Management	VLAN 60	

Scenario

This activity includes many of the skills that you have acquired during your CCNA studies. First, you will complete the documentation for the network. Make sure you have a printed version of the instructions. During implementation, you will configure VLANs, trunking, port security, and SSH remote access on a switch. Then, you will implement inter-VLAN routing and NAT on a router. Finally, you will use your documentation to verify your implementation by testing end-to-end connectivity.

Documentation

You are required to fully document the network. You will need a print out of this instruction set, which will include an unlabeled topology diagram:

- Label all the device names, network addresses, and other important information that Packet Tracer generated.

- Complete the Addressing Table and VLANs and Port Assignments Table.

- Fill in any blanks in the **Implementation** and **Verification** steps. The information is supplied when you launch the Packet Tracer activity.

Implementation

Note: All devices in the topology except [[R1Name]], [[S1Name]], and [[PC1Name]] are fully configured. You do not have access to the other routers. You can access all the servers and PCs for testing purposes.

Implement the following requirements using your documentation:

[[S1Name]]

- Configure remote management access including IP addressing and SSH:

  - Domain is cisco.com

  - Enable secret ciscoenpass

  - User **[[UserText]]** with password **[[UserPass]]**

  - Crypto key length of 1024

  - SSH version 2, limited to 2 authentication attempts and a 60 second timeout

  - Plaintext passwords should be encrypted.

- Configure, name, and assign VLANs. Ports should be manually configured as access ports.

- Configure trunking.

- Implement port security:
  - On F0/1, allow 2 MAC addresses that are automatically added to the configuration file when detected. The port should not be disabled, but a syslog message should be captured if a violation occurs.
  - Disable all other unused ports.

[[R1Name]]

- Configure inter-VLAN routing.
- Configure DHCP services for VLAN 30. Use **LAN** as the case-sensitive name for the pool.
- Implement routing:
  - Use RIPv2.
  - Configure one network statement for the entire **[[DisplayNet]]** address space.
  - Disable interfaces that should not send RIPv2 messages.
  - Configure a default route to the Internet.
- Implement NAT:
  - Configure a standard, one statement ACL number 1. All IP addresses belonging to the **[[DisplayNet]]** address space are allowed.
  - Refer to your documentation and configure static NAT for the File Server.
  - Configure dynamic NAT with PAT using a pool name of your choice, a /30 mask, and these two public addresses:

    [[NATPoolText]]

    [[PC1Name]]
- Verify **[[PC1Name]]** has received full addressing information from **[[R1Name]]**.

Verification

All devices should now be able to ping all other devices. If not, troubleshoot your configurations to isolate and solve problems. A few tests include:

- Verify remote access to **[[S1Name]]** by using SSH from a PC.
- Verify VLANs are assigned to appropriate ports and port security is in force.
- Verify a complete routing table.
- Verify NAT translations and statistics.
  - **Outside Host** should be able to access **File Server** at the public address.
  - Inside PCs should be able to access **Web Server**.
- Document any problems you encountered and the solutions in the **Troubleshooting Documentation** table below.

Troubleshooting Documentation

Problem	Solution

Suggested Scoring Rubric

Packet Tracer scores 75 points. Documentation is worth 25 points.

CHAPTER 2

Scaling VLANs

Several tools allow you to scale your VLANs. VLAN Trunking Protocol (VTP) reduces administration in a switched network. Using an extended VLAN range you can increase the number of VLANs you can configure. The Dynamic Trunking Protocol (DTP) provides the capability for ports to automatically negotiate trunking between switches. Layer 3 switches allow you to consolidate Layer 2 switch and Layer 3 router functionality in one device. This chapter reviews VTP, extended VLANs, DTP, and Layer 3 switching. It also describes issues encountered when implementing VTP, DTP, and inter-VLAN routing.

Study Guide

VTP, Extended VLANs, and DTP

VTP, extended VLANs, and DTP are tools you can use to scale your network.

VTP Concepts and Operation

As the number of switches increases on a small or medium-sized business network, the overall administration required to manage VLANs and trunks in a network becomes a challenge. Cisco engineers invented the VLAN Trunking Protocol (VTP), a technology that helps network administrators automate some of the tasks related to VLAN creation, deletion, and synchronization.

Match the definition on the left with a term on the right. All definitions and terms are used exactly one time.

Definition

___ Switches share VLAN information; boundary is defined by a Layer 3 device.

___ Can only create, delete, and modify local VLANs.

___ Advertises VLAN configuration information; can create, delete, and modify VLANs.

___ By default, this is disabled.

___ Stores VLAN information only in RAM.

___ Carries VLAN configuration information.

Terms

a. VTP advertisements

b. VTP client

c. VTP domain

d. VTP pruning

e. VTP server

f. VTP transparent

VTP Modes

Finish Table 2-1 by first indicating the VTP mode and then answering Yes or No for each of the features listed.

Table 2-1   VTP Mode Comparisons

Feature	_____ Mode	_____ Mode	_____ Mode
Source VTP messages			
Listen to VTP messages			
Create VLANs	Yes	No	Yes*
Remember VLANs			

*Locally significant only

VTP Advertisements

Refer to Figure 2-1. When a network administrator adds a new VLAN in a VTP domain, the following process takes place:

1. The new VLAN is added to the VTP server S1.

2. S1 informs other switches in the same VTP domain that the revision number has changed.

3. S2 has a lower revision number, so it asks for more information.

4. S1 replies with the changes to the VLAN database.

In Figure 2-1, label the correct name for these VTP advertisements.

Figure 2-1   VTP Advertisements

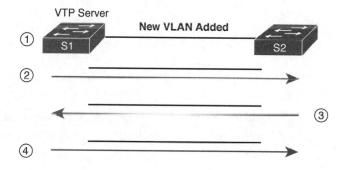

Default VTP Configuration

Fill in the default VTP settings for a Cisco 2960 switch.

- VTP Version: _____

- VTP Domain Name: _____

- VTP Pruning Mode: _____

- VTP Traps Generation: _____

- VTP Mode: _____

- Configuration Revision Number: _____

VTP Caveats

Assuming a new switch was configured with the correct domain name, what would happen if you added a VTP client or server switch with a higher configuration revision number to the network?

_____

_____

_____

_____

_____

_____

List two ways to reset the configuration revision number on a switch.

VTP Configuration

VTP configuration is straightforward, so this exercise uses a rather large topology, shown in Figure 2-2, to give you extra practice. Table 2-2 shows the addressing scheme used for this exercise.

Figure 2-2   VTP Configuration Topology

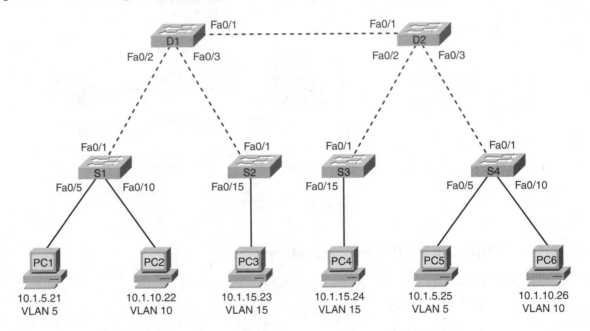

Table 2-2   Addressing Table for VTP Configuration Exercise

Device	Interface	IP Address	Subnet Mask	Default Gateway
D1	VLAN 99	10.1.1.1	255.255.255.0	N/A
D2	VLAN 99	10.1.1.2	255.255.255.0	N/A
S1	VLAN 99	10.1.1.11	255.255.255.0	N/A
S2	VLAN 99	10.1.1.12	255.255.255.0	N/A
S3	VLAN 99	10.1.1.13	255.255.255.0	N/A
S4	VLAN 99	10.1.1.14	255.255.255.0	N/A
PC1	NIC	10.1.5.21	255.255.255.0	10.1.5.1
PC2	NIC	10.1.10.22	255.255.255.0	10.1.10.1
PC3	NIC	10.1.15.23	255.255.255.0	10.1.15.1
PC4	NIC	10.1.15.24	255.255.255.0	10.1.15.1
PC5	NIC	10.1.5.25	255.255.255.0	10.1.5.1
PC6	NIC	10.1.10.26	255.255.255.0	10.1.10.1

Specifications for configuring VLANs and VTP are as follows:

- **D1** is responsible for sending VLAN configuration information to all other switches.
- The other switches are clients.
- The domain is **CCNA**.
- The password is **cisco**.
- The VLANs are as follows:
    - VLAN 5: Engineering
    - VLAN 10: Sales
    - VLAN 15: Administration
    - VLAN 99: Management

Enter the commands, including the switch prompt, to configure D1 as the VTP server:

_____

_____

_____

_____

_____

_____

_____

_____

_____

_____

Enter the commands, including the switch prompt, to configure the remaining switches as VTP clients. You need to list the commands only once.

_____

_____

_____

_____

What command displays the following output? Also, indicate which switch this output is from.

```
VTP Version                        : 2

Configuration Revision             : 8

Maximum VLANs supported locally : 64

Number of existing VLANs           : 9

VTP Operating Mode                 : Server

VTP Domain Name                    : CCNA

VTP Pruning Mode                   : Disabled

VTP V2 Mode                        : Disabled
```

```
VTP Traps Generation           : Disabled

MD5 digest                     : 0xA0 0xA3 0xB8 0xC9 0x49 0xE2 0x44 0xA6

Configuration last modified by 0.0.0.0 at 3-1-93 00:12:32

Local updater ID is 10.1.1.1 on interface Vl99 (lowest numbered VLAN interface found)
```

You need to configure another switch for the CCNA domain and you forgot the VTP password. How would you find out what the password is?

_____

_____

_____

_____

Packet Tracer Exercise 2-1: VTP Configuration

Now you are ready to use Packet Tracer to apply your documented configuration. Download and open the file LSG03-0201.pka found at the companion website for this book. Refer to the Introduction of this book for specifics on accessing files.

Note: The following instructions are also contained within the Packet Tracer Exercise.

In this Packet Tracer activity, you will configure a router and a switch with basic settings and verify connectivity. Use the commands you documented in the section "VTP Configuration." You will then verify that switches can ping each other and PCs in the same VLAN can ping each other.

Requirements

Configure the switches with the following settings:

- Configure VTP on the switches.
- Configure VLANs on the VTP server.
- Configure trunking between the switches. Assign VLAN 99 as the native VLAN.
- After the network converges, use **show vtp status** and **show vlan brief** to verify that:
  - D1 is the VTP server.
  - The remaining switches are VTP clients.
  - The remaining switches have all VLANs from D1.
- Configure access ports and assign VLANs for the PCs.
- All switches should now be able to ping each other. PCs belonging to the same VLAN should be able to ping each other.

Your completion percentage should be 100%. All the connectivity tests should show a status of "successful." If not, click **Check Results** to see which required components are not yet completed.

Extended VLANs

In Table 2-3, indicate whether the characteristic applies to normal range VLANs or extended range VLANs.

Table 2-3   Characteristics of VLAN Ranges

Characteristic	Normal Range VLANs	Extended Range VLANs
Used by service providers and large organizations.		
Configurations are stored within the vlan.dat file.		
Support fewer VLAN features than the other range.		
Used in small and medium-sized business and enterprise networks.		
Configurations are saved in the running configuration file.		
Identified by VLAN IDs between 1 and 1005.		
Identified by a VLAN ID between 1006 and 4094.		

DTP

DTP is a Cisco proprietary protocol that negotiates both the status of trunk ports and the trunk encapsulation of trunk ports. To enable trunking from a Cisco switch to a device that does not support DTP, use the _____ and _____ interface configuration mode commands. This causes the interface to become a trunk, but not generate DTP frames.

A switch port on a Cisco Catalyst switch supports a number of trunking modes. Identify the commands used to configure the trunking mode:

- _____: Puts the interface into permanent nontrunking mode and negotiates to convert the link into a nontrunk link.

- _____: Puts the interface into permanent trunking mode and negotiates to convert the neighboring link into a trunk link. The interface becomes a trunk interface even if the neighboring interface is not a trunk interface.

- _____: Makes the interface actively attempt to convert the link to a trunk link. The interface becomes a trunk interface if the neighboring interface is set to _____, _____, or _____ mode. This is the default switchport mode on older switches, such as the Catalyst 2950 and 3550 series switches.

- _____: Prevents the interface from generating DTP frames. You can use this command only when the interface switchport mode is **access** or **trunk**. You must manually configure the neighboring interface as a trunk interface to establish a trunk link.

- _____: Enables the interface to convert the link to a trunk link. The interface becomes a trunk interface if the neighboring interface is set to _____ or _____. This is the default switchport mode for all Ethernet interfaces.

In Table 2-4, the arguments for the **switchport mode** command are listed for the local side of the link down the first column and for the remote side of the link across the first row. Indicate whether the link will transition to access mode or trunk mode after the two switches have sent DTP messages.

Table 2-4   Trunk Negotiation Combinations

	Dynamic Auto	Dynamic Desirable	Trunk	Access
Dynamic auto				
Dynamic desirable				
Trunk				Limited Connectivity
Access			Limited Connectivity	

In Figure 2-3, indicate which DTP combinations between two switches will become trunk links and which will become access links.

Figure 2-3   Predict DTP Behavior

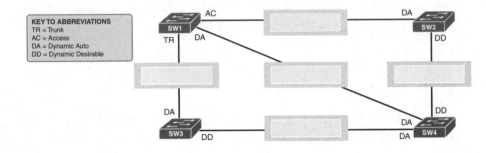

Troubleshoot Multi-VLAN Issues

As you know, the **ping** and **tracert/traceroute** can be helpful in isolating the general location of a connectivity problem. But to further isolate an inter-VLAN routing issue, you might need several additional commands.

In Examples 2-1 and 2-2, fill in the command used to generate the output. Highlight relevant parts of the output that would help in isolating inter-VLAN routing issues. Then document the error and possible solution.

Example 2-1   Inter-VLAN Troubleshooting Scenario 1

```
Switch# _____

Name: Gi0/23

Switchport: Enabled

Administrative Mode: dynamic auto

Operational Mode: static access

Administrative Trunking Encapsulation: dot1q

Operational Trunking Encapsulation: native

Negotiation of Trunking: On

Access Mode VLAN: 1 (default)

Trunking Native Mode VLAN: 1 (default)

(output omitted)
```

What error or errors do you see in Example 2-1?

_____

What solution would you recommend?

_____

_____

_____

Example 2-2   Inter-VLAN Troubleshooting Scenario 2

```
Interface                      IP-Address     OK? Method Status                 Protocol

Embedded-Service-Engine0/0     unassigned     YES unset  administratively down  down

GigabitEthernet0/0             unassigned     YES unset  administratively down  down

GigabitEthernet0/0.10          172.17.10.1    YES manual up                     up

GigabitEthernet0/0.30          172.17.30.1    YES manual up                     up

GigabitEthernet0/1             unassigned     YES unset  administratively down  down

Serial0/0/0                    unassigned     YES unset  administratively down  down

Serial0/0/1                    unassigned     YES unset  administratively down  down
```

What error or errors do you see in Example 2-2?

_____

What solution would you recommend?

_____

_____

_____

Refer to the topology in Figure 2-4.

Figure 2-4   Inter-VLAN Troubleshooting Scenario 3

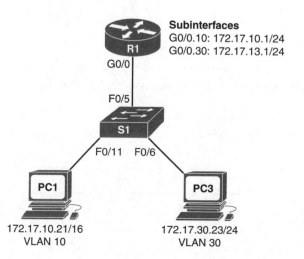

Subinterfaces
G0/0.10: 172.17.10.1/24
G0/0.30: 172.17.13.1/24

R1

G0/0

F0/5

S1

F0/11   F0/6

PC1

PC3

172.17.10.21/16
VLAN 10

172.17.30.23/24
VLAN 30

What error or errors do you see?

_____

_____

What solution would you recommend?

_____

_____

Layer 3 Switching

Router-on-a-stick is simple to implement because routers are usually available in every network. But most enterprise networks use multilayer switches to achieve high-packet processing rates using hardware-based switching.

Layer 3 Switching Operation

All Catalyst multilayer switches support the following types of Layer 3 interfaces:

- _____ : A pure Layer 3 interface similar to a physical interface on a Cisco IOS router.

- _____ **(SVI):** A virtual VLAN interface for inter-VLAN routing. In other words, SVIs are the virtual-routed VLAN interfaces.

What kind of switch forwarding do high-performance Catalyst switches use?

_____

What are some reasons and advantages for configuring SVIs?

_____

_____

_____

_____

_____

_____

What is the purpose of the **no switchport** command?

_____

What are two advantages of using a multilayer switch port?

_____

_____

Layer 3 Switching Troubleshooting Scenarios

Use Figure 2-5 for each of the following Layer 3 switching troubleshooting scenarios.

Figure 2-5   Layer 3 Switching Troubleshooting Topology

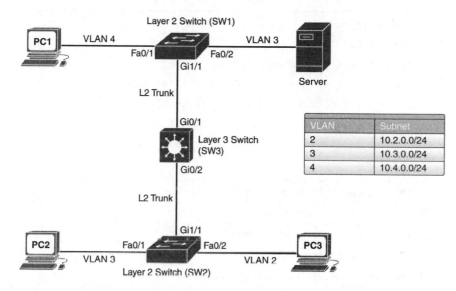

PC2 is unable to communicate with PC3 but can communicate with all other devices. Refer to the command output in Example 2-3. Then select the most likely causes for this issue. More than one answer choice may be selected.

Example 2-3   Layer 3 Switching Troubleshooting Scenario 1

```
SW3# show ip route
<output omitted>
Gateway of last resort is not set
     10.0.0.0/8 is variably subnetted, 3 subnets, 3 masks
C       10.2.0.0/24 is directly connected, Vlan5
C       10.3.0.0/24 is directly connected, Vlan3
C       10.4.0.0/24 is directly connected, Vlan4
```

VLAN 5 IP address is not correct.

VLAN 4 has no IP address.

VLAN 3 IP address is not correct.

VLAN 2 is not configured.

VLAN 3 and 4 are shut down.

PC3 is unable to communicate with any of the other devices, including its own gateway. Refer to the command output in Example 2-4. Then select the most likely causes for this issue. More than one answer choice may be selected.

Example 2-4   Layer 3 Switching Troubleshooting Scenario 2

```
SW3# show ip route
<output omitted>
Gateway of last resort is not set
     10.0.0.0/8 is variably subnetted, 3 subnets, 3 masks
C        10.2.0.0/30 is directly connected, Vlan2
C        10.3.0.0/24 is directly connected, Vlan3
C        10.4.0.0/24 is directly connected, Vlan4
```

VLAN 4 subnet mask is not correct.

VLAN 4 IP address is not correct.

VLAN 2 subnet mask is not correct.

VLAN 2 is not configured.

VLAN 3 IP address is not correct.

PC1 is unable to communicate with PC2 or PC3 but can communicate with the server. Refer to the command output in Example 2-5. Then select the most likely causes for this issue. More than one answer choice may be selected.

Example 2-5   Layer 3 Switching Troubleshooting Scenario 3

```
SW3# show interface trunk
Port        Mode        Encapsulation    Status      Native vlan
Gig0/1      auto        n-802.1q         trunking    1
```

VLAN 2 and 3 are being pruned from the trunk links.

SW2 is shut down.

The trunk encapsulation is not correct.

The gigabit 0/2 port is not configured as a trunk.

The gigabit 0/1 port is not configured as a trunk.

VLAN 2 is not configured.

Labs and Activities

Command Reference

In Table 2-5, record the command, including the correct router or switch prompt, that fits the description. Fill in any blanks with the appropriate missing information.

Table 2-5   Commands for Chapter 2, Scaling VLANs

Command	Description
	Configure S1 as the VTP server.
	Configure S2 as a VTP client.
	Configure S3 for local VLANs and to ignore VTP advertisements.
	Configure CCNA as the VTP domain.
	Configure cisco as the VTP password.
	Verify that S1 is the VTP server.
	Display the VTP password.
	Configure an interface into a permanent nontrunking mode.
	Configure an interface into a permanent trunking mode.
	Configure an interface to actively attempt to convert the link to a trunk.
	Configure an interface to convert to a trunk if the other side of the link is set to trunk or desirable.
	Disable DTP on an interface.

2.1.4.4 Packet Tracer–Configure VLANs, VTP, and DTP

Topology

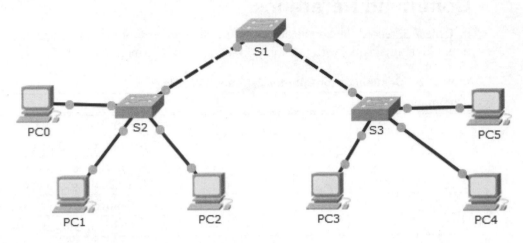

Addressing Table

Device	Interface	IP Address	Subnet Mask
PC0	NIC	192.168.10.1	255.255.255.0
PC1	NIC	192.168.20.1	255.255.255.0
PC2	NIC	192.168.30.1	255.255.255.0
PC3	NIC	192.168.30.2	255.255.255.0
PC4	NIC	192.168.20.2	255.255.255.0
PC5	NIC	192.168.10.2	255.255.255.0
S1	VLAN 99	192.168.99.1	255.255.255.0
S2	VLAN 99	192.168.99.2	255.255.255.0
S3	VLAN 99	192.168.99.3	255.255.255.0

Objectives

Part 1: Configure and Verify DTP

Part 2: Configure and Verify VTP

Background/Scenario

As the number of switches in a network increases, the administration necessary to manage the VLANs and trunks can be challenging. To ease some of the VLAN and trunking configurations, VLAN trunking protocol (VTP) allows a network administration to automate the management of VLANs. Trunk negotiation between network devices is managed by the Dynamic Trunking Protocol (DTP), and is automatically enabled on Catalyst 2960 and Catalyst 3560 switches.

In this activity, you will configure trunk links between the switches. You will configure a VTP server and VTP clients in the same VTP domain. You will also observe the VTP behavior when a switch is in

VTP transparent mode. You will assign ports to VLANs and verify end-to-end connectivity with the same VLAN.

Part 1: Configure and Verify DTP

In Part 1, you will configure trunk links among the switches, and you will configure VLAN 999 as the native VLAN.

Step 1.   Verify VLAN configuration.

Verify the configured VLANs on the switches.

a.   On S1, click the **CLI** tab. At the prompt, enter **enable** and enter the **show vlan brief** command to verify the configured VLANs on S1.

```
S1# show vlan brief
```

```
VLAN Name                             Status    Ports
---- -------------------------------- --------- -------------------------------
1    default                          active    Fa0/1, Fa0/2, Fa0/3, Fa0/4
                                                Fa0/5, Fa0/6, Fa0/7, Fa0/8
                                                Fa0/9, Fa0/10, Fa0/11, Fa0/12
                                                Fa0/13, Fa0/14, Fa0/15, Fa0/16
                                                Fa0/17, Fa0/18, Fa0/19, Fa0/20
                                                Fa0/21, Fa0/22, Fa0/23, Fa0/24
                                                Gig0/1, Gig0/2
99   Management                       active
999  VLAN0999                         active
1002 fddi-default                     active
1003 token-ring-default               active
1004 fddinet-default                  active
1005 trnet-default                    active
```

b.   Repeat step a. on S2 and S3. What VLANs are configured on the switches?

Step 2.   Configure Trunks on S1, S2, and S3.

Dynamic trunking protocol (DTP) manages the trunk links between Cisco switches. Currently all the switch ports are in the default trunking mode, which is dynamic auto. In this step, you will change the trunking mode to dynamic desirable for the link between switches S1 and S2. For the link between switches S1 and S3, the link will be set as a static trunk. Use VLAN 999 as the native VLAN in this topology.

a.   On S1, configure the trunk link to dynamic desirable on the GigabitEthernet 0/1 interface.

```
S1(config)# interface g0/1
S1(config-if)# switchport mode dynamic desirable
```

b.   For the trunk link between S1 and S3, configure a static trunk link on the GigabitEthernet 0/2 interface.

```
S1(config)# interface g0/2
S1(config-if)# switchport mode trunk
S3(config)# interface g0/2
S3(config-if)# switchport mode trunk
```

c. Verify trunking is enabled on all the switches using the **show interfaces trunk** command.

```
S1# show interfaces trunk
Port         Mode         Encapsulation   Status       Native vlan
Gig0/1       desirable    n-802.1q        trunking     1
Gig0/2       on           802.1q          trunking     1


Port         Vlans allowed on trunk
Gig0/1       1-1005
Gig0/2       1-1005


Port         Vlans allowed and active in management domain
Gig0/1       1,99,999
Gig0/2       1,99,999


Port         Vlans in spanning tree forwarding state and not pruned
Gig0/1       none
Gig0/2       none
```

What is the native VLAN for these trunks currently? _____

d. Configure VLAN 999 as the native VLAN for the trunk links on S1.

```
S1(config)# interface range g0/1 - 2
S1(config-if-range)# switchport trunk native vlan 999
```

What messages did you receive on S1? How would you correct them?

_____

_____

_____

_____

_____

_____

e. On S2 and S3, configure VLAN 999 as the native VLAN.

f. Verify trunking is successfully configured on all the switches. You should be able to ping one switch from another switch in the topology using the IP addresses configured on the SVI.

Part 2: Configure and Verify VTP

S1 will be configured as the VTP server and S2 will be configured as VTP clients. All the switches will be configured to be in the VTP domain **CCNA** and use the VTP password **cisco**.

VLANs can be created on the VTP server and distributed to other switches in the VTP domain. In this part, you will create three new VLANs on the VTP server, S1. These VLANs will be distributed to S2 using VTP. Observe how the transparent VTP mode behaves.

Step 1.   Configure S1 as the VTP server.

Configure S1 as the VTP server in the **CCNA** domain with the password **cisco**.

a. Configure S1 as a VTP server.

```
S1(config)# vtp mode server
Setting device to VTP SERVER mode.
```

b. Configure **CCNA** as the VTP domain name.

```
S1(config)# vtp domain CCNA
Changing VTP domain name from NULL to CCNA
```

c. Configure **cisco** as the VTP password.

```
S1(config)# vtp password cisco
Setting device VLAN database password to cisco
```

Step 2. Verify VTP on S1.

a. Use the **show vtp status** command on the switches to confirm that the VTP mode and domain are configured correctly.

```
S1# show vtp status
VTP Version                     : 2
Configuration Revision          : 0
Maximum VLANs supported locally : 255
Number of existing VLANs        : 7
VTP Operating Mode              : Server
VTP Domain Name                 : CCNA
VTP Pruning Mode                : Disabled
VTP V2 Mode                     : Disabled
VTP Traps Generation            : Disabled
MD5 digest                      : 0x8C 0x29 0x40 0xDD 0x7F 0x7A 0x63 0x17
Configuration last modified by 0.0.0.0 at 0-0-00 00:00:00
Local updater ID is 192.168.99.1 on interface Vl99 (lowest numbered VLAN inter-
face found)
```

b. To verify the VTP password, use the **show vtp password** command.

```
S1# show vtp password
VTP Password: cisco
```

Step 3. Add S2 and S3 to the VTP domain.

Before S2 and S3 will accept VTP advertisements from S1, they must belong to the same VTP domain. Configure S2 and S3 as VTP clients with **CCNA** as the VTP domain name and **cisco** as the VTP password. Remember that VTP domain names are case sensitive.

a. Configure S2 as a VTP client in the **CCNA** VTP domain with the VTP password **cisco**.

```
S2(config)# vtp mode client
Setting device to VTP CLIENT mode.
S2(config)# vtp domain CCNA
Changing VTP domain name from NULL to CCNA
S2(config)# vtp password cisco
Setting device VLAN database password to cisco
```

b. To verify the VTP password, use the **show vtp password** command.

```
S2# show vtp password
VTP Password: cisco
```

c. Configure S3 to be in the **CCNA** VTP domain with the VTP password **cisco**. Switch S3 will stay in VTP transparent mode.

```
S3(config)# vtp domain CCNA
Changing VTP domain name from NULL to CCNA
S3(config)# vtp password cisco
Setting device VLAN database password to cisco
```

d. Enter **show vtp status** command on all the switches to answer the following question. Notice that the configuration revision number is 0 on all three switches. Explain.

_____

_____

_____

Step 4.   Create more VLANs on S1.

a. On S1, create VLAN 10 and name it Red.

```
S1(config)# vlan 10
S1(config-vlan)# name Red
```

b. Create VLANs 20 and 30 according to the table below.

VLAN Number	VLAN Name
10	Red
20	Blue
30	Yellow

Verify the addition of the new VLANs. Enter **show vlan brief** at the privileged EXEC mode.

Which VLANs are configured on S1?

_____

c. Confirm configuration changes using the **show vtp status** command on S1 and S2 to confirm that the VTP mode and domain are configured correctly. Output for S2 is shown here.

```
S2# show vtp status
VTP Version                        : 2
Configuration Revision             : 6
Maximum VLANs supported locally : 255
Number of existing VLANs           : 10
VTP Operating Mode                 : Client
VTP Domain Name                    : CCNA
VTP Pruning Mode                   : Disabled
VTP V2 Mode                        : Disabled
VTP Traps Generation               : Disabled
MD5 digest                         : 0xE6 0x56 0x05 0xE0 0x7A 0x63 0xFB 0x33
Configuration last modified by 192.168.99.1 at 3-1-93 00:21:07
```

How many VLANs are configured on S2? Does S2 have the same VLANs as S1? Explain.

_____

_____

Step 5. Observe VTP transparent mode.

S3 is currently configured as VTP transparent mode.

    a. Use **show vtp status** command to answer the following question.

       How many VLANs are configured on S3 currently? What is the configuration revision number? Explain your answer.

       _____

       _____

       How would you change the number of VLANs on S3?

       _____

       _____

    b. Change VTP mode to client on S3.

       Use show commands to verify the changes on VTP mode. How many VLANs exist on S3 now?

       _____

Note: VTP advertisements are flooded throughout the management domain every five minutes, or whenever a change occurs in VLAN configurations. To accelerate this process, you can switch between Realtime mode and Simulation mode until the next round of updates. However, you may have to do this multiple times because this will only forward Packet Tracer's clock by 10 seconds each time. Alternatively, you can change one of the client switches to transparent mode and then back to client mode.

Step 6. Assign VLANs to Ports

Use the **switchport mode access** command to set access mode for the access links. Use the **switchport access vlan** *vlan-id* command to assign a VLAN to an access port.

Ports	Assignments	Network
S1 F0/1 – 8	VLAN 10 (Red)	192.168.10.0 /24
S2 F0/1 – 8		
S1 F0/9 – 16	VLAN 20 (Blue)	192.168.20.0 /24
S2 F0/9 – 16		
S1 F0/17 – 24	VLAN 30 (Yellow)	192.168.30.0 /24
S2 F0/17 – 24		

    a. Assign VLANs to ports on S2 using assignments from the table above.

```
S2(config-if)# interface range f0/1 - 8
S2(config-if-range)# switchport mode access
S2(config-if-range)# switchport access vlan 10
S2(config-if-range)# interface range f0/9 -16
S2(config-if-range)# switchport mode access
S2(config-if-range)# switchport access vlan 20
```

```
S2(config-if-range)# interface range f0/17 - 24
S2(config-if-range)# switchport mode access
S2(config-if-range)# switchport access vlan 30
```

   b. Assign VLANs to ports on S3 using assignment from the table above.

Step 7. Verify end-to-end connectivity.

   a. From PC0 ping PC5.

   b. From PC1 ping PC4.

   c. From PC2 ping PC3.

2.1.4.5 Lab–Configure Extended VLANs, VTP, and DTP

Topology

Addressing Table

Table Heading	Interface	IP Address	Subnet Mask
S1	VLAN 99	192.168.99.1	255.255.255.0
S2	VLAN 99	192.168.99.2	255.255.255.0
S3	VLAN 99	192.168.99.3	255.255.255.0
PC-A	NIC	192.168.10.1	255.255.255.0
PC-B	NIC	192.168.20.1	255.255.255.0
PC-C	NIC	192.168.10.2	255.255.255.0

Objectives

Part 1: Configure VTP

Part 2: Configure DTP

Part 3: Add VLANs and Assign Ports

Part 4: Configure Extended VLAN

Background/Scenario

It can become challenging to manage VLANs and trunks in a network, as the number of switches increases. VLAN trunking protocol (VTP) allows a network administrator to automate the management of VLANs. Automated trunk negotiation between network devices is managed by the Dynamic Trunking Protocol (DTP). DTP is enabled by default on Catalyst 2960 and Catalyst 3560 switches.

In this lab, you will configure trunk links between the switches. You will also configure a VTP server and VTP clients in the same VTP domain. Furthermore, you will configure an extended VLAN on one of the switches, assign ports to VLANs and verify end-to-end connectivity within the same VLAN.

Note: The switches used are Cisco Catalyst 2960s with Cisco IOS Release 15.0(2) (lanbasek9 image). Other switches and Cisco IOS versions can be used. Depending on the model and Cisco IOS version, the commands available and output produced might vary from what is shown in the labs.

Note: Make sure that the switches have been erased and have no startup configurations. If you are unsure, contact your instructor.

Required Resources

- 3 Switches (Cisco 2960 with Cisco IOS Release 15.0(2) lanbasek9 image or comparable)
- 3 PCs (Windows 7 or 8 with terminal emulation program, such as Tera Term)
- Console cables to configure the Cisco IOS devices via the console ports
- Ethernet cables as shown in the topology

Part 1: Configure VTP

All the switches will be configured to use VTP for VLAN updates. S2 will be configured as the server. Switches S1 and S3 will be configured as clients. They will be in the **CCNA** VTP domain using the password **cisco**.

a. Configure S2 as a VTP server in the **CCNA** VTP domain using **cisco** as the VTP password.

```
S2(config)# vtp domain CCNA
Changing VTP domain name from NULL to CCNA
S2(config)#
*Mar  1 00:03:44.193: %SW_VLAN-6-VTP_DOMAIN_NAME_CHG: VTP domain name changed
to CCNA.
S2(config)# vtp mode server
Device mode already VTP Server for VLANS.
S2(config)# vtp password cisco
Setting device VTP password to cisco
```

b. Configure S1 and S3 as VTP clients in the **CCNA** VTP domain using **cisco** as the VTP password. VTP configurations are displayed below.

```
S1(config)# vtp domain CCNA
Changing VTP domain name from NULL to CCNA
S1(config)#
*Mar  1 00:03:44.193: %SW_VLAN-6-VTP_DOMAIN_NAME_CHG: VTP domain name changed
to CCNA.
S1(config)# vtp mode client
Device mode VTP client for VLANS.
S1(config)# vtp password cisco
Setting device VTP password to cisco
```

c. Verify VTP configurations by entering the **show vtp status** command on all switches. The VTP status for S3 is displayed below.

```
S3# show vtp status
VTP Version capable             : 1 to 3
VTP version running             : 1
VTP Domain Name                 : CCNA
```

```
VTP Pruning Mode                    : Disabled
VTP Traps Generation                : Disabled
Device ID                           : 0cd9.96d2.3580
Configuration last modified by 0.0.0.0 at 0-0-00 00:00:00


Feature VLAN:
--------------
VTP Operating Mode                  : Client
Maximum VLANs supported locally     : 255
Number of existing VLANs            : 5
Configuration Revision              : 0
MD5 digest                          : 0x8B 0x58 0x3D 0x9D 0x64 0xBE 0xD5 0xF6
                                      0x62 0xCB 0x4B 0x50 0xE5 0x9C 0x6F 0xF6
```

Part 2: Configure DTP

Step 1.   Configure dynamic trunk links between S1 and S2.

    a.   Enter the **show interfaces f0/1 switchport** command on S1 and S2.

    What is the administrative and operational mode of switchport f0/1?

    _____

    _____

    _____

    _____

    _____

    _____

    b.   In interface configuration mode, configure a dynamic trunk link between S1 and S2. Because the default mode is dynamic auto, only one side of the link needs to be configured as dynamic desirable.

```
S1(config)# interface f0/1
S1(config-if)# switchport mode dynamic desirable
S1(config-if)#

*Mar  1 00:30:45.082: %LINEPROTO-5-UPDOWN: Line protocol on Interface
FastEthernet0/1, changed state to down

*Mar  1 00:30:48.102: %LINEPROTO-5-UPDOWN: Line protocol on Interface
FastEthernet0/1, changed state to up
```

    c.   Verify trunking link between S1 and S2 using the **show interfaces trunk** command.

```
S1# show interfaces trunk

Port        Mode         Encapsulation  Status      Native vlan
Fa0/1       desirable    802.1q         trunking    1


Port        Vlans allowed on trunk
Fa0/1       1-4094
```

```
Port         Vlans allowed and active in management domain
Fa0/1        1


Port         Vlans in spanning tree forwarding state and not pruned
Fa0/1        none


S2# show interfaces trunk

Port         Mode             Encapsulation  Status        Native vlan
Fa0/1        auto             802.1q         trunking      1


Port         Vlans allowed on trunk
Fa0/1        1-4094


Port         Vlans allowed and active in management domain
Fa0/1        1


Port         Vlans in spanning tree forwarding state and not pruned
Fa0/1        1
```

Step 2.   Configure static trunk link between S1 and S3.

  a.   Between S1 and S3, configure a static trunk link using the **switchport mode trunk** command in the interface configuration mode for port F0/3.

```
S1(config)# interface f0/3
S1(config-if)# switchport mode trunk
```

  b.   Verify the trunks using **show interfaces trunk** command on S1.

```
S1# show interface trunk

Port         Mode             Encapsulation  Status        Native vlan
Fa0/1        desirable        802.1q         trunking      1
Fa0/3        on               802.1q         trunking      1


Port         Vlans allowed on trunk
Fa0/1        1-4094
Fa0/3        1-4094


Port         Vlans allowed and active in management domain
Fa0/1        1
Fa0/3        1


Port         Vlans in spanning tree forwarding state and not pruned
Fa0/1        none
Fa0/3        none
```

  c.   Configure a permanent trunk between S2 and S3.

  d.   Record the commands you used to create the static trunk.

_____

_____

_____

_____

Part 3: Add VLANs and Assign Ports

Step 1. Add VLANs on the switches.

a. On S1, add VLAN 10.

```
S1(config)# vlan 10
```

Were you able to create VLAN 10 on S1? Explain.

_____

b. On S2, add the following VLANs.

VLAN	Name
10	Red
20	Blue
30	Yellow
99	Management

```
S2(config)# vlan 10
S2(config-vlan)# name Red
S2(config-vlan)# vlan 20
S2(config-vlan)# name Blue
S2(config-vlan)# vlan 30
S2(config-vlan)# name Yellow
S2(config-vlan)# vlan 99
S2(config-vlan)# name Management
S2(config-vlan)# end

S2# show vlan brief

VLAN Name                             Status    Ports
---- -------------------------------- --------- -------------------------------
1    default                          active    Fa0/2, Fa0/4, Fa0/5, Fa0/6
                                                Fa0/7, Fa0/8, Fa0/9, Fa0/10
                                                Fa0/11, Fa0/12, Fa0/13, Fa0/14
                                                Fa0/15, Fa0/16, Fa0/17, Fa0/18
                                                Fa0/19, Fa0/20, Fa0/21, Fa0/22
                                                Fa0/23, Fa0/24, Gi0/1, Gi0/2
10   Red                              active
20   Blue                             active
30   Yellow                           active
99   Management                       active
<output omitted>
```

Step 2. Verify VTP updates on S1 and S3.

Because S2 is configured as a VTP server, and S1 and S3 are configured as VTP clients, S1 and S3 should learn and implement the VLAN information from S2.

What **show** commands did you use to verify the VTP updates on S1 and S3?

```
S1# show vlan brief

VLAN Name                           Status     Ports
---- -------------------------------- ---------  -------------------------------
1    default                         active     Fa0/2, Fa0/4, Fa0/5, Fa0/6
                                                 Fa0/7, Fa0/8, Fa0/9, Fa0/10
                                                 Fa0/11, Fa0/12, Fa0/13, Fa0/14
                                                 Fa0/15, Fa0/16, Fa0/17, Fa0/18
                                                 Fa0/19, Fa0/20, Fa0/21, Fa0/22
                                                 Fa0/23, Fa0/24, Gi0/1, Gi0/2

10   Red                             active
20   Blue                            active
30   Yellow                          active
99   Management                      active
1002 fddi-default                    act/unsup
1003 token-ring-default              act/unsup
1004 fddinet-default                 act/unsup
1005 trnet-default                   act/unsup


S1# show vtp status
VTP Version capable             : 1 to 3
VTP version running             : 1
VTP Domain Name                 : CCNA
VTP Pruning Mode                : Disabled
VTP Traps Generation            : Disabled
Device ID                       : 0cd9.96e2.3d00
Configuration last modified by 0.0.0.0 at 3-1-93 00:58:46


Feature VLAN:
--------------
VTP Operating Mode              : Client
Maximum VLANs supported locally : 255
Number of existing VLANs        : 9
Configuration Revision          : 4
MD5 digest                      : 0xB2 0x9A 0x11 0x5B 0xBF 0x2E 0xBF 0xAA
                                  0x31 0x18 0xFF 0x2C 0x5E 0x54 0x0A 0xB7
```

Step 3.   Assign ports to VLANs.

In this step, you will associate ports to VLANs and configure IP addresses according to the table below.

Port Assignment	VLAN	Attached PC IP Address and Prefix

S1 F0/6	VLAN 10	PC-A: 192.168.10.1 / 24
S2 F0/18	VLAN 20	PC-B: 192.168.20.1 /24
S3 F0/18	VLAN 10	PC-C: 192.168.10.2 /24

    a. On S1, configure F0/6 to access mode and assign F0/6 to VLAN 10.

```
S1(config)# interface f0/6
S1(config-if)# switchport mode access
S1(config-if)# switchport access vlan 10
```

    b. Repeat the procedure for switchport F0/18 on S2 and S3. Assign the VLAN according to the table above.

    c. Assign the IP addresses to the PCs according to the table above.

Step 4. Configure IP addresses on the switches.

    a. On S1, assign an IP address to the SVI for VLAN 99 according to the Addressing Table and activate the interface.

```
S1(config)# interface vlan 99
S1(config-if)# ip address 192.168.99.1 255.255.255.0
S1(config-fi)# no shutdown
```

    b. Repeat step a. for S2 and S3.

Step 5. Verify end-to-end connectivity

    a. Ping PC-A from PC-B. Was it successful? Explain.

    _____

    b. Ping PC-A from PC-C. Was it successful? Explain.

    _____

    c. Ping PC-A from S1. Was it successful? Explain.

    _____

    d. Ping S1 from S2. Was it successful? Explain.

    _____

Part 4: Configure Extended VLAN

An extended VLAN is a VLAN between 1025 and 4096. Because the extended VLANs cannot be managed with VTP, VTP must be configured in transparent mode. In this part, you will change the VTP mode on S1 to transparent and create an extended VLAN on S1.

Step 1. Configure VTP mode to transparent on S1.

    a. On switch S1, set VTP mode to transparent.

```
S1(config)# vtp mode transparent
Setting device to VTP Transparent mode for VLANS.
S1(config)# exit
```

    b. Verify the VTP mode on S1.

```
S1# show vtp status
VTP Version capable             : 1 to 3
VTP version running             : 1
VTP Domain Name                 : CCNA
VTP Pruning Mode                : Disabled
VTP Traps Generation            : Disabled
Device ID                       : 0cd9.96e2.3d00
Configuration last modified by 0.0.0.0 at 3-1-93 02:36:11


Feature VLAN:
--------------
VTP Operating Mode              : Transparent
Maximum VLANs supported locally : 255
Number of existing VLANs        : 9
Configuration Revision          : 0
MD5 digest                      : 0xB2 0x9A 0x11 0x5B 0xBF 0x2E 0xBF 0xAA
                                  0x31 0x18 0xFF 0x2C 0x5E 0x54 0x0A 0xB7
```

Step 2. Configure an extended VLAN on S1.

    a. Display the current VLAN configurations on S1.

    b. Create an extended VLAN 2000.

```
S1# conf t
Enter configuration commands, one per line.  End with CNTL/Z.
S1(config)# vlan 2000
S1(config-vlan)# end
```

    c. Verify the VLAN creation.

```
S1# show vlan brief

VLAN Name                             Status    Ports
---- -------------------------------- --------- -------------------------------
1    default                          active    Fa0/2, Fa0/4, Fa0/5, Fa0/7
                                                Fa0/8, Fa0/9, Fa0/10, Fa0/11
                                                Fa0/12, Fa0/13, Fa0/14, Fa0/15
                                                Fa0/16, Fa0/17, Fa0/18, Fa0/19
                                                Fa0/20, Fa0/21, Fa0/22, Fa0/23
                                                Fa0/24, Gi0/1, Gi0/2
10   Red                              active    Fa0/6
20   Blue                             active
30   Yellow                           active
99   Management                       active
1002 fddi-default                     act/unsup
```

```
1003 token-ring-default              act/unsup
1004 fddinet-default                 act/unsup
1005 trnet-default                   act/unsup
2000 VLAN2000                        active
```

Reflection

What are the advantages and disadvantages of using VTP?

_____

_____

_____

_____

Router Interface Summary Table

Router Interface Summary

Router Model	Ethernet Interface #1	Ethernet Interface #2	Serial Interface #1	Serial Interface #2
1800	Fast Ethernet 0/0 (F0/0)	Fast Ethernet 0/1 (F0/1)	Serial 0/0/0 (S0/0/0)	Serial 0/0/1 (S0/0/1)
1900	Gigabit Ethernet 0/0 (G0/0)	Gigabit Ethernet 0/1 (G0/1)	Serial 0/0/0 (S0/0/0)	Serial 0/0/1 (S0/0/1)
2801	Fast Ethernet 0/0 (F0/0)	Fast Ethernet 0/1 (F0/1)	Serial 0/1/0 (S0/1/0)	Serial 0/1/1 (S0/1/1)
2811	Fast Ethernet 0/0 (F0/0)	Fast Ethernet 0/1 (F0/1)	Serial 0/0/0 (S0/0/0)	Serial 0/0/1 (S0/0/1)
2900	Gigabit Ethernet 0/0 (G0/0)	Gigabit Ethernet 0/1 (G0/1)	Serial 0/0/0 (S0/0/0)	Serial 0/0/1 (S0/0/1)

Note: To find out how the router is configured, look at the interfaces to identify the type of router and how many interfaces the router has. There is no way to effectively list all the combinations of configurations for each router class. This table includes identifiers for the possible combinations of Ethernet and Serial interfaces in the device. The table does not include any other type of interface, even though a specific router may contain one. An example of this might be an ISDN BRI interface. The string in parentheses is the legal abbreviation that can be used in Cisco IOS commands to represent the interface.

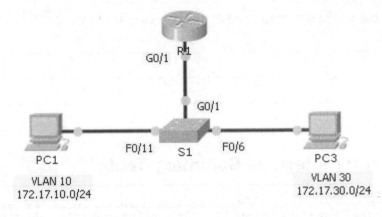

| Packet Tracer
☐ Activity | |

2.2.2.4 Packet Tracer–Troubleshooting Inter-VLAN Routing

Topology

Addressing Table

Device	Interface	IP Address	Subnet Mask	Default Gateway	VLAN
R1	G0/1.10	172.17.10.1	255.255.255.0	N/A	VLAN 10
	G0/1.30	172.17.30.1	255.255.255.0	N/A	VLAN 30
PC1	NIC	172.17.10.10	255.255.255.0	172.17.10.1	VLAN 10
PC3	NIC	172.17.30.10	255.255.255.0	172.17.30.1	VLAN 30

Objectives

Part 1: Locate Network Problems

Part 2: Implement the Solution

Part 3: Verify Network Connectivity

Scenario

In this activity, you will troubleshoot connectivity problems caused by improper configurations related to VLANs and inter-VLAN routing.

Part 1: Locate the Network Problems

Examine the network and locate the source of any connectivity issues.

- Test connectivity and use the necessary **show** commands to verify configurations.
- List all of the problems and possible solutions in the **Documentation Table**.

Documentation Table

Problems	Solutions

Part 2: Implement the Solutions

Make changes according to your recommended solutions.

Part 3: Verify Network Connectivity

Verify the PCs can ping other PCs and R1. If not, continue to troubleshoot until the pings are successful.

Suggested Scoring Rubric

Packet Tracer scores 60 points. Completing the **Documentation Table** is worth 40 points.

2.2.2.5 Lab–Troubleshooting Inter-VLAN Routing

Topology

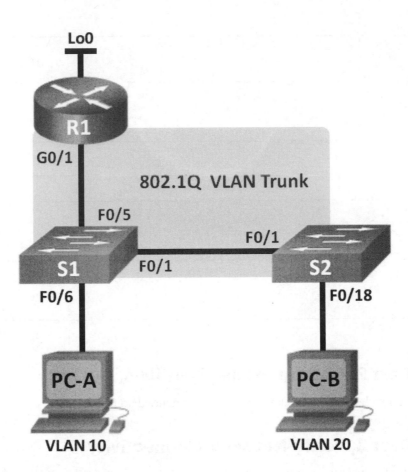

Addressing Table

Device	Interface	IP Address	Subnet Mask	Default Gateway
R1	G0/1.1	192.168.1.1	255.255.255.0	N/A
	G0/1.10	192.168.10.1	255.255.255.0	N/A
	G0/1.20	192.168.20.1	255.255.255.0	N/A
	Lo0	209.165.200.225	255.255.255.224	N/A
S1	VLAN 1	192.168.1.11	255.255.255.0	192.168.1.1
S2	VLAN 1	192.168.1.12	255.255.255.0	192.168.1.1
PC-A	NIC	192.168.10.3	255.255.255.0	192.168.10.1
PC-B	NIC	192.168.20.3	255.255.255.0	192.168.20.1

Switch Port Assignment Specifications

Ports	Assignment	Network
S1 F0/1	802.1Q Trunk	N/A
S2 F0/1	802.1Q Trunk	N/A
S1 F0/5	802.1Q Trunk	N/A
S1 F0/6	VLAN 10 – R&D	192.168.10.0/24
S2 F0/18	VLAN 20 – Engineering	192.168.20.0/24

Objectives

Part 1: Build the Network and Load Device Configurations

Part 2: Troubleshoot the Inter-VLAN Routing Configuration

Part 3: Verify VLAN Configuration, Port Assignment, and Trunking

Part 4: Test Layer 3 Connectivity

Background/Scenario

The network has been designed and configured to support three VLANs. Inter-VLAN routing is provided by an external router using an 802.1Q trunk, also known as router-on-a-stick. Routing to a remote Web Server, which is simulated by Lo0, is also provided by R1. However, it is not working as designed, and user complaints have not given much insight into the source of the problems.

In this lab, you must first define what is not working as expected, and then analyze the existing configurations to determine and correct the source of the problems. This lab is complete when you can demonstrate IP connectivity between each of the user VLANs and the external Web Server network, and between the switch management VLAN and the Web Server network.

Note: The routers used with CCNA hands-on labs are Cisco 1941 Integrated Services Routers (ISRs) with Cisco IOS Release 15.2(4)M3 (universalk9 image). The switches used are Cisco Catalyst 2960s with Cisco IOS Release 15.0(2) (lanbasek9 image). Other routers, switches, and Cisco IOS versions can be used. Depending on the model and Cisco IOS version, the commands available and output produced might vary from what is shown in the labs. Refer to the Router Interface Summary Table at the end of this lab for the correct interface identifiers.

Note: Make sure that the routers and switches have been erased and have no startup configurations. If you are unsure, contact your instructor.

Required Resources

- 1 Router (Cisco 1941 with Cisco IOS Release 15.2(4)M3 universal image or comparable)
- 2 Switches (Cisco 2960 with Cisco IOS Release 15.0(2) lanbasek9 image or comparable)
- 2 PCs (Microsoft Windows with terminal emulation program, such as Tera Term)
- Console cables to configure the Cisco IOS devices via the console ports
- Ethernet cables as shown in the topology

Part 1: Build the Network and Load Device Configurations

In Part 1, you will set up the network topology and configure basic settings on the PC hosts, switches, and router.

Step 1.   Cable the network as shown in the topology.

Step 2.   Configure PC hosts.

Refer to the Addressing Table for PC host address information.

Step 3.   Load router and switch configurations.

Load the following configurations into the appropriate router or switch. All devices have the same passwords; the enable password is **class**, and the line password is **cisco**.

Router R1 Configuration:

```
hostname R1
enable secret class
no ip domain lookup
line con 0
 password cisco
 login
 logging synchronous
line vty 0 4
 password cisco
 login
interface loopback0
 ip address 209.165.200.225 255.255.255.224
interface gigabitEthernet0/1
 no ip address
```

_____

```
interface gigabitEthernet0/1.1
 encapsulation dot1q 11
```

_____

```
 ip address 192.168.1.1 255.255.255.0
interface gigabitEthernet0/1.10
 encapsulation dot1q 10
 ip address 192.168.11.1 255.255.255.0
```

_____

```
interface gigabitEthernet0/1.20
 encapsulation dot1q 20
 ip address 192.168.20.1 255.255.255.0
end
```

Switch S1 Configuration:

```
hostname S1
enable secret class
no ip domain-lookup
line con 0
 password cisco
 login
 logging synchronous
```

```
line vty 0 15
 password cisco
 login
vlan 10
 name R&D
 exit
```



```
interface fastethernet0/1
 switchport mode access
```

```
interface fastethernet0/5
 switchport mode trunk
```



```
interface vlan1
 ip address 192.168.1.11 255.255.255.0
ip default-gateway 192.168.1.1
end
```

Switch S2 Configuration:

```
hostname S2
enable secret class
no ip domain-lookup
line con 0
 password cisco
 login
 logging synchronous
line vty 0 15
 password cisco
 login
```



```
vlan 20
 name Engineering
 exit
interface fastethernet0/1
 switchport mode trunk
interface fastethernet0/18
 switchport access vlan 10
 switchport mode access
```

```
interface vlan1
 ip address 192.168.1.12 255.255.255.0
ip default-gateway 192.168.1.1
end
```

Step 4.   Save the running configuration to the startup configuration.

Part 2: Troubleshoot the Inter-VLAN Routing Configuration

In Part 2, you will verify the inter-VLAN routing configuration.

   a.   On R1, enter the **show ip route** command to view the routing table.

   Which networks are listed?

   _____

   Are there any networks missing in the routing table? If so, which networks?

   _____

   What is one possible reason that a route would be missing from the routing table?

   _____

   b.   On R1, issue the **show ip interface brief** command.

   Based on the output, are there any interface issues on the router? If so, what commands would resolve the issues?

   _____

   _____

   _____

   c.   On R1, re-issue the **show ip route** command.

Verify that all networks are available in the routing table. If not, continue to troubleshoot until all networks are present.

Part 3: Verify VLAN Configuration, Port Assignment, and Trunking

In Part 3, you will verify that the correct VLANs exist on both S1 and S2 and that trunking is configured correctly.

Step 1.   Verify VLAN configuration and port assignments.

   a.   On S1, enter the **show vlan brief** command to view the VLAN database.

   Which VLANs are listed? Ignore VLANs 1002 to 1005.

   _____

   Are there any VLANs numbers or names missing in the output? If so, list them.

   _____

   Are the access ports assigned to the correct VLANs? If not, list the missing or incorrect assignments.

   _____

If required, what commands would resolve the VLAN issues?

_____

_____

_____

_____

_____

_____

b. On S1, re-issue the **show vlan brief** command to verify configuration.

c. On S2, enter the **show vlan brief** command to view the VLAN database.

Which VLANs are listed? Ignore VLANs 1002 to 1005.

_____

Are there any VLANs numbers or names missing in the output? If so, list them.

_____

Are the access ports assigned to the correct VLANs? If not, list the missing or incorrect assignments.

_____

If required, what commands would resolve the VLAN issues?

_____

_____

_____

_____

d. On S2, re-issue the **show vlan brief** command to verify any configuration changes.

Step 2.   Verify trunking interfaces.

a. On S1, enter the **show interface trunk** command to view the trunking interfaces.

Which ports are in trunking mode?

_____

Are there any ports missing in the output? If so, list them.

_____

If required, what commands would resolve the port trunking issues?

_____

_____

b. On S1, re-issue the **show interface trunk** command to verify any configuration changes.

c. On S2, enter the **show interface trunk** command to view the trunking interfaces.

Which ports are in trunking mode?

_____

Are there any ports missing in the output? If so, list them.

_____

If required, what commands would resolve the port trunking issues?

_____

_____

Part 4: Test Layer 3 Connectivity

a. Now that you have corrected multiple configuration issues, let's test connectivity.

From PC-A, is it possible to ping the default gateway for VLAN 10? _____

From PC-A, is it possible to ping PC-B? _____

From PC-A, is it possible to ping Lo0? _____

If the answer is **no** to any of these questions, troubleshoot the configurations and correct the error.

Note: It may be necessary to disable the PC firewall for pings between PCs to be successful.

From PC-A, is it possible to ping S1? _____

From PC-A, is it possible to ping S2? _____

List some of the issues that could still be preventing successful pings to the switches.

_____

_____

b. One way to help resolve where the error is occurring is to do a **tracert** from PC-A to S1.

```
C:\Users\User1> tracert 192.168.1.11
Tracing route to 192.168.1.11 over a maximum of 30 hops
  1    <1 ms    <1 ms    <1 ms  192.168.10.1
  2    *        *        *      Request timed out.
  3    *        *        *      Request timed out.
<output omitted>
```

This output shows that the request from PC-A is reaching the default gateway on R1 g0/1.10, but the packet stops at the router.

c.   You have already verified the routing table entries for R1, now execute the **show run | section interface** command to verify VLAN configuration. List any configuration errors.

_____

_____

_____

_____

_____

_____

_____

_____

_____

_____

_____

_____

_____

_____

_____

What commands would resolve any issues found?

_____

_____

_____

d.   Verify that pings from PC-A now reach both S1 and S2.

From PC-A, is it possible to ping S1? _____

From PC-A, is it possible to ping S2? _____

Reflection

What are the advantages of viewing the routing table for troubleshooting purposes?

_____

_____

Router Interface Summary Table

Router Interface Summary				
Router Model	Ethernet Interface #1	Ethernet Interface #2	Serial Interface #1	Serial Interface #2
1800	Fast Ethernet 0/0 (F0/0)	Fast Ethernet 0/1 (F0/1)	Serial 0/0/0 (S0/0/0)	Serial 0/0/1 (S0/0/1)
1900	Gigabit Ethernet 0/0 (G0/0)	Gigabit Ethernet 0/1 (G0/1)	Serial 0/0/0 (S0/0/0)	Serial 0/0/1 (S0/0/1)
2801	Fast Ethernet 0/0 (F0/0)	Fast Ethernet 0/1 (F0/1)	Serial 0/1/0 (S0/1/0)	Serial 0/1/1 (S0/1/1)
2811	Fast Ethernet 0/0 (F0/0)	Fast Ethernet 0/1 (F0/1)	Serial 0/0/0 (S0/0/0)	Serial 0/0/1 (S0/0/1)
2900	Gigabit Ethernet 0/0 (G0/0)	Gigabit Ethernet 0/1 (G0/1)	Serial 0/0/0 (S0/0/0)	Serial 0/0/1 (S0/0/1)

Note: To find out how the router is configured, look at the interfaces to identify the type of router and how many interfaces the router has. There is no way to effectively list all the combinations of configurations for each router class. This table includes identifiers for the possible combinations of Ethernet and Serial interfaces in the device. The table does not include any other type of interface, even though a specific router may contain one. An example of this might be an ISDN BRI interface. The string in parentheses is the legal abbreviation that can be used in Cisco IOS commands to represent the interface.

2.2.3.3 Packet Tracer–Troubleshoot VTP and DTP

Topology

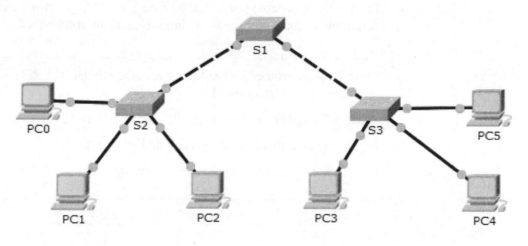

Addressing Table

Device	IP Address	Subnet Mask
PC0	172.16.10.1	255.255.255.0
PC1	172.16.20.1	255.255.255.0
PC2	172.16.30.1	255.255.255.0
PC3	172.16.30.2	255.255.255.0
PC4	172.16.20.2	255.255.255.0
PC5	172.16.10.2	255.255.255.0
S1	172.16.99.1	255.255.255.0
S2	172.16.99.2	255.255.255.0
S3	172.16.99.3	255.255.255.0

Objectives

Part 1: Troubleshoot DTP

Part 2: Troubleshoot VTP

Background/Scenario

In this activity, the switches S2 and S3 are not implementing VTP information. You will verify that DTP and VTP configurations are correctly implemented. When all the issues are resolved, the PCs in the same VLAN will be able to communicate with each other.

Part 1: Troubleshoot DTP

In Part 1, you will troubleshoot the trunk links among the switches. You will verify that permanent trunk links are used between the switches.

a. Enter **show interfaces trunk** at the privileged EXEC prompt on all the switches to determine the status of the trunk links. How many trunk links are configured currently?

_____

b. Enter **show interfaces g0/1 switchport** at the privileged EXEC prompt on S1. Do the same for g0/2 interface on S1.

What is the operational mode on the GigabitEthernet interfaces on S1?_____

c. Repeat the commands for g0/1 on S2 and g0/2 on S3.

Correct the trunk links. Record the commands you used to correct the trunking issue.

_____

_____

_____

_____

_____

_____

d. Verify the trunk links using the **show** commands.

Part 2: Troubleshoot VTP

S1 will be configured as the VTP server. S2 and S3 will be configured as VTP clients, and will be receiving VTP updates from S1. The VTP domain should be **CCNA** and the VTP password should be **cisco**. Currently all the desired VLANs are already configured on S1.

Step 1. Verify VLAN information.

Use the **show vlan brief** command on all the switches. Do all the switches have the same number of VLANs? How many does each switch have?

_____

Step 2. Verify VTP configurations.

Use the **show vtp status** and **show vtp password** commands on all the switches to verify the VTP status.

Record the VTP status information in the table below.

Device	Domain Name	Operating Mode	VTP Password
S1			
S2			
S3			

Step 3.   Correct the VTP configurations.

Record the commands used to correct the VTP configurations.

_____

_____

_____

_____

_____

_____

_____

_____

Step 4.   Verify port assignment.

The switchports connecting to the PCs need to be configured in the correct VLANs so the PCs can communicate with each other.

Use the **show vlan brief** command on S2 and S3 to determine if VLANs have been assigned to the switchports. Which VLAN is associated with these switchports? _____

Ports	Assignments	Network
S2 F0/1	VLAN 10 (Staff)	172.16.10.0/24
S3 F0/8		
S2 F0/9	VLAN 20 (Student)	172.16.20.0 /24
S3 F0/16		
S2 F0/17	VLAN 30 (Faculty)	172.16.30.0 /24
S3 F0/24		

Using the table above, correct the VLAN assignments on S2 and S3. Record the VLAN assignment configurations below.

_____

_____

_____

_____

_____

_____

_____

_____

_____

_____

_____

Step 5. Verify end-to-end connectivity.

    a. From PC0 ping PC5.

    b. From PC1 ping PC4.

    c. From PC2 ping PC3.

2.3.1.5 Packet Tracer–Configure Layer 3 Switching and Inter-VLAN Routing

Topology

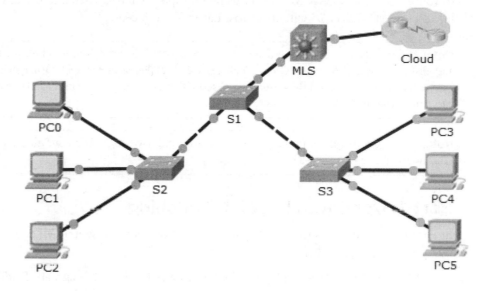

Addressing Table

Device	Interface	IP Address	Subnet Mask
MLS	VLAN 10	192.168.10.254	255.255.255.0
	VLAN 20	192.168.20.254	255.255.255.0
	VLAN 30	192.168.30.254	255.255.255.0
	VLAN 99	192.168.99.254	255.255.255.0
	G0/2	209.165.200.225	255.255.255.252
PC0	NIC	192.168.10.1	255.255.255.0
PC1	NIC	192.168.20.1	255.255.255.0
PC2	NIC	192.168.30.1	255.255.255.0
PC3	NIC	192.168.30.2	255.255.255.0
PC4	NIC	192.168.20.2	255.255.255.0
PC5	NIC	192.168.10.2	255.255.255.0
S1	VLAN 99	192.168.99.1	255.255.255.0
S2	VLAN 99	192.168.99.2	255.255.255.0
S3	VLAN 99	192.168.99.3	255.255.255.0

Objectives

Part 1: Configure Layer 3 Switching

Part 2: Configure Inter-VLAN Routing

Background/Scenario

A multilayer switch like the Cisco Catalyst 3560 is capable of both Layer 2 switching and Layer 3 routing. One of the advantages of using a multilayer switch is this dual functionality. A benefit for a small- to medium-sized company would be the ability to purchase a single multilayer switch instead of separate switching and routing network devices. Capabilities of a multilayer switch include the ability to route from one VLAN to another using multiple switched virtual interfaces (SVIs), as well as the ability to convert a Layer 2 switchport to a Layer 3 interface.

Note: The switches used in this lab are a Cisco Catalyst 3560 with Cisco IOS Release 12.2(37) (advipservicesk9) and Cisco Catalyst 2960s with Cisco IOS Release 15.0(2) (lanbasek9 image). Other switches and Cisco IOS versions can be used. Depending on the model and Cisco IOS version, the commands available and output produced might vary from what is shown in the labs.

Note: Make sure that the switches have been erased and have no startup configurations. If you are unsure, contact your instructor.

Part 1: Configure Layer 3 Switching

In Part 1, you will configure the GigabitEthernet 0/2 port on switch MLS as a routed port and verify that you can ping another Layer 3 address.

a. On MLS, configure G0/2 as a routed port and assign an IP address according to the Addressing Table.

```
MLS(config)# interface g0/2
MLS(config-if)# no switchport
MLS(config-if)# ip address 209.165.200.225 255.255.255.252
```

b. Verify connectivity to **Cloud** by pinging 209.165.200.226.

```
MLS# ping 209.165.200.226

Type escape sequence to abort.
Sending 5, 100-byte ICMP Echos to 209.165.200.226, timeout is 2 seconds:
!!!!!
Success rate is 100 percent (5/5), round-trip min/avg/max = 0/0/0 ms
```

Part 2: Configure Inter-VLAN Routing

Step 1.   Add VLANs.

Add VLANs to MLS according to the table below.

VLAN Number	VLAN Name
10	Staff
20	Student
30	Faculty

Step 2.   Configure SVI on MLS.

Configure and activate the SVI interface for VLANs 10, 20, 30, and 99 according to the Addressing Table. The configuration for VLAN 10 is shown below.

```
MLS(config)# interface vlan 10
MLS(config-if)# ip address 192.168.10.254 255.255.255.0
```

Step 3.   Enable routing.

a.   Use the **show ip route** command. Are there any active routes? _____

b.   Enter the **ip routing** command to enable routing in global configuration mode.

```
MLS(config)# ip routing
```

c.   Use the **show ip route** command to verify routing is enabled.

```
MLS# show ip route
Codes: C - connected, S - static, I - IGRP, R - RIP, M - mobile, B - BGP
       D - EIGRP, EX - EIGRP external, O - OSPF, IA - OSPF inter area
       N1 - OSPF NSSA external type 1, N2 - OSPF NSSA external type 2
       E1 - OSPF external type 1, E2 - OSPF external type 2, E - EGP
       i - IS-IS, L1 - IS-IS level-1, L2 - IS-IS level-2, ia - IS-IS inter area
       * - candidate default, U - per-user static route, o - ODR
       P - periodic downloaded static route

Gateway of last resort is not set

C    192.168.10.0/24 is directly connected, Vlan10
C    192.168.20.0/24 is directly connected, Vlan20
C    192.168.30.0/24 is directly connected, Vlan30
C    192.168.99.0/24 is directly connected, Vlan99
     209.165.200.0/30 is subnetted, 1 subnets
C       209.165.200.224 is directly connected, GigabitEthernet0/2
```

Step 4.   Verify end-to-end connectivity.

a.   From PC0, ping PC3 or MLS to verify connectivity within VLAN 10.

b.   From PC1, ping PC4 or MLS to verify connectivity within VLAN 20.

c.   From PC2, ping PC5 or MLS to verify connectivity within VLAN 30.

d.   From S1, ping S2, S3, or MLS to verify connectivity with VLAN 99.

e.   To verify inter-VLAN routing, ping devices outside the sender's VLAN.

f.   From any device, ping this address inside **Cloud,** 209.165.200.226

CHAPTER 3

STP

Computer networks are inextricably linked to productivity in today's small and medium-sized businesses. Consequently, IT administrators have to implement redundancy in their hierarchical networks. When a switch connection is lost, another link needs to quickly take its place without introducing any traffic loops. This chapter investigates how Spanning Tree Protocol (STP) logically blocks physical loops in the network and how STP has evolved into a robust protocol that rapidly calculates which ports should be blocked in a VLAN-based network.

Study Guide

Spanning Tree Concepts

Redundancy increases the availability of a network topology by protecting the network from a single point of failure, such as a failed network cable or switch. STP was developed to address the issue of loops in a redundant Layer 2 design.

Draw a Redundant Topology

In Figure 3-1, draw redundant links between the access, distribution, and core switches. Each access switch should have two links to the distribution layer with each link connecting to a different distribution layer switch. Each distribution layer switch should have two links to the core layer with each link connecting to a different core layer switch.

Figure 3-1   Redundant Topology

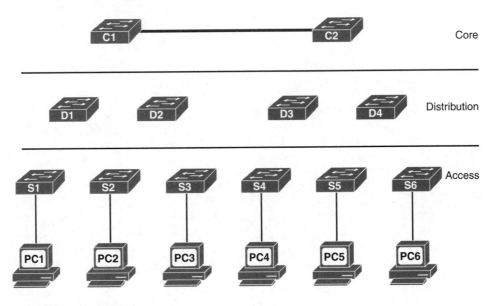

Purpose of Spanning Tree

STP prevents specific types of issues in a redundant topology like the one in Figure 3-1. Specifically, three potential issues would occur if STP was not implemented. Describe each of the following issues:

- MAC database instability:

  _____

  _____

  _____

- Broadcast storms:

  _____

  _____

■ Multiple frame transmission:

_____

_____

_____

You should be prepared to use a topology like Figure 3-1 to explain exactly how these three issues would occur if STP was not implemented.

Spanning Tree Operation

Because _____, which is documented in IEEE _____-2004, supersedes the original STP documented in IEEE _____-1998, all references to STP assume RSTP unless otherwise indicated.

STP ensures that there is only one logical path between all destinations on the network by intentionally blocking redundant paths that could cause a _____. A switch port is considered _____ when network traffic is prevented from entering or leaving that port.

STP uses the _____ (STA) to determine which switch ports on a network need to be _____ to prevent _____ from occurring. The STA designates a single switch as the root bridge and uses it as the reference point for all subsequent calculations. Switches participating in STP determine which switch has the lowest _____ (BID) on the network. This switch automatically becomes the _____ bridge.

A _____ (BPDU) is a frame containing STP information exchanged by switches running STP. Each BPDU contains a BID that identifies the switch that sent the BPDU. The _____ BID value determines which switch is root.

After the root bridge has been determined, the STA calculates the shortest path to the root bridge. If there is more than one path to choose from, STA chooses the path with the lowest _____.

When the STA has determined the "best" paths emanating from the root bridge, it configures the switch ports into distinct port roles. The port roles describe their relation in the network to the root bridge and whether they are allowed to forward traffic:

■ _____ **ports:** Switch ports closest to the root bridge

■ _____ **ports:** Nonroot ports that are still permitted to forward traffic on the network

■ _____ **ports:** Ports in a blocking state to prevent loops

■ _____ **port:** Ports that are administratively shut down

After a switch boots, it sends BPDU frames containing the switch BID and the root ID every 2 seconds. Initially, each switch identifies itself as the root bridge after boot.

How would a switch determine that another switch is now the root bridge?

_____

_____

How does the STA determine path cost?

_____

_____

Record the default port costs for various link speeds in Table 3-1.

Table 3-1 Port Costs

Link Speed	Cost (Revised IEEE Specification)	Cost (Previous IEEE Specification)
10 Gbps		
1 Gbps		
100 Mbps		
10 Mbps		

Although switch ports have a default port cost associated with them, the port cost is configurable.

To configure the port cost of an interface, enter the **spanning-tree cost value** command in interface configuration mode. The range value can be between 1 and 200,000,000.

Record the commands, including the switch prompt, to configure the port cost for F0/1 as 15:

_____

_____

To verify the port and path cost to the root bridge, enter the **show spanning-tree** privileged EXEC mode command, as shown here:

```
S2# _____
VLAN0001
  Spanning tree enabled protocol ieee
  Root ID    Priority    32769
             Address     c025.5cd7.ef00
             Cost        15
             Port        1 (FastEthernet0/1)
             Hello Time   2 sec  Max Age 20 sec  Forward Delay 15 sec

  Bridge ID  Priority    32769  (priority 32768 sys-id-ext 1)
             Address     c07b.bcc4.a980
             Hello Time   2 sec  Max Age 20 sec  Forward Delay 15 sec
             Aging Time  15  sec


Interface          Role Sts Cost      Prio.Nbr Type
------------------ ---- --- --------- -------- -------------------------------
Fa0/1              Root FWD 15        128.1    P2p
Fa0/2              Altn BLK 19        128.2    P2p
Fa0/3              Desg LIS 19        128.3    P2p
Fa0/4              Desg LIS 19        128.4    P2p
Fa0/6              Desg FWD 19        128.6    P2p
<output omitted>
```

The BID field of a BPDU frame contains three separate fields: _____, _____, and _____.

Of these three fields, the _____ is a customizable value that you can use to influence which switch becomes the root bridge. The default value for this field is

_____.

Cisco enhanced its implementation of STP to include support for the extended system ID field, which contains the ID of the _____ with which the BPDU is associated.

Because using the extended system ID changes the number of bits available for the bridge priority, the customizable values can only be multiples of _____.

When two switches are configured with the same priority and have the same extended system ID, the switch with the lowest _____ has the lower BID.

Identify the 802.1D Port Roles

The topologies in the next three figures do not necessarily represent an appropriate network design. However, they provide good exercise topologies for you to practice determining the STP port roles. In Figures 3-2 through 3-4, use the priority values and MAC addresses to determine the root bridge. Then label the ports with one of the following:

- RP: Root Port

- DP: Designated Port

- AP: Alternate Port

Figure 3-2   802.1D Port Roles - Scenario 1

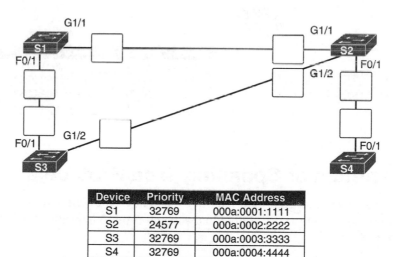

Device	Priority	MAC Address
S1	32769	000a:0001:1111
S2	24577	000a:0002:2222
S3	32769	000a:0003:3333
S4	32769	000a:0004:4444

Figure 3-3   802.1D Port Roles - Scenario 2

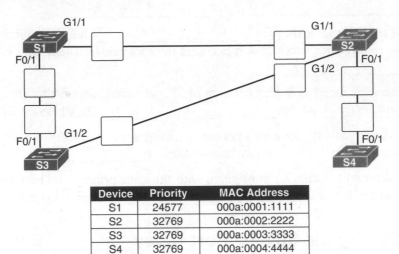

Device	Priority	MAC Address
S1	24577	000a:0001:1111
S2	32769	000a:0002:2222
S3	32769	000a:0003:3333
S4	32769	000a:0004:4444

Figure 3-4   802.1D Port Roles - Scenario 3

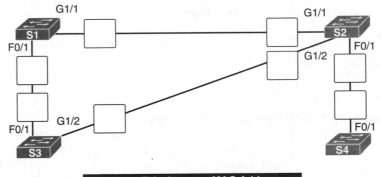

Device	Priority	MAC Address
S1	32769	000a:0001:1111
S2	32769	000a:0002:2222
S3	24577	000a:0003:3333
S4	32769	000a:0004:4444

Varieties of Spanning Tree Protocols

STP has been improved multiple times since its introduction in the original IEEE 802.1D specification. A network administrator should know which type to implement based on the equipment and topology needs.

Comparing the STP Varieties

Identify each of the STP varieties described in the following list:

- _____: This is the original IEEE 802.1D version (802.1D-1998 and earlier) that provides a loop-free topology in a network with redundant links.

- _____: This is a Cisco enhancement of STP that provides a separate 802.1D spanning tree instance for each VLAN configured in the network.

- _____ : This is an updated version of the STP standard, incorporating IEEE 802.1w.

- _____ : This is an evolution of STP that provides faster convergence than STP.

- _____ : This is a Cisco enhancement that provides a separate instance of 802.1w per VLAN.

- _____ : This is an IEEE that maps multiple VLANs into the same spanning tree instance.

Complete the cells in Table 3-2 to identify the characteristics of each STP variety.

Table 3-2   STP Characteristics - Exercise 1

Protocol	Standard	Resources Needed	Convergence	Tree Calculation
STP		Low		
	Cisco			
	802.1w			
Rapid PVST+				
	802.1s, Cisco	Medium or high		

In Table 3-3, indicate which varieties of STP are best described by the characteristic. Some characteristics apply to more than one STP variety.

Table 3-3   STP Characteristics - Exercise 2

Characteristic	STP	PVST+	RSTP	Rapid PVST+	MSTP	MST
A Cisco implementation of 802.1s that provides up to 16 instances of RSTP.						
Cisco enhancement of RSTP.						
The default STP mode for Cisco Catalyst switches.						
Has the highest CPU and memory requirements.						
Can lead to suboptimal traffic flows.						
Cisco proprietary versions of STP.						
Cisco enhancement of STP. Provides a separate 802.1D spanning-tree instance for each VLAN.						
There is only 1 root bridge and 1 tree.						
Uses 1 IEEE 802.1D spanning-tree instance for the entire bridged network, regardless of the number of VLANs.						
Supports PortFast, BPDU guard, BPDU filter, root guard, and loop guard.						
An evolution of STP that provides faster STP convergence.						
Maps multiple VLANs that have the same traffic flow requirements into the same spanning-tree instance.						
First version of STP to address convergence issues, but still provided only one STP instance.						

PVST+ Operation

After a switch boots, the spanning tree is immediately determined as ports transition through five possible states and three BPDU timers on the way to convergence. Briefly describe each state:

■   Blocking:

_____

_____

_____

■   Listening:

_____

_____

_____

_____

_____

■   Learning:

_____

_____

■   Forwarding:

_____

_____

■   Disabled:

_____

_____

Once stable, every active port in the switched network is either in the _____ state or the _____ state.

List and briefly describe the four steps PVST+ performs for each VLAN to provide a loop-free logical topology.

_____

_____

_____

_____

_____

In Table 3-4, answer the "Operation Allowed" question with "yes" or "no" for each port state.

Table 3-4   Operations Allowed at Each Port State

Operation Allowed	Port State				
	Blocking	**Listening**	**Learning**	**Forwarding**	**Disabled**
Can receive and process BPDUs					
Can forward data frames received on interface					
Can forward data frames switched from another interface					
Can learn MAC addresses					

Rapid PVST+ Operation

RSTP (IEEE _____) is an evolution of the original _____
standard and is incorporated into the IEEE _____ -2004 standard. Rapid PVST+
is the Cisco implementation of RSTP on a per-VLAN basis. What is the primary difference between
Rapid PVST+ and RSTP?

_____

Briefly describe the RSTP concept that corresponds to the PVST+ PortFast feature.

_____

_____

_____

What command implements Cisco's version of an edge port?

_____

In Table 3-5, indicate whether the characteristic describes PVST+, Rapid PVST+, or both.

Table 3-5   Comparing PVST+ and Rapid PVST+

Characteristic	PVST+	Rapid PVST+	Both
Cisco proprietary protocol.			
Port roles: root, designated, alternate, edge, backup.			
CPU processing and trunk bandwidth usage is greater than with STP.			
Ports can transition to forwarding state without relying on a timer.			
The root bridge is determined by the lowest BID + VLAN ID + MAC.			
Runs a separate IEEE 802.1D STP instance for each VLAN.			
Possible to have load sharing with some VLANs forwarding on each trunk.			
Sends a BPDU "hello message" every 2 seconds.			

Spanning Tree Configuration

It is crucial to understand the impact of a default switch configuration on STP convergence and what
configurations can be applied to adjust the default behavior.

PVST+ and Rapid PVST+ Configuration

Complete Table 3-6 to show the default spanning-tree configuration for a Cisco Catalyst 2960 series switch.

Table 3-6 Default Switch Configuration

Feature	Default Setting
Enable state	Enabled on VLAN 1
Spanning-tree mode	
Switch priority	
Spanning-tree port priority configurable on a per-interface basis)	
Spanning-tree port cost (configurable on a per-interface basis)	1000 Mbps: 100 Mbps: 10 Mbps:
Spanning-tree VLAN port priority (configurable on a per-VLAN basis)	
Spanning-tree VLAN port cost (configurable on a per-VLAN basis)	1000 Mbps: 100 Mbps: 10 Mbps:
Spanning-tree timers	Hello time: ____ seconds Forward-delay time: ____ seconds Maximum-aging time: ____ seconds Transmit hold count: ____ BPDUs

Document the two different configuration commands that you can use to configure the bridge priority value so that the switch is root for VLAN 1. Use the value 4096 when necessary:

_____

_____

_____

Record the command to verify that the local switch is now root:

S1# _____

```
VLAN0001
  Spanning tree enabled protocol ieee
  Root ID    Priority    24577
             Address     000A.0033.3333
             This bridge is the root
             Hello Time   2 sec  Max Age 20 sec  Forward Delay 15 sec

  Bridge ID  Priority    24577  (priority 24576 sys-id-ext 1)
             Address     0019.aa9e.b000
```

```
Hello Time   2 sec   Max Age 20 sec   Forward Delay 15 sec
Aging Time 300


Interface         Role Sts Cost      Prio.Nbr Type
----------------  ---- --- --------- -------- --------------------------------
Fa0/1             Desg FWD 4         128.1    Shr
Fa0/2             Desg FWD 4         128.2    Shr
```

Explain the purpose of the BPDU guard feature on Cisco switches.

_____

_____

What command interface configuration command enables BPDU guard?

_____

What global configuration command will configure all nontrunking ports as edge ports?

_____

What global configuration command will configure BPDU guard on all PortFast-enabled ports?

_____

The power of PVST+ is that it can load balance across redundant links. By default, the least-favored redundant link is not used. So, you must manually configure PVST+ to use the link.

Figure 3-5 represents a small section of Figure 3-1, showing only two distribution layer switches and one access layer switch. For this example, we have attached PC2 to S1. PC1 is assigned to VLAN 15, and PC2 is assigned to VLAN 25. D1 should be the primary root for VLAN 1 and VLAN 15 and the secondary root for VLAN 25 and VLAN 99. D2 should be the primary root for VLAN 25 and VLAN 99 and the secondary root for VLAN 1 and VLAN 15.

Figure 3-5   PVST+ Configuration Topology

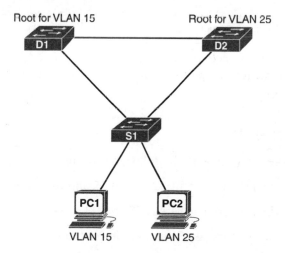

Based on these requirements, document the commands to modify the default PVST+ operation on D1 and D2.

D1 commands

_____

_____

_____

_____

D2 commands

_____

_____

_____

_____

Document the commands to configure all nontrunking ports on S1 as edge ports with BPDU guard enabled.

_____

_____

Now, assume that you want to run rapid PVST+ on all three switches. What command is required?

_____

Packet Tracer Exercise 3-1: STP Configuration

Packet Tracer
☐ Activity

Now you are ready to use Packet Tracer to apply your documented configuration. Download and open the file LSG03-0301.pka found at the companion website for this book. Refer to the Introduction of this book for specifics on accessing files.

Note: The following instructions are also contained within the Packet Tracer Exercise.

In this Packet Tracer activity, you will configure Rapid PVST+ to load balance VLAN traffic between two switches. Use the commands you documented in the section "PVST+ and Rapid PVST+ Configuration."

Requirements

Configure the switches with the following settings:

- D1 is the primary for VLAN 1 and 15 and the secondary root for VLAN 25 and VLAN 99.
- D2 is the primary for VLAN 25 and 99 and the secondary root for VLAN 1 and 15.
- All nontrunk links on S1 should be configured with portfast.
- The links to PC1 and PC2 should be configured to block BPDUs.

Note: Packet Tracer does not support the global command for blocking BPDUs.

Your completion percentage should be 100%. If not, click **Check Results** to see which required components are not yet completed.

Labs and Activities

Command Reference

In Table 3-7, record the command, including the correct router or switch prompt, that fits the description. Fill in any blanks with the appropriate missing information.

Table 3-7   Commands for Chapter 3, STP

Command	Description
	Change the STP cost for S1's Fa0/1 interface to 20.
	Verify the port and path costs for all interfaces on S1.
	Configure S1 as the root for VLAN 1.
	Configure S1 as the backup root for VLAN 10.
	Configure S1's Fa0/5 interface to drop all BPDUs.
	Configure all nontrunk links as portfast.
	Configure S1's Fa0/5 interface as portfast.
	Configure S1 to use Rapid PVST+

3.0.1.2 Class Activity–Stormy Traffic

Objective

Explain the purpose of the Spanning Tree Protocol (STP) in a switched LAN environment with redundant switch links.

Scenario

It is your first day on the job as a network administrator for a small- to medium-sized business. The previous network administrator left suddenly after a network upgrade took place for the business.

During the upgrade, a new switch was added. Since the upgrade, many employees complain that they are having trouble accessing the Internet and servers on your network. In fact, most of them cannot access the network at all. Your corporate manager asks you to immediately research what could be causing these connectivity problems and delays.

So you take a look at the equipment operating on your network at your main distribution facility in the building. You notice that the network topology seems to be visually correct and that cables have been connected correctly, routers and switches are powered on and operational, and switches are connected together to provide backup or redundancy.

However, one thing you do notice is that all of your switches' status lights are constantly blinking at a very fast pace to the point that they almost appear solid. You think you have found the problem with the connectivity issues your employees are experiencing.

Use the Internet to research STP. As you research, take notes and describe:

- Broadcast storm
- Switching loops
- The purpose of STP
- Variations of STP

Complete the reflection questions that accompany the PDF file for this activity. Save your work and be prepared to share your answers with the class.

Resources

- Internet access to the World Wide Web

Reflection

1. What is a definition of a broadcast storm? How does a broadcast storm develop?

_____

_____

_____

_____

2. What is a definition of a switching loop? What causes a switching loop?

_____

_____

_____

_____

3. How can you mitigate broadcast storms and switching loops caused by introducing redundant switches to your network?

_____

_____

_____

_____

4. What is the IEEE standard for STP and some other STP variations, as mentioned in the hyperlinks provided?

_____

_____

_____

_____

5. In answer to this scenario, what would be your first step (after visually checking your network) to correcting the described network problem?

_____

_____

_____

_____

3.1.1.5 Packet Tracer–Examining a Redundant Design

Topology

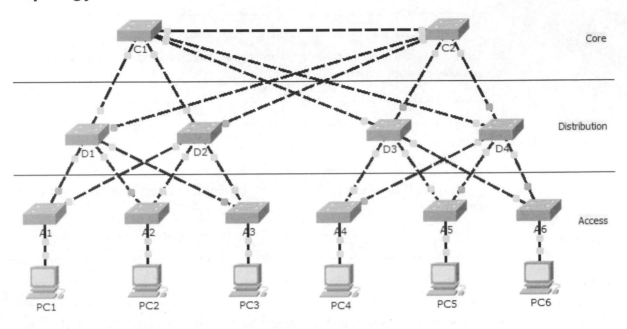

Objectives

Part 1: Check for STP Convergence

Part 2: Examine the ARP Process

Part 3: Test Redundancy in a Switched Network

Background

In this activity, you will observe how STP operates, by default, and how it reacts when faults occur. Switches have been added to the network "out of the box." Cisco switches can be connected to a network without any additional action required by the network administrator. For the purpose of this activity, the bridge priority was modified.

Part 1: Check for STP Convergence

When STP is fully converged, the following conditions exist:

- All PCs have green link lights on the switched ports.

- Access layer switches have one forwarding uplink (green link) to a distribution layer switch and a blocking uplink (amber link) to a second distribution layer switch.

- Distribution layer switches have one forwarding uplink (green link) to a core layer switch and a blocking uplink (amber link) to another core layer switch.

Part 2: Examine the ARP Process

Step 1.   Switch to Simulation mode.

Step 2.   Ping from PC1 to PC6.

    a.   Use the **Add Simple PDU** tool to create a PDU from **PC1** to **PC6**. Verify that ARP and ICMP are selected in the **Event List Filters**. Click **Capture/Forward** to examine the ARP process as the switched network learns the MAC addresses of **PC1** and **PC6**. Notice that all possible loops are stopped by blocking ports. For example, the ARP request from **PC1** travels from **A1** to **D2** to **C1** to **D1** and then back to **A1**. However, because STP is blocking the link between **A1** and **D1**, no loop occurs.

    b.   Notice that the ARP reply from **PC6** travels back along one path. Why?

    _____

    c.   Record the loop-free path between **PC1** and **PC6**.

    _____

Step 3.   Examine the ARP process again.

    a.   Below the **Scenario 0** drop-down list, click **New** to create **Scenario 1**. Examine the ARP process again by pinging between two different PCs.

    b.   What part of the path changed from the last set of pings?

    _____

Part 3: Test Redundancy in a Switched Network

Step 1.   Delete the link between A1 and D2.

Switch to **Realtime** mode. Delete the link between **A1** and **D2**. It takes some time for STP to converge and establish a new, loop-free path. Because only **A1** is affected, watch for the amber light on the link between **A1** and **D1** to change to green. You can click **Fast Forward Time** to accelerate the STP convergence process.

Step 2.   Ping between PC1 and PC6.

    a.   After the link between **A1** and **D1** is active (indicated by a green light), switch to **Simulation** mode and create **Scenario 2**. Ping between **PC1** and **PC6** again.

    b.   Record the new loop-free path.

    _____

Step 3.   Delete the link between C1 and D3.

    a.   Switch to **Realtime** mode. Notice that the links between **D3** and **D4** to **C2** are amber. Delete the link between **C1** and **D3**. It takes some time for STP to converge and establish a new, loop-free path. Watch the amber links on **D3** and **D4**. You can click **Fast Forward Time** to accelerate the STP convergence process.

    b.   Which link is now the active link to **C2**?

    _____

Step 4.   Ping between PC1 and PC6.

    a.   Switch to **Simulation** mode and create **Scenario 3**. Ping between **PC1** and **PC6**.

b.   Record the new loop-free path.

_____

Step 5.   Delete D4.

Switch to **Realtime** mode. Notice that **A4**, **A5**, and **A6** are all forwarding traffic to **D4**. Delete **D4**. It takes some time for STP to converge and establish a new, loop-free path. Watch for the links between **A4**, **A5**, and **A6** to **D3** transition to forwarding (green). All three switches should now be forwarding to **D3**.

Step 6.   Ping between PC1 and PC6.

a.   Switch to **Simulation** mode and create **Scenario 4**. Ping between **PC1** and **PC6**.

b.   Record the new loop-free path.

_____

c.   What is unique about the new path that you have not seen before?

_____

_____

Step 7.   Delete C1.

Switch to **Realtime** mode. Notice that **D1** and **D2** are both forwarding traffic to **C1**. Delete **C1**. It takes some time for STP to converge and establish a new, loop-free path. Watch for the links between **D1** and **D2** to **C2** to transition to forwarding (green). Once converged, both switches should now be forwarding to **C2**.

Step 8.   Ping between PC1 and PC6.

a.   Switch to **Simulation** mode and create **Scenario 5**. Ping between **PC1** and **PC6**.

b.   Record the new loop-free path.

_____

Suggested Scoring Rubric

Activity Section	Question Location	Possible Points	Earned Points
Part 2: Examine the ARP Process	Step 2b	5	
	Step 2c	15	
	Step 3	5	
	Part 2 Total	25	
Part 3: Test Redundancy in a Switched Network	Step 2	15	
	Step 3	5	
	Step 4	15	
	Step 6b	15	
	Step 6c	10	
	Step 8	15	
	Part 3 Total	75	
	Total Score	100	

3.1.2.12 Lab–Building a Switched Network with Redundant Links

Topology

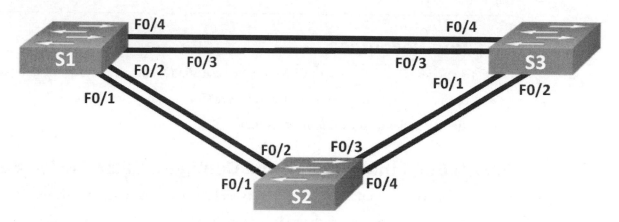

Addressing Table

Device	Interface	IP Address	Subnet Mask
S1	VLAN 1	192.168.1.1	255.255.255.0
S2	VLAN 1	192.168.1.2	255.255.255.0
S3	VLAN 1	192.168.1.3	255.255.255.0

Objectives

Part 1: Build the Network and Configure Basic Device Settings

Part 2: Determine the Root Bridge

Part 3: Observe STP Port Selection Based on Port Cost

Part 4: Observe STP Port Selection Based on Port Priority

Background/Scenario

Redundancy increases the availability of devices in the network topology by protecting the network from a single point of failure. Redundancy in a switched network is accomplished through the use of multiple switches or multiple links between switches. When physical redundancy is introduced into a network design, loops and duplicate frames can occur.

The Spanning Tree Protocol (STP) was developed as a Layer 2 loop-avoidance mechanism for redundant links in a switched network. STP ensures that there is only one logical path between all destinations on the network by intentionally blocking redundant paths that could cause a loop.

In this lab, you will use the **show spanning-tree** command to observe the STP election process of the root bridge. You will also observe the port selection process based on cost and priority.

Note: The switches used are Cisco Catalyst 2960s with Cisco IOS Release 15.0(2) (lanbasek9 image). Other switches and Cisco IOS versions can be used. Depending on the model and Cisco IOS version, the commands available and output produced might vary from what is shown in the labs.

Note: Make sure that the switches have been erased and have no startup configurations. If you are unsure, contact your instructor.

Required Resources

- 3 Switches (Cisco 2960 with Cisco IOS Release 15.0(2) lanbasek9 image or comparable)
- Console cables to configure the Cisco IOS devices via the console ports
- Ethernet cables as shown in the topology

Part 1: Build the Network and Configure Basic Device Settings

In Part 1, you will set up the network topology and configure basic settings on the switches.

Step 1. Cable the network as shown in the topology.

Attach the devices as shown in the topology diagram, and cable as necessary.

Step 2. Initialize and reload the switches as necessary.

Step 3. Configure basic settings for each switch.

    a. Disable DNS lookup.

    b. Configure the device name as shown in the topology.

    c. Assign **class** as the encrypted privileged EXEC mode password.

    d. Assign **cisco** as the console and vty passwords and enable login for console and vty lines.

    e. Configure logging synchronous for the console line.

    f. Configure a message of the day (MOTD) banner to warn users that unauthorized access is prohibited.

    g. Configure the IP address listed in the Addressing Table for VLAN 1 on all switches.

    h. Copy the running configuration to the startup configuration.

Step 4. Test connectivity.

Verify that the switches can ping one another.

Can S1 ping S2? _____

Can S1 ping S3? _____

Can S2 ping S3? _____

Troubleshoot until you are able to answer yes to all questions.

Part 2: Determine the Root Bridge

Every spanning-tree instance (switched LAN or broadcast domain) has a switch designated as the root bridge. The root bridge serves as a reference point for all spanning-tree calculations to determine which redundant paths to block.

An election process determines which switch becomes the root bridge. The switch with the lowest bridge identifier (BID) becomes the root bridge. The BID is made up of a bridge priority value, an extended system ID, and the MAC address of the switch. The priority value can range from 0 to 65,535, in increments of 4,096, with a default value of 32,768.

Step 1.   Deactivate all ports on the switches.

Step 2.   Configure connected ports as trunks.

Step 3.   Activate ports F0/2 and F0/4 on all switches.

Step 4.   Display spanning tree information.

Issue the **show spanning-tree** command on all three switches. The Bridge ID Priority is calculated by adding the priority value and the extended system ID. The extended system ID is always the VLAN number. In the example below, all three switches have equal Bridge ID Priority values (32769 = 32768 + 1, where default priority = 32768, VLAN number = 1); therefore, the switch with the lowest MAC address becomes the root bridge (S2 in the example).

```
S1# show spanning-tree


VLAN0001
  Spanning tree enabled protocol ieee
  Root ID      Priority     32769
               Address      0cd9.96d2.4000
               Cost         19
               Port         2 (FastEthernet0/2)
               Hello Time   2 sec  Max Age 20 sec  Forward Delay 15 sec

  Bridge ID    Priority     32769   (priority 32768 sys-id-ext 1)
               Address      0cd9.96e8.8a00
               Hello Time   2 sec  Max Age 20 sec  Forward Delay 15 sec
               Aging Time   300 sec


Interface            Role Sts Cost      Prio.Nbr Type
-------------------  ---- --- ------    -------- --------------------------------
Fa0/2                Root FWD 19        128.2    P2p
Fa0/4                Altn BLK 19        128.4    P2p


S2# show spanning-tree


VLAN0001
  Spanning tree enabled protocol ieee
  Root ID      Priority     32769
               Address      0cd9.96d2.4000
               This bridge is the root
               Hello Time   2 sec  Max Age 20 sec  Forward Delay 15 sec

  Bridge ID    Priority     32769   (priority 32768 sys-id-ext 1)
               Address      0cd9.96d2.4000
               Hello Time   2 sec  Max Age 20 sec  Forward Delay 15 sec
               Aging Time   300 sec
```

```
Interface          Role Sts Cost      Prio.Nbr Type
------------------ ---- --- --------- -------- ------------------------------
Fa0/2              Desg FWD 19        128.2    P2p
Fa0/4              Desg FWD 19        128.4    P2p


S3# show spanning-tree


VLAN0001
  Spanning tree enabled protocol ieee
  Root ID    Priority    32769
             Address     0cd9.96d2.4000
             Cost        19
             Port        2 (FastEthernet0/2)
             Hello Time  2 sec  Max Age 20 sec  Forward Delay 15 sec

  Bridge ID  Priority    32769  (priority 32768 sys-id-ext 1)
             Address     0cd9.96e8.7400
             Hello Time  2 sec  Max Age 20 sec  Forward Delay 15 sec
             Aging Time  300 sec


Interface          Role Sts Cost      Prio.Nbr Type
------------------ ---- --- --------- -------- ------------------------------
Fa0/2              Root FWD 19        128.2    P2p
Fa0/4              Desg FWD 19        128.4    P2p
```

Note: The default STP mode on the 2960 switch is Per VLAN Spanning Tree (PVST).

In the diagram below, record the Role and Status (Sts) of the active ports on each switch in the Topology.

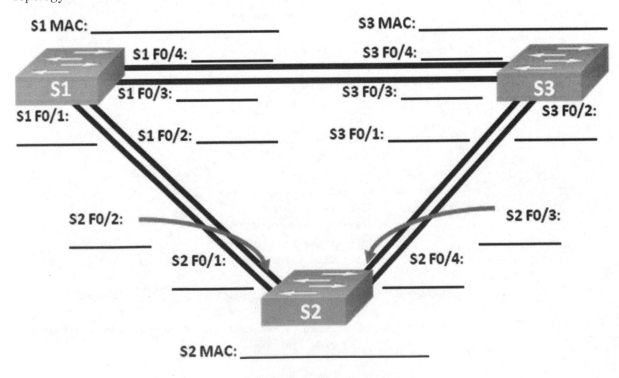

Based on the output from your switches, answer the following questions.

Which switch is the root bridge? _____

Why did spanning tree select this switch as the root bridge?

_____

Which ports are the root ports on the switches? _____

Which ports are the designated ports on the switches? _____

What port is showing as an alternate port and is currently being blocked? _____

Why did spanning tree select this port as the non-designated (blocked) port?

_____

_____

_____

_____

Part 3: Observe STP Port Selection Based on Port Cost

The spanning tree algorithm (STA) uses the root bridge as the reference point and then determines which ports to block, based on path cost. The port with the lower path cost is preferred. If port costs are equal, then spanning tree compares BIDs. If the BIDs are equal, then the port priorities are used to break the tie. Lower values are always preferred. In Part 3, you will change the port cost to control which port is blocked by spanning tree.

Step 1.   Locate the switch with the blocked port.

With the current configuration, only one switch should have a port that is blocked by STP. Issue the **show spanning-tree** command on both non-root switches. In the example below, spanning tree is blocking port F0/4 on the switch with the highest BID (S1).

```
S1# show spanning-tree


VLAN0001
  Spanning tree enabled protocol ieee
  Root ID    Priority    32769
             Address     0cd9.96d2.4000
             Cost        19
             Port        2 (FastEthernet0/2)
             Hello Time  2 sec  Max Age 20 sec  Forward Delay 15 sec

  Bridge ID  Priority    32769  (priority 32768 sys-id-ext 1)
             Address     0cd9.96e8.8a00
             Hello Time  2 sec  Max Age 20 sec  Forward Delay 15 sec
             Aging Time  300 sec

Interface           Role Sts Cost       Prio.Nbr Type
------------------- ---- --- --------- -------- --------------------------------
Fa0/2               Root FWD 19          128.2    P2p
Fa0/4               Altn BLK 19          128.4    P2p


S3# show spanning-tree
```

```
VLAN0001
  Spanning tree enabled protocol ieee
  Root ID    Priority    32769
             Address     0cd9.96d2.4000
             Cost        19
             Port        2 (FastEthernet0/2)
             Hello Time   2 sec  Max Age 20 sec  Forward Delay 15 sec

  Bridge ID  Priority    32769  (priority 32768 sys-id-ext 1)
             Address     0cd9.96e8.7400
             Hello Time   2 sec  Max Age 20 sec  Forward Delay 15 sec
             Aging Time  15  sec


Interface          Role Sts Cost      Prio.Nbr Type
------------------ ---- --- --------- -------- --------------------------------
Fa0/2              Root FWD 19        128.2    P2p
Fa0/4              Desg FWD 19        128.4    P2p
```

Note: Root bridge and port selection may differ in your topology.

Step 2.   Change port cost.

In addition to the blocked port, the only other active port on this switch is the port designated as the root port. Lower the cost of this root port to 18 by issuing the **spanning-tree cost 18** interface configuration mode command.

```
S1(config)# interface f0/2
S1(config-if)# spanning-tree cost 18
```

Step 3.   Observe spanning tree changes.

Re-issue the **show spanning-tree** command on both non-root switches. Observe that the previously blocked port (S1 - F0/4) is now a designated port and spanning tree is now blocking a port on the other non-root switch (S3 - F0/4).

```
S1# show spanning-tree

VLAN0001
  Spanning tree enabled protocol ieee
  Root ID    Priority    32769
             Address     0cd9.96d2.4000
             Cost        18
             Port        2 (FastEthernet0/2)
             Hello Time   2 sec  Max Age 20 sec  Forward Delay 15 sec

  Bridge ID  Priority    32769  (priority 32768 sys-id-ext 1)
             Address     0cd9.96e8.8a00
             Hello Time   2 sec  Max Age 20 sec  Forward Delay 15 sec
             Aging Time  300 sec


Interface          Role Sts Cost      Prio.Nbr Type
------------------ ---- --- --------- -------- --------------------------------
Fa0/2              Root FWD 18        128.2    P2p
Fa0/4              Desg FWD 19        128.4    P2p
```

```
S3# show spanning-tree

VLAN0001
  Spanning tree enabled protocol ieee
  Root ID     Priority    32769
              Address     0cd9.96d2.4000
              Cost        19
              Port        2 (FastEthernet0/2)
              Hello Time    2 sec  Max Age 20 sec  Forward Delay 15 sec

  Bridge ID   Priority    32769   (priority 32768 sys-id-ext 1)
              Address     0cd9.96e8.7400
              Hello Time    2 sec  Max Age 20 sec  Forward Delay 15 sec
              Aging Time  300 sec


Interface              Role Sts Cost      Prio.Nbr Type
-------------------    ---- --- --------- -------- --------------------------------

Fa0/2                  Root FWD 19        128.2    P2p
Fa0/4                  Altn BLK 19        128.4    P2p
```

Why did spanning tree change the previously blocked port to a designated port, and block the port that was a designated port on the other switch?

Step 4. Remove port cost changes.

a. Issue the **no spanning-tree cost 18** interface configuration mode command to remove the cost statement that you created earlier.

```
S1(config)# interface f0/2
S1(config-if)# no spanning-tree cost 18
```

b. Re-issue the **show spanning-tree** command to verify that STP has reset the port on the non-root switches back to the original port settings. It takes approximately 30 seconds for STP to complete the port transition process.

Part 4: Observe STP Port Selection Based on Port Priority

If port costs are equal, then spanning tree compares BIDs. If the BIDs are equal, then the port priorities are used to break the tie. The default port priority value is 128. STP aggregates the port priority with the port number to break ties. Lower values are always preferred. In Part 4, you will activate redundant paths to each switch to observe how STP selects a port using the port priority.

a. Activate ports F0/1 and F0/3 on all switches.

b. Wait 30 seconds for STP to complete the port transition process, and then issue the **show spanning-tree** command on the non-root switches. Observe that the root port has moved to the lower numbered port linked to the root switch, and blocked the previous root port.

```
S1# show spanning-tree

VLAN0001
  Spanning tree enabled protocol ieee
  Root ID     Priority    32769
```

```
            Address      0cd9.96d2.4000
            Cost         19
            Port         1 (FastEthernet0/1)
            Hello Time   2 sec  Max Age 20 sec  Forward Delay 15 sec

  Bridge ID  Priority    32769  (priority 32768 sys-id-ext 1)
            Address      0cd9.96e8.8a00
            Hello Time   2 sec  Max Age 20 sec  Forward Delay 15 sec
            Aging Time   15  sec


Interface           Role Sts Cost      Prio.Nbr Type
------------------- ---- --- --------- -------- -------------------------------
Fa0/1               Root FWD 19        128.1    P2p
Fa0/2               Altn BLK 19        120.2    P2p
Fa0/3               Altn BLK 19        128.3    P2p
Fa0/4               Altn BLK 19        128.4    P2p


S3# show spanning-tree


VLAN0001
  Spanning tree enabled protocol ieee
  Root ID    Priority    32769
            Address      0cd9.96d2.4000
            Cost         19
            Port         1 (FastEthernet0/1)'
            Hello Time   2 sec  Max Age 20 sec  Forward Delay 15 sec


  Bridge ID  Priority    32769  (priority 32768 sys-id-ext 1)
            Address      0cd9.96e8.7400
            Hello Time   2 sec  Max Age 20 sec  Forward Delay 15 sec
            Aging Time   15  sec


Interface           Role Sts Cost      Prio.Nbr Type
------------------- ---- --- --------- -------- -------------------------------
Fa0/1               Root FWD 19        128.1    P2p
Fa0/2               Altn BLK 19        128.2    P2p
Fa0/3               Desg FWD 19        128.3    P2p
Fa0/4               Desg FWD 19        128.4    P2p
```

What port did STP select as the root port on each non-root switch? _____

_____

Why did STP select these ports as the root port on these switches?

_____

_____

Reflection

1. After a root bridge has been selected, what is the first value STP uses to determine port selection?

   _____

2. If the first value is equal on the two ports, what is the next value that STP uses to determine port selection?

   _____

3. If both values are equal on the two ports, what is the next value that STP uses to determine port selection?

   _____

3.3.1.5 Packet Tracer–Configuring PVST+

Topology

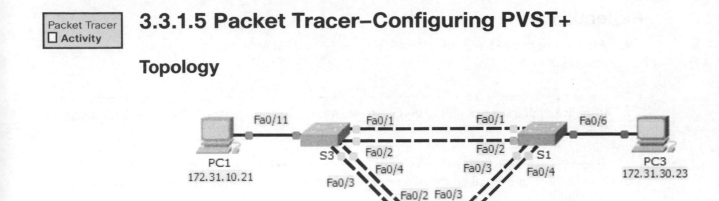

Addressing Table

Device	Interface	IP Address	Subnet Mask	Default Gateway
S1	VLAN 99	172.31.99.1	255.255.255.0	N/A
S2	VLAN 99	172.31.99.2	255.255.255.0	N/A
S3	VLAN 99	172.31.99.3	255.255.255.0	N/A
PC1	NIC	172.31.10.21	255.255.255.0	172.31.10.254
PC2	NIC	172.31.20.22	255.255.255.0	172.31.20.254
PC3	NIC	172.31.30.23	255.255.255.0	172.31.30.254

Switch Port Assignment Specifications

Ports	Assignments	Network
S1 F0/6	VLAN 30	172.17.30.0/24
S2 F0/18	VLAN 20	172.17.20.0/24
S3 F0/11	VLAN 10	172.17.10.0/24

Objectives

Part 1: Configure VLANs

Part 2: Configure Spanning Tree PVST+ and Load Balancing

Part 3: Configure PortFast and BPDU Guard

Background

In this activity, you will configure VLANs and trunks, and examine and configure the Spanning Tree Protocol primary and secondary root bridges. You will also optimize the switched topology using PVST+, PortFast, and BPDU guard.

Part 1: Configure VLANs

Step 1.   Enable the user ports on S1, S2, and S3 in access mode.

Refer to the topology diagram to determine which switch ports (**S1, S2,** and **S3**) are activated for end-user device access. These three ports will be configured for access mode and enabled with the **no shutdown** command.

Step 2.   Create VLANs.

Using the appropriate command, create VLANs 10, 20, 30, 40, 50, 60, 70, 80, and 99 on all of the switches.

Step 3.   Assign VLANs to switch ports.

Port assignments are listed in the table at the beginning of the activity. Save your configurations after assigning switch ports to the VLANs.

Step 4.   Verify the VLANs.

Use the **show vlan brief** command on all switches to verify that all VLANs are registered in the VLAN table.

Step 5.   Assign the trunks to native VLAN 99.

Use the appropriate command to configure ports F0/1 to F0/4 on each switch as trunk ports, and assign these trunk ports to native VLAN 99.

Step 6.   Configure the management interface on all three switches with an address.

Verify that the switches are correctly configured by pinging between them.

Part 2: Configure Spanning Tree PVST+ and Load Balancing

Because there is a separate instance of the spanning tree for every active VLAN, a separate root election is conducted for each instance. If the default switch priorities are used in root selection, the same root is elected for every spanning tree instance, as we have seen. This could lead to an inferior design. Some reasons to control the selection of the root switch include:

- The root switch is responsible for generating BPDUs for STP 802.1D and is the focal point for spanning tree to control traffic. The root switch must be capable of handling this additional load.

- The placement of the root defines the active switched paths in the network. Random placement is likely to lead to suboptimal paths. Ideally the root is in the distribution layer.

- Consider the topology used in this activity. Of the six trunks configured, only three are carrying traffic. While this prevents loops, it is a waste of resources. Because the root can be defined on the basis of the VLAN, you can have some ports blocking for one VLAN and forwarding for another. This is demonstrated below.

Step 1.   Configure STP mode.

Use the **spanning-tree mode** command to configure the switches so they use PVST as the STP mode.

Step 2.   Configure Spanning Tree PVST+ load balancing.

    a.   Configure **S1** to be the primary root for VLANs 1, 10, 30, 50, and 70. Configure **S3** to be the primary root for VLANs 20, 40, 60, 80, and 99. Configure **S2** to be the secondary root for all VLANs.

    b.   Verify your configurations using the **show spanning-tree** command.

Part 3: Configure PortFast and BPDU Guard

Step 1.   Configure PortFast on the switches.

PortFast causes a port to enter the forwarding state almost immediately by dramatically decreasing the time of the listening and learning states. PortFast minimizes the time it takes for the server or workstation to come online. Configure PortFast on the switch interfaces that are connected to PCs.

Step 2.   Configure BPDU guard on the switches.

The STP PortFast BPDU guard enhancement allows network designers to enforce the STP domain borders and keep the active topology predictable. The devices behind the ports that have STP PortFast enabled are unable to influence the STP topology. At the reception of BPDUs, the BPDU guard operation disables the port that has PortFast configured. The BPDU guard transitions the port into the err-disable state, and a message appears on the console. Configure BPDU guard on switch interfaces that are connected to PCs.

Step 3.   Verify your configuration.

Use the **show running-configuration** command to verify your configuration.

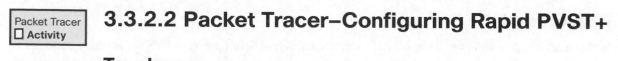

3.3.2.2 Packet Tracer–Configuring Rapid PVST+

Topology

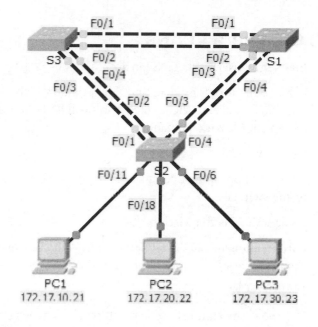

Addressing Table

Device	Interface	IP Address	Subnet Mask	Default Gateway
S1	VLAN 99	172.17.99.11	255.255.255.0	N/A
S2	VLAN 99	172.17.99.12	255.255.255.0	N/A
S3	VLAN 99	172.17.99.13	255.255.255.0	N/A
PC1	NIC	172.17.10.21	255.255.255.0	172.17.10.254
PC2	NIC	172.17.20.22	255.255.255.0	172.17.20.254
PC3	NIC	172.17.30.23	255.255.255.0	172.17.30.254

Switch Port Assignment Specifications

Ports	Assignments	Network
S2 F0/6	VLAN 30	172.17.30.0/24
S2 F0/18	VLAN 20	172.17.20.0/24
S2 F0/11	VLAN 10	172.17.10.0/24

Objectives

Part 1: Configure VLANs

Part 2: Configure Rapid Spanning Tree PVST+ Load Balancing

Part 3: Configure PortFast and BPDU Guard

Background

In this activity, you will configure VLANs and trunks, Rapid Spanning Tree PVST+, primary and secondary root bridges, and examine the configuration results. You will also optimize the network by configuring PortFast, and BPDU Guard on edge ports.

Part 1: Configure VLANs

Step 1.   Enable the user ports on S2 in access mode.

Refer to the topology diagram to determine which switch ports on **S2** are activated for end-user device access. These three ports will be configured for access mode and enabled with the **no shutdown** command.

Step 2.   Create VLANs.

Using the appropriate command, create VLANs 10, 20, 30, 40, 50, 60, 70, 80, and 99 on all of the switches.

Step 3.   Assign VLANs to switch ports.

Port assignments are listed in the table at the beginning of the activity. Save your configurations after assigning switch ports to the VLANs.

Step 4.   Verify the VLANs.

Use the **show vlan brief** command on all switches to verify that all VLANs are registered in the VLAN table.

Step 5.   Assign the trunks to native VLAN 99.

Use the appropriate command to configure ports F0/1 to F0/4 on each switch as trunk ports and assign these trunk ports to native VLAN 99.

_____

_____

_____

_____

_____

_____

_____

_____

Step 6.   Configure the management interface on all three switches with an address.

Verify that the switches are correctly configured by pinging between them.

Part 2: Configure Rapid Spanning Tree PVST+ Load Balancing

The Rapid Spanning Tree Protocol (RSTP; IEEE 802.1w) can be seen as an evolution of the 802.1D standard more so than a revolution. The 802.1D terminology remains primarily the same. Most parameters have been left unchanged so users familiar with 802.1D can rapidly configure the new protocol comfortably. In most cases, RSTP performs better than proprietary extensions of Cisco without any additional configuration. 802.1w can also revert back to 802.1D in order to interoperate with legacy bridges on a per-port basis.

Step 1. Configure STP mode.

Use the **spanning-tree mode** command to configure the switches to use rapid PVST as the STP mode.

Step 2. Configure Rapid Spanning Tree PVST+ load balancing.

Configure **S1** to be the primary root for VLANs 1, 10, 30, 50, and 70. Configure **S3** to be the primary root for VLANs 20, 40, 60, 80, and 99. Configure **S2** to be the secondary root for all of the VLANs.

Verify your configurations by using the **show spanning-tree** command.

Part 3: Configure PortFast and BPDU Guard

Step 1. Configuring PortFast on S2.

PortFast causes a port to enter the forwarding state almost immediately by dramatically decreasing the time of the listening and learning states. PortFast minimizes the time it takes for the server or workstation to come online. Configure PortFast on **S2** interfaces that are connected to PCs.

Step 2. Configuring BPDU Guard on S2.

The STP PortFast BPDU Guard enhancement allows network designers to enforce the STP domain borders and keep the active topology predictable. The devices behind the ports that have STP PortFast enabled are not able to influence the STP topology. At the reception of BPDUs, the BPDU Guard operation disables the port that has PortFast configured. The BPDU Guard transitions the port into err-disable state, and a message appears on the console. Configure BPDU Guard on **S2** interfaces that are connected to PCs.

Step 3. Verify your configuration.

Use the **show run** command to verify your configuration.

3.3.2.3 Lab–Configuring Rapid PVST+, PortFast, and BPDU Guard

Topology

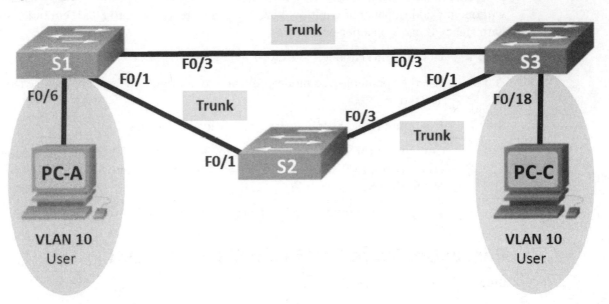

Addressing Table

Device	Interface	IP Address	Subnet Mask
S1	VLAN 99	192.168.1.11	255.255.255.0
S2	VLAN 99	192.168.1.12	255.255.255.0
S3	VLAN 99	192.168.1.13	255.255.255.0
PC-A	NIC	192.168.0.2	255.255.255.0
PC-C	NIC	192.168.0.3	255.255.255.0

VLAN Assignments

VLAN	Name
10	User
99	Management

Objectives

Part 1: Build the Network and Configure Basic Device Settings

Part 2: Configure VLANs, Native VLAN, and Trunks

Part 3: Configure the Root Bridge and Examine PVST+ Convergence

Part 4: Configure Rapid PVST+, PortFast, BPDU Guard, and Examine Convergence

Background/Scenario

The Per-VLAN Spanning Tree (PVST) protocol is Cisco proprietary. Cisco switches default to PVST. Rapid PVST+ (IEEE 802.1w) is an enhanced version of PVST+ and allows for faster spanning-tree calculations and convergence in response to Layer 2 topology changes. Rapid PVST+ defines three port states: discarding, learning, and forwarding, and provides multiple enhancements to optimize network performance.

In this lab, you will configure the primary and secondary root bridge, examine PVST+ convergence, configure Rapid PVST+ and compare its convergence to PVST+. In addition, you will configure edge ports to transition immediately to a forwarding state using PortFast and prevent the edge ports from forwarding BDPUs using BDPU guard.

Note: This lab provides minimal assistance with the actual commands necessary for configuration. However, the required commands are provided in Appendix A. Test your knowledge by trying to configure the devices without referring to the appendix.

Note: The switches used with CCNA hands-on labs are Cisco Catalyst 2960s with Cisco IOS Release 15.0(2) (lanbasek9 image). Other switches and Cisco IOS versions can be used. Depending on the model and Cisco IOS version, the commands available and output produced might vary from what is shown in the labs.

Note: Make sure that the switches have been erased and have no startup configurations. If you are unsure, contact your instructor.

Required Resources

- 3 Switches (Cisco 2960 with Cisco IOS Release 15.0(2) lanbasek9 image or comparable)
- 2 PCs (Windows 7, Vista, or XP with terminal emulation program, such as Tera Term)
- Console cables to configure the Cisco IOS devices via the console ports
- Ethernet cables as shown in the topology

Part 1: Build the Network and Configure Basic Device Settings

In Part 1, you will set up the network topology and configure basic settings, such as the interface IP addresses, device access, and passwords.

Step 1.   Cable the network as shown in the topology.

Step 2.   Configure PC hosts.

Step 3.   Initialize and reload the switches as necessary.

Step 4.   Configure basic settings for each switch.

    a.   Disable DNS lookup.

    b.   Configure the device name as shown in the topology.

    c.   Assign **cisco** as the console and vty passwords and enable login.

    d.   Assign **class** as the encrypted privileged EXEC mode password.

    e.   Configure **logging synchronous** to prevent console messages from interrupting command entry.

f. Shut down all switch ports.

g. Copy the running configuration to startup configuration.

Part 2: Configure VLANs, Native VLAN, and Trunks

In Part 2, you will create VLANs, assign switch ports to VLANs, configure trunk ports, and change the native VLAN for all switches.

Note: The required commands for Part 2 are provided in Appendix A. Test your knowledge by trying to configure the VLANs, native VLAN, and trunks without referring to the appendix.

Step 1. Create VLANs.

Use the appropriate commands to create VLANs 10 and 99 on all of the switches. Name VLAN 10 as **User** and VLAN 99 as **Management**.

```
S1(config)# vlan 10
S1(config-vlan)# name User
S1(config-vlan)# vlan 99
S1(config-vlan)# name Management

S2(config)# vlan 10
S2(config-vlan)# name User
S2(config-vlan)# vlan 99
S2(config-vlan)# name Management

S3(config)# vlan 10
S3(config-vlan)# name User
S3(config-vlan)# vlan 99
S3(config-vlan)# name Management
```

Step 2. Enable user ports in access mode and assign VLANs.

For S1 F0/6 and S3 F0/18, enable the ports, configure them as access ports, and assign them to VLAN 10.

Step 3. Configure trunk ports and assign to native VLAN 99.

For ports F0/1 and F0/3 on all switches, enable the ports, configure them as trunk ports, and assign them to native VLAN 99.

Step 4. Configure the management interface on all switches.

Using the Addressing Table, configure the management interface on all switches with the appropriate IP address.

Step 5. Verify configurations and connectivity.

What is the default setting for spanning-tree mode on Cisco switches?

_____

Verify connectivity between PC-A and PC-C. Was your ping successful? _____

If your ping was unsuccessful, troubleshoot the configurations until the issue is resolved.

Note: It may be necessary to disable the PC firewall to successfully ping between PCs.

Part 3: Configure the Root Bridge and Examine PVST+ Convergence

In Part 3, you will determine the default root in the network, assign the primary and secondary root, and use the **debug** command to examine convergence of PVST+.

Note: The required commands for Part 3 are provided in Appendix A. Test your knowledge by trying to configure the root bridge without referring to the appendix.

Step 1.   Determine the current root bridge.

Which command allows a user to determine the spanning-tree status of a Cisco Catalyst switch for all VLANs? Write the command in the space provided.

_____

Use the command on all three switches to determine the answers to the following questions:

Note: There are three instances of the spanning tree on each switch. The default STP configuration on Cisco switches is PVST+, which creates a separate spanning tree instance for each VLAN (VLAN 1 and any user-configured VLANs).

What is the bridge priority of switch S1 for VLAN 1? _____

What is the bridge priority of switch S2 for VLAN 1? _____

What is the bridge priority of switch S3 for VLAN 1? _____

Which switch is the root bridge? _____

Why was this switch elected as the root bridge?

_____

Step 2.   Configure a primary and secondary root bridge for all existing VLANs.

Having a root bridge (switch) elected by MAC address may lead to a suboptimal configuration. In this lab, you will configure switch S2 as the root bridge and S1 as the secondary root bridge.

a.   Configure switch S2 to be the primary root bridge for all existing VLANs. Write the command in the space provided.

_____

b.   Configure switch S1 to be the secondary root bridge for all existing VLANs. Write the command in the space provided.

_____

Use the **show spanning-tree** command to answer the following questions:

What is the bridge priority of S1 for VLAN 1? _____

What is the bridge priority of S2 for VLAN 1? _____

Which interface in the network is in a blocking state? _____

Step 3.   Change the Layer 2 topology and examine convergence.

To examine PVST+ convergence, you will create a Layer 2 topology change while using the **debug** command to monitor spanning-tree events.

a.   Enter the **debug spanning-tree events** command in privileged EXEC mode on switch S3.

```
S3# debug spanning-tree events
Spanning Tree event debugging is on
```

b.   Create a topology change by disabling interface F0/1 on S3.

```
S3(config)# interface f0/1
S3(config-if)# shutdown
*Mar  1 00:58:56.225: STP: VLAN0001 new root port Fa0/3, cost 38
*Mar  1 00:58:56.225: STP: VLAN0001 Fa0/3 > listening
*Mar  1 00:58:56.225: STP[1]: Generating TC trap for port FastEthernet0/1
*Mar  1 00:58:56.225: STP: VLAN0010 new root port Fa0/3, cost 38
*Mar  1 00:58:56.225: STP: VLAN0010 Fa0/3 -> listening
*Mar  1 00:58:56.225: STP[10]: Generating TC trap for port FastEthernet0/1
*Mar  1 00:58:56.225: STP: VLAN0099 new root port Fa0/3, cost 38
*Mar  1 00:58:56.225: STP: VLAN0099 Fa0/3 -> listening
*Mar  1 00:58:56.225: STP[99]: Generating TC trap for port FastEthernet0/1
*Mar  1 00:58:56.242: %LINEPROTO-5-UPDOWN: Line protocol on Interface Vlan1,
changed state to down
*Mar  1 00:58:56.242: %LINEPROTO-5-UPDOWN: Line protocol on Interface Vlan99,
changed state to down
*Mar  1 00:58:58.214: %LINK-5-CHANGED: Interface FastEthernet0/1, changed state
to administratively down
*Mar  1 00:58:58.230: STP: VLAN0001 sent Topology Change Notice on Fa0/3
*Mar  1 00:58:58.230: STP: VLAN0010 sent Topology Change Notice on Fa0/3
*Mar  1 00:58:58.230: STP: VLAN0099 sent Topology Change Notice on Fa0/3
*Mar  1 00:58:59.220: %LINEPROTO-5-UPDOWN: Line protocol on Interface
FastEthernet0/1, changed state to down
*Mar  1 00:59:11.233: STP: VLAN0001 Fa0/3 -> learning
*Mar  1 00:59:11.233: STP: VLAN0010 Fa0/3 -> learning
*Mar  1 00:59:11.233: STP: VLAN0099 Fa0/3 -> learning
*Mar  1 00:59:26.240: STP[1]: Generating TC trap for port FastEthernet0/3
*Mar  1 00:59:26.240: STP: VLAN0001 Fa0/3 -> forwarding
*Mar  1 00:59:26.240: STP[10]: Generating TC trap for port FastEthernet0/3
*Mar  1 00:59:26.240: STP: VLAN0010 sent Topology Change Notice on Fa0/3
*Mar  1 00:59:26.240: STP: VLAN0010 Fa0/3 -> forwarding
*Mar  1 00:59:26.240: STP[99]: Generating TC trap for port FastEthernet0/3
*Mar  1 00:59:26.240: STP: VLAN0099 Fa0/3 -> forwarding
*Mar  1 00:59:26.248: %LINEPROTO-5-UPDOWN: Line protocol on Interface Vlan1,
changed state to up
*Mar  1 00:59:26.248: %LINEPROTO-5-UPDOWN: Line protocol on Interface Vlan99,
changed state to up
```

Note: Before proceeding, use the **debug** output to verify that all VLANs on F0/3 have reached a forwarding state then use the command **no debug spanning-tree events** to stop the **debug** output.

Through which port states do each VLAN on F0/3 proceed during network convergence?

_____

Using the time stamp from the first and last STP debug message, calculate the time (to the nearest second) that it took for the network to converge. **Hint:** The debug time-stamp format is date hh.mm.ss:msec.

_____

Part 4: Configure Rapid PVST+, PortFast, BPDU Guard, and Examine Convergence

In Part 4, you will configure Rapid PVST+ on all switches. You will configure PortFast and BPDU guard on all access ports, and then use the **debug** command to examine Rapid PVST+ convergence.

Note: The required commands for Part 4 are provided in Appendix A. Test your knowledge by trying to configure the Rapid PVST+, PortFast, and BPDU guard without referring to the appendix.

Step 1.   Configure Rapid PVST+.

   a.   Configure S1 for Rapid PVST+. Write the command in the space provided.

_____

   b.   Configure S2 and S3 for Rapid PVST+.

_____

_____

   c.   Verify configurations with the **show running-config | include spanning-tree mode** command.

```
S1# show running-config | include spanning-tree mode
spanning-tree mode rapid-pvst

S2# show running-config | include spanning-tree mode
spanning-tree mode rapid-pvst

S3# show running-config | include spanning-tree mode
spanning-tree mode rapid-pvst
```

Step 2.   Configure PortFast and BPDU Guard on access ports.

PortFast is a feature of spanning tree that transitions a port immediately to a forwarding state as soon as it is turned on. This is useful in connecting hosts so that they can start communicating on the VLAN instantly, rather than waiting on spanning tree. To prevent ports that are configured with PortFast from forwarding BPDUs, which could change the spanning tree topology, BPDU guard can be enabled. At the receipt of a BPDU, BPDU guard disables a port configured with PortFast.

   a.   Configure interface F0/6 on S1 with PortFast. Write the command in the space provided.

_____

b. Configure interface F0/6 on S1 with BPDU guard. Write the command in the space provided.

_____

c. Globally configure all non-trunking ports on switch S3 with PortFast. Write the command in the space provided.

_____

d. Globally configure all non-trunking PortFast ports on switch S3 with BPDU guard. Write the command in the space provided.

_____

Step 3. Examine Rapid PVST+ convergence.

a. Enter the **debug spanning-tree events** command in privileged EXEC mode on switch S3.

b. Create a topology change by enabling interface F0/1 on switch S3.

```
S3(config)# interface f0/1
S3(config-if)# no shutdown
*Mar  1 01:28:34.946: %LINK-3-UPDOWN: Interface FastEthernet0/1, changed state
to up
*Mar  1 01:28:37.588: RSTP(1): initializing port Fa0/1
*Mar  1 01:28:37.588: RSTP(1): Fa0/1 is now designated
*Mar  1 01:28:37.588: RSTP(10): initializing port Fa0/1
*Mar  1 01:28:37.588: RSTP(10): Fa0/1 is now designated
*Mar  1 01:28:37.588: RSTP(99): initializing port Fa0/1
*Mar  1 01:28:37.588: RSTP(99): Fa0/1 is now designated
*Mar  1 01:28:37.597: RSTP(1): transmitting a proposal on Fa0/1
*Mar  1 01:28:37.597: RSTP(10): transmitting a proposal on Fa0/1
*Mar  1 01:28:37.597: RSTP(99): transmitting a proposal on Fa0/1
*Mar  1 01:28:37.597: RSTP(1): updt roles, received superior bpdu on Fa0/1
*Mar  1 01:28:37.597: RSTP(1): Fa0/1 is now root port
*Mar  1 01:28:37.597: RSTP(1): Fa0/3 blocked by re-root
*Mar  1 01:28:37.597: RSTP(1): synced Fa0/1
*Mar  1 01:28:37.597: RSTP(1): Fa0/3 is now alternate
*Mar  1 01:28:37.597: RSTP(10): updt roles, received superior bpdu on Fa0/1
*Mar  1 01:28:37.597: RSTP(10): Fa0/1 is now root port
*Mar  1 01:28:37.597: RSTP(10): Fa0/3 blocked by re-root
*Mar  1 01:28:37.597: RSTP(10): synced Fa0/1
*Mar  1 01:28:37.597: RSTP(10): Fa0/3 is now alternate
*Mar  1 01:28:37.597: RSTP(99): updt roles, received superior bpdu on Fa0/1
*Mar  1 01:28:37.605: RSTP(99): Fa0/1 is now root port
*Mar  1 01:28:37.605: RSTP(99): Fa0/3 blocked by re-root
*Mar  1 01:28:37.605: RSTP(99): synced Fa0/1
*Mar  1 01:28:37.605: RSTP(99): Fa0/3 is now alternate
*Mar  1 01:28:37.605: STP[1]: Generating TC trap for port FastEthernet0/1
*Mar  1 01:28:37.605: STP[10]: Generating TC trap for port FastEthernet0/1
*Mar  1 01:28:37.605: STP[99]: Generating TC trap for port FastEthernet0/1
*Mar  1 01:28:37.622: RSTP(1): transmitting an agreement on Fa0/1 as a response
to a proposal
```

```
*Mar  1 01:28:37.622: RSTP(10): transmitting an agreement on Fa0/1 as a
response to a proposal
*Mar  1 01:28:37.622: RSTP(99): transmitting an agreement on Fa0/1 as a
response to a proposal
*Mar  1 01:28:38.595: %LINEPROTO-5-UPDOWN: Line protocol on Interface
FastEthernet0/1, changed state to up
```

Using the time stamp from the first and last RSTP debug message, calculate the time that it took for the network to converge.

Reflection

1. What is the main benefit of using Rapid PVST+?

2. How does configuring a port with PortFast allow for faster convergence?

3. What protection does BPDU guard provide?

Appendix A – Switch Configuration Commands

Switch S1

```
S1(config)# vlan 10
S1(config-vlan)# name User
S1(config-vlan)# vlan 99
S1(config-vlan)# name Management
S1(config-vlan)# exit
S1(config)# interface f0/6
S1(config-if)# no shutdown
S1(config-if)# switchport mode access
S1(config-if)# switchport access vlan 10
S1(config-if)# interface f0/1
S1(config-if)# no shutdown
S1(config-if)# switchport mode trunk
S1(config-if)# switchport trunk native vlan 99
S1(config-if)# interface f0/3
S1(config-if)# no shutdown
S1(config-if)# switchport mode trunk
S1(config-if)# switchport trunk native vlan 99
S1(config-if)# interface vlan 99
S1(config-if)# ip address 192.168.1.11 255.255.255.0
S1(config-if)# exit
S1(config)# spanning-tree vlan 1,10,99 root secondary
S1(config)# spanning-tree mode rapid-pvst
S1(config)# interface f0/6
S1(config-if)# spanning-tree portfast
S1(config-if)# spanning-tree bpduguard enable
```

Switch S2

```
S2(config)# vlan 10
S2(config-vlan)# name User
S2(config-vlan)# vlan 99
S2(config-vlan)# name Management
S2(config-vlan)# exit
S2(config)# interface f0/1
S2(config-if)# no shutdown
S2(config-if)# switchport mode trunk
S2(config-if)# switchport trunk native vlan 99
S2(config-if)# interface f0/3
S2(config-if)# no shutdown
S2(config-if)# switchport mode trunk
S2(config-if)# switchport trunk native vlan 99
S2(config-if)# interface vlan 99
S2(config-if)# ip address 192.168.1.12 255.255.255.0
S2(config-if)# exit
S2(config)# spanning-tree vlan 1,10,99 root primary
S2(config)# spanning-tree mode rapid-pvst
```

Switch S3

```
S3(config)# vlan 10
S3(config-vlan)# name User
S3(config-vlan)# vlan 99
S3(config-vlan)# name Management
S3(config-vlan)# exit
S3(config)# interface f0/18
S3(config-if)# no shutdown
S3(config-if)# switchport mode access
S3(config-if)# switchport access vlan 10
S3(config-if)# spanning-tree portfast
S3(config-if)# spanning-tree bpduguard enable
S3(config-if)# interface f0/1
S3(config-if)# no shutdown
S3(config-if)# switchport mode trunk
S3(config-if)# switchport trunk native vlan 99
S3(config-if)# interface f0/3
S3(config-if)# no shutdown
S3(config-if)# switchport mode trunk
S3(config-if)# switchport trunk native vlan 99
S3(config-if)# interface vlan 99
S3(config-if)# ip address 192.168.1.13 255.255.255.0
S3(config-if)# exit
S3(config)# spanning-tree mode rapid-pvst
```

3.4.1.1 Class Activity–Documentation Tree

Objective

Identify common STP configuration issues.

Scenario

The employees in your building are having difficulty accessing a Web Server on the network. You look for the network documentation that the previous network engineer used before he transitioned to a new job; however, you cannot find any network documentation whatsoever.

Therefore, you decide to create your own network recordkeeping system. You decide to start at the access layer of your network hierarchy. This is where redundant switches are located, as well as the company servers, printers, and local hosts.

You create a matrix to record your documentation and include access layer switches on the list. You also decide to document switch names, ports in use, cabling connections, and root ports, designated ports, and alternate ports.

For more detailed instructions on how to design your model, use the student PDF that accompanies this activity.

Resources

- Packet Tracer software
- Word processing software

Directions

Step 1.   Create the topology diagram with three redundant switches.

Step 2.   Connect host devices to the switches.

Step 3.   Create the switch documentation matrix.

    a.   Name and switch location

    b.   General switch description

    c.   Model, IOS version, and image name

    d.   Switch serial number

    e.   MAC address

    f.   Ports currently in use

    g.   Cable connections

    h.   Root ports

    i.   Designated ports, status, and cost

    j.   Alternate ports, status, and cost

Step 4.   Use show commands to locate Layer 2 switch information.

     a.   show version

     b.   show cdp neighbors detail

     c.   show spanning-tree

CHAPTER 4

EtherChannel and HSRP

Link aggregation is the ability to create one logical link using multiple physical links between two devices. This allows load sharing among the physical links, rather than having an STP block one or more of the links. EtherChannel is a form of link aggregation used in switched networks. This chapter describes EtherChannel and the methods used to create an EtherChannel.

Redundant devices, such as multilayer switches or routers, provide the capability for a client to use an alternate default gateway should the primary default gateway fail. First Hop Redundancy Protocols (FHRPs) are used to manage multiple Layer 3 devices that serve as a default gateway or alternate default gateway. This chapter focuses on operations and configuration of one FHRP, Hot Standby Router Protocol (HSRP).

Study Guide

Link Aggregation Concepts

One of the best ways to reduce the time it takes for STP convergence is to simply avoid STP. EtherChannel is a form of link aggregation used in switched networks.

EtherChannel Advantages

EtherChannel technology was originally developed by Cisco as a technique of grouping several Fast Ethernet or Gigabit Ethernet switch ports into one logical channel.

List at least three advantages to using EtherChannel:

_____

_____

_____

_____

_____

EtherChannel Operation

You can configure EtherChannel as static or unconditional. However, there are also two protocols that can be used to configure the negotiation process: Port Aggregation Protocol (PAgP—Cisco proprietary) and Link Aggregation Control Protocol (LACP—IEEE 802.3ad).

These two protocols ensure that both sides of the link have compatible configurations—same speed, duplex setting, and VLAN information. The modes for each differ slightly.

For PAgP, briefly describe each of the following modes:

- **On:** _____

- **Desirable:** _____

- **Auto:** _____

For LACP, briefly describe each of the following modes:

- **On:** _____

- **Active:** _____

- **Passive:** _____

In Table 4-1, indicate the mode that is described.

Table 4-1   PAgP and LACP Modes

Mode	PAgP and/or LACP Mode Description
	Initiates LACP negotiations with other interfaces.
	Forces EtherChannel state without PAgP or LACP initiated negotiations.
	Places an interface in a passive, responding state. Does not initiate PAgP negotiations.
	Actively initiates PAgP negotiations with other interfaces.
	Places an interface in a passive, responding state. Does not initiate LACP negotiations.

The mode that is configured on each side of the EtherChannel link determines whether EtherChannel will be operational.

In Table 4-2, two switches are using PAgP. Indicate with "yes" or "no" whether EtherChannel is established.

Table 4-2   EtherChannel Negotiation Using PAgP

Switch 1 Mode	Switch 2 Mode	EtherChannel Established?
Auto	Auto	
Auto	Desirable	
On	Desirable	
On	Off	
Desirable	Desirable	

In Table 4-3, two switches are using LACP. Indicate with "yes" or "no" whether EtherChannel is established.

Table 4-3   EtherChannel Negotiation Using LACP

Switch 1 Mode	Switch 2 Mode	EtherChannel Established?
Passive	On	
Passive	Active	
On	On	
Passive	Passive	
On	Active	

Link Aggregation Configuration

EtherChannel configuration is straightforward once you decide on which protocol you will use. In fact, the easiest method is to just force both sides to be on.

Configuring EtherChannel

To configure EtherChannel, complete the following steps:

Step 1. Specify the interfaces that participate in the EtherChannel group using the **interface range** *interface* command.

What are the requirements for each interface before they can form an EtherChannel?

_____

_____

_____

Step 2. Create the port channel interface with the **channel-group** *identifier* **mode {on | auto | desirable | active | passive}** command in interface range configuration mode. The keyword _____ forces the port to channel without PAgP or LACP. The keywords _____ and _____ enable PAgP. The keywords _____ and _____ enable LACP.

Step 3. The **channel-group** command automatically creates a port channel interface using the *identifier* as the number. Use the **interface port-channel** *identifier* command to configure channel-wide settings like trunking, native VLANs, or allowed VLANs.

As you can see from the configuration steps, the way you specify whether to use PAgP, LACP, or no negotiations is by configuring one keyword in the **channel-group** command.

So, with those steps in mind, consider Figure 4-1 in each of the following configuration scenarios.

Figure 4-1   EtherChannel Topology

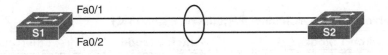

EtherChannel Configuration Scenario 1

Record the commands, including the switch prompt, to configure the S1 Fa0/1 and Fa0/2 into an EtherChannel without negotiations. Then force the channel to trunk using native VLAN 99.

`S1(config)#` _____

_____

_____

_____

_____

EtherChannel Configuration Scenario 2

Record the commands, including the switch prompt, to configure the S1 Fa0/1 and Fa0/2 into an EtherChannel using PAgP. S1 should initiate the negotiations. The channel should trunk, allowing only VLANs 1, 10, and 20.

```
S1(config)# _____
_____
_____
_____
_____
```

EtherChannel Configuration Scenario 3

Record the commands, including the switch prompt, to configure the S1 Fa0/1 and Fa0/2 into an EtherChannel using LACP. S1 should not initiate the negotiations. The channel should trunk, allowing all VLANs.

```
_____
_____
_____
_____
```

Verifying and Troubleshooting EtherChannel

Record the commands used to display the output in Example 4-1.

Example 4-1   EtherChannel Verification Commands

```
S1# _____
Port-channel1 is up, line protocol is up (connected)
  Hardware is EtherChannel, address is 0cd9.96e8.8a01 (bia 0cd9.96e8.8a01)
  MTU 1500 bytes, BW 200000 Kbit/sec, DLY 100 usec,
     reliability 255/255, txload 1/255, rxload 1/255
<output omitted>


S1# _____
Flags:  D - down        P - bundled in port-channel
        I - stand-alone s - suspended
        H - Hot-standby (LACP only)
        R - Layer3       S - Layer2
        U - in use       f - failed to allocate aggregator

        M - not in use, minimum links not met
        u - unsuitable for bundling
        w - waiting to be aggregated
        d - default port


Number of channel-groups in use: 1
Number of aggregators:            1


Group  Port-channel  Protocol    Ports
```

```
------+--------------+-----------+------------------------------------------------
1       Po1(SU)           LACP      Fa0/1(P)     Fa0/2(P)


S1# _____
               Channel-group listing:

               ----------------------


Group: 1
----------
               Port-channels in the group:

               --------------------------


Port-channel: Po1     (Primary Aggregator)


------------


Age of the Port-channel   = 0d:00h:25m:17s

Logical slot/port    = 2/1          Number of ports = 2

HotStandBy port = null

Port state             = Port-channel Ag-Inuse

Protocol            =   LACP

Port security        = Disabled


Ports in the Port-channel:


Index   Load   Port    EC state          No of bits

------+------+------+------------------+-----------

  0     00     Fa0/1   Active               0

  0     00     Fa0/2   Active               0


Time since last port bundled:    0d:00h:05m:41s    Fa0/2

Time since last port Un-bundled: 0d:00h:05m:48s    Fa0/2


S1# _____
Port state     = Up Mstr Assoc In-Bndl

Channel group = 1              Mode = Active          Gcchange = -

Port-channel = Po1            GC   =   -              Pseudo port-channel = Po1

Port index    = 0             Load = 0x00             Protocol =    LACP


Flags:   S - Device is sending Slow LACPDUs    F - Device is sending fast LACPDUs.

         A - Device is in active mode.         P - Device is in passive mode.


Local information:
```

```
LACP port        Admin    Oper    Port        Port
Port       Flags   State    Priority     Key       Key       Number      State
Fa0/1      SA      bndl     32768        0x1       0x1       0x102       0x3D


Partner's information:


                   LACP port                        Admin  Oper   Port    Port
Port       Flags   Priority  Dev ID          Age    key    Key    Number  State
Fa0/1      SA      32768     0cd9.96d2.4000  4s     0x0    0x1    0x102   0x3D


Age of the port in the current state: 0d:00h:24m:59s
S1#
```

When troubleshooting an EtherChannel issue, keep in mind the configuration restrictions for interfaces that participate in the channel. List at least four restrictions.

_____

_____

_____

_____

_____

Refer to the output for S1 and S2 in Example 4-2. Record the command that generated the output.

Example 4-2   Troubleshooting an EtherChannel Issue

```
S1# _____
Flags:  D - down         P - bundled in port-channel
        I - stand-alone s - suspended
        H - Hot-standby (LACP only)
        R - Layer3       S - Layer2
        U - in use       f - failed to allocate aggregator
        M - not in use, minimum links not met
        u - unsuitable for bundling
        w - waiting to be aggregated
        d - default port
Number of channel-groups in use: 1
Number of aggregators:           1
Group  Port-channel  Protocol    Ports
------+-------------+-----------+-------------------------------------------
1      Po1(SD)           -        Fa0/1(D)    Fa0/2(D)
S1# _____
interface Port-channel1
 switchport mode trunk
!
```

```
interface FastEthernet0/1
 switchport mode trunk
 channel-group 1 mode auto
!
interface FastEthernet0/2
 switchport mode trunk
 channel-group 1 mode auto
!
<output omitted>
S 1#
S2# _____
interface Port-channel1
 switchport mode trunk
!
interface FastEthernet0/1
 switchport mode trunk
 channel-group 1 mode auto
!
interface FastEthernet0/2
 switchport mode trunk
 channel-group 1 mode auto
!
<output omitted>
S2#
```

Explain why the EtherChannel between S1 and S2 is down.

_____

_____

EtherChannel and spanning tree must interoperate. For this reason, the order in which EtherChannel-related commands are entered is important. To correct this issue, you must first remove the port channel. Otherwise, spanning-tree errors cause the associated ports to go into blocking or errdisabled state. With that in mind, what would you suggest to correct the issue shown in Example 4-2 if the requirement is to use PAgP? What commands would be required?

_____

_____

_____

_____

_____

_____

_____

First Hop Redundancy Protocols

Up to this point, we've been reviewing STP and how to manipulate the election of root bridges and load balance across redundant links. In addition to Layer 1 and Layer 2 redundancy, a high-availability network might also implement Layer 3 redundancy by sharing the default gateway responsibility across multiple devices. Through the use of a virtual IP address, two Layer 3 devices can share the default gateway responsibility. This section reviews First Hop Redundancy Protocols (FHRPs) that provide Layer 3 redundancy.

Identify FHRP Terminology

Match the definition on the left with the terms on the right. This is a one-to-one matching exercise.

Definitions

___ The ability to dynamically recover from the failure of a device acting as the default gateway

___ Two or more routers sharing a single MAC and IP address

___ A device that is part of a virtual router group assigned to the role of default gateway

___ Provides the mechanism for determining which router should take the active role in forwarding traffic

___ A device that routes traffic destined to network segments beyond the source network segment

___ A device that is part of a virtual router group assigned the role of alternate default gateway

___ A Layer 3 address assigned to a protocol that shares the single address among multiple devices

___ The Layer 2 address returned by ARP for an FHRP gateway

Terms

a. Default gateway

b. First hop redundancy

c. Forwarding router

d. Redundancy protocol

e. Standby router

f. Virtual IP address

g. Virtual MAC address

h. Virtual router

Identify the Type of FHRP

In Table 4-4, indicate whether the characteristic describes HSRP, VRRP, or GLBP.

Table 4-4   FHRP Characteristics

FHRP Characteristic	HSRP	VRRP	GLBP
Used in a group of routers for selecting an active device and a standby device.			
A nonproprietary election protocol that allows several routers on a multi-access link to use the same virtual IPv4 address.			
Cisco-proprietary FHRP protocol designed to allow for transparent failover of first hop IPv4 devices.			
Cisco-proprietary FHRP protocol that protects data traffic from a failed router or circuit while also allowing load sharing between a group of redundant routers.			
One router is elected as the virtual router master, with the other routers acting as backups in case the virtual router master fails.			

Identify the HSRP Version

In Table 4-5, identify the HSRP state based on the characteristic description.

Table 4-5   Identify the HSRP Version

Characteristic	HSRPv1	HSRPv2
Uses the multicast address 224.0.0.102		
Supports MD5 authentication		
Supports group numbers 0 to 255		
Uses MAC address range 0000.0C07.AC00 to 0000.0C07.ACFF		
Uses IPv6 multicast address FF02::66		
Adds support for MD5 authentication		
Uses the multicast address 224.0.0.2		

Determine the HSRP State

In Table 4-6, indicate the HSRP state based on the scenario description.

Table 4-6   Determine the HSRP State

Scenario	Initial	Learn	Listen	Speak	Standby	Active
The router has not determined the virtual IP address and has not yet seen a hello message from the active router. In this state, the router waits to hear from the active router.						
The router currently forwards packets that are sent to the group virtual MAC address. The router sends periodic hello messages.						
A new HSRP interface is activated.						

Scenario	Initial	Learn	Listen	Speak	Standby	Active
The router will become active if it does not receive a hello message from the active router after 10 seconds.						
The router knows the virtual IP address, but the router is neither the active router nor the standby router. It listens for hello messages from those routers.						
The router sends periodic hello messages and actively participates in the election of the active and/or standby router.						
The router is a candidate to become the next active router and sends periodic hello messages.						
The router is configured with a priority of 200. The other router is not configured with an HSRP priority.						
This state is entered through a configuration change.						

HSRP Implementation

Refer to the topology in Figure 4-2. R2 has been configured for HSRP group 20, priority 120, IP address 192.168.1.20, and virtual IP address 192.168.1.1.

Figure 4-2   HSRP Configuration Topology

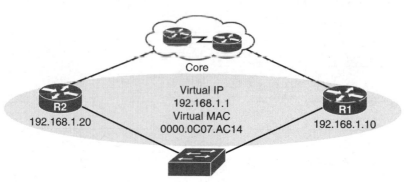

HSRP Configuration

Example 4-3 shows the HSRP configuration for R2.

Example 4-3   R2 HSRP Configuration

```
R2# show run interface g0/1
<output omitted>
interface GigabitEthernet0/1
 ip address 192.168.1.20 255.255.255.0
 standby 20 ip 192.168.1.1
 standby 20 priority 120
<output omitted>
```

Using the information in Example 4-3, document the commands to configure R1 as the HSRP active router in group 20 using a priority of 210. R1 should become the active router even if R2 is already the active router.

_____

_____

_____

_____

_____

_____

HSRP Verification

What command would generate the following output to verify the HSRP configuration?

```
R1# _____
GigabitEthernet0/1 - Group 20
  State is Active
    8 state changes, last state change 00:11:58
  Virtual IP address is 192.168.1.1
  Active virtual MAC address is 0000.0C07.AC14
    Local virtual MAC address is 0000.0C07.AC14 (v1 default)
  Hello time 3 sec, hold time 10 sec
    Next hello sent in 1.969 secs
  Preemption enabled
  Active router is local
  Standby router is 192.168.1.20, priority 120 (expires in 6 sec)
  Priority 210 (configured 210)
  Group name is hsrp-Gig0/1-20 (default)
R1#
R1# _____
                    P indicates configured to preempt.
                    |
Interface   Grp  Pri P State   Active       Standby       Virtual IP
Gi0/1       20   210   Active  local        192.168.1.20  192.168.1.1
```

HSRP Troubleshooting

HSRP failure can occur for a number of reasons including

- Active router is not elected because IP addressing is incorrectly configured.
- Standby and active routers are not configured for the same HSRP group.
- End devices are not configured with the virtual IP address as the default gateway.

Use debugging commands to troubleshoot HSRP. Fill in the correct command for the following output:

```
R2# _____
*Apr  3 12:34:12.347: HSRP: Gi0/1 Grp 20 Hello  in  192.168.1.20 Active  pri 120 vIP 192.168.1.1
```

```
*Apr  3 12:34:12.643: HSRP: Gi0/1 Grp 20 Hello  out 192.168.1.10 Standby pri 210 vIP 192.168.1.1

R2# _____

HSRP:
  HSRP Errors debugging is on
  HSRP Events debugging is on
     (protocol, neighbor, redundancy, track, arp, interface)
  HSRP Packets debugging is on
     (Coup, Resign)
*Apr  3 12:52:31.855: HSRP: Gi0/1 Grp 20 Standby: c/Active timer expired (192.168.1.20)
*Apr  3 12:52:31.855: HSRP: Gi0/1 Grp 20 Active router is local, was 192.168.1.20
*Apr  3 12:52:31.855: HSRP: Gi0/1 Nbr 192.168.1.20 no longer active for group 20 (Standby)
*Apr  3 12:52:31.855: HSRP: Gi0/1 Nbr 192.168.1.20 Was active or standby - start passive
holddown
*Apr  3 12:52:31.855: HSRP: Gi0/1 Grp 20 Standby router is unknown, was local
*Apr  3 12:52:31.855: HSRP: Gi0/1 Grp 20 Standby -> Active
<output omitted>
R2#
```

Packet Tracer Exercise 4-1: EtherChannel and HSRP Configuration

Download and open the file LSG03-0401.pka found at the companion website for this book. Refer to the Introduction of this book for specifics on accessing files.

Note: The following instructions are also contained within the Packet Tracer Exercise.

In this Packet Tracer activity, you will configure EtherChannel and HSRP.

Requirements

- Configure the links between S1 and S2 to be part of EtherChannel group 1.
- Enable trunking on the port channel interface.
- R1 and R2 use the following virtual IP addresses
    - VLAN 10: 10.1.10.254
    - VLAN 20: 10.1.20.254
- Configure R1 to be the active HSRP router for VLAN 10.
    - Set priority to 150.
    - R1 should resume active role after a reboot.
- Configure R2 to be the active HSRP router for VLAN 20.
    - Set priority to 150.
    - R2 should resume active role after a reboot.

Your completion percentage should be 100%. If not, click **Check Results** to see which required components are not yet completed.

Labs and Activities

Command Reference

In Table 4-7, record the command, including the correct router or switch prompt, that fits the description. Fill in any blanks with the appropriate missing information.

Table 4-7 Commands for Chapter 4, EtherChannel and HSRP

Command	Description
	Enter interface configuration mode on S1 for both Fa0/1 and Fa0/2.
	Configure EtherChannel group 1 without LACP or PAgP negotiations.
	Enter port channel configuration mode.
	Configure the port channel to trunk.
	Verify the EtherChannel is up and in use.
	Configure R1 to use the virtual IP 10.1.1.1 for group 10.
	Configure R1 with HSRP priority 110.
	Configure R1 to immediately take over active role when rebooting.
	Verify the HSRP information for R1.
	View the receiving and sending of HSRP hello packets.
	View the election process as an HSRP router becomes the new active router.

4.0.1.2 Class Activity–Imagine This

Objective

Explain the operation of link aggregation in a switched LAN environment.

Scenario

It is the end of the work day. In your small- to medium-sized business, you are trying to explain to the network engineers about EtherChannel and how it looks when it is physically set up. The network engineers have difficulties envisioning how two switches could possibly be connected via several links that collectively act as one channel or connection. Your company is definitely considering implementing an EtherChannel network.

Therefore, you end the meeting with an assignment for the engineers. To prepare for the next day's meeting, they are to perform some research and bring to the meeting one graphic representation of an EtherChannel network connection. They are tasked with explaining how an EtherChannel network operates to the other engineers.

When researching EtherChannel, a good question to search for is "What docs EtherChannel look like?" Prepare a few slides to demonstrate your research that will be presented to the network engineering group. These slides should provide a solid grasp of how EtherChannels are physically created within a network topology. Your goal is to ensure that everyone leaving the next meeting will have a good idea as to why they would consider moving to a network topology using EtherChannel as an option.

Required Resources

- Internet connectivity for research
- Software program for presentation model

Step 1. Use the Internet to research graphics depicting EtherChannel.

Step 2. Prepare a three-slide presentation to share with the class.

    a. The first slide should show a very short, concise definition of a switch-to-switch EtherChannel.

    b. The second slide should show a graphic of how a switch-to-switch EtherChannel physical topology would look if used in a small- to medium-sized business.

    c. The third slide should list three advantages of using EtherChannel.

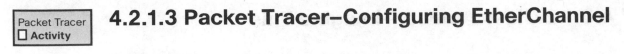

4.2.1.3 Packet Tracer–Configuring EtherChannel

Topology

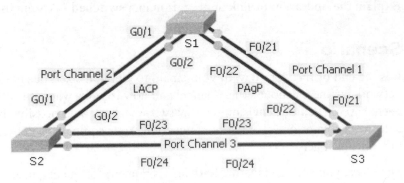

Objectives

Part 1: Configure Basic Switch Settings

Part 2: Configure an EtherChannel with Cisco PAgP

Part 3: Configure an 802.3ad LACP EtherChannel

Part 4: Configure a Redundant EtherChannel Link

Background

Three switches have just been installed. There are redundant uplinks between the switches. Usually, only one of these links could be used; otherwise, a bridging loop might occur. However, using only one link utilizes only half of the available bandwidth. EtherChannel allows up to eight redundant links to be bundled together into one logical link. In this lab, you will configure Port Aggregation Protocol (PAgP), a Cisco EtherChannel protocol, and Link Aggregation Control Protocol (LACP), an IEEE 802.3ad open standard version of EtherChannel.

Part 1: Configure Basic Switch Settings

Step 1.   Configure basic switch parameters.

     a.   Assign each switch a hostname according to the topology diagram.

     b.   Configure all required ports as trunks, depending on the connections between devices.

Note: If the ports are configured with dynamic auto mode, and you do not set the mode of the ports to trunk, the links do not form trunks and remain access ports. The default mode on a 2960 switch is dynamic auto.

Part 2: Configure an EtherChannel with Cisco PAgP

Note: When configuring EtherChannels, it is recommended to shut down the physical ports being grouped on both devices before configuring them into channel groups. Otherwise, the EtherChannel Misconfig Guard may place these ports into err-disabled state. The ports and port channels can be re-enabled after EtherChannel is configured.

Step 1.   Configure Port Channel 1.

  a.   The first EtherChannel created for this activity aggregates ports F0/22 and F0/21 between **S1** and **S3**. Use the **show interfaces trunk** command to ensure that you have an active trunk link for those two links.

  b.   On both switches, add ports F0/21 and F0/22 to Port Channel 1 with the **channel-group 1 mode desirable** command. The **mode desirable** option enables the switch to actively negotiate to form a PAgP link.

  c.   Configure the logical interface to become a trunk by first entering the **interface port-channel** *number* command and then the **switchport mode trunk** command. Add this configuration to both switches.

Step 2.   Verify Port Channel 1 status.

  a.   Issue the **show etherchannel summary** command to verify that EtherChannel is working on both switches. This command displays the type of EtherChannel, the ports utilized, and port states.

  b.   If the EtherChannel does not come up, shut down the physical interfaces on both ends of the EtherChannel and then bring them back up again. This involves using the **shutdown** command on those interfaces, followed by a **no shutdown** command a few seconds later.

  The **show interfaces trunk** and **show spanning-tree** commands also show the port channel as one logical link.

Part 3: Configure an 802.3ad LACP EtherChannel

Step 1.   Configure Port Channel 2.

  a.   In 2000, the IEEE released 802.3ad, which is an open standard version of EtherChannel. Using the previous commands, configure the link between **S1** and **S2** on ports G0/1 and G0/2 as an LACP EtherChannel. You must use a different port channel number on **S1** than 1, because you already used that in the previous step. To configure a port channel as LACP, use the interface configuration mode **channel-group** *number* **mode active** command. Active mode indicates that the switch actively tries to negotiate that link as LACP, as opposed to PAgP.

Step 2.   Verify Port Channel 2 status.

  a.   Use the **show** commands from Part 1 Step 2 to verify the status of Port Channel 2. Look for the protocol used by each port.

Part 4: Configure a Redundant EtherChannel Link

Step 1.   Configure Port Channel 3.

There are various ways to enter the **channel-group** *number* **mode** command:

```
S2(config)# interface range f0/23 - 24
S2(config-if-range)# channel-group 3 mode ?
  active     Enable LACP unconditionally
  auto       Enable PAgP only if a PAgP device is detected
  desirable  Enable PAgP unconditionally
  on         Enable Etherchannel only
  passive    Enable LACP only if a LACP device is detected
```

    a.   On switch **S2**, add ports F0/23 and F0/24 to Port Channel 3 with the **channel-group 3 mode passive** command. The **passive** option indicates that you want the switch to use LACP only if another LACP device is detected. Statically configure Port Channel 3 as a trunk interface.

    b.   On switch **S3**, add ports F0/23 and F0/24 to Port Channel 3 with the **channel-group 3 mode active** command. The **active** option indicates that you want the switch to use LACP unconditionally. Statically configure Port Channel 3 as a trunk interface.

Step 2.   Verify Port Channel 3 status.

    a.   Use the **show** commands from Part 1 Step 2 to verify the status of Port Channel 3. Look for the protocol used by each port.

    b.   Port Channel 2 is not operative because spanning tree protocol placed some ports into blocking mode. Unfortunately, those ports were Gigabit ports. To restore these ports, configure **S1** to be **primary** root for VLAN 1 or set the priority to **24576**.

4.2.1.4 Lab–Configuring EtherChannel

Topology

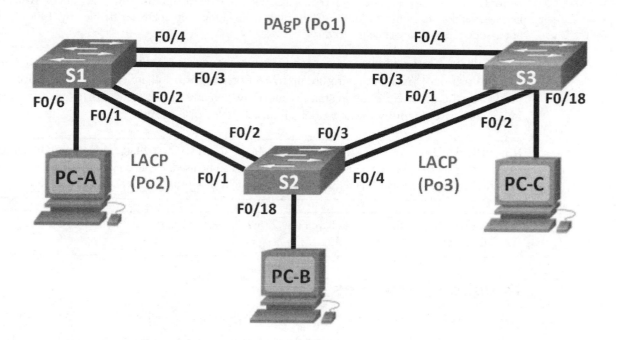

Addressing Table

Device	Interface	IP Address	Subnet Mask
S1	VLAN 99	192.168.99.11	255.255.255.0
S2	VLAN 99	192.168.99.12	255.255.255.0
S3	VLAN 99	192.168.99.13	255.255.255.0
PC-A	NIC	192.168.10.1	255.255.255.0
PC-B	NIC	192.168.10.2	255.255.255.0
PC-C	NIC	192.168.10.3	255.255.255.0

Objectives

Part 1: Configure Basic Switch Settings

Part 2: Configure PAgP

Part 3: Configure LACP

Background/Scenario

Link aggregation allows the creation of logical links that are comprised of two or more physical links. This provides increased throughput beyond using only one physical link. Link aggregation also provides redundancy if one of the links fails.

In this lab, you will configure EtherChannel, a form of link aggregation used in switched networks. You will configure EtherChannel using Port Aggregation Protocol (PAgP) and Link Aggregation Control Protocol (LACP).

Note: PAgP is a Cisco-proprietary protocol that you can only run on Cisco switches and on switches that are licensed vendors to support PAgP. LACP is a link aggregation protocol that is defined by IEEE 802.3ad, and it is not associated with any specific vendor.

LACP allows Cisco switches to manage Ethernet channels between switches that conform to the 802.3ad protocol. You can configure up to 16 ports to form a channel. Eight of the ports are in active mode and the other eight are in standby mode. When any of the active ports fail, a standby port becomes active. Standby mode works only for LACP, not for PAgP.

Note: The switches used with CCNA hands-on labs are Cisco Catalyst 2960s with Cisco IOS Release 15.0(2) (lanbasek9 image). Other switches and Cisco IOS versions can be used. Depending on the model and Cisco IOS version, the commands available and output produced might vary from what is shown in the labs.

Note: Make sure that the switches have been erased and have no startup configurations. If you are unsure, contact your instructor.

Required Resources

- 3 Switches (Cisco 2960 with Cisco IOS Release 15.0(2) lanbasek9 image or comparable)
- 3 PCs (Windows 7, Vista, or XP with terminal emulation program, such as Tera Term)
- Console cables to configure the Cisco IOS devices via the console ports
- Ethernet cables as shown in the topology

Part 1: Configure Basic Switch Settings

In Part 1, you will set up the network topology and configure basic settings, such as the interface IP addresses, device access, and passwords.

Step 1.   Cable the network as shown in the topology.

Attach the devices as shown in the topology diagram, and cable as necessary.

Step 2.   Initialize and reload the switches.

Step 3.   Configure basic settings for each switch.

    a.   Disable DNS lookup.

    b.   Configure the device name as displayed in the topology.

    c.   Encrypt plain text passwords.

    d.   Create a MOTD banner warning users that unauthorized access is prohibited.

    e.   Assign **class** as the encrypted privileged EXEC mode password.

    f.   Assign **cisco** as the console and vty password and enable login.

    g.   Configure logging synchronous to prevent console message from interrupting command entry.

    h.   Shut down all switch ports except the ports connected to PCs.

    i. Configure VLAN 99 and name it **Management**.

    j. Configure VLAN 10 and name it **Staff**.

    k. Configure the switch ports with attached hosts as access ports in VLAN 10.

    l. Assign the IP addresses according to the Addressing Table.

    m. Copy the running configuration to startup configuration.

Step 4. Configure the PCs.

Assign IP addresses to the PCs according to the Addressing Table.

Part 2: Configure PAgP

PAgP is a Cisco proprietary protocol for link aggregation. In Part 2, a link between S1 and S3 will be configured using PAgP.

Step 1. Configure PAgP on S1 and S3.

For a link between S1 and S3, configure the ports on S1 with PAgP desirable mode and the ports on S3 with PAgP auto mode. Enable the ports after PAgP modes have been configured.

```
S1(config)# interface range f0/3-4
S1(config-if-range)# channel-group 1 mode desirable
Creating a port-channel interface Port-channel 1

S1(config-if-range)# no shutdown

S3(config)# interface range f0/3-4
S3(config-if-range)# channel-group 1 mode auto
Creating a port-channel interface Port-channel 1

S3(config-if-range)# no shutdown
*Mar  1 00:09:12.792: %LINK-3-UPDOWN: Interface FastEthernet0/3, changed state to up
*Mar  1 00:09:12.792: %LINK-3-UPDOWN: Interface FastEthernet0/4, changed state to up
S3(config-if-range)#
*Mar  1 00:09:15.384: %LINEPROTO-5-UPDOWN: Line protocol on Interface
FastEthernet0/3, changed state to up
*Mar  1 00:09:16.265: %LINEPROTO-5-UPDOWN: Line protocol on Interface
FastEthernet0/4, changed state to up
S3(config-if-range)#
*Mar  1 00:09:16.357: %LINK-3-UPDOWN: Interface Port-channel1, changed state to up
*Mar  1 00:09:17.364: %LINEPROTO-5-UPDOWN: Line protocol on Interface Port-channel1,
changed state to up
*Mar  1 00:09:44.383: %LINEPROTO-5-UPDOWN: Line protocol on Interface Vlan1, changed
state to up
```

Step 2. Examine the configuration on the ports.

Currently the F0/3, F0/4, and Po1 (Port-channel1) interfaces on both S1 and S3 are in access operational mode with the administrative mode in dynamic auto. Verify the configuration using the **show run interface** *interface-id* and **show interfaces** *interface-id* **switchport** commands, respectively. The example configuration outputs for F0/3 on S1 are as follows:

```
S1# show run interface f0/3
Building configuration...
```

```
Current configuration : 103 bytes
!
interface FastEthernet0/3
 channel-group 1 mode desirable
```

S1# **show interfaces f0/3 switchport**
```
Name: Fa0/3
Switchport: Enabled
Administrative Mode: dynamic auto
Operational Mode: static access (member of bundle Po1)
Administrative Trunking Encapsulation: dot1q
Operational Trunking Encapsulation: native
Negotiation of Trunking: On
Access Mode VLAN: 1 (default)
Trunking Native Mode VLAN: 1 (default)
Administrative Native VLAN tagging: enabled
Voice VLAN: none
Administrative private-vlan host-association: none
Administrative private-vlan mapping: none
Administrative private-vlan trunk native VLAN: none
Administrative private-vlan trunk Native VLAN tagging: enabled
Administrative private-vlan trunk encapsulation: dot1q
Administrative private-vlan trunk normal VLANs: none
Administrative private-vlan trunk associations: none
Administrative private-vlan trunk mappings: none
Operational private-vlan: none
Trunking VLANs Enabled: ALL
Pruning VLANs Enabled: 2-1001
Capture Mode Disabled
Capture VLANs Allowed: ALL

Protected: false
Unknown unicast blocked: disabled
Unknown multicast blocked: disabled
Appliance trust: none
```

Step 3.   Verify that the ports have been aggregated.

S1# **show etherchannel summary**
```
Flags:  D - down       P - bundled in port-channel
        I - stand-alone s - suspended
        H - Hot-standby (LACP only)
        R - Layer3      S - Layer2
        U - in use      f - failed to allocate aggregator

        M - not in use, minimum links not met
        u - unsuitable for bundling
        w - waiting to be aggregated
        d - default port
```

```
Number of channel-groups in use: 1
Number of aggregators:         1

Group  Port-channel  Protocol    Ports
------+-------------+-----------+----------------------------------------------
1      Po1(SU)        PAgP        Fa0/3(P)    Fa0/4(P)
```

```
S3# show etherchannel summary
Flags:  D - down         P - bundled in port-channel
        I - stand-alone  s - suspended
        H - Hot-standby (LACP only)
        R - Layer3       S - Layer2
        U - in use       f - failed to allocate aggregator

        M - not in use, minimum links not met
        u - unsuitable for bundling
        w - waiting to be aggregated
        d - default port


Number of channel-groups in use: 1
Number of aggregators:         1

Group  Port-channel  Protocol    Ports
------+-------------+-----------+----------------------------------------------
1      Po1(SU)        PAgP        Fa0/3(P)    Fa0/4(P)
```

What do the flags, SU and P, indicate in the Ethernet summary?

_____

_____

Step 4. Configure trunk ports.

After the ports have been aggregated, commands applied at the port channel interface affect all the links that were bundled together. Manually configure the Po1 ports on S1 and S3 as trunk ports and assign them to native VLAN 99.

```
S1(config)# interface port-channel 1
S1(config-if)# switchport mode trunk
S1(config-if)# switchport trunk native vlan 99

S3(config)# interface port-channel 1
S3(config-if)# switchport mode trunk
S3(config-if)# switchport trunk native vlan 99
```

Step 5.   Verify that the ports are configured as trunk ports.

    a.   Issue the **show run interface** *interface-id* commands on S1 and S3. What commands are listed for F0/3 and F0/4 on both switches? Compare the results to the running configuration for the Po1 interface? Record your observation.

_____

_____

_____

_____

_____

_____

_____

_____

_____

_____

    b.   Issue the **show interfaces trunk** and **show spanning-tree** commands on S1 and S3. What trunk port is listed? What is the native VLAN? What is the concluding result from the output?

_____

From the **show spanning-tree** output, what is port cost and port priority for the aggregated link?

_____

Part 3: Configure LACP

LACP is an open source protocol for link aggregation developed by the IEEE. In Part 3, the link between S1 and S2, and the link between S2 and S3 will be configured using LACP. Also, the individual links will be configured as trunks before they are bundled together as EtherChannels.

Step 1.   Configure LACP between S1 and S2.

```
S1(config)# interface range f0/1-2
S1(config-if-range)# switchport mode trunk
S1(config-if-range)# switchport trunk native vlan 99
S1(config-if-range)# channel-group 2 mode active
Creating a port-channel interface Port-channel 2

S1(config-if-range)# no shutdown


S2(config)# interface range f0/1-2
S2(config-if-range)# switchport mode trunk
S2(config-if-range)# switchport trunk native vlan 99
S2(config-if-range)# channel-group 2 mode passive
Creating a port-channel interface Port-channel 2

S2(config-if-range)# no shutdown
```

Step 2.   Verify that the ports have been aggregated.

What protocol is Po2 using for link aggregation? Which ports are aggregated to form Po2? Record the command used to verify.

_____

_____

Step 3.   Configure LACP between S2 and S3.

   a.   Configure the link between S2 and S3 as Po3 and use LACP as the link aggregation protocol.

```
S2(config)# interface range f0/3-4
S2(config-if-range)# switchport mode trunk
S2(config-if-range)# switchport trunk native vlan 99
S2(config-if-range)# channel-group 3 mode active
Creating a port-channel interface Port-channel 3
S2(config-if-range)# no shutdown


S3(config)# interface range f0/1-2
S3(config-if-range)# switchport mode trunk
S3(config-if-range)# switchport trunk native vlan 99
S3(config-if-range)# channel-group 3 mode passive
Creating a port-channel interface Port-channel 3

S3(config-if-range)# no shutdown
```

   b.   Verify that the EtherChannel has formed.

Step 4.   Verify end-to-end connectivity.

Verify that all devices can ping each other within the same VLAN. If not, troubleshoot until there is end-to-end connectivity.

Note: It may be necessary to disable the PC firewall to ping between PCs.

Reflection

What could prevent EtherChannels from forming?

_____

4.2.2.3 Packet Tracer–Troubleshooting EtherChannel

Topology

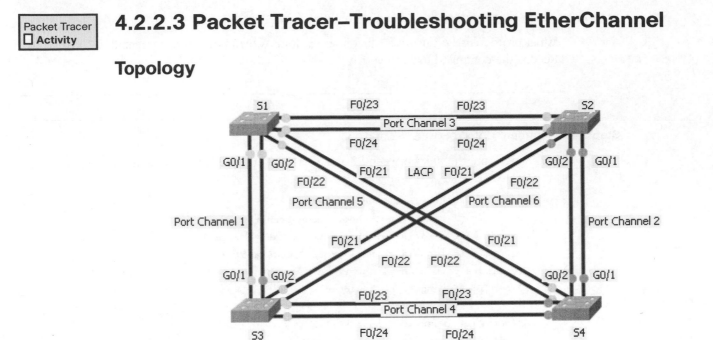

Objectives

Part 1: Examine the Physical Layer and Correct Switch Port Mode Issues

Part 2: Identify and Correct Port Channel Assignment Issues

Part 3: Identify and Correct Port Channel Protocol Issues

Background

Four switches were recently configured by a junior technician. Users are complaining that the network is running slow and would like you to investigate.

Part 1: Examine the Physical Layer and Correct Switch Port Mode Issues

Step 1. Look for access ports.

Examine the switches. When physical ports are assigned to an EtherChannel port, they behave as one. Each pair will either be operational or down. They will not be mixed with one port green and the other port orange.

Step 2. Set ports to trunking mode.

a. Verify that all physical ports in the topology are set to trunking. Correct any that are in access mode.

b. Correct any EtherChannel ports that are not set to trunking mode.

Part 2: Identify and Correct Port Channel Assignment Issues

Step 1.   Examine port channel assignments.

The topology illustrates physical ports and their EtherChannel assignments. Verify that the switches are configured as indicated.

Step 2.   Correct port channel assignments.

Correct any switch ports that are not assigned to the correct EtherChannel port.

Part 3: Identify and Correct Port Channel Protocol Issues

Step 1.   Identify protocol issues.

In 2000, the IEEE released 802.3ad (LACP), which is an open standard version of EtherChannel. For compatibility reasons, the network design team chose to use LACP across the network. All ports that participate in EtherChannel need to actively negotiate the link as LACP, as opposed to PAgP. Verify that the physical ports are configured as indicated.

Step 2.   Correct protocol issues.

Correct any switch ports that are not negotiating using LACP.

4.2.2.4 Lab–Troubleshooting EtherChannel

Topology

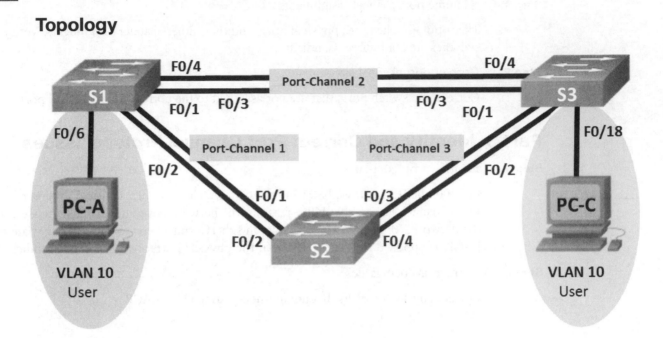

Addressing Table

Device	Interface	IP Address	Subnet Mask
S1	VLAN 99	192.168.1.11	255.255.255.0
S2	VLAN 99	192.168.1.12	255.255.255.0
S3	VLAN 99	192.168.1.13	255.255.255.0
PC-A	NIC	192.168.0.2	255.255.255.0
PC-C	NIC	192.168.0.3	255.255.255.0

VLAN Assignments

VLAN	Name
10	User
99	Management

Objectives

Part 1: Build the Network and Load Device Configurations

Part 2: Troubleshoot EtherChannel

Background/Scenario

The switches at your company were configured by an inexperienced network administrator. Several errors in the configuration have resulted in speed and connectivity issues. Your manager has asked you to troubleshoot and correct the configuration errors and document your work. Using your knowledge of EtherChannel and standard testing methods, find and correct the errors. Ensure that all of the EtherChannels use Port Aggregation Protocol (PAgP), and that all hosts are reachable.

Note: The switches used are Cisco Catalyst 2960s with Cisco IOS Release 15.0(2) (lanbasek9 image). Other switches and Cisco IOS versions can be used. Depending on the model and Cisco IOS version, the commands available and output produced might vary from what is shown in the labs.

Note: Make sure that the switches have been erased and have no startup configurations. If you are unsure, contact your instructor.

Required Resources

- 3 Switches (Cisco 2960 with Cisco IOS Release 15.0(2) lanbasek9 image or comparable)
- 2 PCs (Windows 7, Vista, or XP with a terminal emulation program, such as Tera Term)
- Console cables to configure the Cisco IOS devices via the console ports
- Ethernet cables as shown in the topology

Part 1: Build the Network and Load Device Configurations

In Part 1, you will set up the network topology, configure basic settings on the PC hosts, and load configurations on the switches.

Step 1. Cable the network as shown in the topology.

Step 2. Configure the PC hosts.

Step 3. Erase the startup and VLAN configurations and reload the switches.

Step 4. Load switch configurations.

Load the following configurations into the appropriate switch. All switches have the same passwords. The privileged EXEC password is **class**. The password for console and vty access is **cisco**. As all switches are Cisco devices, the network administrator decided to use Cisco's PAgP on all port channels configured with EtherChannel. Switch S2 is the root bridge for all VLANs in the topology.

Switch S1 Configuration:

```
hostname S1
interface range f0/1-24, g0/1-2
shutdown
exit
enable secret class
no ip domain lookup
line vty 0 15
password cisco
login
line con 0
```

```
   password cisco
   logging synchronous
   login
   exit
 vlan 10
   name User
 vlan 99
   Name Management
 interface range f0/1-2
   switchport mode trunk
   channel-group 1 mode active
   switchport trunk native vlan 99
   no shutdown
 interface range f0/3-4
   channel-group 2 mode desirable
   switchport trunk native vlan 99
   no shutdown
 interface f0/6
   switchport mode access
   switchport access vlan 10
   no shutdown
 interface vlan 99
   ip address 192.168.1.11 255.255.255.0
 interface port-channel 1
   switchport trunk native vlan 99
   switchport mode trunk
 interface port-channel 2
   switchport trunk native vlan 99
   switchport mode access
```

Switch S2 Configuration:

```
hostname S2
interface range f0/1-24, g0/1-2
 shutdown
 exit
enable secret class
no ip domain lookup
line vty 0 15
 password cisco
 login
line con 0
 password cisco
 logging synchronous
 login
 exit
vlan 10
 name User
vlan 99
 name Management
spanning-tree vlan 1,10,99 root primary
interface range f0/1-2
```

```
 switchport mode trunk
 channel-group 1 mode desirable
 switchport trunk native vlan 99
 no shutdown
interface range f0/3-4
 switchport mode trunk
 channel-group 3 mode desirable
 switchport trunk native vlan 99
interface vlan 99
 ip address 192.168.1.12 255.255.255.0
interface port-channel 1
 switchport trunk native vlan 99
 switchport trunk allowed vlan 1,99
interface port-channel 3
 switchport trunk native vlan 99
 switchport trunk allowed vlan 1,10,99
 switchport mode trunk
```

Switch S3 Configuration:

```
hostname S3
interface range f0/1-24, g0/1-2
 shutdown
 exit
enable secret class
no ip domain lookup
line vty 0 15
 password cisco
 login
line con 0
 password cisco
 logging synchronous
 login
 exit
vlan 10
 name User
vlan 99
 name Management
interface range f0/1-2
interface range f0/3-4
 switchport mode trunk
 channel-group 3 mode desirable
 switchport trunk native vlan 99
 no shutdown
interface f0/18
 switchport mode access
 switchport access vlan 10
 no shutdown
interface vlan 99
 ip address 192.168.1.13 255.255.255.0
interface port-channel 3
```

```
switchport trunk native vlan 99
switchport mode trunk
```

Step 5.   Save your configuration.

Part 2: Troubleshoot EtherChannel

In Part 2, you must examine the configurations on all switches, make corrections if needed, and verify full functionality.

Step 1.   Troubleshoot S1.

    a.   Use the **show interfaces trunk** command to verify that the port channels are functioning as trunk ports.

        Do port channels 1 and 2 appear as trunked ports? _____

    b.   Use the **show etherchannel summary** command to verify that interfaces are configured in the correct port channel, the proper protocol is configured, and the interfaces are in use.

        Based on the output, are there any EtherChannel issues? If issues are found, record them in the space provided below.

        _____

        _____

    c.   Use the command **show run | begin interface Port-channel** command to view the running configuration beginning with the first port channel interface.

    d.   Resolve all problems found in the outputs from the previous **show** commands. Record the commands used to correct the configurations.

        _____

        _____

        _____

        _____

    e.   Use the **show interfaces trunk** command to verify trunk settings.

    f.   Use the **show etherchannel summary** command to verify that the port channels are up and in use.

Step 2.   Troubleshoot S2.

    a.   Issue the command to verify that the port channels are functioning as trunk ports. Record the command used in the space provided below.

        Based on the output, are there any issues with the configurations? If issues are found, record them in the space provided below.

        _____

        _____

    b.   Issue the command to verify that interfaces are configured in the correct port channel and the proper protocol is configured.

Based on the output, are there any EtherChannel issues? If issues are found, record them in the space provided below.

_____

c. Use the command **show run | begin interface Port-channel** to view the running configuration beginning with the first port-channel interface.

d. Resolve all problems found in the outputs from the previous **show** commands. Record the commands used to correct the configuration.

_____

_____

_____

_____

_____

e. Issue the command to verify trunk settings.

f. Issue the command to verify that the port channels are functioning. Remember that port channel issues can be caused by either end of the link.

Step 3. Troubleshoot S3.

a. Issue the command to verify that the port channels are functioning as trunk ports.

Based on the output, are there any issues with the configurations? If issues are found, record them in the space provided below.

_____

_____

b. Issue the command to verify that the interfaces are configured in the correct port channel and that the proper protocol is configured.

Based on the output, are there any EtherChannel issues? If issues are found, record them in the space provided below.

_____

_____

c. Use the **show run | begin interface Port-channel** command to view the running configuration beginning with the first port channel interface.

d. Resolve all problems found. Record the commands used to correct the configuration.

_____

_____

_____

_____

_____

_____

e. Issue the command to verify trunk settings. Record the command used in the space provided below.

_____

_____

_____

_____

_____

_____

f. Issue the command to verify that the port channels are functioning. Record the command used in the space provided below.

_____

_____

_____

_____

_____

_____

_____

_____

_____

_____

_____

_____

Step 4.   Verify EtherChannel and Connectivity.

a. Use the **show interfaces etherchannel** command to verify full functionality of the port channels.

b. Verify connectivity of the management VLAN.

Can S1 ping S2? _____

Can S1 ping S3? _____

Can S2 ping S3? _____

c. Verify connectivity of PCs.

Can PC-A ping PC-C? _____

If EtherChannels are not fully functional, connectivity between switches does not exist, or connectivity between hosts does not exist. Troubleshoot to resolve any remaining issues.

Note: It may be necessary to disable the PC firewall for pings between the PCs to succeed.

4.3.3.4 Lab–Configuring HSRP

Topology

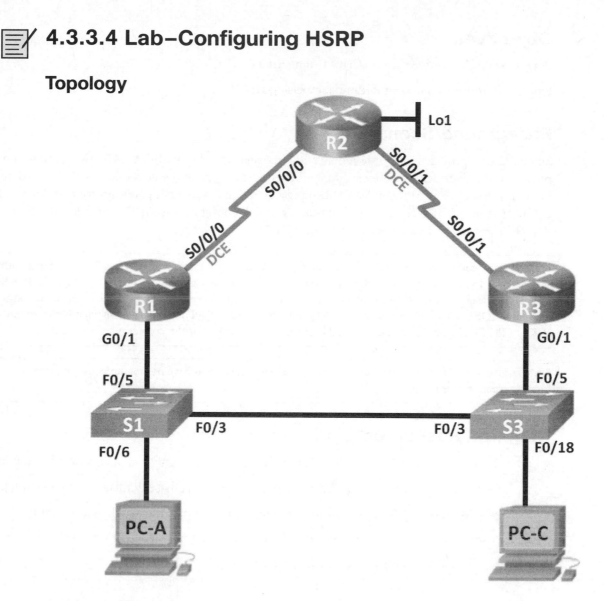

Addressing Table

Device	Interface	IP Address	Subnet Mask	Default Gateway
R1	G0/1	192.168.1.1	255.255.255.0	N/A
	S0/0/0 (DCE)	10.1.1.1	255.255.255.252	N/A
R2	S0/0/0	10.1.1.2	255.255.255.252	N/A
	S0/0/1 (DCE)	10.2.2.2	255.255.255.252	N/A
	Lo1	209.165.200.225	255.255.255.224	N/A
R3	G0/1	192.168.1.3	255.255.255.0	N/A
	S0/0/1	10.2.2.1	255.255.255.252	N/A
S1	VLAN 1	192.168.1.11	255.255.255.0	192.168.1.1
S3	VLAN 1	192.168.1.13	255.255.255.0	192.168.1.3
PC-A	NIC	192.168.1.31	255.255.255.0	192.168.1.1
PC-C	NIC	192.168.1.33	255.255.255.0	192.168.1.3

Objectives

Part 1: Build the Network and Verify Connectivity

Part 2: Configure First Hop Redundancy Using HSRP

Background/Scenario

Spanning tree provides loop-free redundancy between switches within a LAN. However, it does not provide redundant default gateways for end-user devices within the network if one of the routers fails. First Hop Redundancy Protocols (FHRPs) provide redundant default gateways for end devices with no end-user configuration necessary. In this lab, you will configure Cisco's Hot Standby Routing Protocol (HSRP), a First Hop Redundancy Protocol (FHRP).

Note: The routers used with CCNA hands-on labs are Cisco 1941 Integrated Services Routers (ISRs) with Cisco IOS Release 15.2(4)M3 (universalk9 image). The switches used are Cisco Catalyst 2960s with Cisco IOS Release 15.0(2) (lanbasek9 image). Other routers, switches, and Cisco IOS versions can be used. Depending on the model and Cisco IOS version, the commands available and output produced might vary from what is shown in the labs. Refer to the Router Interface Summary Table at the end of this lab for the correct interface identifiers.

Note: Make sure that the routers and switches have been erased and have no startup configurations. If you are unsure, contact your instructor.

Required Resources

- 3 Routers (Cisco 1941 with Cisco IOS Release 15.2(4)M3 universal image or comparable)
- 2 Switches (Cisco 2960 with Cisco IOS Release 15.0(2) lanbasek9 image or comparable)
- 2 PCs (Windows 8, 7, or Vista with terminal emulation program, such as Tera Term)
- Console cables to configure the Cisco IOS devices via the console ports
- Ethernet and serial cables as shown in the topology

Part 1: Build the Network and Verify Connectivity

In Part 1, you will set up the network topology and configure basic settings, such as the interface IP addresses, static routing, device access, and passwords.

Step 1.   Cable the network as shown in the topology.

Attach the devices as shown in the topology diagram, and cable as necessary.

Step 2.   Configure PC hosts.

Step 3.   Initialize and reload the routers and switches as necessary.

Step 4.   Configure basic settings for each router.

    a.   Disable DNS lookup.

    b.   Configure the device name as shown in the topology.

    c.   Configure IP addresses for the routers as listed in the Addressing Table.

    d.   Set clock rate to **128000** for all DCE serial interfaces.

e. Assign **class** as the encrypted privileged EXEC mode password.

f. Assign **cisco** for the console and vty password and enable login.

g. Configure **logging synchronous** to prevent console messages from interrupting command entry.

h. Copy the running configuration to the startup configuration.

Step 5. Configure basic settings for each switch.

a. Disable DNS lookup.

b. Configure the device name as shown in the topology.

c. Assign **class** as the encrypted privileged EXEC mode password.

d. Configure IP addresses for the switches as listed in the Addressing Table.

e. Configure the default gateway on each switch.

f. Assign **cisco** for the console and vty password and enable login.

g. Configure **logging synchronous** to prevent console messages from interrupting command entry.

h. Copy the running configuration to the startup configuration.

Step 6. Verify connectivity between PC-A and PC-C.

Ping from PC-A to PC-C. Were the ping results successful? _____

If the pings are not successful, troubleshoot the basic device configurations before continuing.

Note: It may be necessary to disable the PC firewall to successfully ping between PCs.

Step 7. Configure routing.

a. Configure RIP version 2 on all routers. Add all the networks, except 209.165.200.224/27 into the RIP process.

b. Configure a default route on R2 using Lo1 as the exit interface to 209.165.200.224/27 network.

c. On R2, use the following commands to redistribute the default route into the RIP process.

```
R2(config)# router rip
R2(config-router)# default-information originate
```

Step 8. Verify connectivity.

a. From PC-A, you should be able to ping every interface on R1, R2, R3, and PC-C. Were all pings successful? _____

If the pings are not successful, troubleshoot the basic device configurations before continuing.

b. From PC-C, you should be able to ping every interface on R1, R2, R3, and PC-A. Were all pings successful? _____

If the pings are not successful, troubleshoot the basic device configurations before continuing.

Part 2: Configure First Hop Redundancy Using HSRP

Even though the topology has been designed with some redundancy (two routers and two switches on the same LAN network), both PC-A and PC-C are configured with only one gateway address. PC-A is using R1 and PC-C is using R3. If either of these routers or the interfaces on the routers went down, the PC could lose its connection to the Internet.

In Part 2, you will test how the network behaves both before and after configuring HSRP. To do this, you will determine the path that packets take to the loopback address on R2.

Step 1.   Determine the path for Internet traffic for PC-A and PC-C.

    a.   From a command prompt on PC-A, issue a **tracert** command to the 209.165.200.225 loopback address of R2.

```
C:\ tracert 209.165.200.225
Tracing route to 209.165.200.225 over a maximum of 30 hops

  1     1 ms     1 ms     1 ms  192.168.1.1
  2    13 ms    13 ms    13 ms  209.165.200.225


Trace complete.
```

    What path did the packets take from PC-A to 209.165.200.225? _____

_____

    b.   From a command prompt on PC-C, issue a **tracert** command to the 209.165.200.225 loopback address of R2.

    What path did the packets take from PC-C to 209.165.200.225? _____

_____

Step 2.   Start a ping session on PC-A, and break the connection between S1 and R1.

    a.   From a command prompt on PC-A, issue a **ping –t** command to the **209.165.200.225** address on R2. Make sure you leave the command prompt window open.

Note: The pings continue until you press Ctrl+C, or until you close the command prompt window.

```
C:\ ping -t 209.165.200.225
Pinging 209.165.200.225 with 32 bytes of data:
Reply from 209.165.200.225: bytes=32 time=9ms TTL=254
Reply from 209.165.200.225: bytes=32 time=9ms TTL=254
Reply from 209.165.200.225: bytes=32 time=9ms TTL=254
<output omitted>
```

    b.   As the ping continues, disconnect the Ethernet cable from F0/5 on S1. You can also shut down the S1 F0/5 interface, which creates the same result.

    What happened to the ping traffic?

_____

    c.   What would the results be if you repeat Steps 2a and 2b on PC-C and S3?

_____

    d.   Reconnect the Ethernet cables to F0/5 or enable the F0/5 interface on both S1 and S3, respectively. Re-issue pings to 209.165.200.225 from both PC-A and PC-C to make sure connectivity is re-established.

Step 3.   Configure HSRP on R1 and R3.

In this step, you will configure HSRP and change the default gateway address on PC-A, PC-C, S1, and S2 to the virtual IP address for HSRP. R1 becomes the active router via configuration of the HSRP priority command.

a.   Configure HSRP on R1.

```
R1(config)# interface g0/1
R1(config-if)# standby version 2
R1(config-if)# standby 1 ip 192.168.1.254
R1(config-if)# standby 1 priority 150
R1(config-if)# standby 1 preempt
```

b.   Configure HSRP on R3.

```
R3(config)# interface g0/1
R3(config-if)# standby version 2
R3(config-if)# standby 1 ip 192.168.1.254
```

c.   Verify HSRP by issuing the **show standby** command on R1 and R3.

```
R1# show standby
GigabitEthernet0/1 - Group 1 (version 2)
  State is Active
    4 state changes, last state change 00:00:30
  Virtual IP address is 192.168.1.254
  Active virtual MAC address is 0000.0c9f.f001
    Local virtual MAC address is 0000.0c9f.f001 (v2 default)
  Hello time 3 sec, hold time 10 sec
    Next hello sent in 1.696 secs
  Preemption enabled
  Active router is local
  Standby router is 192.168.1.3, priority 100 (expires in 11.120 sec)
  Priority 150 (configured 150)
  Group name is "hsrp-Gi0/1-1" (default)


R3# show standby
GigabitEthernet0/1 - Group 1 (version 2)
  State is Standby
    4 state changes, last state change 00:02:29
  Virtual IP address is 192.168.1.254
  Active virtual MAC address is 0000.0c9f.f001
    Local virtual MAC address is 0000.0c9f.f001 (v2 default)
  Hello time 3 sec, hold time 10 sec
    Next hello sent in 0.720 secs
  Preemption disabled
  Active router is 192.168.1.1, priority 150 (expires in 10.128 sec)
    MAC address is d48c.b5ce.a0c1
  Standby router is local
  Priority 100 (default 100)
  Group name is "hsrp-Gi0/1-1" (default)
```

Using the output shown above, answer the following questions:

Which router is the active router? _____

What is the MAC address for the virtual IP address? _____

What is the IP address and priority of the standby router?

_____

_____

d.   Use the **show standby brief** command on R1 and R3 to view an HSRP status summary.

e.   Change the default gateway address for PC-A, PC-C, S1, and S3. Which address should you use?

_____

f.   Verify the new settings. Issue a ping from both PC-A and PC-C to the loopback address of R2. Are the pings successful? _____

Step 4.   Start a ping session on PC-A and break the connection between the switch that is connected to the Active HSRP router (R1).

a.   From a command prompt on PC-A, issue a **ping –t** command to the 209.165.200.225 address on R2. Ensure that you leave the command prompt window open.

b.   As the ping continues, disconnect the Ethernet cable from F0/5 on S1 or shut down the F0/5 interface.

What happened to the ping traffic?

_____

_____

_____

Step 5.   Verify HSRP settings on R1 and R3.

a.   Issue the **show standby brief** command on R1 and R3.

Which router is the active router? _____

b.   Reconnect the cable between the switch and the router or enable interface F0/5. Now which router is the active router? Explain.

_____

Step 6.   Change HSRP priorities.

a.   Change the HSRP priority to 200 on R3. Which is the active router?

_____

b.   Issue the command to change the active router to R3 without changing the priority. What command did you use?

_____

```
R3(config)# interface g0/1
R3(config-if)# standby 1 preempt
```

c.   Use a **show** command to verify that R3 is the active router.

Reflection

Why would there be a need for redundancy in a LAN?

_____

_____

Router Interface Summary Table

Router Interface Summary

Router Model	Ethernet Interface #1	Ethernet Interface #2	Serial Interface #1	Serial Interface #2
1800	Fast Ethernet 0/0 (F0/0)	Fast Ethernet 0/1 (F0/1)	Serial 0/0/0 (S0/0/0)	Serial 0/0/1 (S0/0/1)
1900	Gigabit Ethernet 0/0 (G0/0)	Gigabit Ethernet 0/1 (G0/1)	Serial 0/0/0 (S0/0/0)	Serial 0/0/1 (S0/0/1)
2801	Fast Ethernet 0/0 (F0/0)	Fast Ethernet 0/1 (F0/1)	Serial 0/1/0 (S0/1/0)	Serial 0/1/1 (S0/1/1)
2811	Fast Ethernet 0/0 (F0/0)	Fast Ethernet 0/1 (F0/1)	Serial 0/0/0 (S0/0/0)	Serial 0/0/1 (S0/0/1)
2900	Gigabit Ethernet 0/0 (G0/0)	Gigabit Ethernet 0/1 (G0/1)	Serial 0/0/0 (S0/0/0)	Serial 0/0/1 (S0/0/1)

Note: To find out how the router is configured, look at the interfaces to identify the type of router and how many interfaces the router has. There is no way to effectively list all the combinations of configurations for each router class. This table includes identifiers for the possible combinations of Ethernet and Serial interfaces in the device. The table does not include any other type of interface, even though a specific router may contain one. An example of this might be an ISDN BRI interface. The string in parentheses is the legal abbreviation that can be used in Cisco IOS commands to represent the interface.

4.3.4.4 Packet Tracer–Troubleshoot HSRP

Topology

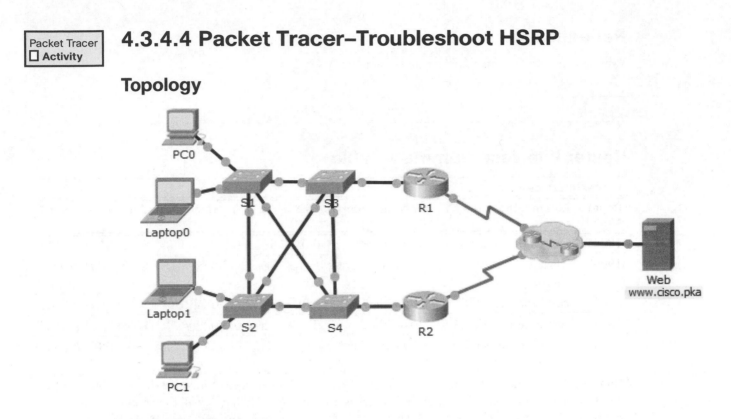

Addressing Table

Device	Interface	IP Address	Subnet Mask	Default Gateway
R1	G0/1	192.168.1.1	255.255.255.0	N/A
	S0/0/0	209.165.200.226	255.255.255.252	N/A
R2	G0/1	192.168.1.2	255.255.255.0	N/A
	S0/0/1	209.165.200.230	255.255.255.252	N/A
PC0	NIC	192.168.1.10	255.255.255.0	192.168.1.254
Laptop0	NIC	192.168.1.11	255.255.255.0	192.168.1.254
Laptop1	NIC	192.168.1.12	255.255.255.0	192.168.1.254
PC1	NIC	192.168.1.13	255.255.255.0	192.168.1.254
Web	NIC	209.165.202.156	255.255.255.224	209.165.202.158

Objective

In this activity, you will troubleshoot and resolve the HSRP issues in the network. You will also verify that all the HSRP configurations meet the network requirement.

Background/Scenario

Currently the users can access www.cisco.pka. The network has been updated to use HSRP to ensure the network availability to the users. You must verify that the users can still access the website if one of the routers is down. R1 should always be the active router if it is functioning.

Network Requirement:

- HSRP virtual router is 192.168.1.254.
- HSRP standby group is 1.
- DNS server is 209.165.202.157.
- R1 should always be the active router when it is functioning properly.
- R2 uses the default HSRP priority.
- All users should be able to access www.cisco.pka as long as one of the routers is functioning.

Troubleshooting Process

Step 1.   PCs and Laptops

   a. Verify the PCs and laptops are configured correctly using the provided network requirement.

   b. Based on the Network Requirement shown above, verify that the PCs and laptops can navigate to www.cisco.pka successfully.

Step 2.   Troubleshoot R1.

   a. Disable the interface G0/1 on R2.

   b. Use **show** commands to determine issues. Record and correct any issues found on R1.

   _____

   _____

   _____

   _____

   o. Re enable the interface G0/1 on R2.

Step 3.   Troubleshoot R2.

   a. Disable the interface G0/1 on R1.

   b. Use **show** commands to determine any issues. Record and correct any issues found on R2.

   _____

   _____

   _____

   _____

   c. After verifying that the PCs and laptops can navigate to www.cisco.pka successfully, re-enable the interface G0/1 on R1.

Step 4.   Verify connectivity.

   a. Verify all PCs and laptops can navigate to www.cisco.pka.

   b. Verify all the HSRP requirements have been met.

Running Scripts

PC0 and Laptop1

The default gateway should be configured at 192.168.1.254.

R1 Configuration

_____

_____

_____

_____

_____

R2 Configuration

_____

_____

_____

4.4.1.1 Class Activity–Linking Up

Objective

Describe link aggregation.

Scenario

Many bottlenecks occur on your small- to medium-sized business network, even though you have configured VLANs, STP, and other network traffic options on the company's switches.

Instead of keeping the switches as they are currently configured, you would like to try EtherChannel as an option for, at least, part of the network to see if it will lessen traffic congestion between your access and distribution layer switches.

Your company uses Catalyst 3560 switches at the distribution layer and Catalyst 2960 and 2950 switches at the access layer of the network. To verify if these switches can perform EtherChannel, you visit the *System Requirements to Implement EtherChannel on Catalyst Switches*. This site allows you to gather more information to determine if EtherChannel is a good option for the equipment and network currently in place.

After researching the models, you decide to use a simulation software program to practice configuring EtherChannel before implementing it live on your network. As a part of this procedure, you ensure that the equipment simulated in Packet Tracer will support these practice configurations.

Resources

- World Wide Web connectivity
- Packet Tracer software
- Word processing or spreadsheet software

Directions

Step 1.   Visit *System Requirements to Implement EtherChannel on Catalyst Switches*.

    a.   Pay particular attention to the Catalyst 3560, 2960, and 2950 model information.

    b.   Record any information you feel would be useful to deciding whether to use EtherChannel in your company.

Step 2.   Create a matrix to record the information you recorded in Step 1b, including:

    a.   Number of ports allowed to be bundled for an EtherChannel group

    b.   Maximum group bandwidth supported by bundling the ports

    c.   IOS version needed to support EtherChannel on the switch model

    d.   Load balancing availability

    e.   Load balancing configuration options

    f.   Network layers supported for EtherChannel operation

Step 3.   Open Packet Tracer.

    a. Notice how many ports are available to bundle for EtherChannel on all three switch models.

    b. Check all three models to see how many EtherChannel groups you could create on each model.

    c. Make sure the IOS version is recent enough to support all EtherChannel configurations.

    d. Do not configure your simulated network, but do check the models available in the Packet Tracer to make sure they will support all the EtherChannel configuration options.

Step 4.   Share your matrix with another group or the class.

4.4.1.2 Packet Tracer–Skills Integration Challenge

Topology

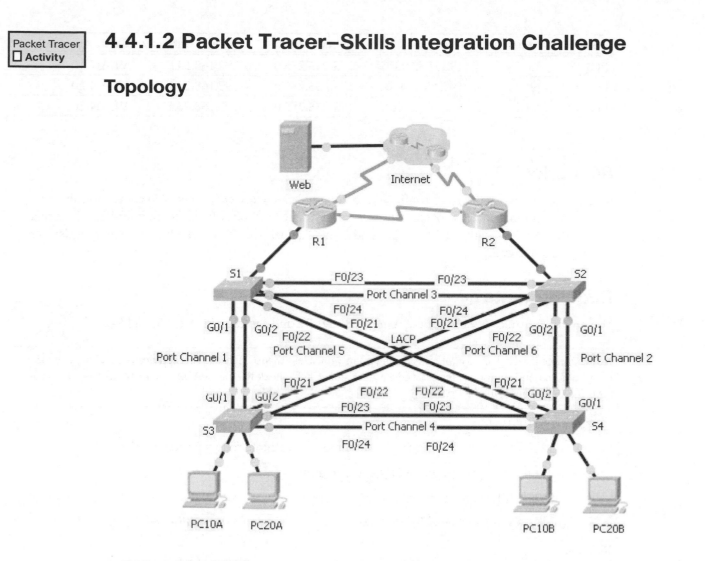

Addressing Table

Device	Interface	IP Address	Subnet Mask	Default Gateway	VLAN Association
R1	G0/0.1	192.168.99.1	255.255.255.0	N/A	VLAN 99
	G0/0.10	192.168.10.1	255.255.255.0	N/A	VLAN 10
	G0/0.20	192.168.20.1	255.255.255.0	N/A	VLAN 20
	S0/0/0	209.165.200.238	255.255.255.224	N/A	N/A
	S0/0/1	192.168.1.1	255.255.255.0	N/A	N/A
R2	G0/0.1	192.168.99.2	255.255.255.0	N/A	VLAN 99
	G0/0.10	192.168.10.2	255.255.255.0	N/A	VLAN 10
	G0/0.20	192.168.20.2	255.255.255.0	N/A	VLAN 20
	S0/0/0	192.168.1.2	255.255.255.0	N/A	N/A
	S0/0/1	209.165.202.158	255.255.255.224	N/A	N/A
ISP	S0/0/0	209.165.200.225	255.255.255.224	N/A	N/A
	S0/0/1	209.165.202.129	255.255.255.224	N/A	N/A
Web	NIC	64.104.13.130	255.255.255.252	64.104.13.129	N/A
PC10A	NIC	192.168.10.101	255.255.255.0	192.168.10.1	VLAN 10

Device	Interface	IP Address	Subnet Mask	Default Gateway	VLAN Association
PC10B	NIC	192.168.10.102	255.255.255.0	192.168.10.1	VLAN 10
PC20A	NIC	192.168.20.101	255.255.255.0	192.168.20.1	VLAN 20
PC20B	NIC	192.168.20.102	255.255.255.0	192.168.20.1	VLAN 20

Scenario

In this activity, two routers are configured to communicate with each other. You are responsible for configuring subinterfaces to communicate with the switches. You will configure inter-VLAN routing with RIPv2, VLANs with VTP, trunking, and EtherChannel with PVST. The PCs and Internet devices are all preconfigured.

Requirements

You are responsible for configuring routers **R1** and **R2** and switches **S1**, **S2**, **S3**, and **S4**.

Note: Packet Tracer does not allow assigning point values less than 1. Because this activity is checking over 150 items, not all configurations are assigned a point value. Click **Check Results > Assessment Items** to verify you have correctly configured all items.

Inter-VLAN Routing

On **R1** and **R2**, enable and configure the subinterfaces with the following requirement:

- Configure the appropriate dot1Q encapsulation.
- Configure VLAN 99 as the native VLAN.
- Configure the IP address for the subinterface according to the Addressing Table.

Routing

Configure RIPv2 using the following requirements:

- Do not advertise the network connected to the Internet.
- Disable autosummarization.
- Disable RIP updates for each subinterface.

VTP and VLANs

- Configure S1 as the VTP server. Configure all other switches as VTP clients. They are not allowed to create VLANs.
    - VTP domain is **CCNA**.
    - VTP password is **cisco123**.
- Create VLAN 10, 20, and 99 on **S1**.
- Configure the following static ports for **S1** and **S2**:
    - F0/1 – 9 as access ports in VLAN 10.
    - F0/10 – 19 as access ports in VLAN 20.
    - F0/20 – F24 and G0/1 – 0/2 as the native trunk for VLAN 99.

- Configure the following static ports for **S3** and **S4:**
  - F0/1 – 9 as access ports in VLAN 10.
  - F0/10 – 20 as access ports in VLAN 20.
  - F0/21 – F24 and G0/1 – 0/2 as the native trunk for VLAN 99.

EtherChannels

- All EtherChannels are configured as LACP.
- All EtherChannels are statically configured to trunk all VLANs including VLAN 99 as the native VLAN.
- Use the following table to configure the appropriate switch ports to form EtherChannels:

Port Channel	Device: Ports	Device: Ports
1	S1: G0/1 – 2	S3: G0/1 – 2
2	S2: G0/1 – 2	S4: G0/1 – 2
3	S1: F0/23 – 24	S2: F0/23 – 24
4	S3: F0/23 – 24	S4: F0/23 – 24
5	S1: F0/21 – 22	S4: F0/21 – 22
6	S2: F0/21 – 22	S3: F0/21 - 22

Spanning Tree

- Configure per-VLAN rapid spanning tree mode for all switches.
- Configure spanning tree priorities according to the table below:

Device	VLAN 10 Priority	VLAN 20 Priority
S1	4096	8192
S2	8192	4096
S3	32768	32768
S4	32768	32768

Connectivity

- All PCs should be able to ping the **Web** and other PCs.

Dynamic Routing

Routers forward packets by using information in the routing table. Routes to remote networks can be learned by the router in two ways: static routes and dynamic routes. In a large network with numerous networks and subnets, configuring and maintaining static routes between these networks requires a great deal of administrative and operational overhead. Implementing dynamic routing protocols can ease the burden of configuration and maintenance tasks and give the network scalability.

Study Guide

Dynamic Routing Protocols

Dynamic routing protocols have been used in networks since the late 1980s. As networks evolved and became more complex, new routing protocols emerged. To support the communication based on IPv6, newer versions of the IP routing protocols have been developed.

Dynamic Routing Protocols Classification Chart

The chart in Figure 5-1 is a succinct way to represent the major classifications of dynamic routing protocols. For each of the empty boxes, write in the missing protocol.

Figure 5-1   Classifying Dynamic Routing Protocols

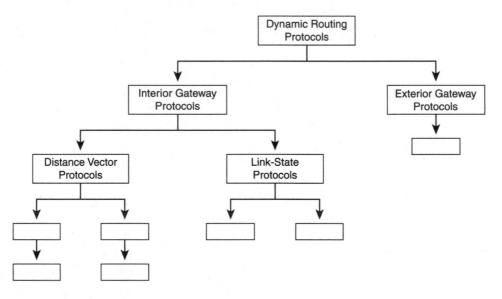

Routing Protocols Characteristics

Briefly explain each of the following routing protocol characteristics.

Speed of Convergence

_____

_____

_____

_____

Scalability

_____

_____

Classful or Classless (Use of VLSM)

_____

_____

_____

Resource Usage

_____

_____

_____

Implementation and Maintenance

_____

_____

_____

Comparing Routing Protocol Characteristics

In Table 5-1, routing protocols are compared based on the characteristics you briefly described in the previous exercise. For each characteristic, circle the description that applies to each routing protocol. For example, RIP is slow to converge. So, you would circle Slow in the Speed of Convergence row under both RIPv1 and RIPv2.

Table 5-1   Routing Protocol Characteristics

	Distance Vector			Link-State		
	RIPv1	RIPv2	IGRP	EIGRP	OSPF	IS-IS
Speed of Convergence				Slow	Slow	Slow
	Fast	Fast	Fast			
Scalability (Size of Network)				Small	Small	Small
	Large	Large	Large			
Use of VLSM	Yes		Yes			
		No		No	No	No
Resource Usage				Low	Low	Low
	Medium	Medium	Medium		Medium	Medium
	High	High	High	High		
Implementation and Maintenance				Simple	Simple	Simple
	Complex	Complex	Complex			

Dynamic Routing Protocol Operation

List at least three purposes of a dynamic routing protocol.

_____

_____

_____

Briefly describe the three main components of dynamic routing protocols.

- Data structures:

  _____

  _____

- Routing protocol messages:

  _____

  _____

- Algorithm:

  _____

  _____

Distance Vector Dynamic Routing

Distance vector routing protocols share updates between neighbors. Each router is only aware of the network addresses of its own interfaces and the remote network addresses it can reach through its neighbors. Routers using distance vector routing are not aware of the network topology.

From Cold Start to Convergence

Cold Start

What does a router know when it first boots?

_____

After it boots, what does the router know about the network topology?

_____

In Figure 5-2, the routers have booted. However, they have not yet discovered any neighbors. In the tables below each router, fill in the networks, interfaces, and hop counts that each router has installed in its routing table.

Figure 5-2   Network Discovery: Cold Start

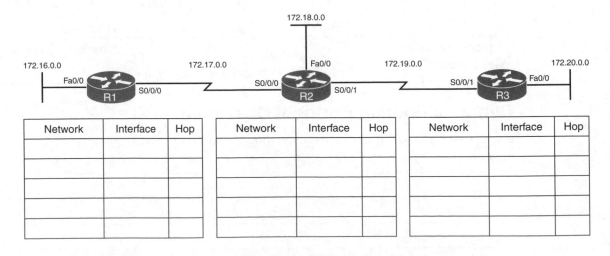

Network	Interface	Hop

Network	Interface	Hop

Network	Interface	Hop

Exchanging the Routing Information

What is required before the routers will start sending each other updates?

_____

For the first round of updates after a cold start, what information will the updates include?

_____

In Figure 5-3, the routers have completed their initial exchange of routing updates. In the tables that follow each router, fill in the networks, interfaces, and hop counts that each router now has installed in its routing table.

Figure 5-3   Network Discovery: Initial Exchange

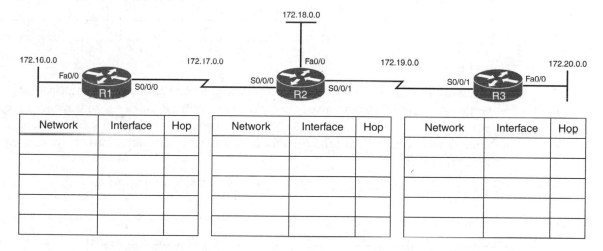

At this point in the network discovery process, the routing tables are incomplete. In other words, the network has not yet converged.

Which routing tables and which networks still need to be discovered?

_____

_____

Next Update

Continuing the journey toward convergence, the routers exchange the next round of periodic updates.

In Figure 5-4, the routers have completed their next round of updates. In the tables after each router, fill in the networks, interfaces, and hop counts that each router now has installed in its routing table.

Figure 5-4   Network Discovery: Next Update

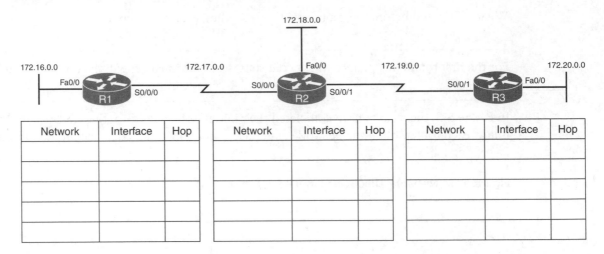

Convergence

The network has converged when all routers have complete and accurate information about the entire network, as should be shown in your completed table for Figure 5-4. Convergence time is the time it takes routers to share information, calculate best paths, and update their routing tables. A network is not completely operable until the network has converged; therefore, most networks require short convergence times.

Convergence is both collaborative and independent. Explain what this means.

_____

_____

Distance Vector Operation and Terminology

At the core of the distance vector protocol is the routing algorithm. The algorithm is used to calculate the best paths and then send that information to the neighbors. The algorithm is responsible for what three processes?

_____

_____

_____

Match the distance vector term on the left with the description on the right. This exercise is a one-to-one matching. Each term has exactly one matching description.

Term

  a. algorithm

  b. Bellman-Ford

  c. broadcast updates

  d. DUAL

  e. neighbors

  f. periodic updates

Description

___ A timed process, with updates sent to neighboring routers at regular intervals.

___ A process where neighboring routers receive network updates at a specific network address.

___ EIGRP uses this algorithm process as developed by Cisco.

___ RIP uses this algorithm process.

___ Process that calculates the best paths to networks.

___ Describes routers that share a link and the same routing protocol.

Comparing RIP and EIGRP

In Table 5-2, indicate the routing protocol for each characteristic or feature.

Table 5-2   RIP and EIGRP Comparison

Characteristic or Feature	RIP	EIGRP
Multicasts bounded, triggered updates to 224.0.0.10.		
Broadcasts routing updates to 255.255.255.255.		
Version 2 supports VLSM and classless routing.		
Forms neighbor adjacencies table.		
Uses administrative distance of 120.		
Fastest converging routing protocol.		
Uses DUAL algorithm.		
Maximum limit of 255 hops.		
Routing updates sent every 30 seconds.		
Maximum limit of 15 hops.		
Sends hello packets.		
Version 2 multicasts updates to 224.0.0.9.		
Uses administrative distance of 90 for internal routes.		

Link-State Dynamic Routing

Distance vector routing protocols are like road signs; routers must make preferred path decisions based on a distance or metric to a network. Just as travelers trust a road sign to accurately state the distance to the next town, a distance vector router trusts that another router is advertising the true distance to the destination network.

Link-state routing protocols take a different approach. Link-state routing protocols are more like a road map because they create a topological map of the network and each router uses this map to determine the shortest path to each network. Just as you refer to a map to find the route to another town, link-state routers use a map to determine the preferred path to reach another destination.

Link-State Routing Protocol Operation

Link-state routing protocols are also known as _____ (SPF) protocols and are built around Edsger _____ SPF algorithm.

The IPv4 link-state routing protocols include

_____

_____

Just like RIP and EIGRP, basic OSPF operations can be configured using the

_____ global configuration command

_____ command to advertise networks

The SPF algorithm accumulates _____ along each path, from source to destination. Each router calculates the SPF algorithm and determines the _____ from its own perspective.

Using Figure 5-5, complete the following tables filling in the appropriate information for each router. As an example, Table 5-3 for R1 is partially complete.

Figure 5-5 Topology of Link-State Routers

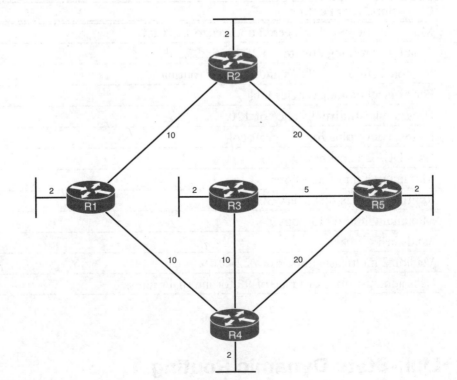

Table 5-3   SPF Tree for R1

Destination	Shortest Path	Cost
R2 LAN	R1 to R2	12
R3 LAN	R1 to R4 to R3	22
R4 LAN		
R5 LAN		

Table 5-4   SPF Tree for R2

Destination	Shortest Path	Cost
R1 LAN		
R3 LAN		
R4 LAN		
R5 LAN		

Table 5-5   SPF Tree for R3

Destination	Shortest Path	Cost
R1 LAN		
R2 LAN		
R4 LAN		
R5 LAN		

Table 5-6   SPF Tree for R4

Destination	Shortest Path	Cost
R1 LAN		
R2 LAN		
R3 LAN		
R5 LAN		

Table 5-7   SPF Tree for R5

Destination	Shortest Path	Cost
R1 LAN		
R2 LAN		
R3 LAN		
R4 LAN		

Building the Link-State Database

All routers in the area will complete the following generic link-state routing process to reach a state of convergence:

1. Each router learns about its own links and its own directly connected networks. This is done by detecting that an interface is in the _____ state.

2. Each router is responsible for meeting its neighbors on directly connected networks. Link-state routers do this by exchanging _____ packets with other link-state routers on _____ networks.

3. Each router builds a link-state packet (LSP) containing the state of each _____ link. This is done by recording all the pertinent information about each neighbor, including _____, _____, and _____.

4. Each router floods the LSP to all neighbors, who then store all LSPs received in a _____. Neighbors then flood the LSPs to their neighbors until all routers in the area have received the LSPs. Each router stores a copy of each LSP received from its neighbors in a local _____.

5. Each router uses the _____ to construct a complete map of the _____ and computes the best path to each destination network.

The topology in Figure 5-6 now shows the network addresses and interfaces for R5.

Figure 5-6   Topology from the Perspective of R5

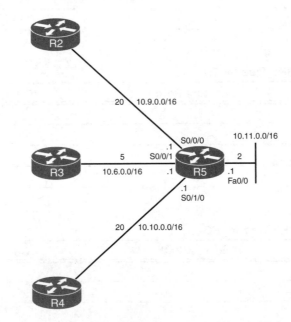

The first step in the link-state routing process is that each router learns about its own links and its own directly connected networks. This occurs when you correctly configure and activate the interfaces.

In Table 5-8, list the link-state information for R5, including the network address, type of interface, the address, cost, and neighbor.

Table 5-8   Link-State Information for R5

Network Address	Interface	IP Address	Cost	Neighbor

The second step in the link-state routing process is that each router is responsible for meeting its neighbors on directly connected networks.

Routers with link-state routing protocols use a _____ protocol to discover any neighbors on its links. In relation to link state routing, what is a neighbor?

_____

Small hello packets are periodically exchanged between two adjacent neighbors and serve as a _____ function to monitor the state of the neighbor. If a router stops receiving hello packets from a neighbor, that neighbor is considered _____ and the adjacency is broken.

The third step in the link-state routing process is that each router builds a link-state packet (LSP) containing the state of each directly connected link.

Once a router has established its adjacencies, it can build its LSPs that contain the link-state information about its links. Table 5-8 you filled out previously should contain all of the information for R5's LSP.

The fourth step in the link-state routing process is that each router floods the LSP to all neighbors, who then store all LSPs received in a database.

What happens when a router receives an LSP from a neighbor?

_____

_____

The final step in the link-state routing process is for a router to use its own database to construct a complete map of the topology and compute the best path to each destination network.

After each router has propagated its own LSPs using the link-state flooding process, each router will then have an LSP from every link-state router in the routing area. These LSPs are stored in the link state database. Each router in the routing area can now use the SPF algorithm to construct the SPF trees that you saw earlier.

Figure 5-7 shows the entire topology with network addresses.

Figure 5-7   Topology of Link-State Routers with Network Address

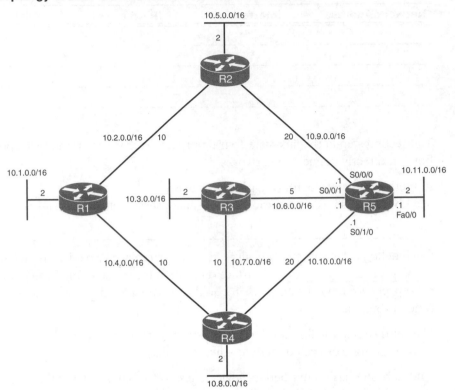

Table 5-9 shows partial information in the link-state database for R5 after all LSPs have been received and R5 is ready to calculate the SPF algorithm. Fill in the missing information

Table 5-9   Link-State Database for R5

LSPs from R1

- Connected to neighbor _____ on network _____,
cost of _____

- Connected to neighbor _____ on network _____,
cost of _____

- Has a network _____, cost of _____

LSPs from R2

- Connected to neighbor R1 on network 10.2.0.0/16, cost of _____

- Connected to neighbor R5 on network _____, cost of
_____

- Has a network _____, cost of _____

LSPs from R3

- Connected to neighbor _____ on network _____,
cost of _____

- Connected to neighbor _____ on network _____,
cost of _____

- Has a network _____ cost of _____

LSPs from R4

- Connected to neighbor _____ on network _____ ,
cost of _____

- Connected to neighbor _____ on network _____ ,
cost of _____

- Connected to neighbor _____ on network _____ ,
cost of _____

- Has a network _____ , cost of _____

R5 Link States

- Connected to neighbor _____ on network _____ ,
cost of _____

- Connected to neighbor _____ on network _____ ,
cost of _____

- Connected to neighbor _____ on network _____ ,
cost of _____

- Has a network _____ , cost of _____

Because all LSPs have been processed using the SPF algorithm, R5 has now constructed the complete SPF tree. Table 5-10 repeats the SPF tree for R5 that you determined earlier. Fill in the table again here.

Table 5-10   SPF Tree for R5

Destination	Shortest Path	Cost
R1 LAN		
R2 LAN		
R3 LAN		
R4 LAN		

Using this tree, the SPF algorithm results indicate the shortest path to each network. Only the LANs are shown in the table, but SPF can also be used to determine the shortest path to each WAN link network shown in Figure 5-7 earlier. Complete the missing information in the following list for R5's shortest path to each network:

- Network 10.1.0.0/16 via _____ serial _____ at a cost of _____
- Network 10.2.0.0/16 via _____ serial _____ at a cost of _____
- Network 10.3.0.0/16 via _____ serial _____ at a cost of _____
- Network 10.4.0.0/16 via _____ serial _____ at a cost of _____
- Network 10.5.0.0/16 via _____ serial _____ at a cost of _____
- Network 10.7.0.0/16 via _____ serial _____ at a cost of _____
- Network 10.8.0.0/16 via _____ serial _____ at a cost of _____

Using Link-State Routing Protocols

List three advantages and disadvantages of using link-state routing protocols when compared to distance vector routing protocols.

Advantages

_____

_____

_____

_____

Disadvantages

_____

_____

_____

Labs and Activities

Command Reference

Chapter 5, "Dynamic Routing," does not include any new commands.

5.0.1.2 Class Activity–How Much Does This Cost?

Objectives

Explain the operation of dynamic routing protocols.

_____

_____

_____

_____

Scenario

This modeling activity illustrates the network concept of routing cost.

You will be a member of a team of five students who travel routes to complete the activity scenarios. Each group will be required to have one digital camera or any device that has a camera, a stopwatch, and the provided student file for this activity. One person will function as the photographer and event recorder, as selected by each group. The remaining four team members will actively participate in the scenarios below.

A school or university classroom, hallway, outdoor track area, school parking lot, or any other location can serve as the venue for these activities.

Activity 1

The tallest person in the group establishes a start and finish line by marking 15 steps from start to finish, indicating the distance of the team route. Each student will take 15 steps from the start line toward the finish line and then stop on the 15th step—no further steps are allowed.

Note: Not all of the students may reach the same distance from the start line due to their height and stride differences. The photographer will take a group picture of the entire team's final location after taking the 15 steps required.

Activity 2

A new start and finish line will be established; however, this time, a longer distance for the route will be established than the distance specified in Activity 1. No maximum steps are to be used as a basis for creating this particular route. One at a time, students will "walk the new route from beginning to end twice."

Each team member will count the steps taken to complete the route. The recorder will time each student and at the end of each team member's route, record the time that it took to complete the full route and how many steps were taken, as recounted by each team member and recorded on the team's student file.

Once both activities have been completed, teams will use the digital picture taken for Activity 1 and their recorded data from the Activity 2 file to answer the reflection questions.

Group answers can be discussed as a class, time permitting.

Required Resources

- Digital or BYOD camera to record Activity 1's team results. Activity 2's data is based solely upon number of steps taken and the time it took to complete the route and no camera is necessary for Activity 2.

- Stopwatch

- Student file accompanying this modeling activity so that Activity 2 results can be recorded as each student finishes the route.

Scenario – Part 2 Recording Matrix

Student Team Member Name	Time Used to Finish the Route	Number of Steps Taken to Finish the Route

Reflection Questions

1. The photographer took a picture of the team's progress after taking 15 steps for Activity 1. Most likely, some team members did not reach the finish line on their 15th step due to height and stride differences. What do you think would happen if network data did not reach the finish line, or destination, in the allowed number of hops or steps?

2. What could be done to help team members reach the finish line if they did not reach it in Activity 1?

3. Which person would best be selected to deliver data using the network route completed in Activity 2? Justify your answer.

4. Using the data recorded in Activity 2 and a limit of 255 steps, or hops, did all members of the team take more than 255 steps to finish their route? What would happen if they had to stop on the 254th step, or hop?

_____

_____

5. Use the data that was recorded in Activity 2. Would you say the parameters for the route were enough to finish it successfully if all team members reached the finish line with 255 or less steps, or hops? Justify your answer.

_____

_____

_____

6. In network routing, different parameters are set for routing protocols. Use the data recorded for Activity 2. Would you select time, or number of steps, or hops, or a combination of both as your preferred routing type? List at least three reasons for your answers.

_____

_____

_____

5.2.1.6 Packet Tracer–Investigating Convergence

Topology

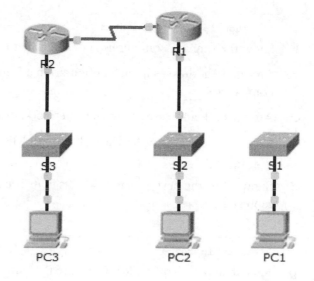

Addressing Table

Device	Interface	IP Address	Subnet Mask	Default Gateway
R1	G0/0	209.165.0.1	255.255.255.0	N/A
	G0/1	64.100.0.1	255.0.0.0	N/A
	S0/0/0	192.168.1.2	255.255.255.0	N/A
R2	G0/0	10.0.0.1	255.0.0.0	N/A
	S0/0/0	192.168.1.1	255.255.255.0	N/A
PC1	NIC	64.100.0.2	255.0.0.0	64.100.0.1
PC2	NIC	209.165.0.2	255.255.255.0	209.165.0.1
PC3	NIC	10.0.0.2	255.0.0.0	10.0.0.1

Objectives

Part 1: View the Routing Table of a Converged Network

Part 2: Add a New LAN to the Topology

Part 3: Watch the Network Converge

Background

This activity will help you identify important information in routing tables and witness the process of network convergence.

Part 1: View the Routing Table of a Converged Network

Step 1. Use **show** commands and interpret the output.

    a. Show the directly connected networks of **R1**. How many routes are connected to **R1**?

    _____

    `R1# show ip route connected`

    b. Show the running configuration of **R1**. What routing protocol is in use? _____

    c. Are the IP addresses in the configuration advertised by RIP the same as those that are connected? _____

    d. Are these IP addresses assignable, network, or broadcast? _____

    e. Show the networks of **R1** learned through RIP. How many routes are there? _____

    `R1# show ip route rip`

    f. Show all of the networks that **R1** has in its routing table. What do the leading letters represent?

    _____

    `R1# show ip route`

    g. Repeat step 1, a to f on **R2**. Compare the output of the two routers.

Step 2. Verify the state of the topology.

    a. Ping **PC3** from **PC2**. The ping should be successful.

    b. Show the interface status on **R2**. Two interfaces should have assigned addresses. Each address corresponds to a connected network.

    `R2# show ip interface brief`

    c. Show the interface status on **R1**. How many interfaces have assigned addresses? _____

    `R1# show ip interface brief`

Part 2: Add a New LAN to the Topology

Step 1. Add an Ethernet cable.

    a. Connect the correct Ethernet cable from **S1** to the appropriate port on **R1**.

    b. Ping from **PC1** to **PC2** after the affected **S1** port turns green. Was the ping successful?

    _____

    c. Ping from **PC1** to **PC3**. Was the ping successful? Why?

    _____

Step 2. Configure a route.

    a. Switch from Realtime mode to Simulation mode.

    b. Enter a new route on **R1** for the 64.0.0.0 network.

    `R1(config)# router rip`
    `R1(config-router)# network 64.0.0.0`

    c. Examine the PDUs leaving **R1**. What type are they? _____

Part 3: Watch the Network Converge

Step 1.   Use debug commands.

    a.   Enable debugging on **R2**.

```
R2# debug ip rip
R2# debug ip routing
```

    b.   For reference, show the routing table of **R2** as in step 1f.

    c.   Click **Capture / Forward** from simulation mode. What notification appeared in the terminal of **R2**?

_____

    d.   According to the debugging output, how many hops away from R2 is 64.0.0.0? _____

    e.   What interface does **R2** use to send packets destined for the 64.0.0.0 network? _____

    f.   Show the routing table of **R2**. Record the new entry.

_____

Step 2.   Verify the state of the topology.

Ping from **PC1** to **PC3**. Was the ping successful? Why?

_____

Suggested Scoring Rubric

Activity Section	Question Location	Possible Points	Earned Points
Part 1: View the Routing Table of a Converged Network.	Step 1-a	6	
	Step 1-b	6	
	Step 1-c	6	
	Step 1-d	6	
	Step 1-e	6	
	Step 1-f	6	
	Step 2-c	6	
	Part 1 Total	42	
Part 2: Add a New LAN to the Topology	Step 1-b	6	
	Step 1-c	6	
	Step 2-c	6	
	Part 2 Total	18	
Part 3: Watch the Network Converge	Step 1-c	6	
	Step 1-d	6	
	Step 1-e	6	
	Step 1-f	6	
	Step 2-a	6	
	Part 3 Total	30	
	Packet Tracer Score	10	
	Total Score	100	

5.2.3.4 Packet Tracer–Comparing RIP and EIGRP Path Selection

Topology

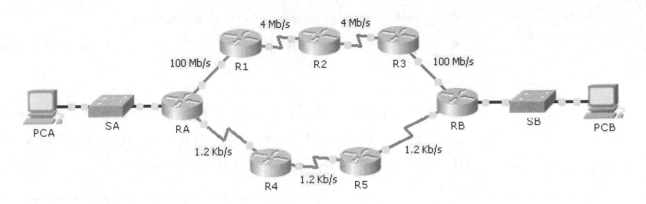

Objectives

Part 1: Predict the Path

Part 2: Trace the Route

Part 3: Reflection Questions

Scenario

PCA and PCB need to communicate. The path that the data takes between these end devices can travel through **R1**, **R2**, and **R3**, or it can travel through **R4** and **R5**. The process by which routers select the best path depends on the routing protocol. We will examine the behavior of two distance vector routing protocols, Enhanced Interior Gateway Routing Protocol (EIGRP) and Routing Information Protocol version 2 (RIPv2).

Part 1: Predict the Path

Metrics are factors that can be measured. Routing protocols are each designed to consider various metrics when considering which route is the best to send data along. These metrics include hop count, bandwidth, delay, reliability, path cost, and more.

Step 1.   Consider EIGRP metrics.

   a.   EIGRP can consider many metrics. By default, however, bandwidth and delay are used to determine best path selection.

   b.   Based on the metrics, what path would you predict data would take from **PCA** to **PCB**?

Step 2.   Consider RIP metrics.

    a.   What metric(s) are used by RIP? _____

    b.   Based on the metrics, what path would you predict data would take from **PCA** to **PCB**?

    _____

Part 2: Trace the Route

Step 1.   Examine the EIGRP path.

    a.   On **RA**, view the routing table using the appropriate command. Which protocol codes are listed in the table and what protocols do they represent?

    _____

    b.   Trace the route from **PCA** to **PCB**.

    What path does the data take?

    _____

    How many hops away is the destination? _____

    What is the minimum bandwidth on the path? _____

Step 2.   Examine the RIPv2 path.

You may have noticed that, while RIPv2 is configured, the routers ignore the routes that it generates, because they prefer EIGRP. Cisco routers use a scale called administrative distance and we need to change that number for RIPv2 in **RA** to make the router prefer the protocol.

    a.   For reference purposes, show the routing table of **RA** using the appropriate command. What is the first number between the brackets in each EIGRP route entry?

    _____

    b.   Set the administrative distance for RIPv2 using the following commands. This forces **RA** to choose RIP routes over EIGRP routes.

```
RA(config)# router rip
RA(config-router)# distance 89
```

    c.   Wait a minute and show the routing table again. Which protocol codes are listed in the table and what protocols do they represent? _____

    d.   Trace the route from **PCA** to **PCB**.

    What path does the data take? _____

    How many hops away is the destination? _____

    What is the minimum bandwidth on the path? _____

    e.   What is the first number between the brackets in each RIP entry? _____

Part 3: Reflection Questions

1. What metrics does the RIPv2 routing protocol ignore? _____

   How could this affect its performance? _____

2. What metrics does the EIGRP routing protocol ignore? _____

   How could this affect its performance?

   _____

3. Which do you prefer for your own Internet access, lower hops or more bandwidth?

   _____

4. Is one routing protocol suitable for all applications? Why? _____

Suggested Scoring Rubric

Activity Section	Question Location	Possible Points	Earned Points
Part 1: Predict the Path	Step 1-b	8	
	Step 2-a	8	
	Step 2-b	8	
	Part 1 Total	24	
Part 2: Trace the Route	Step 1-a	8	
	Step 1-b	8	
	Step 2-a	8	
	Step 2-c	8	
	Step 2-d	8	
	Step 2-e	8	
	Part 2 Total	48	
Part 3: Reflection Questions	1	7	
	2	7	
	3	7	
	4	7	
	Part 3 Total	28	
	Total Score	100	

CHAPTER 6

EIGRP

The main purpose in Cisco's development of Enhanced Interior Gateway Routing Protocol (EIGRP) was to create a classless version of IGRP. EIGRP includes several features that are not commonly found in other distance vector routing protocols such as RIP (RIPv1 and RIPv2) and IGRP. Although EIGRP may act like a link-state routing protocol, it is still a distance vector routing protocol.

Study Guide

EIGRP Characteristics

EIGRP is considered an advanced distance vector routing protocol because it has characteristics not found in other distance vector protocols like RIP and IGRP.

Describe Basic EIGRP Features

A major difference between EIGRP and other distance vector protocols is the algorithm it uses to calculate the best rate. Name and briefly describe this algorithm.

_____

_____

_____

What protocol, unique to EIGRP, provides for the delivery of EIGRP packets to neighbors?

_____

What is meant by the statement, "EIGRP provides partial and bounded updates"?

_____

_____

_____

Protocol-dependent modules (PDMs) allow EIGRP to route several different network layer protocols. List at least four functions of EIGRP's PDMs.

_____

_____

_____

_____

_____

_____

What are the IPv4 and IPv6 multicast addresses used by EIGRP's RTP?

_____

Identify and Describe EIGRP Packet Types

Like the Open Shortest Path First (OSPF) protocol, EIGRP relies on different types of packets to maintain its tables and establish relationships with neighbor routers. In Table 6-1, provide a brief description for each EIGRP packet type.

Table 6-1   EIGRP Packet Types

Packet Type	Description
Hello	
Acknowledgment	
Update	
Query	
Reply	

Complete the missing elements in this exercise by filling in appropriate words or phrases. When encountered, circle whether the packet is reliable or unreliable and whether it is unicast or multicast.

Hello packets:

- (Reliable/unreliable) (unicast/multicast) sent to the address, _____, to discover and maintain neighbors; contains the router's neighbor table

- Default _____ interval depends on the bandwidth:

    - ≤ 1.544 Mbps = _____ sec. _____
      interval (_____ holdtime)

    - > 1.544 Mbps = _____ sec. _____
      interval (_____ holdtime)

Update packets. Sent (reliably/unreliably), there are two types:

- (Unicast/multicast) to new neighbor discovered; contains routing information

- (Unicast/multicast) to all neighbors when topology changes

Query packets. Queries can use unicast or multicast and are sent (reliably/unreliably) during route recomputation, asking neighbors for a new successor to a lost route.

Reply packets. Neighbors (unicast/multicast) a reply to a query whether they have a route.

Acknowledgment packets. "Dataless" (unicast/multicast) packet that acknowledges the receipt of a packet that was sent reliably. This type is actually a Hello packet with a nonzero value in the Acknowledgment field.

An EIGRP router assumes that as long as it is receiving Hello packets from a neighbor, the neighbor and its routes remain viable. _____ tells the router the maximum time the router should wait to receive the next Hello before declaring that neighbor as _____. By default, this waiting period is _____ times the _____ interval, or _____ seconds on most networks and _____ seconds on networks with speeds of T1 or slower. If the time expires, EIGRP will declare the route as down, and DUAL will search for a new path by sending out queries.

Identify Elements of the EIGRP Message Formats

Figure 6-1 shows an example of an encapsulated EIGRP message. Fill in the missing field contents.

Figure 6-1   Encapsulated EIGRP Message

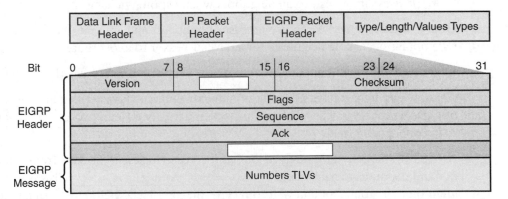

Data Link Frame Header	IP Packet Header	EIGRP Packet Header	Type/Length/Values Types

Data Link Frame

MAC Source Address = Address of Sending Interface
MAC Destination Address = Multicast: 01-00-5E-00-00-0A

IP Packet

IP Source Address = Address of Sending Interface
IP Destination Address = Multicast: ☐
Protocol Field = ☐ for EIGRP

EIGRP Packet Header

Opcode for EIGRP Packet Type
☐

TLV Types

Some Types Include:
0x0001 ☐
0x0102 ☐
0x0103 ☐

The EIGRP packet _____ is included with every EIGRP packet, regardless of its type. In the IP packet header, the Protocol field is set to _____ to indicate EIGRP, and the destination address is set to the multicast _____.

Every EIGRP message includes the header as shown in Figure 6-2. Fill in the missing field contents.

Figure 6-2   EIGRP Packet Header

Data Link Frame Header	IP Packet Header	EIGRP Packet Header	Type/Length/Values Types

Bit   0   7 | 8   15 | 16   23 | 24   31

EIGRP Header:
Version | ☐ | Checksum
Flags
Sequence
Ack
☐

EIGRP Message:
Numbers TLVs

Important fields for our discussion include the Opcode field and the Autonomous System (AS) field. _____ specifies the EIGRP packet type, one of the following:

_____

_____

_____

_____

The number in the AS field is used to track multiple instances of EIGRP.

Encapsulated in the EIGRP packet header is the TLV (Type/Length/Values) shown in Figure 6-3. Fill in the missing field contents.

Figure 6-3   EIGRP Parameters TLV

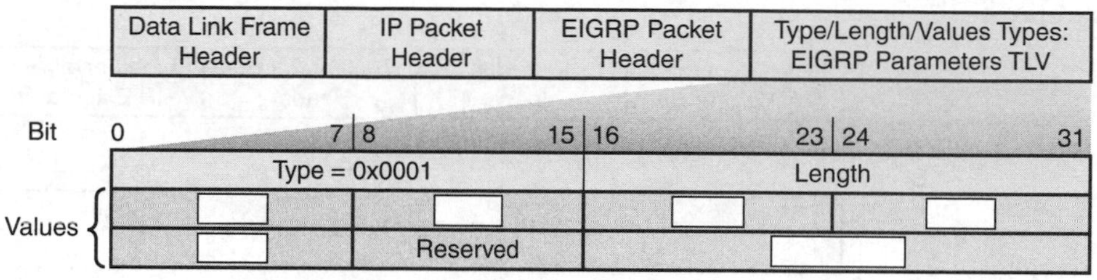

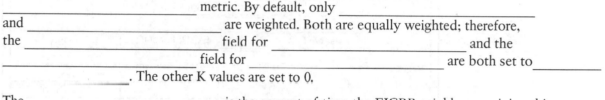

This EIGRP parameters message includes the weights that EIGRP uses for its _____ metric. By default, only _____ and _____ are weighted. Both are equally weighted; therefore, the _____ field for _____ and the _____ field for _____ are both set to_____. _____. The other K values are set to 0.

The _____ is the amount of time the EIGRP neighbor receiving this message should wait before considering the advertising router to be down.

Figure 6-4 shows the IP Internal message that is used to advertise EIGRP routes within an autonomous system. Fill in the missing field contents.

Figure 6-4   IP Internal Routes TLV

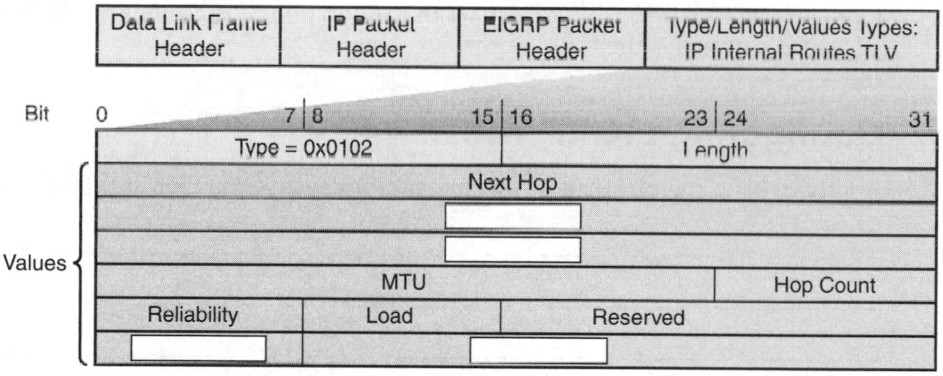

Important fields include the metric fields (_____ and _____), the subnet mask field (_____), and the _____ field.

Explain how the delay value is calculated.

_____

Explain how the bandwidth value is determined.

_____

The subnet mask is specified as the _____ or the number of _____ bits in the subnet mask. For example, the subnet mask 255.255.255.0 has a _____ of _____.

Figure 6-5 shows the IP External message that is used when external routes are imported into the EIGRP routing process. Notice that the bottom half of the IP External TLV includes all the fields used by the IP Internal TLV. Fill in the missing field contents.

Figure 6-5   IP External Routes TLV

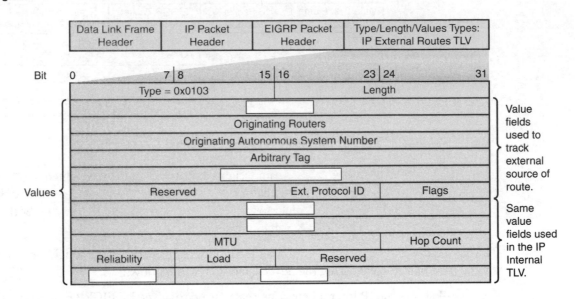

Configuring EIGRP for IPv4

Implementing EIGRP for IPv4 with basic configurations is straightforward. Tweaking EIGRP with more advanced settings is the topic of the next chapter.

Configuring EIGRP with IPv4

Briefly explain the purpose of the autonomous system number in EIGRP configurations.

_____

_____

_____

What are the steps a Cisco router uses to choose its router ID?

_____

_____

_____

What are the two main reasons for using the **passive-interface** command?

_____

_____

_____

_____

We will use the topology in Figure 6-6 and the addressing in Table 6-2 to configure a dual-stacked network running EIGRP for IPv4 and IPv6.

Figure 6-6   Dual-Stacked Multiarea EIGRP Topology

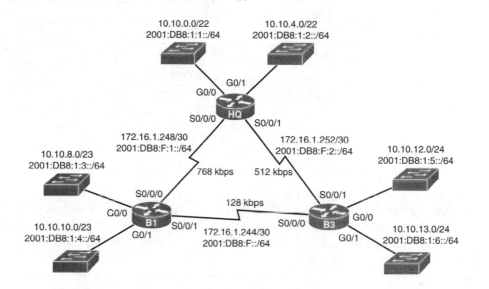

Table 6-2   Addressing for the Dual-Stacked EIGRP Topology

Device	Interface	Addressing Information	
HQ	G0/0	10.10.0.1	255.255.252.0
		2001:DB8:1:1::1/64	
	G0/1	10.10.4.1	255.255.252.0
		2001:DB8:1:2::1/64	
	S0/0/0	172.16.1.249	255.255.255.252
		2001:DB8:F:1::1/64	
	S0/0/1	172.16.1.253	255.255.255.252
		2001:DB8:F:2::1/64	
	Link-Local	FE80::2	
	Router ID	2.2.2.2	
B1	G0/0	10.10.8.1	255.255.254.0
		2001:DB8:1:3::1/64	
	G0/1	10.10.10.1	255.255.254.0
		2001:DB8:1:4::1/64	
	S0/0/0	172.16.1.250	255.255.255.252
		2001:DB8:F:1::2/64	
	S0/0/1	172.16.1.245	255.255.255.252
		2001:DB8:F::1/64	
	Link-Local	FE80::1	
	Router ID	1.1.1.1	

Device	Interface	Addressing Information	
B3	G0/0	10.10.12.1	255.255.255.0
		2001:DB8:1:5::1/64	
	G0/1	10.10.13.1	255.255.255.0
		2001:DB8:1:6::1/64	
	S0/0/0	172.16.1.246	255.255.255.252
		2001:DB8:F::2/64	
	S0/0/1	172.16.1.254	255.255.255.252
		2001:DB8:F:2::2/64	
	Link-Local	FE80::3	
	Router ID	3.3.3.3	

Document the most basic routing commands you could use to configure EIGRP for IPv4. Use AS number 1. Include the commands to configure the LAN interfaces as passive. The commands for all three routers are the same, except for the router ID configuration for each router.

_____

_____

_____

_____

_____

_____

_____

_____

_____

_____

_____

_____

_____

_____

_____

_____

_____

_____

_____

Now, for each router, document the network commands you would configure if the policy stated that you must also configure the wildcard mask for each interface participating in the EIGRP routing domain.

_____

_____

_____

_____

_____

_____

_____

_____

_____

_____

_____

_____

_____

_____

_____

_____

_____

_____

Verifying EIGRP with IPv4

Before any updates can be sent or received by EIGRP, routers must establish adjacencies with their neighbors. EIGRP routers establish adjacencies with neighbor routers by exchanging EIGRP Hello packets.

Use the _____ command to view the neighbor table and verify that EIGRP has established an adjacency with its neighbors. This command enables you to verify and troubleshoot EIGRP. Example 6-1 shows the neighbor table for HQ.

Example 6-1   EIGRP Neighbor Table for HQ

```
HQ# _____

EIGRP-IPv4 Neighbors for AS(1)

H   Address         Interface        Hold Uptime   SRTT   RTO  Q   Seq
                                          (sec)           (ms)     Cnt Num

1   172.16.1.254        Se0/0/1          14 00:28:35    2   100  0   33

0   172.16.1.250        Se0/0/0          10 00:28:48    1   100  0   36
```

As with OSPF, you can use the _____ command shown in Example 6-2 to verify that EIGRP is enabled. Because this configuration was done on a router with IOS 15.1, automatic summarization is disabled by default.

Example 6-2   Verifying EIGRP Is Enabled on HQ

```
HQ# _____
*** IP Routing is NSF aware ***


Routing Protocol is "eigrp 1"
  Outgoing update filter list for all interfaces is not set
  Incoming update filter list for all interfaces is not set
  Default networks flagged in outgoing updates
  Default networks accepted from incoming updates
  EIGRP-IPv4 Protocol for AS(1)
    Metric weight K1=1, K2=0, K3=1, K4=0, K5=0
    NSF-aware route hold timer is 240
    Router-ID: 2.2.2.2
    Topology : 0 (base)
      Active Timer: 3 min
      Distance: internal 90 external 170
      Maximum path: 4
      Maximum hopcount 100
      Maximum metric variance 1

  Automatic Summarization: disabled
  Maximum path: 4
  Routing for Networks:
    10.10.0.0/22
    10.10.4.0/22
    172.16.1.248/30
    172.16.1.252/30
  Passive Interface(s):
    GigabitEthernet0/0
    GigabitEthernet0/1
  Routing Information Sources:
```

```
    Gateway          Distance        Last Update
    172.16.1.254            90        00:29:47
    172.16.1.250            90        00:29:47
 Distance: internal 90 external 170
```

Another way to verify that EIGRP and other functions of the router are configured properly is to examine the routing tables with the _____ command. EIGRP routes are denoted in the routing table with a _____, which stands for DUAL.

Example 6-3 shows output from the routing table for B1 with only the EIGRP routes shown. Also, notice that the output begins at the "Gateway of last resort is not set" statement. What command generated this output?

Example 6-3   B1 Routing Table with EIGRP Routes

```
B1# _____

Gateway of last resort is not set


     10.0.0.0/8 is variably subnetted, 8 subnets, 4 masks
D       10.10.0.0/22 [90/2172416] via 172.16.1.249, 00:43:44, Serial0/0/0
D       10.10.4.0/22 [90/2172416] via 172.16.1.249, 00:43:44, Serial0/0/0
D       10.10.12.0/24 [90/2684416] via 172.16.1.249, 00:43:31, Serial0/0/0
D       10.10.13.0/24 [90/2684416] via 172.16.1.249, 00:43:31, Serial0/0/0
    172.16.0.0/16 is variably subnetted, 5 subnets, 2 masks
D       172.16.1.252/30 [90/2681856] via 172.16.1.246, 00:00:05, Serial0/0/1
B1#
```

EIGRP Operation

EIGRP uses the Diffusing Update Algorithm (DUAL) to select the best routes based on a composite metric. This section reviews the values of the EIGRP metric and how EIGRP performs the calculation to arrive at the metric displayed in the routing table.

EIGRP Metric Concepts

List the values EIGRP uses in its composite metric to calculate the preferred path to a network:

_____

_____

_____

_____

Record the formula used to calculate the *default* EIGRP composite metric.

_____

What command can you use to change the default K values?

_____

What command do you use to verify the K values used by EIGRP?

_____

What command enables you to verify the actual values of the EIGRP metric?

_____

The _____ metric is displayed in Kbit (kilobits). The WIC-2T and HWIC-2T use the default value of _____ bps, which is the value for a _____ connection. The value may or may not reflect the actual physical _____ of the interface. If actual _____ of the link differs from the default value, you should modify the value. We will review modifying the bandwidth calculation to reflect actual values in the next chapter.

_____ is a measure of the time it takes for a packet to traverse a route. This metric is a static value and is expressed in _____.

Complete Table 6-3.

Table 6-3   Interface Delay Values

Media	Delay
Ethernet	
Fast Ethernet	
Gigabit Ethernet	
FDDI	
T1 (serial default)	
DS0 (64 Kbps)	
1024 Kbps	
56 Kbps	

_____ is based on the worst value on a particular link and is computed based on keep-alives.

_____ is based on the worst value on a particular link and is computed based on packet rates.

However, because the EIGRP composite metric defaults to _____ and _____ only, _____ and _____ are not normally considered in the calculation of metric.

DUAL Concepts Exercise

Dual provides the following:

- _____ paths
- _____ backup paths that can be used immediately
- Fast _____
- Minimum _____ usage with _____ updates

Briefly explain the term *successor*.

_____

_____

Briefly explain what is meant by *feasible distance*.

_____

Examine the following output for B1's routing table shown in Example 6-4.

Example 6-4   Feasible Distance and Successors in the B1 Routing Table

```
B1# show ip route eigrp | begin Gateway
Gateway of last resort is not set


     10.0.0.0/8 is variably subnetted, 8 subnets, 4 masks
D        10.10.0.0/22 [90/2172416] via 172.16.1.249, 03:06:49, Serial0/0/0
D        10.10.4.0/22 [90/2172416] via 172.16.1.249, 03:06:49, Serial0/0/0
D        10.10.12.0/24 [90/2684416] via 172.16.1.249, 03:06:49, Serial0/0/0
D        10.10.13.0/24 [90/2684416] via 172.16.1.249, 03:06:49, Serial0/0/0
     172.16.0.0/16 is variably subnetted, 5 subnets, 2 masks
D        172.16.1.252/30 [90/2681856] via 172.16.1.249, 03:06:50, Serial0/0/0
```

Answer the questions that follow:

What is the IP address of the successor for network 10.10.4.0/22? _____

What is the feasible distance to 10.10.4.0/22? _____

What is the IP address of the successor for network 10.10.12.0/24? _____

What is the feasible distance to 10.10.12.0/24? _____

Briefly explain the term *feasible successor*.

_____

_____

Briefly explain *feasibility condition*.

_____

_____

Briefly explain *reported distance*.

_____

_____

The successor, feasible distance, and any feasible successors with their reported distances are kept by a router in its EIGRP topology table or topology database. This table can be viewed using the _____ command, as shown in Example 6-5.

Example 6-5   Successors and Feasible Successors in the B1 Topology Table

```
B1# _____
EIGRP-IPv4 Topology Table for AS(1)/ID(1.1.1.1)
Codes: P - Passive, A - Active, U - Update, Q - Query, R - Reply,
       r - reply Status, s - sia Status


P 10.10.8.0/23, 1 successors, FD is 28160
        via Connected, GigabitEthernet0/0
P 172.16.1.248/30, 1 successors, FD is 2169856
        via Connected, Serial0/0/0
P 172.16.1.244/30, 1 successors, FD is 3845120
        via Connected, Serial0/0/1
P 10.10.12.0/24, 1 successors, FD is 2684416
        via 172.16.1.249 (2684416/2172416), Serial0/0/0
        via 172.16.1.246 (3847680/28160), Serial0/0/1
P 10.10.4.0/22, 1 successors, FD is 2172416
        via 172.16.1.249 (2172416/28160), Serial0/0/0
P 172.16.1.252/30, 1 successors, FD is 2681856
        via 172.16.1.249 (2681856/2169856), Serial0/0/0
        via 172.16.1.246 (4357120/2169856), Serial0/0/1
P 10.10.0.0/22, 1 successors, FD is 2172416
        via 172.16.1.249 (2172416/28160), Serial0/0/0
P 10.10.13.0/24, 1 successors, FD is 2684416
        via 172.16.1.249 (2684416/2172416), Serial0/0/0
        via 172.16.1.246 (3847680/28160), Serial0/0/1
P 10.10.10.0/23, 1 successors, FD is 28160
        via Connected, GigabitEthernet0/1
```

The topology table lists all successors and feasible successors that DUAL has calculated to destination networks. Use the partial output in Example 6-5 to answer the following questions:

For route 10.10.12.0/24...

What is the IP address of the successor? _____

What is the reported distance of the successor? _____

What is the feasible distance of the successor? _____

What is the IP address of the feasible successor? _____

What is the reported distance of the feasible successor? _____

What is the feasible distance of the feasible successor? _____

Notice that the reported distance of the feasible successor is less than the feasible distance of the successor.

What happens if an EIGRP router doesn't have feasible successor in the topology table and the router loses connection to the successor?

DUAL FSM Completion Exercise

A finite state machine (FSM) is an abstract machine, not a mechanical device with moving parts. FSMs define a set of possible states that something can go through, what events cause those states, and what events result from those states. Designers use FSMs to describe how a device, computer program, or routing algorithm will react to a set of input events.

Figure 6-7 is a simplified flowchart of DUAL's FSM. Fill in the flowchart with the states EIGRP moves through when it loses connectivity with a successor. The flowchart should serve as a visual study aid to help you remember how DUAL converges on new routes.

Figure 6-7   DUAL FSM Flowchart

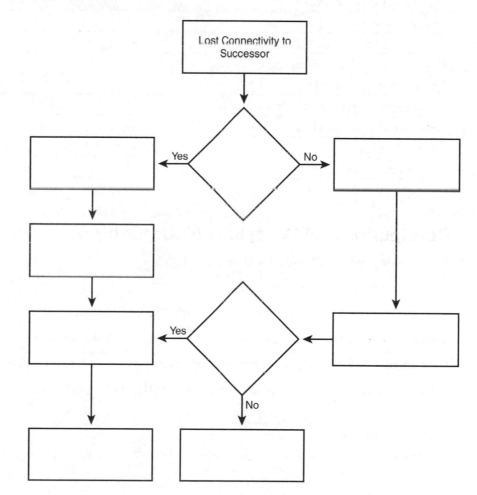

Configuring EIGRP for IPv6

EIGRP for IPv4 and EIGRP for IPv6 are almost identical in their operation. Configuring EIGRP for IPv6 is actually easier than IPv4. No need to configure network statements. Simply enable EIGRP for IPv6 globally, assigning a router ID. Then enable EIGRP on each interface you want to participate in the EIGRP routing process.

Comparing EIGRP for IPv4 and EIGRP for IPv6

In Table 6-4, indicate whether an EIGRP feature is associated with EIGRP for IPv4, EIGRP for IPv6, or both.

Table 6-4   Comparing EIGRP for IPv4 and IPv6

Features	EIGRP for IPv4	EIGRP for IPv6	Both
Advertised IPv4 networks			
Advertised IPv6 networks			
Distance vector			
DUAL algorithm			
Default metric: bandwidth and delay			
Transport protocol: RTP			
Incremental, partial, and bounded updates			
Neighbor discovery: Hello packets			
224.0.0.10 multicast			
FF02::A multicast			

Configuring and Verifying EIGRP for IPv6

The steps to configure EIGRP for IPv6 are as follows:

Step 1.   Enable IPv6 routing.

Step 2.   Enable EIGRP for IPv6 globally with AS number 1 and configure the router ID.

Step 3.   Enable the interfaces that are to participate in EIGRP for IPv6.

With those steps in mind, document the configurations for each router shown in Figure 6-6.

What command enables you to verify adjacency with other EIGRP routers?

```
B1# _____

EIGRP-IPv6 Neighbors for AS(1)

H   Address              Interface       Hold Uptime   SRTT   RTO  Q   Seq
                                         (sec)         (ms)        Cnt Num

1   Link-local address:  Se0/0/1         11 00:14:52    1     186  0   50
    FE80::3

0   Link-local address:  0Se0/0/0        12 00:14:53    1     100  0   25
    FE80::2
```

What command enables you to display the EIGRP parameters, including the K values, router ID, process ID, and administrative distances?

```
B1# _____

IPv6 Routing Protocol is "connected"

IPv6 Routing Protocol is "eigrp 1"

EIGRP-IPv6 Protocol for AS(1)

  Metric weight K1=1, K2=0, K3=1, K4=0, K5=0

  NSF-aware route hold timer is 240

  Router-ID: 1.1.1.1

  Topology : 0 (base)

    Active Timer: 3 min

    Distance: internal 90 external 170

    Maximum path: 16

    Maximum hopcount 100

    Maximum metric variance 1


  Interfaces:

    Serial0/0/0

    Serial0/0/1

    GigabitEthernet0/0

    GigabitEthernet0/1

  Redistribution:

    None

IPv6 Routing Protocol is "ND"
```

What command enables you to verify the EIGRP routes are installed in the routing table?

```
B1# _____

IPv6 Routing Table - default - 14 entries

Codes: C - Connected, L - Local, S - Static, U - Per-user Static route

       B - BGP, R - RIP, H - NHRP, I1 - ISIS L1

       I2 - ISIS L2, IA - ISIS interarea, IS - ISIS summary, D - EIGRP

       EX - EIGRP external, ND - ND Default, NDp - ND Prefix, DCE - Destination

       NDr - Redirect, O - OSPF Intra, OI - OSPF Inter, OE1 - OSPF ext 1

       OE2 - OSPF ext 2, ON1 - OSPF NSSA ext 1, ON2 - OSPF NSSA ext 2

D   2001:DB8:1:1::/64 [90/2172416]

      via FE80::2, Serial0/0/0

D   2001:DB8:1:2::/64 [90/2172416]

      via FE80::2, Serial0/0/0

D   2001:DB8:1:5::/64 [90/2684416]

      via FE80::2, Serial0/0/0

D   2001:DB8:1:6::/64 [90/2684416]

      via FE80::2, Serial0/0/0

D   2001:DB8:F:2::/64 [90/2681856]

      via FE80::2, Serial0/0/0
```

Packet Tracer Exercise 6-1: Implement Dual Stack EIGRP

Now you are ready to use Packet Tracer to apply your documented configuration. Download and open the file LSG03-0601.pka found at the companion website for this book. Refer to the Introduction of this book for specifics on accessing files.

Note: The following instructions are also contained within the Packet Tracer Exercise.

In this Packet Tracer activity, you will configure HQ, B1, and B3 with EIGRP routing for IPv4 and for IPv6. You will then verify that PCs can ping each other using IPv4 and IPv6 addresses. Use the addressing table and the commands you documented in this chapter.

Requirements

Configure each router with the following:

- Router ID
- EIGRP routing for IPv4 using the most basic network commands and setting LAN interfaces to passive.
- EIGRP routing for IPv6 and setting the LAN interfaces to passive.
- Verify IPv4 and IPv6 connectivity between the PCs.

Your completion percentage should be 100%. All the connectivity tests should show a status of "successful." If not, click **Check Results** to see which required components are not yet completed.

Labs and Activities

Command Reference

In Table 6-5, record the command, including the correct router or switch prompt, that fits the description. Fill in any blanks with the appropriate missing information.

Table 6-5   Commands for Chapter 6, EIGRP

Command	Description
	Configure R1 with EIGRP for IPv4 using AS number 20.
	Configure R1 with an EIGRP for IPv4 router ID of 1.1.1.1.
	Configure R1 to advertised network 172.16.1.0/24 in EIGRP for IPv4. Use the most basic command.
	Configure R1 to advertised network 172.16.1.0/24 in EIGRP for IPv4. Use the wild card mask argument to specify the subnet mask.
	Configure interface S0/0/0 to not send out EIGRP for IPv4 updates.
	List the command that will display all of R1's EIGRP for IPv4 neighbors.
	List the command that will display the status of EIGRP for IPv4 automatic summarization.
	List the command that will only show the EIGRP for IPv4 routes.
	List the command that will show EIGRP for IPv4 feasible successors.
	Configure R1 to route IPv6 packets.
	Configure R1 with EIGRP for IPv6 using AS number 20.
	Configure R1 with an EIGRP for IPv6 router ID of 1.1.1.1.
	Activate the EIGRP for IPv6 routing process.
	Configure R1 to use EIGRP for IPv6 to advertise an interface's IPv6 network address.
	List the command that will display all of R1's EIGRP for IPv6 neighbors.
	List the command that will display the interfaces that are participating in EIGRP for IPv6 routing.
	List the command that will only show the EIGRP for IPv6 routes.

6.0.1.2 Class Activity–Classless EIGRP

Objectives

Describe the basic features of EIGRP.

_____

_____

_____

_____

Scenario

EIGRP was introduced as a distance vector routing protocol in 1992. It was originally designed to work as a proprietary protocol on Cisco devices only. In 2013, EIGRP became a multi-vendor routing protocol, meaning that it can be used by other device vendors in addition to Cisco devices.

View the *Fundamental Configuration and Verification of EIGRP* video located at http://www.cisco.com/E-Learning/bulk/subscribed/tac/netbits/iprouting/eigrp/01_fundamental_eigrp/start.htm. In order to view the video you must have a cisco.com account. If you do not have a cisco.com account, please register to create one.

While viewing the video, pay close attention to the following concepts and terms:

- Subnet mask reporting to routing tables for classful and classless networks
- Auto-summarization of networks in routing tables
- Autonomous system numbers
- Wildcard masks
- Passive interfaces
- EIGRP configuration commands
- EIGRP verification commands

Complete the reflection questions that accompany the PDF file for this activity. Save your work and be prepared to share your answers with the class.

Resources

Internet access

Reflection

1. Explain classful routing protocols.

    _____

2. Explain classless routing protocols.

    _____

3. What is network auto-summarization?

_____

_____

_____

4. What is an autonomous system number?

_____

_____

_____

5. What are wildcard masks?

_____

_____

_____

6. What is a passive interface?

_____

_____

_____

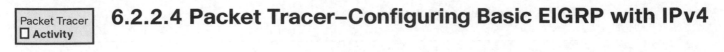

6.2.2.4 Packet Tracer–Configuring Basic EIGRP with IPv4

Topology

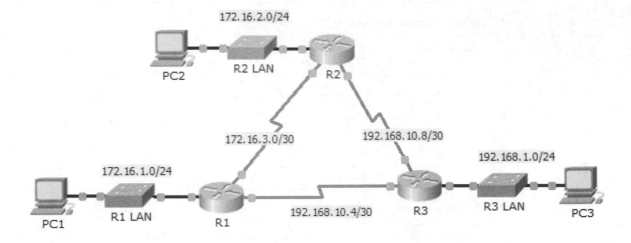

Addressing Table

Device	Interface	IP Address	Subnet Mask	Default Gateway
R1	G0/0	172.16.1.1	255.255.255.0	N/A
	S0/0/0	172.16.3.1	255.255.255.252	N/A
	S0/0/1	192.168.10.5	255.255.255.252	N/A
R2	G0/0	172.16.2.1	255.255.255.0	N/A
	S0/0/0	172.16.3.2	255.255.255.252	N/A
	S0/0/1	192.168.10.9	255.255.255.252	N/A
R3	G0/0	192.168.1.1	255.255.255.0	N/A
	S0/0/0	192.168.10.6	255.255.255.252	N/A
	S0/0/1	192.168.10.10	255.255.255.252	N/A
PC1	NIC	172.16.1.10	255.255.255.0	172.16.1.1
PC2	NIC	172.16.2.10	255.255.255.0	172.16.2.1
PC3	NIC	192.168.1.10	255.255.255.0	192.168.1.1

Objectives

Part 1: Configure EIGRP

Part 2: Verify EIGRP Routing

Background

In this activity, you will implement basic EIGRP configurations including network commands, passive interfaces, and disabling automatic summarization. You will then verify your EIGRP configuration using a variety of show commands and testing end-to-end connectivity.

Part 1: Configure EIGRP

Step 1.   Enable the EIGRP routing process.

Enable the EIGRP routing process on each router using AS number 1. The configuration for **R1** is shown.

```
R1(config)# router eigrp 1
```

What is the range of numbers that can be used for AS numbers? _____

Step 2.   Advertise directly connected networks.

a.   Use the **show ip route** command to display the directly connected networks on each router.

How can you tell the difference between subnet addresses and interface addresses?

_____

b.   On each router, configure EIGRP to advertise the specific directly connected subnets. The configuration for **R1** is shown.

```
R1(config-router)# network 172.16.1.0 0.0.0.255
R1(config-router)# network 172.16.3.0 0.0.0.3
R1(config-router)# network 192.168.10.4 0.0.0.3
```

Step 3.   Configure passive interfaces.

Configure the LAN interfaces to not advertise EIGRP updates. The configuration for R1 is shown.

```
R1(config-router)# passive-interface g0/0
```

Step 4.   Disable automatic summarization.

The topology contains discontiguous networks. Therefore, disable automatic summarization on each router. The configuration for **R1** is shown.

```
R1(config-router)# no auto-summary
```

Note: Prior to IOS 15 auto-summary had to be manually disabled.

Step 5.   Save the configurations.

Part 2: Verify EIGRP Routing

Step 1.   Examine neighbor adjacencies.

a.   Which command displays the neighbors discovered by EIGRP?

_____

b.   All three routers should have two neighbors listed. The output for **R1** should look similar to the following.

```
IP-EIGRP neighbors for process 1
H   Address          Interface       Hold Uptime     SRTT   RTO    Q    Seq
                                     (sec)           (ms)          Cnt  Num
0   172.16.3.2       Se0/0/0         14   00:25:05   40     1000   0    28
1   192.168.10.6     Se0/0/1         12   00:13:29   40     1000   0    31
```

Step 2. Display the EIGRP routing protocol parameters.

    a. What command displays the parameters and other information about the current state of any active IPv4 routing protocol processes configured on the router?

    _____

    b. On **R2**, enter the command you listed for 2a and answer the following questions.

    How many routers are sharing routing information with **R2**? _____

    Where is this information located under? _____

    What is the maximum hop count? _____

Step 3. Verify end-to-end connectivity

PC1, PC2, and PC3 should now be able to ping each other. If not, troubleshoot your EIGRP configurations.

Suggested Scoring Rubric

Activity Section	Question Location	Possible Points	Earned Points
Part 1: Configure EIGRP	Step 1	2	
	Step 2a	2	
	Part 1 Total	**4**	
Part 2: Verify EIGRP Routing	Step 1a	5	
	Step 2a	5	
	Step 2b	6	
	Part 2 Total	**16**	
	Packet Tracer Score	80	
	Total Score	**100**	

6.2.2.5 Lab—Configuring Basic EIGRP for IPv4

Topology

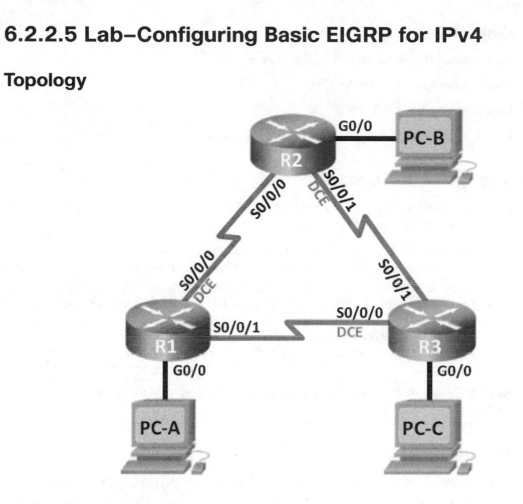

Addressing Table

Device	Interface	IP Address	Subnet Mask	Default Gateway
R1	G0/0	192.168.1.1	255.255.255.0	N/A
	S0/0/0 (DCE)	10.1.1.1	255.255.255.252	N/A
	S0/0/1	10.3.3.1	255.255.255.252	N/A
R2	G0/0	192.168.2.1	255.255.255.0	N/A
	S0/0/0	10.1.1.2	255.255.255.252	N/A
	S0/0/1 (DCE)	10.2.2.2	255.255.255.252	N/A
R3	G0/0	192.168.3.1	255.255.255.0	N/A
	S0/0/0 (DCE)	10.3.3.2	255.255.255.252	N/A
	S0/0/1	10.2.2.1	255.255.255.252	N/A
PC-A	NIC	192.168.1.3	255.255.255.0	192.168.1.1
PC-B	NIC	192.168.2.3	255.255.255.0	192.168.2.1
PC-C	NIC	192.168.3.3	255.255.255.0	192.168.3.1

Objectives

Part 1: Build the Network and Verify Connectivity

Part 2: Configure EIGRP Routing

Part 3: Verify EIGRP Routing

Part 4: Configure Bandwidth and Passive Interfaces

Background/Scenario

Enhanced Interior Gateway Routing Protocol (EIGRP) is a powerful distance vector routing protocol and is relatively easy to configure for basic networks.

In this lab, you will configure EIGRP for the topology and networks shown above. You will modify bandwidth and configure passive interfaces to allow EIGRP to function more efficiently.

Note: The routers used with CCNA hands-on labs are Cisco 1941 Integrated Services Routers (ISRs) with Cisco IOS Release 15.2(4)M3 (universalk9 image). Other routers and Cisco IOS versions can be used. Depending on the model and Cisco IOS version, the commands available and output produced might vary from what is shown in the labs. Refer to the Router Interface Summary Table at the end of this lab for the correct interface identifiers.

Note: Make sure that the routers have been erased and have no startup configurations. If you are unsure, contact your instructor.

Required Resources

- 3 Routers (Cisco 1941 with Cisco IOS Release 15.2(4)M3 universal image or comparable)
- 3 PCs (Windows 7, Vista, or XP with terminal emulation program, such as Tera Term)
- Console cables to configure the Cisco IOS devices via the console ports
- Ethernet and serial cables as shown in the topology

Part 1: Build the Network and Verify Connectivity

In Part 1, you will set up the network topology and configure basic settings, such as the interface IP addresses, device access, and passwords.

Step 1.   Cable the network as shown in the topology.

Step 2.   Configure PC hosts.

Step 3.   Initialize and reload the routers as necessary.

Step 4.   Configure basic settings for each router.

    a.   Disable DNS lookup.

    b.   Configure IP addresses for the routers, as listed in the Addressing Table.

    c.   Configure device name as shown in the topology.

    d.   Assign **cisco** as the console and vty passwords.

    e.   Assign **class** as the privileged EXEC password.

f. Configure **logging synchronous** to prevent console and vty messages from interrupting command entry.

g. Configure a message of the day.

h. Copy the running configuration to the startup configuration.

Step 5. Verify connectivity.

The routers should be able to ping one another, and each PC should be able to ping its default gateway. The PCs will not be able to ping other PCs until EIGRP routing is configured. Verify and troubleshoot if necessary.

Part 2: Configure EIGRP Routing

Step 1. Enable EIGRP routing on R1. Use AS number 10.

```
R1(config)# router eigrp 10
```

Step 2. Advertise the directly connected networks on R1 using the wildcard mask.

```
R1(config-router)# network 10.1.1.0 0.0.0.3
R1(config-router)# network 192.168.1.0 0.0.0.255
R1(config-router)# network 10.3.3.0 0.0.0.3
```

Why is it a good practice to use wildcard masks when advertising networks? Could the mask have been omitted from any of the network statements above? If so, which one(s)?

_____

_____

_____

Step 3. Enable EIGRP routing and advertise the directly connected networks on R2 and R3.

You will see neighbor adjacency messages as interfaces are added to the EIGRP routing process. The messages on R2 are displayed as an example.

```
*Apr 14 15:24:59.543: %DUAL-5-NBRCHANGE: EIGRP-IPv4 10: Neighbor 10.1.1.1
(Serial0/0/0) is up: new adjacency
```

Step 4. Verify end-to-end connectivity.

All devices should be able to ping each other if EIGRP is configured correctly.

Note: Depending on the operating system, it may be necessary to disable the firewall for the pings to the host PCs to be successful.

Part 3: Verify EIGRP Routing

Step 1. Examine the EIGRP neighbor table.

On R1, issue the **show ip eigrp neighbors** command to verify that the adjacency has been established with its neighboring routers.

```
R1# show ip eigrp neighbors
EIGRP-IPv4 Neighbors for AS(10)
```

H	Address	Interface	Hold (sec)	Uptime	SRTT (ms)	RTO	Q Cnt	Seq Num
1	10.3.3.2	Se0/0/1	13	00:24:58	8	100	0	17
0	10.1.1.2	Se0/0/0	13	00:29:23	7	100	0	23

Step 2.   Examine the IP EIGRP routing table.

```
R1# show ip route eigrp
Codes: L - local, C - connected, S - static, R - RIP, M - mobile, B - BGP
       D - EIGRP, EX - EIGRP external, O - OSPF, IA - OSPF inter area
       N1 - OSPF NSSA external type 1, N2 - OSPF NSSA external type 2
       E1 - OSPF external type 1, E2 - OSPF external type 2
       i - IS-IS, su - IS-IS summary, L1 - IS-IS level-1, L2 - IS-IS level-2
       ia - IS-IS inter area, * - candidate default, U - per-user static route
       o - ODR, P - periodic downloaded static route, H - NHRP, l - LISP
       + - replicated route, % - next hop override


Gateway of last resort is not set

      10.0.0.0/8 is variably subnetted, 5 subnets, 2 masks
D        10.2.2.0/30 [90/2681856] via 10.3.3.2, 00:29:01, Serial0/0/1
                     [90/2681856] via 10.1.1.2, 00:29:01, Serial0/0/0
D     192.168.2.0/24 [90/2172416] via 10.1.1.2, 00:29:01, Serial0/0/0
D     192.168.3.0/24 [90/2172416] via 10.3.3.2, 00:27:56, Serial0/0/1
```

Why does R1 have two paths to the 10.2.2.0/30 network?

Step 3.   Examine the EIGRP topology table.

```
R1# show ip eigrp topology
EIGRP-IPv4 Topology Table for AS(10)/ID(192.168.1.1)
Codes: P - Passive, A - Active, U - Update, Q - Query, R - Reply,
       r - reply Status, s - sia Status

P 192.168.3.0/24, 1 successors, FD is 2172416
        via 10.3.3.2 (2172416/28160), Serial0/0/1
P 192.168.2.0/24, 1 successors, FD is 2172416
        via 10.1.1.2 (2172416/28160), Serial0/0/0
P 10.2.2.0/30, 2 successors, FD is 2681856
        via 10.1.1.2 (2681856/2169856), Serial0/0/0
        via 10.3.3.2 (2681856/2169856), Serial0/0/1
P 10.3.3.0/30, 1 successors, FD is 2169856
        via Connected, Serial0/0/1
P 192.168.1.0/24, 1 successors, FD is 2816
        via Connected, GigabitEthernet0/0
P 10.1.1.0/30, 1 successors, FD is 2169856
        via Connected, Serial0/0/0
```

Why are there no feasible successors listed in the R1 topology table?

Step 4.   Verify the EIGRP routing parameters and networks advertised.

Issue the **show ip protocols** command to verify the EIGRP routing parameters used.

```
R1# show ip protocols
*** IP Routing is NSF aware ***

Routing Protocol is "eigrp 10"
```

```
      Outgoing update filter list for all interfaces is not set
      Incoming update filter list for all interfaces is not set
      Default networks flagged in outgoing updates
      Default networks accepted from incoming updates
      EIGRP-IPv4 Protocol for AS(10)
        Metric weight K1=1, K2=0, K3=1, K4=0, K5=0
        NSF-aware route hold timer is 240
        Router-ID: 192.168.1.1
        Topology : 0 (base)
          Active Timer: 3 min
          Distance: internal 90 external 170
          Maximum path: 4
          Maximum hopcount 100
          Maximum metric variance 1

      Automatic Summarization: disabled
      Maximum path: 4
      Routing for Networks:
        10.1.1.0/30
        10.3.3.0/30
        192.168.1.0
      Routing Information Sources:
        Gateway         Distance      Last Update
        10.3.3.2              90      02:38:34
        10.1.1.2              90      02:38:34
      Distance: internal 90 external 170
```

Based on the output of issuing the **show ip protocols** command, answer the following questions.

What AS number is used? _____

What networks are advertised?

_____

What is the administrative distance for EIGRP? _____

How many equal cost paths does EIGRP use by default? _____

Part 4: Configure Bandwidth and Passive Interfaces

EIGRP uses a default bandwidth based on the type of interface in the router. In Part 4, you will modify the bandwidth so that the link between R1 and R3 has a lower bandwidth than the link between R1/R2 and R2/R3. In addition, you will set passive interfaces on each router.

Step 1.   Observe the current routing settings.

    a.   Issue the **show interface s0/0/0** command on R1.

```
R1# show interface s0/0/0
Serial0/0/0 is up, line protocol is up
  Hardware is WIC MBRD Serial
  Internet address is 10.1.1.1/30
  MTU 1500 bytes, BW 1544 Kbit/sec, DLY 20000 usec,
```

```
    reliability 255/255, txload 1/255, rxload 1/255
  Encapsulation HDLC, loopback not set
  Keepalive set (10 sec)
  Last input 00:00:01, output 00:00:02, output hang never
  Last clearing of "show interface" counters 03:43:45
  Input queue: 0/75/0/0 (size/max/drops/flushes); Total output drops: 0
  Queueing strategy: fifo
  Output queue: 0/40 (size/max)
  5 minute input rate 0 bits/sec, 0 packets/sec
  5 minute output rate 0 bits/sec, 0 packets/sec
     4050 packets input, 270294 bytes, 0 no buffer
     Received 1554 broadcasts (0 IP multicasts)
     0 runts, 0 giants, 0 throttles
     1 input errors, 0 CRC, 0 frame, 0 overrun, 0 ignored, 1 abort
     4044 packets output, 271278 bytes, 0 underruns
     0 output errors, 0 collisions, 5 interface resets
     4 unknown protocol drops
     0 output buffer failures, 0 output buffers swapped out
     12 carrier transitions
     DCD=up  DSR=up  DTR=up  RTS=up  CTS=up
```

What is the default bandwidth for this serial interface?

---

b. How many routes are listed in the routing table to reach the 10.2.2.0/30 network?

_____

Step 2.   Modify the bandwidth on the routers.

a.   Modify the bandwidth on R1 for the serial interfaces.

```
R1(config)# interface s0/0/0
R1(config-if)# bandwidth 2000
R1(config-if)# interface s0/0/1
R1(config-if)# bandwidth 64
```

Issue **show ip route** command on R1. Is there a difference in the routing table? If so, what is it?

```
Codes: L - local, C - connected, S - static, R - RIP, M - mobile, B - BGP
       D - EIGRP, EX - EIGRP external, O - OSPF, IA - OSPF inter area
       N1 - OSPF NSSA external type 1, N2 - OSPF NSSA external type 2
       E1 - OSPF external type 1, E2 - OSPF external type 2
       i - IS-IS, su - IS-IS summary, L1 - IS-IS level-1, L2 - IS-IS level-2
       ia - IS-IS inter area, * - candidate default, U - per-user static route
       o - ODR, P - periodic downloaded static route, H - NHRP, l - LISP
       + - replicated route, % - next hop override

Gateway of last resort is not set

      10.0.0.0/8 is variably subnetted, 5 subnets, 2 masks
C        10.1.1.0/30 is directly connected, Serial0/0/0
L        10.1.1.1/32 is directly connected, Serial0/0/0
D        10.2.2.0/30 [90/2681856] via 10.1.1.2, 00:03:09, Serial0/0/0
C        10.3.3.0/30 is directly connected, Serial0/0/1
```

```
L           10.3.3.1/32 is directly connected, Serial0/0/1
            192.168.1.0/24 is variably subnetted, 2 subnets, 2 masks
C           192.168.1.0/24 is directly connected, GigabitEthernet0/0
L           192.168.1.1/32 is directly connected, GigabitEthernet0/0
D        192.168.2.0/24 [90/1794560] via 10.1.1.2, 00:03:09, Serial0/0/0
D        192.168.3.0/24 [90/2684416] via 10.1.1.2, 00:03:08, Serial0/0/0
```

_____

_____

_____

_____

b. Modify the bandwidth on the R2 and R3 serial interfaces.

```
R2(config)# interface s0/0/0
R2(config-if)# bandwidth 2000
R2(config-if)# interface s0/0/1
R2(config-if)# bandwidth 2000

R3(config)# interface s0/0/0
R3(config-if)# bandwidth 64
R3(config-if)# interface s0/0/1
R3(config-if)# bandwidth 2000
```

Step 3. Verify the bandwidth modifications.

a. Verify bandwidth modifications. Issue a **show interface serial 0/0/x** command, with x being the appropriate serial interface on all three routers to verify that bandwidth is set correctly. R1 is shown as an example.

```
R1# show interface s0/0/0
Serial0/0/0 is up, line protocol is up
  Hardware is WIC MBRD Serial
  Internet address is 10.1.1.1/30
  MTU 1500 bytes, BW 2000 Kbit/sec, DLY 20000 usec,
     reliability 255/255, txload 1/255, rxload 1/255
  Encapsulation HDLC, loopback not set
  Keepalive set (10 sec)
  Last input 00:00:01, output 00:00:02, output hang never
  Last clearing of "show interface" counters 04:06:06
  Input queue: 0/75/0/0 (size/max/drops/flushes); Total output drops: 0
  Queueing strategy: fifo
  Output queue: 0/40 (size/max)
  5 minute input rate 0 bits/sec, 0 packets/sec
  5 minute output rate 0 bits/sec, 0 packets/sec
     4767 packets input, 317155 bytes, 0 no buffer
     Received 1713 broadcasts (0 IP multicasts)
     0 runts, 0 giants, 0 throttles
     1 input errors, 0 CRC, 0 frame, 0 overrun, 0 ignored, 1 abort
     4825 packets output, 316451 bytes, 0 underruns
     0 output errors, 0 collisions, 5 interface resets
```

```
        4 unknown protocol drops
        0 output buffer failures, 0 output buffers swapped out
        12 carrier transitions
        DCD=up  DSR=up  DTR=up  RTS=up  CTS=up
```

Based on your bandwidth configuration, try and determine what the R2 and R3 routing tables will look like before you issue a **show ip route** command. Are their routing tables the same or different?

_____

_____

_____

Step 4.   Configure G0/0 interface as passive on R1, R2, and R3.

A passive interface does not allow outgoing and incoming routing updates over the configured interface. The **passive-interface** *interface* command causes the router to stop sending and receiving Hello packets over an interface; however, the network associated with the interface is still advertised to other routers through the non-passive interfaces. Router interfaces connected to LANs are typically configured as passive.

```
R1(config)# router eigrp 10
R1(config-router)# passive-interface g0/0


R2(config)# router eigrp 10
R2(config-router)# passive-interface g0/0


R3(config)# router eigrp 10
R3(config-router)# passive-interface g0/0
```

Step 5.   Verify the passive interface configuration.

Issue a **show ip protocols** command on R1, R2, and R3 and verify that G0/0 has been configured as passive.

```
R1# show ip protocols
*** IP Routing is NSF aware ***

Routing Protocol is "eigrp 10"
  Outgoing update filter list for all interfaces is not set
  Incoming update filter list for all interfaces is not set
  Default networks flagged in outgoing updates
  Default networks accepted from incoming updates
  EIGRP-IPv4 Protocol for AS(10)
    Metric weight K1=1, K2=0, K3=1, K4=0, K5=0
    NSF-aware route hold timer is 240
    Router-ID: 192.168.1.1
    Topology : 0 (base)
      Active Timer: 3 min
      Distance: internal 90 external 170
      Maximum path: 4
      Maximum hopcount 100
      Maximum metric variance 1

Automatic Summarization: disabled
```

```
     Maximum path: 4
     Routing for Networks:
       10.1.1.0/30
       10.3.3.0/30
       192.168.1.0
     Passive Interface(s):
       GigabitEthernet0/0
     Routing Information Sources:
       Gateway           Distance        Last Update
       10.3.3.2                90        00:48:09
       10.1.1.2                90        00:48:26
     Distance: internal 90 external 170
```

Reflection

You could have used only static routing for this lab. What is an advantage of using EIGRP?

_____

_____

_____

Router Interface Summary Table

Router Interface Summary				
Router Model	Ethernet Interface #1	Ethernet Interface #2	Serial Interface #1	Serial Interface #2
1800	Fast Ethernet 0/0 (F0/0)	Fast Ethernet 0/1 (F0/1)	Serial 0/0/0 (S0/0/0)	Serial 0/0/1 (S0/0/1)
1900	Gigabit Ethernet 0/0 (G0/0)	Gigabit Ethernet 0/1 (G0/1)	Serial 0/0/0 (S0/0/0)	Serial 0/0/1 (S0/0/1)
2801	Fast Ethernet 0/0 (F0/0)	Fast Ethernet 0/1 (F0/1)	Serial 0/1/0 (S0/1/0)	Serial 0/1/1 (S0/1/1)
2811	Fast Ethernet 0/0 (F0/0)	Fast Ethernet 0/1 (F0/1)	Serial 0/0/0 (S0/0/0)	Serial 0/0/1 (S0/0/1)
2900	Gigabit Ethernet 0/0 (G0/0)	Gigabit Ethernet 0/1 (G0/1)	Serial 0/0/0 (S0/0/0)	Serial 0/0/1 (S0/0/1)

Note: To find out how the router is configured, look at the interfaces to identify the type of router and how many interfaces the router has. There is no way to effectively list all the combinations of configurations for each router class. This table includes identifiers for the possible combinations of Ethernet and Serial interfaces in the device. The table does not include any other type of interface, even though a specific router may contain one. An example of this might be an ISDN BRI interface. The string in parentheses is the legal abbreviation that can be used in Cisco IOS commands to represent the interface.

6.3.4.4 Packet Tracer–Investigating DUAL FSM

Topology

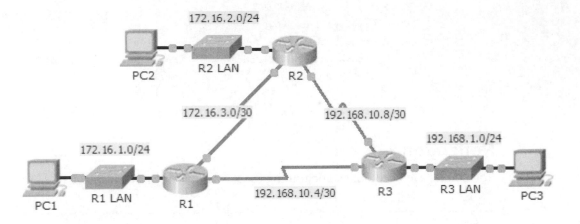

Addressing Table

Device	Interface	IP Address	Subnet Mask	Default Gateway
R1	G0/0	172.16.1.254	255.255.255.0	N/A
	S0/0/0	172.16.3.1	255.255.255.252	N/A
	S0/0/1	192.168.10.5	255.255.255.252	N/A
R2	G0/0	172.16.2.254	255.255.255.0	N/A
	S0/0/0	172.16.3.2	255.255.255.252	N/A
	S0/0/1	192.168.10.9	255.255.255.252	N/A
R3	G0/0	192.168.1.254	255.255.255.0	N/A
	S0/0/0	192.168.10.6	255.255.255.252	N/A
	S0/0/1	192.168.10.10	255.255.255.252	N/A
PC1	NIC	172.16.1.1	255.255.255.0	172.16.1.254
PC2	NIC	192.168.1.1	255.255.255.0	192.168.1.254
PC3	NIC	192.168.2.1	255.255.255.0	192.168.2.254

Objectives

Part 1: Verify the EIGRP Configuration

Part 2: Observe the EIGRP DUAL FSM

Background

In this activity, you will modify the EIGRP metric formula to cause a change in the topology. This will allow you to see how EIGRP reacts when a neighbor goes down due to unforeseen circumstances. You will then use the debug command to view topology changes and how the DUAL Finite State Machine determines successor and feasible successor paths to re-converge the network.

Part 1: Verify EIGRP Configuration

Step 1.   Examine the routing tables of each router and verify that there is a path to every network in the topology.

What command displays the routing table? _____

Are any of the routers load balancing between any network?

_____

Step 2.   Verify that each router has entries in its neighbor table.

What command displays the neighbor table?_____

How many neighbors does each router have? _____

Step 3.   Analyze the topology table of each router.

a.   What command displays the topology table? _____

Based on the output in the topology table, how many successor paths does each router have? _____

Why are there more successor paths than networks?

_____

_____

b.   Copy the output for **R1**'s topology table to a text editor so that you can refer to it later.

Part 2: Observe the EIGRP DUAL FSM

Step 1.   On R1, turn on the debugging feature that will display DUAL FSM notifications.

What command enables debugging for the EIGRP DUAL FSM? _____

Step 2.   Force a DUAL FSM update to generate debug output.

a.   Place the R1 and R3 windows side by side so that you can observe the debug output. Then on R3, disable the serial 0/0/0 interface.

```
R3(config)# interface s0/0/0
R3(config-if)# shutdown
```

b.   Do not disable debugging yet. What debug output indicated changes to the routing table?

_____

_____

_____

_____

Step 3.   Display the routing table of R1.

Verify that 192.168.10.4/30 network is no longer in **R1**'s routing table.

Describe any other changes to the **R1** routing table?

_____

Step 4.   Determine the difference in the topology table.

Examine the topology table of **R1** and compare it to the previous output from Part 1.

Are there any other changes to **R1**'s topology table?

_____

_____

Step 5.   Document changes in each router's neighbor table.

Examine the neighbor table of each router and compare it to the previous one from Part 1.

Are there any changes to the neighbor table?

_____

Step 6.   Restore connectivity between R1 and R2.

a.   With the R1 and R3 windows side by side, on R3 activate the serial 0/0/0 interface and observe the debug output on R1.

b.   Disable debugging by entering the **no** form of the debug command or simply enter **undebug** all. What debug output indicated changes to the routing table?

_____

_____

How did the DUAL FSM handle the change in topology when the route to **R1** came back up?

_____

_____

Suggested Scoring Rubric

Activity Section	Question Location	Possible Points	Earned Points
Part 1: Verify EIGRP Configuration	Step 1	12	
	Step 2	12	
	Step 3	12	
	Part 1 Total	36	
Part 2: Observe the EIGRP DUAL FSM	Step 1	10	
	Step 2	12	
	Step 3	10	
	Step 4	10	
	Step 5	10	
	Step 6	12	
	Part 2 Total	64	
	Total Score	100	

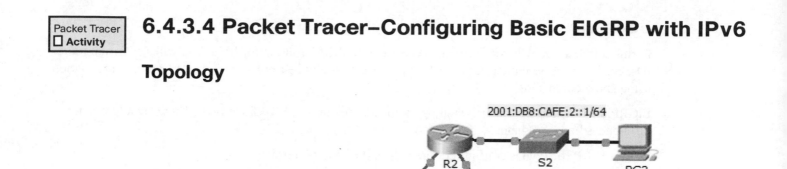

6.4.3.4 Packet Tracer–Configuring Basic EIGRP with IPv6

Packet Tracer
☐ Activity

Topology

2001:DB8:CAFE:2::1/64

R2

S2

PC2

2001:DB8:CAFE:A001::1/64

2001:DB8:CAFE:A002::1/64

2001:DB8:CAFE:1::1/64

2001:DB8:CAFE:3::1/64

PC1

S1

R1

2001:DB8:CAFE:A003::1/64

R3

S3

PC3

Addressing Table

Device	Interface	IPv6 Address	Default Gateway
R1	G0/0	2001:DB8:CAFE:1::1/64	N/A
	S0/0/0	2001:DB8:CAFE:A001::1/64	N/A
	S0/0/1	2001:DB8:CAFE:A003::1/64	N/A
	Link-local	FE80::1	N/A
R2	G0/0	2001:DB8:CAFE:2::1/64	N/A
	S0/0/0	2001:DB8:CAFE:A001::2/64	N/A
	S0/0/1	2001:DB8:CAFE:A002::1/64	N/A
	Link-local	FE80::2	N/A
R3	G0/0	2001:DB8:CAFE:3::1/64	N/A
	S0/0/0	2001:DB8:CAFE:A003::2/64	N/A
	S0/0/1	2001:DB8:CAFE:A002::2/64	N/A
	Link-local	FE80::3	N/A
PC1	NIC	2001:DB8:CAFE:1::3/64	Fe80::1
PC2	NIC	2001:DB8:CAFE:2::3/64	Fe80::2
PC3	NIC	2001:DB8:CAFE:3::3/64	Fe80::3

Objectives

Part 1: Configure EIGRP for IPv6 Routing

Part 2: Verify IPv6 EIGRP for IPv6 Routing

Scenario

In this activity, you will configure the network with EIGRP routing for IPv6. You will also assign router IDs, configure passive interfaces, verify the network is fully converged, and display routing information using **show** commands.

EIGRP for IPv6 has the same overall operation and features as EIGRP for IPv4. There are a few major differences between them:

- EIGRP for IPv6 is configured directly on the router interfaces.
- With EIGRP for IPv6, a router-id is required on each router or the routing process will not start.
- The EIGRP for IPv6 routing process uses a "shutdown" feature.

Part 1: Configure EIGRP for IPv6 Routing

Step 1.   Enable IPv6 routing on each router.

Step 2.   Enable EIGRP for IPv6 routing on each router.

The IPv6 routing process is shutdown by default. Issue a command that will enable EIGRP for IPv6 routing in R1, R2, and R3.

Enable the EIGRP process on all routers and use **1** as the Autonomous System number.

Step 3.   Assign a router ID to each router.

The router IDs are as follows:

- R1: 1.1.1.1
- R2: 2.2.2.2
- R3: 3.3.3.3

Step 4.   Using AS 1, configure EIGRP for IPv6 on each interface.

Part 2: Verify EIGRP for IPv6 Routing

Step 1.   Examine neighbor adjacencies.

Use the command **show ipv6 eigrp neighbors** to verify that the adjacency has been established with its neighboring routers. The link-local addresses of the neighboring routers are displayed in the adjacency table.

Step 2.   Examine the IPv6 EIGRP routing table.

Use the **show ipv6 route** command to display the IPv6 routing table on all routers. EIGRP for IPv6 routes are denoted in the routing table with a **D**.

Step 3.   Verify the parameters and current state of the active IPv6 routing protocol processes.

Use the command **show ipv6 protocols** to verify the configured parameter.

Step 4.   Verify end-to-end connectivity.

PC1, PC2, and PC3 should now be able to ping each other. If not, troubleshoot your EIGRP configurations.

6.4.3.5 Lab–Configuring Basic EIGRP for IPv6

Topology

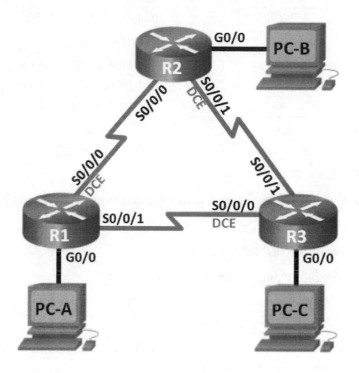

Addressing Table

Device	Interface	IP Address	Default Gateway
R1	G0/0	2001:DB8:ACAD:A::1/64	N/A
		FE80::1 link-local	
	S0/0/0 (DCE)	2001:DB8:ACAD:12::1/64	N/A
		FE80::1 link-local	
	S0/0/1	2001:DB8:ACAD:13::1/64	N/A
		FE80::1 link-local	
R2	G0/0	2001:DB8:ACAD:B::1/64	N/A
		FE80::2 link-local	
	S0/0/0	2001:DB8:ACAD:12::2/64	N/A
		FE80::2 link-local	
	S0/0/1 (DCE)	2001:DB8:ACAD:23::2/64	N/A
		FE80::2 link-local	
R3	G0/0	2001:DB8:ACAD:C::1/64	N/A
		FE80::3 link-local	

Device	Interface	IP Address	Default Gateway
	S0/0/0 (DCE)	2001:DB8:ACAD:13::3/64	N/A
		FE80::3 link-local	
	S0/0/1	2001:DB8:ACAD:23::3/64	N/A
		FE80::3 link-local	
PC-A	NIC	2001:DB8:ACAD:A::3/64	FE80::1
PC-B	NIC	2001:DB8:ACAD:B::3/64	FE80::2
PC-C	NIC	2001:DB8:ACAD:C::3/64	FE80::3

Objectives

Part 1: Build the Network and Verify Connectivity

Part 2: Configure EIGRP for IPv6 Routing

Part 3: Verify EIGRP for IPv6 Routing

Part 4: Configure and Verify Passive Interfaces

Background/Scenario

EIGRP for IPv6 has the same overall operation and features as EIGRP for IPv4. However, there are a few major differences between them:

- EIGRP for IPv6 is configured directly on the router interfaces.

- With EIGRP for IPv6, a router ID is required on each router or the routing process does not start.

- The EIGRP for IPv6 routing process uses a shutdown feature.

In this lab, you will configure the network with EIGRP routing for IPv6. You will also assign router IDs, configure passive interfaces, verify the network is fully converged, and display routing information using CLI **show** commands.

Note: The routers used with CCNA hands-on labs are Cisco 1941 Integrated Services Routers (ISRs) with Cisco IOS Release 15.2(4)M3 (universalk9 image). Other routers and Cisco IOS versions can be used. Depending on the model and Cisco IOS version, the commands available and output produced might vary from what is shown in the labs. Refer to the Router Interface Summary Table at the end of this lab for the correct interface identifiers.

Note: Make sure that the routers have been erased and have no startup configurations. If you are unsure, contact your instructor.

Required Resources

- 3 Routers (Cisco 1941 with Cisco IOS Release 15.2(4)M3 universal image or comparable)

- 3 PCs (Windows 7, Vista, or XP with terminal emulation program, such as Tera Term)

- Console cables to configure the Cisco IOS devices via the console ports

- Ethernet and serial cables as shown in the topology

Part 1: Build the Network and Verify Connectivity

In Part 1, you will set up the network topology and configure basic settings, such as the interface IP addresses, device access, and passwords.

Step 1.   Cable the network as shown in the topology.

Step 2.   Configure PC hosts.

Step 3.   Initialize and reload the routers as necessary.

Step 4.   Configure basic settings for each router.

    a.   Disable DNS lookup.

    b.   Configure IP addresses for the routers as listed in the Addressing Table.

Note: Configure the FE80::x link-local address and the unicast address for each router interface.

---

    c.   Configure the device name as shown in the topology.

    d.   Assign **cisco** as the console and vty passwords.

    e.   Assign **class** as the privileged EXEC password.

    f.   Configure **logging synchronous** to prevent console and vty messages from interrupting command entry.

    g.   Configure a message of the day.

    h.   Copy the running configuration to the startup configuration.

Step 5.   Verify connectivity.

The routers should be able to ping one another, and each PC should be able to ping its default gateway. The PCs will not be able to ping other PCs until EIGRP routing is configured. Verify and troubleshoot if necessary.

Part 2: Configure EIGRP for IPv6 Routing

Step 1.   Enable IPv6 routing on the routers.

```
R1(config)# ipv6 unicast-routing
```

Step 2.   Assign a router ID to each router.

    a.   To begin the EIGRP for IPv6 routing configuration process, issue the **ipv6 router eigrp 1** command, where **1** is the AS number.

```
R1(config)# ipv6 router eigrp 1
```

    b.   EIGRP for IPv6 requires a 32-bit address for the router ID. Use the **eigrp router-id** command to configure the router ID in the router configuration mode.

```
R1(config)# ipv6 router eigrp 1
R1(config-rtr)# eigrp router-id 1.1.1.1

R2(config)# ipv6 router eigrp 1
R2(config-rtr)# eigrp router-id 2.2.2.2

R3(config)# ipv6 router eigrp 1
R3(config-rtr)# eigrp router-id 3.3.3.3
```

Step 3.   Enable EIGRP for IPv6 routing on each router.

The IPv6 routing process is shut down by default. Issue the **no shutdown** command to enable EIGRP for IPv6 routing on all routers.

```
R1(config)# ipv6 router eigrp 1
R1(config-rtr)# no shutdown


R2(config)# ipv6 router eigrp 1
R2(config-rtr)# no shutdown


R3(config)# ipv6 router eigrp 1
R3(config-rtr)# no shutdown
```

Step 4.   Configure EIGRP for IPv6 using AS 1 on the Serial and Gigabit Ethernet interfaces on the routers.

a.   Issue the **ipv6 eigrp 1** command on the interfaces that participate in the EIGRP routing process. The AS number is 1 as assigned in Step 2. The configuration for R1 is displayed below as an example.

```
R1(config)# interface g0/0
R1(config-if)# ipv6 eigrp 1
R1(config-if)# interface s0/0/0
R1(config-if)# ipv6 eigrp 1
R1(config-if)# interface s0/0/1
R1(config-if)# ipv6 eigrp 1
```

b.   Assign EIGRP participating interfaces on R2 and R3. You will see neighbor adjacency messages as interfaces are added to the EIGRP routing process. The messages on R1 are displayed below as an example.

```
R1(config-if)#
*Apr 12 00:25:49.183: %DUAL-5-NBRCHANGE: EIGRP-IPv6 1: Neighbor FE80::2
(Serial0/0/0) is up: new adjacency
*Apr 12 00:26:15.583: %DUAL-5-NBRCHANGE: EIGRP-IPv6 1: Neighbor FE80::3
(Serial0/0/1) is up: new adjacency
```

What address is used to indicate the neighbor in the adjacency messages?

_____

Step 5.   Verify end-to-end connectivity.

Part 3: Verify EIGRP for IPv6 Routing

Step 1.   Examine the neighbor adjacencies.

On R1, issue the **show ipv6 eigrp neighbors** command to verify that the adjacency has been established with its neighboring routers. The link-local addresses of the neighboring routers are displayed in the adjacency table.

```
R1# show ipv6 eigrp neighbors
EIGRP-IPv6 Neighbors for AS(1)
```

H	Address	Interface	Hold (sec)	Uptime	SRTT (ms)	RTO	Q Cnt	Seq Num
1	Link-local address: FE80::3	Se0/0/1	13	00:02:42	1	100	0	7
0	Link-local address: FE80::2	Se0/0/0	13	00:03:09	12	100	0	9

Step 2.   Examine the IPv6 EIGRP routing table.

Use the **show ipv6 route eigrp** command to display IPv6 specific EIGRP routes on all the routers.

```
R1# show ipv6 route eigrp
IPv6 Routing Table - default - 10 entries
Codes: C - Connected, L - Local, S - Static, U - Per-user Static route
       B - BGP, R - RIP, I1 - ISIS L1, I2 - ISIS L2
       IA - ISIS interarea, IS - ISIS summary, D - EIGRP, EX - EIGRP external
       ND - ND Default, NDp - ND Prefix, DCE - Destination, NDr - Redirect
       O - OSPF Intra, OI - OSPF Inter, OE1 - OSPF ext 1, OE2 - OSPF ext 2
       ON1 - OSPF NSSA ext 1, ON2 - OSPF NSSA ext 2
D    2001:DB8:ACAD:B::/64 [90/2172416]
     via FE80::2, Serial0/0/0
D    2001:DB8:ACAD:C::/64 [90/2172416]
     via FE80::3, Serial0/0/1
D    2001:DB8:ACAD:23::/64 [90/2681856]
     via FE80::2, Serial0/0/0
     via FE80::3, Serial0/0/1
```

Step 3.   Examine the EIGRP topology.

```
R1# show ipv6 eigrp topology
EIGRP-IPv6 Topology Table for AS(1)/ID(1.1.1.1)
Codes: P - Passive, A - Active, U - Update, Q - Query, R - Reply,
       r - reply Status, s - sia Status

P 2001:DB8:ACAD:A::/64, 1 successors, FD is 28160
        via Connected, GigabitEthernet0/0
P 2001:DB8:ACAD:C::/64, 1 successors, FD is 2172416
        via FE80::3 (2172416/28160), Serial0/0/1
P 2001:DB8:ACAD:12::/64, 1 successors, FD is 2169856
        via Connected, Serial0/0/0
P 2001:DB8:ACAD:B::/64, 1 successors, FD is 2172416
        via FE80::2 (2172416/28160), Serial0/0/0
P 2001:DB8:ACAD:23::/64, 2 successors, FD is 2681856
        via FE80::2 (2681856/2169856), Serial0/0/0
        via FE80::3 (2681856/2169856), Serial0/0/1
P 2001:DB8:ACAD:13::/64, 1 successors, FD is 2169856
        via Connected, Serial0/0/1
```

Compare the highlighted entries to the routing table. What can you conclude from the comparison?

_____

_____

_____

Step 4. Verify the parameters and current state of the active IPv6 routing protocol processes.

Issue the **show ipv6 protocols** command to verify the configured parameter. From the output, EIGRP is the configured IPv6 routing protocol with 1.1.1.1 as the router ID for R1. This routing protocol is associated with autonomous system 1 with three active interfaces: G0/0, S0/0/0, and S0/0/1.

```
R1# show ipv6 protocols
IPv6 Routing Protocol is "connected"
IPv6 Routing Protocol is "ND"
IPv6 Routing Protocol is "eigrp 1"
EIGRP-IPv6 Protocol for AS(1)
  Metric weight K1=1, K2=0, K3=1, K4=0, K5=0
  NSF-aware route hold timer is 240
  Router-ID: 1.1.1.1
  Topology : 0 (base)
    Active Timer: 3 min
    Distance: internal 90 external 170
    Maximum path: 16
    Maximum hopcount 100
    Maximum metric variance 1

  Interfaces:
    GigabitEthernet0/0
    Serial0/0/0
    Serial0/0/1
  Redistribution:
    None
```

Part 4: Configure and Verify Passive Interfaces

A passive interface does not allow outgoing and incoming routing updates over the configured interface. The **passive-interface** *interface* command causes the router to stop sending and receiving Hello packets over an interface.

Step 1. Configure interface G0/0 as passive on R1 and R2.

```
R1(config)# ipv6 router eigrp 1
R1(config-rtr)# passive-interface g0/0

R2(config)# ipv6 router eigrp 1
R2(config-rtr)# passive-interface g0/0
```

Step 2. Verify the passive interface configuration.

Issue the **show ipv6 protocols** command on R1 and verify that G0/0 has been configured as passive.

```
R1# show ipv6 protocols
IPv6 Routing Protocol is "connected"
IPv6 Routing Protocol is "ND"
IPv6 Routing Protocol is "eigrp 1"
EIGRP-IPv6 Protocol for AS(1)
```

```
Metric weight K1=1, K2=0, K3=1, K4=0, K5=0
NSF-aware route hold timer is 240
Router-ID: 1.1.1.1
Topology : 0 (base)
  Active Timer: 3 min
  Distance: internal 90 external 170
  Maximum path: 16
  Maximum hopcount 100
  Maximum metric variance 1

Interfaces:
  Serial0/0/0
  Serial0/0/1
  GigabitEthernet0/0 (passive)
Redistribution:
  None
```

Step 3.   Configure the G0/0 passive interface on R3.

If a few interfaces are configured as passive, use the **passive-interface default** command to configure all the interfaces on the router as passive. Use the **no passive-interface** *interface* command to allow EIGRP Hello messages in and out of the router interface.

a.   Configure all interfaces as passive on R3.

```
R3(config)# ipv6 router eigrp 1
R3(config-rtr)# passive-interface default
R3(config-rtr)#
*Apr 13 00:07:03.267: %DUAL-5-NBRCHANGE: EIGRP-IPv6 1: Neighbor FE80::1
(Serial0/0/0) is down: interface passive
*Apr 13 00:07:03.267: %DUAL-5-NBRCHANGE: EIGRP-IPv6 1: Neighbor FE80::2
(Serial0/0/1) is down: interface passive
```

b.   After you have issued the **passive-interface default** command, R3 no longer participates in the routing process. What command can you use to verify it?

_____

c.   What command can you use to display the passive interfaces on R3?

_____

d.   Configure the serial interfaces to participate in the routing process.

```
R3(config)# ipv6 router eigrp 1
R3(config-rtr)# no passive-interface s0/0/0
R3(config-rtr)# no passive-interface s0/0/1
R3(config-rtr)#
*Apr 13 00:21:23.807: %DUAL-5-NBRCHANGE: EIGRP-IPv6 1: Neighbor FE80::1
(Serial0/0/0) is up: new adjacency
*Apr 13 00:21:25.567: %DUAL-5-NBRCHANGE: EIGRP-IPv6 1: Neighbor FE80::2
(Serial0/0/1) is up: new adjacency
```

e.   The neighbor relationships have been established again with R1 and R2. Verify that only G0/0 has been configured as passive. What command do you use to verify the passive interface?

_____

Reflection

1. Where would you configure passive interfaces? Why?

    _____

    _____

    _____

2. What are some advantages with using EIGRP as the routing protocol in your network?

    _____

    _____

    _____

Router Interface Summary Table

Router Interface Summary				
Router Model	Ethernet Interface #1	Ethernet Interface #2	Serial Interface #1	Serial Interface #2
1800	Fast Ethernet 0/0 (F0/0)	Fast Ethernet 0/1 (F0/1)	Serial 0/0/0 (S0/0/0)	Serial 0/0/1 (S0/0/1)
1900	Gigabit Ethernet 0/0 (G0/0)	Gigabit Ethernet 0/1 (G0/1)	Serial 0/0/0 (S0/0/0)	Serial 0/0/1 (S0/0/1)
2801	Fast Ethernet 0/0 (F0/0)	Fast Ethernet 0/1 (F0/1)	Serial 0/1/0 (S0/1/0)	Serial 0/1/1 (S0/1/1)
2811	Fast Ethernet 0/0 (F0/0)	Fast Ethernet 0/1 (F0/1)	Serial 0/0/0 (S0/0/0)	Serial 0/0/1 (S0/0/1)
2900	Gigabit Ethernet 0/0 (G0/0)	Gigabit Ethernet 0/1 (G0/1)	Serial 0/0/0 (S0/0/0)	Serial 0/0/1 (S0/0/1)

Note: To find out how the router is configured, look at the interfaces to identify the type of router and how many interfaces the router has. There is no way to effectively list all the combinations of configurations for each router class. This table includes identifiers for the possible combinations of Ethernet and Serial interfaces in the device. The table does not include any other type of interface, even though a specific router may contain one. An example of this might be an ISDN BRI interface. The string in parentheses is the legal abbreviation that can be used in Cisco IOS commands to represent the interface.

6.5.1.1 Class Activity–Portfolio RIP and EIGRP

Objectives

Configure EIGRP for IPv4 in a small routed network (review).

Scenario

You are preparing a portfolio file for comparison of RIP and EIGRP routing protocols.

Think of a network with three interconnected routers with each router providing a LAN for PCs, printers, and other end devices.

In this modeling activity scenario, you will be creating, addressing, and configuring a topology, using verification commands, and comparing/contrasting RIP and EIGRP routing protocol outputs.

Complete the PDF reflection questions. Save your work and be prepared to share your answers with the class. Also save a copy of this activity for later use within this course or for portfolio reference.

Resources

Packet Tracer and word processing software programs

Directions

Step 1.   WAN and LAN topology design

    a.   Use Packet Tracer to design a network with three routers (1941 model, suggested). If necessary, add NIC cards to the routers to provide connectivity to the routers to provide for at least one LAN to each router. Add at least one PC to each LAN.

    b.   Address the networks. You may use a flat addressing scheme or VLSM. Use only IPv4 networks for this entire activity.

Step 2.   Copy the topology

    a.   Highlight the entire topology by using your cursor.

    b.   Use Ctrl+C to make a copy of the highlighted topology.

    c.   Use Ctrl+V to insert a full copy of the topology to the desktop of Packet Tracer. You will now have displayed two exact, IPv4-addressed topologies with which to work for routing protocols configurations.

    d.   While highlighted, move the copied topology to a different location on the Packet Tracer desktop to create room between the two for configuration purposes.

Step 3.   Configure RIP and EIGRP on the separate topologies.

    a.   Configure the RIP routing protocol on the first topology and EIGRP on the second routing topology.

    b.   Once you have successfully configured RIP on one topology and EIGRP on the other, check to make sure your PCs can ping each other.

    c.   Save your work so no configuration information is lost.

Step 4.   Use verification commands to check output for the routing protocols.

   a.   To compare/contrast routing protocol information from the two topologies, issue the **show ip route** command on R1 for topology 1 and 2.

   b.   Copy the output into a table in your word processing program file. Label each column with RIP or EIGRP and place the output you received from the **show ip route** command.

   c.   Issue the **show ip protocols** command on R1 for topology table 1 and 2. Create another table in your word processing software file and place the output information below RIP or EIGRP.

   d.   Issue the **show cdp neighbors** command on R1's topology 1. Copy the output to a third table with RIP as the heading and issue the **show ip eigrp neighbors** command on R1's topology 2. Copy the output from this command in column 2 of table 3 under the heading EIGRP.

Reflection

1. Compare and contrast the output for the **show ip route** verification command.

   _____

   _____

   _____

   _____

   _____

2. Compare and contrast the output for the **show ip protocol** verification command.

   _____

   _____

   _____

   _____

   _____

3. Compare and contrast the **show cdp neighbors** command for the RIP topology and the **show ip eigrp neighbors** command for the EIGRP topology.

   _____

   _____

   _____

   _____

   _____

4. After comparing and contrasting the RIP and EIGRP output, which do you find most informative? Support your answer.

   _____

   _____

   _____

   _____

   _____

CHAPTER 7

EIGRP Tuning and Troubleshooting

This chapter reviews the various ways you can adjust your Enhanced Interior Gateway Routing Protocol (EIGRP) implementation to provide additional capabilities and functionality. In addition, troubleshooting EIGRP is also covered.

Study Guide

Advanced EIGRP Configurations

Now that you are familiar with the basic configuration and verification commands for implementing EIGRP, this section focuses on ways you can tweak the implementation to improve performance.

Automatic Summarization

Before Cisco IOS 15.01(1)M and 12.2(33), automatic summarization in EIGRP was enabled by default. Briefly explain the concept of automatic summarization.

_____

_____

Assume an EIGRP router is using automatic summarization. In Table 7-1, record the classful address advertised by the router for each listing of subnets.

Table 7-1   Determine the Classful Networks Advertised by an EIGRP Router

Subnets	Classful Networks
10.10.10.0/24, 10.10.11.0/24, 10.10.12.0/24	
172.16.16.0/22, 172.16.18.0/22	
192.168.1.0/25, 192.168.1.128/25, 192.168.2.0/25, 192.168.2.128/25	

EIGRP automatic summarization should be used only if you are absolutely sure that you do not have any discontiguous subnets. For example, in Figure 7-1, the addressing scheme is discontiguous.

Figure 7-1   EIGRP Automatic Summarization Topology with Discontiguous Subnets

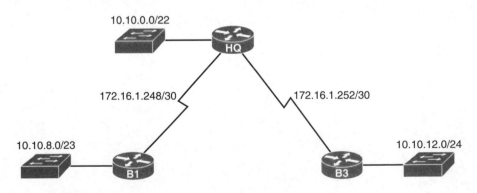

If you enable automatic summarization on the routers, they will not advertise the specific subnets that belong to 10.0.0.0/8 across the 172.16.0.0 WAN links. Instead, they automatically summarize the subnets to 10.0.0.0/8 and advertise the classful network. But each router already has a link in the 10.0.0.0/8 address space, so the update from the neighbor is stored in the topology table. No routes to the subnets are installed.

Automatic summarization is disabled by default in IOS 15 and later. What command including the router prompt will enable automatic summarization?

You can verify whether automatic summarization is enabled with the _____ command displayed in Example 7-1 for HQ from Figure 7-1.

Example 7-1   Verifying Automatic Summarization Is in Effect

```
HQ# _____
*** IP Routing is NSF aware ***


Routing Protocol is "eigrp 1"
  Outgoing update filter list for all interfaces is not set
  Incoming update filter list for all interfaces is not set
  Default networks flagged in outgoing updates
  Default networks accepted from incoming updates
  EIGRP-IPv4 Protocol for AS(1)
    Metric weight K1=1, K2=0, K3=1, K4=0, K5=0
    NSF-aware route hold timer is 240
    Router-ID: 2.2.2.2
    Topology : 0 (base)
      Active Timer: 3 min
      Distance: internal 90 external 170
      Maximum path: 4
      Maximum hopcount 100
      Maximum metric variance 1


  Automatic Summarization: enabled
    172.16.0.0/16 for Gi0/0
      Summarizing 2 components with metric 2169856
    10.0.0.0/8 for Se0/0/0, Se0/0/1
      Summarizing 1 component with metric 28160
  Maximum path: 4
  Routing for Networks:
    10.0.0.0
    172.16.0.0
  Routing Information Sources:
    Gateway         Distance      Last Update
    172.16.1.254          90      00:01:30
    172.16.1.250          90      00:01:30
  Distance: internal 90 external 170
```

To view the entire EIGRP topology table for HQ, use the _____ command to generate the output displayed in Example 7-2.

Example 7-2   Viewing the Complete EIGRP Topology Table

```
HQ# _____
EIGRP-IPv4 Topology Table for AS(1)/ID(2.2.2.2)
Codes: P - Passive, A - Active, U - Update, Q - Query, R - Reply,
       r - reply Status, s - sia Status


P 172.16.1.248/30, 1 successors, FD is 2169856, serno 2
        via Connected, Serial0/0/0
P 172.16.0.0/16, 1 successors, FD is 2169856, serno 4
        via Summary (2169856/0), Null0
P 10.0.0.0/8, 1 successors, FD is 28160, serno 3
        via Summary (28160/0), Null0
        via 172.16.1.250 (2172416/28160), Serial0/0/0
        via 172.16.1.254 (2172416/28160), Serial0/0/1
P 172.16.1.252/30, 1 successors, FD is 2169856, serno 8
        via Connected, Serial0/0/1
P 10.10.0.0/22, 1 successors, FD is 28160, serno 1
        via Connected, GigabitEthernet0/0
```

You can see that HQ has a route for 10.0.0.0/8 from both B1 and B3 in its topology table. However, it also has its own summary route with a better metric. This is the route installed and used by HQ, as verified with the _____ command displayed in Example 7-3.

Example 7-3   Verifying the Summary Route Installed on HQ

```
HQ# _____
Gateway of last resort is not set


      10.0.0.0/8 is variably subnetted, 3 subnets, 3 masks
D        10.0.0.0/8 is a summary, 00:08:42, Null0
      172.16.0.0/16 is variably subnetted, 5 subnets, 3 masks
D        172.16.0.0/16 is a summary, 00:09:01, Null0
```

Briefly explain the purpose of the Null0 interface.

Default Route Propagation

Propagating a default route in EIGRP requires one additional command in your EIGRP configuration. What is the command, including the router prompt, for both IPv4 and IPv6?

IPv4:

IPv6:

Figure 7-2 shows the same EIGRP topology we used in Chapter 6, "EIGRP." However, now the topology shows the contracted bandwidth rates on each of the serial interfaces. We will use that information later to tune how EIGRP chooses the best route.

Figure 7-2 Dual-Stacked EIGRP Topology with Bandwidths

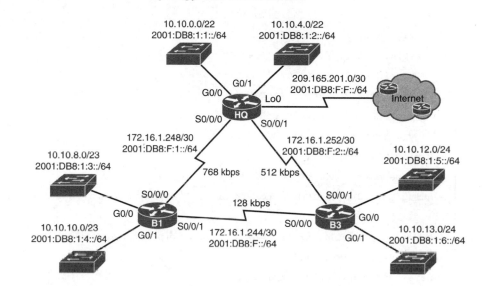

Figure 7-2 is using a loopback interface to simulate a connection to the Internet. Record the commands to configure an IPv4 default route, IPv6 default route, and redistribute the routes to B1 and B3.

If you are following along in a simulator or on lab equipment, your verification output for B1 and B3 should look like Example 7-4.

Example 7-4 EIGRP Routing Tables with Default Route Propagation

```
B1# show ip route eigrp | begin Gateway
Gateway of last resort is 172.16.1.249 to network 0.0.0.0


D*EX  0.0.0.0/0 [170/2297856] via 172.16.1.249, 00:12:58, Serial0/0/0
      10.0.0.0/8 is variably subnetted, 7 subnets, 4 masks
D        10.10.0.0/21 [90/2172416] via 172.16.1.249, 06:04:19, Serial0/0/0
D        10.10.8.0/22 is a summary, 00:05:31, Null0
D        10.10.12.0/23 [90/2172416] via 172.16.1.246, 06:04:19, Serial0/0/1
      172.16.0.0/16 is variably subnetted, 5 subnets, 2 masks
D        172.16.1.252/30 [90/2681856] via 172.16.1.249, 06:04:19, Serial0/0/0
                         [90/2681856] via 172.16.1.246, 06:04:19, Serial0/0/1
B1# show ipv6 route eigrp | begin EX  ::/0
```

```
EX  ::/0 [170/2169856]
        via FE80::2, Serial0/0/0
D   2001:DB8:1:1::/64 [90/2172416]
        via FE80::2, Serial0/0/0
D   2001:DB8:1:2::/64 [90/2172416]
        via FE80::2, Serial0/0/0
D   2001:DB8:1:6::/64 [90/2172416]
        via FE80::3, Serial0/0/1
D   2001:DB8:F:2::/64 [90/2681856]
        via FE80::2, Serial0/0/0
        via FE80::3, Serial0/0/1
B1# ping 209.165.201.1
Type escape sequence to abort.
Sending 5, 100-byte ICMP Echos to 209.165.201.1, timeout is 2 seconds:
!!!!!
Success rate is 100 percent (5/5), round-trip min/avg/max = 1/1/4 ms
B1# ping 2001:db8:f:f::1
Type escape sequence to abort.
Sending 5, 100-byte ICMP Echos to 2001:DB8:F:F::1, timeout is 2 seconds:
!!!!!
Success rate is 100 percent (5/5), round-trip min/avg/max = 1/1/4 ms
```

```
B3# show ip route eigrp | begin Gateway
Gateway of last resort is 172.16.1.253 to network 0.0.0.0


D*EX  0.0.0.0/0 [170/2297856] via 172.16.1.253, 00:13:32, Serial0/0/1
        10.0.0.0/8 is variably subnetted, 7 subnets, 5 masks
D        10.10.0.0/21 [90/2172416] via 172.16.1.253, 06:04:52, Serial0/0/1
D        10.10.8.0/22 [90/2172416] via 172.16.1.245, 06:04:52, Serial0/0/0
D        10.10.12.0/23 is a summary, 06:05:05, Null0
        172.16.0.0/16 is variably subnetted, 5 subnets, 2 masks
D        172.16.1.248/30 [90/2681856] via 172.16.1.253, 06:04:52, Serial0/0/1
                        [90/2681856] via 172.16.1.245, 06:04:52, Serial0/0/0
B3# show ipv6 route eigrp | begin EX  ::/0
EX  ::/0 [170/2169856]
        via FE80::2, Serial0/0/1
D   2001:DB8:1:1::/64 [90/2172416]
        via FE80::2, Serial0/0/1
D   2001:DB8:1:2::/64 [90/2172416]
        via FE80::2, Serial0/0/1
D   2001:DB8:1:4::/64 [90/2172416]
        via FE80::1, Serial0/0/0
D   2001:DB8:F:1::/64 [90/2681856]
        via FE80::1, Serial0/0/0
        via FE80::2, Serial0/0/1
```

```
B3# ping 209.165.201.1
Type escape sequence to abort.
Sending 5, 100-byte ICMP Echos to 209.165.201.1, timeout is 2 seconds:
!!!!!
Success rate is 100 percent (5/5), round-trip min/avg/max = 1/2/4 ms
B3# ping 2001:db8:f:f::1
Type escape sequence to abort.
Sending 5, 100-byte ICMP Echos to 2001:DB8:F:F::1, timeout is 2 seconds:
!!!!!
Success rate is 100 percent (5/5), round-trip min/avg/max = 1/1/4 ms
```

Fine-Tuning EIGRP Interfaces

Bandwidth Utilization

By default, EIGRP will use only up to 50 percent of the bandwidth of an interface for EIGRP information. This prevents the EIGRP process from overutilizing a link and not allowing enough bandwidth for the routing of normal traffic.

The _____ command can be used to configure the percentage of bandwidth that may be used by EIGRP on an interface. Record the full syntax for this command.

_____

This command uses the amount of configured bandwidth (or the default bandwidth) when calculating the percent that EIGRP can use.

Hello Intervals and Holdtimes

Hello intervals and holdtimes are configurable on a per-interface basis and do not have to match with other EIGRP routers to establish adjacencies.

Record the command to configure a different Hello interval.

_____

If you change the Hello interval, make sure that you also change the holdtime to a value equal to or greater than the Hello interval. Otherwise, neighbor adjacency will go down after the holdtime expires and before the next Hello interval.

Record the command to configure a different holdtime.

_____

EIGRP has different default Hello intervals and holdtimes based on the type of link. Complete Table 7-2 with the default values.

Table 7-2   Default Hello Intervals and Holdtimes for EIGRP

Bandwidth	Example Link	Default Hello Interval	Default Holdtime
1.544 Mbps	Multipoint Frame Relay, T1		
Greater Than 1.544 Mbps	Ethernet		

Load Balancing

Briefly describe equal-cost load balancing.

_____

_____

By default, EIGRP uses up to four equal-cost paths to load balance traffic. You can see load balancing in effect in the routing tables shown in the previous Example 7-4.

The reason EIGRP is load balancing is that we have not configured the actual bandwidth shown in Figure 7-2.

Record the commands to configure the routers with the correct bandwidth values.

_____

_____

_____

_____

_____

_____

_____

_____

_____

_____

_____

_____

Once the routers are properly configured with the actual bandwidth values, EIGRP recalculates the metrics and installs the best route in the routing table, as shown in Example 7-5. Notice that B1 and B3 are no longer using the 128-Kbps link to route to each other's LANs. Instead, they are each using the faster path through HQ.

Example 7-5   EIGRP Routing Tables After Bandwidth Configuration

```
B1# show ip route eigrp | begin Gateway
Gateway of last resort is 172.16.1.249 to network 0.0.0.0


D*EX  0.0.0.0/0 [170/3973120] via 172.16.1.249, 00:05:50, Serial0/0/0
      10.0.0.0/8 is variably subnetted, 7 subnets, 4 masks
D        10.10.0.0/21 [90/3847680] via 172.16.1.249, 00:05:50, Serial0/0/0
D      10.10.8.0/22 is a summary, 00:05:21, Null0
D      10.10.12.0/23 [90/6026496] via 172.16.1.249, 00:05:21, Serial0/0/0
      172.16.0.0/16 is variably subnetted, 5 subnets, 2 masks
D      172.16.1.252/30 [90/6023936] via 172.16.1.249, 00:05:31, Serial0/0/0
B1# show ipv6 route eigrp | begin EX  ::/0
EX  ::/0 [170/3845120]
    via FE80::2, Serial0/0/0
```

```
D    2001:DB8:1:1::/64 [90/3847680]
       via FE80::2, Serial0/0/0
D    2001:DB8:1:2::/64 [90/3847680]
       via FE80::2, Serial0/0/0
D    2001:DB8:1:6::/64 [90/6026496]
       via FE80::2, Serial0/0/0
D    2001:DB8:F:2::/64 [90/6023936]
       via FE80::2, Serial0/0/0
B3# show ip route eigrp | begin Gateway
Gateway of last resort is 172.16.1.253 to network 0.0.0.0

D*EX  0.0.0.0/0 [170/5639936] via 172.16.1.253, 00:05:43, Serial0/0/1
        10.0.0.0/8 is variably subnetted, 7 subnets, 5 masks
D         10.10.0.0/21 [90/5514496] via 172.16.1.253, 00:05:43, Serial0/0/1
D         10.10.8.0/22 [90/6026496] via 172.16.1.253, 00:05:43, Serial0/0/1
D         10.10.12.0/23 is a summary, 00:06:11, Null0
        172.16.0.0/16 is variably subnetted, 5 subnets, 2 masks
D         172.16.1.248/30 [90/6023936] via 172.16.1.253, 00:05:43, Serial0/0/1
B3# show ipv6 route eigrp | begin EX  ::/0
EX   ::/0 [170/5511936]
       via FE80::2, Serial0/0/1
D    2001:DB8:1:1::/64 [90/5514496]
       via FE80::2, Serial0/0/1
D    2001:DB8:1:2::/64 [90/5514496]
       via FE80::2, Serial0/0/1
D    2001:DB8:1:4::/64 [90/6026496]
       via FE80::2, Serial0/0/1
D    2001:DB8:F:1::/64 [90/6023936]
       via FE80::2, Serial0/0/1
```

Packet Tracer Exercise 7-1: Fine-Tuning EIGRP

Now you are ready to use Packet Tracer to apply your documented configuration. Download and open the file LSG03-0701.pka found at the companion website for this book. Refer to the Introduction of this book for specifics on accessing files.

Note: The following instructions are also contained within the Packet Tracer Exercise.

In this Packet Tracer activity, you will configure HQ to propagate default routes. You will also configure interfaces to reflect the correct bandwidth. You will then verify that the PCs can ping the Web Server at both the IPv4 and IPv6 address. Use the commands you documented in this chapter.

Requirements

- Configure HQ with an IPv4 and IPv6 default route. Use the exit interface argument.
- Configure HQ to propagate the IPv4 and IPv6 default routes to B1 and B3.

- Configure serial interfaces for the appropriate bandwidth values.
- Verify that the PCs can ping the Web Server.

Your completion percentage should be 100%. All the connectivity tests should show a status of "successful." If not, click **Check Results** to see which required components are not yet completed.

Troubleshoot EIGRP

This section reviews the tools and procedures to troubleshoot EIGRP issues.

Commands for Troubleshooting EIGRP

In Table 7-3, the IPv4 version of the troubleshooting commands for EIGRP are listed. The same commands are available for IPv6. Indicate which command or commands you would use to answer each of the questions.

Table 7-3   Diagnosing EIGRP Connectivity Issues

Command	Is the Neighbor Table Correct?	Is the Routing Table Correct?	Does Traffic Take the Desired Path?
show ip eigrp neighbors			
show ip interface brief			
show ip eigrp interface			
show ip protocols			
show ip route eigrp			

Troubleshoot EIGRP Connectivity Issues

Using the configuration for the devices in Figure 7-2 and the following command outputs, diagnose the EIGRP connectivity issue and recommend a solution.

Connectivity Issue #1

HQ and B1 have not formed a neighbor adjacency. Use the output in Example 7-6 to troubleshoot the first issue.

Example 7-6   Troubleshooting Command Output for Issue #1

```
HQ# show ip eigrp neighbors
EIGRP-IPv4 Neighbors for AS(1)
H   Address                 Interface            Hold Uptime   SRTT   RTO  Q   Seq
                                                 (sec)         (ms)        Cnt Num
0   172.16.1.254            Se0/0/1              10 00:23:18   1      288  0   65
HQ# show ip interface brief
Interface               IP-Address      OK? Method Status                Protocol
Embedded-Service-Engine0/0 unassigned   YES unset  administratively down down
GigabitEthernet0/0      10.10.0.1       YES manual up                    up
```

```
GigabitEthernet0/1          10.10.4.1       YES manual up                    up
Serial0/0/0                 172.16.1.250    YES manual up                    up
Serial0/0/1                 172.16.1.253    YES manual up                    up
Loopback0                   209.165.201.1   YES manual up                    up
B1# show ip eigrp neighbors
EIGRP-IPv4 Neighbors for AS(1)
H   Address                 Interface           Hold Uptime   SRTT    RTO   Q   Seq
                                                (sec)         (ms)          Cnt Num
1   172.16.1.246            Se0/0/1             12 00:26:47   9     1170  0   67
B1# show ip interface brief
Interface                   IP-Address      OK? Method Status              Protocol
Embedded-Service-Engine0/0  unassigned      YES unset  administratively down down
GigabitEthernet0/0          10.10.8.1       YES manual up                    up
GigabitEthernet0/1          10.10.10.1      YES manual up                    up
Serial0/0/0                 172.16.1.250    YES manual up                    up
Serial0/0/1                 172.16.1.245    YES manual up                    up
```

Problem and Solution:

_____

_____

Connectivity Issue #2

HQ and B3 have not formed a neighbor adjacency. Example 7-7 displays the output for the second issue.

Example 7-7   Troubleshooting Command Output for Issue #2

```
HQ# show ipv6 eigrp neighbors
EIGRP-IPv6 Neighbors for AS(1)
H   Address                 Interface           Hold Uptime   SRTT    RTO   Q   Seq
                                                (sec)         (ms)          Cnt Num
0   Link-local address:     Se0/0/0             14 05:12:49   1     186   0   57
    FE80::1
B3# show ipv6 eigrp neighbors
EIGRP-IPv6 Neighbors for AS(2)
```

Problem and Solution:

_____

_____

Connectivity Issue #3

Although the IPv6 routes look correct, B3 is using a less-than-optimal route to reach the B1 and HQ IPv4 LANs. Use the output in Example 7-8 to troubleshoot the third issue.

Example 7-8   Troubleshooting Command Output for Issue #3

```
HQ# show ip protocols
*** IP Routing is NSF aware ***


Routing Protocol is "eigrp 1"
  Outgoing update filter list for all interfaces is not set
  Incoming update filter list for all interfaces is not set
  Default networks flagged in outgoing updates
  Default networks accepted from incoming updates
  Redistributing: static
  EIGRP-IPv4 Protocol for AS(1)
    Metric weight K1=1, K2=0, K3=1, K4=0, K5=0
    NSF-aware route hold timer is 240
    Router-ID: 2.2.2.2
    Topology : 0 (base)
      Active Timer: 3 min
      Distance: internal 90 external 170
      Maximum path: 4
      Maximum hopcount 100
      Maximum metric variance 1


  Automatic Summarization: disabled
  Address Summarization:
    10.10.0.0/21 for Se0/0/0, Se0/0/1
      Summarizing 2 components with metric 28160
  Maximum path: 4
  Routing for Networks:
    10.0.0.0
    172.16.0.0
  Passive Interface(s):
    GigabitEthernet0/0
    GigabitEthernet0/1
    Serial0/0/1
  Routing Information Sources:
    Gateway         Distance      Last Update
    172.16.1.254          90      00:17:55
    172.16.1.250          90      00:00:41
  Distance: internal 90 external 170
B3# show ip route eigrp | begin Gateway
Gateway of last resort is 172.16.1.245 to network 0.0.0.0


D*EX  0.0.0.0/0 [170/21152000] via 172.16.1.245, 00:08:32, Serial0/0/0
      10.0.0.0/8 is variably subnetted, 7 subnets, 5 masks
```

```
D         10.10.0.0/21 [90/21026560] via 172.16.1.245, 00:08:32, Serial0/0/0
D         10.10.8.0/22 [90/20514560] via 172.16.1.245, 00:08:32, Serial0/0/0
D         10.10.12.0/23 is a summary, 04:39:57, Null0
      172.16.0.0/16 is variably subnetted, 5 subnets, 2 masks
D         172.16.1.248/30 [90/21024000] via 172.16.1.245, 00:08:32, Serial0/0/0
B3# show ipv6 route eigrp | begin EX  ::/0
EX  ::/0 [170/5511936]
    via FE80::2, Serial0/0/1
D   2001:DB8:1:1::/64 [90/5514496]
    via FE80::2, Serial0/0/1
D   2001:DB8:1:2::/64 [90/5514496]
    via FE80::2, Serial0/0/1
D   2001:DB8:1:4::/64 [90/6026496]
    via FE80::2, Serial0/0/1
D   2001:DB8:F:1::/64 [90/6023936]
    via FE80::2, Serial0/0/1
```

Problem and Solution:

Labs and Activities

Command Reference

In Table 7-4, record the command, including the correct router or switch prompt, that fits the description. Fill in any blanks with the appropriate missing information.

Table 7-4   Commands for Chapter 7, EIGRP Tuning and Troubleshooting

Command	Description
	Enable EIGRP automatic summarization for R1.
	List the command that will verify that automatic summarization is enabled.
	List the command that will display entire EIGRP for IPv4 topology table.
	List the command to propagate a default route in the EIGRP for IPv4 routing process.
	List the command to propagate a default route in the EIGRP for IPv6 routing process.
	Configure an interface to only use 25% of its bandwidth for EIGRP updates.
	Configure an interface to send out EIGRP hello packets every 10 seconds.
	Configure an interface to use 2048 kbps as the bandwidth.

7.0.1.2 Class Activity–EIGRP–Back to the Future

Objectives

Implement advanced EIGRP features to enhance operation in a small to medium-sized business network.

Scenario

Many of these concepts in the bulleted list below were mentioned in the previous chapter's curriculum content and will be the focus of this chapter:

- Auto-summarization
- Load balancing
- Default routes
- Hold-down timers

With a partner, write 10 EIGRP review questions based on the previous chapter's curriculum content. Three of the questions must focus on the bulleted items above. Ideally, Multiple Choice, True/False, or Fill in the Blank question types will be designed. As you design your questions, make sure you record the curriculum section and page numbers of the supporting content in case you need to refer back for answer verification.

Save your work and then meet with another group, or the entire class, and quiz them using the questions you developed.

Resources

- Word processing software program
- Curriculum content from the previous chapter

Packet Tracer
☐ Activity

7.1.2.4 Packet Tracer–Propagating a Default Route in EIGRP for IPv4 and IPv6

Topology

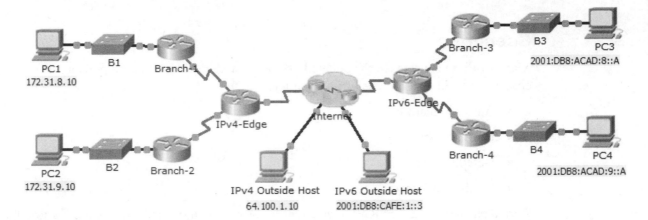

Addressing Table

Device	Interface	IPv4 Address	Subnet Mask
		IPv6 Address/Prefix	
IPv4-Edge	S0/0/0	172.31.6.1	255.255.255.0
	S0/0/1	172.31.7.1	255.255.255.0
	S0/1/0	209.165.200.226	255.255.255.224
Branch-1	G0/0	172.31.8.1	255.255.255.0
	S0/0/0	172.31.6.2	255.255.255.0
Branch-2	G0/0	172.31.9.1	255.255.255.0
	S0/0/1	172.31.7.2	255.255.255.0
IPv6-Edge	S0/0/0	2001:DB8:ACAD:7::1/64	
	S0/0/1	2001:DB8:ACAD:6::1/64	
	S0/1/0	2001:DB8:CAFE:ABCD::2/164	
Branch-3	G0/0	2001:DB8:ACAD:8::1/64	
	S0/0/0	2001:DB8:ACAD:7::2/64	
Branch-4	G0/0	2001:DB8:ACAD:9::1/64	
	S0/0/1	2001:DB8:ACAD:6:::2/64	

Objectives

Part 1: Propagate an IPv4 Default Route

Part 2: Propagate an IPv6 Default Route

Part 3: Verify Connectivity to Outside Hosts

Scenario

In this activity, you will configure and propagate a default route in EIGRP for IPv4 and IPv6 networks. EIGRP is already configured. However, you are required to configure an IPv4 and an IPv6 default route. Then, you will configure the EIGRP routing process to propagate the default route to downstream EIGRP neighbors. Finally, you will verify the default routes by pinging hosts outside the EIGRP routing domain.

Part 1: Propagate a Default Route in EIGRP for IPv4

Step 1.   Verify EIGRP configuration on each IPv4 enabled router.

Display the routing table of each IPv4 enabled router and verify that all IPv4 routes are visible.

Step 2.   Configure an IPv4 default route.

Configure a directly connected IPv4 default route on **IPv4-Edge**.

Step 3.   Propagate the default route in EIGRP.

Configure the EIGRP routing process to propagate the default route.

Step 4.   Verify IPv4 default route is propagating.

Display the routing tables for **Branch-1** and **Branch-2** to verify the default route is now installed.

Part 2: Propagate a Default Route in EIGRP for IPv6

Step 1.   Verify EIGRP configuration on each IPv6 enabled router.

Display the routing table of each IPv6 enabled router and verify that all IPv6 routes are visible.

Step 2.   Configure an IPv6 default route.

Configure a directly connected IPv6 default route on **IPv6-Edge**.

Step 3.   Propagate the default route in EIGRP.

Configure the EIGRP routing process to propagate the default route.

Step 4.   Verify IPv6 default route is propagating.

Display the routing tables for **Branch-3** and **Branch-4** to verify the default route is now installed.

Part 3: Verify Connectivity to Outside Hosts

- PC1 and PC2 should now be able to ping **IPv4 Outside Host**.
- PC3 and PC4 should now be able to ping **IPv6 Outside Host**.

7.1.3.6 Lab–Configuring Advanced EIGRP for IPv4 Features

Topology

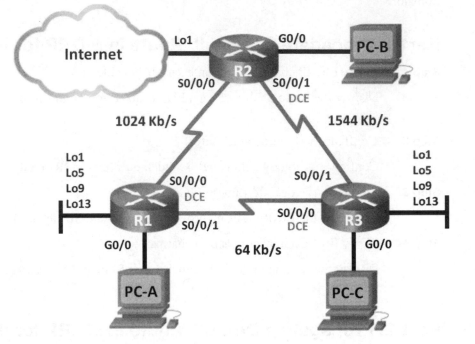

Addressing Table

Device	Interface	IP Address	Subnet Mask	Default Gateway
R1	G0/0	192.168.1.1	255.255.255.0	N/A
	S0/0/0 (DCE)	192.168.12.1	255.255.255.252	N/A
	S0/0/1	192.168.13.1	255.255.255.252	N/A
	Lo1	192.168.11.1	255.255.255.252	N/A
	Lo5	192.168.11.5	255.255.255.252	N/A
	Lo9	192.168.11.9	255.255.255.252	N/A
	Lo13	192.168.11.13	255.255.255.252	N/A
R2	G0/0	192.168.2.1	255.255.255.0	N/A
	S0/0/0	192.168.12.2	255.255.255.252	N/A
	S0/0/1 (DCE)	192.168.23.1	255.255.255.252	N/A
	Lo1	192.168.22.1	255.255.255.252	N/A

Device	Interface	IP Address	Subnet Mask	Default Gateway
R3	G0/0	192.168.3.1	255.255.255.0	N/A
	S0/0/0 (DCE)	192.168.13.2	255.255.255.252	N/A
	S0/0/1	192.168.23.2	255.255.255.252	N/A
	Lo1	192.168.33.1	255.255.255.252	N/A
	Lo5	192.168.33.5	255.255.255.252	N/A
	Lo9	192.168.33.9	255.255.255.252	N/A
	Lo13	192.168.33.13	255.255.255.252	N/A
PC-A	NIC	192.168.1.3	255.255.255.0	192.168.1.1
PC-B	NIC	192.168.2.3	255.255.255.0	192.168.2.1
PC-C	NIC	192.168.3.3	255.255.255.0	192.168.3.1

Objectives

Part 1: Build the Network and Configure Basic Device Settings

Part 2: Configure EIGRP and Verify Connectivity

Part 3: Configure EIGRP for Automatic Summarization

Part 4: Configure and Propagate a Default Static Route

Part 5: Fine-Tune EIGRP

- Configure bandwidth utilization for EIGRP.

- Configure the hello interval and hold timer for EIGRP.

Background/Scenario

EIGRP has advanced features to allow changes related to summarization, default route propagation, bandwidth utilization, and metrics.

In this lab, you will configure automatic summarization for EIGRP, configure EIGRP route propagation, and fine-tune EIGRP metrics.

Note: The routers used with CCNA hands-on labs are Cisco 1941 Integrated Services Routers (ISRs) with Cisco IOS Release 15.2(4)M3 (universalk9 image). Other routers and Cisco IOS versions can be used. Depending on the model and Cisco IOS version, the commands available and output produced might vary from what is shown in the labs. Refer to the Router Interface Summary Table at the end of this lab for the correct interface identifiers.

Note: Ensure that the routers have been erased and have no startup configurations. If you are unsure, contact your instructor.

Required Resources

- 3 Routers (Cisco 1941 with Cisco IOS Release 15.2(4)M3 universal image or comparable)
- 3 PCs (Windows with a terminal emulation program, such as Tera Term)
- Console cables to configure the Cisco IOS devices via the console ports
- Ethernet and serial cables as shown in the topology

Part 1: Build the Network and Configure Basic Device Settings

In Part 1, you will set up the network topology and configure basic settings on the PC hosts and routers.

Step 1. Cable the network as shown in the topology.

Step 2. Configure PC hosts.

Step 3. Initialize and reload the routers as necessary.

Step 4. Configure basic settings for each router.

   a. Disable DNS lookup.

   b. Configure device name as shown in the topology.

   c. Assign **cisco** as the console and vty passwords.

   d. Assign **class** as the privileged EXEC password.

   e. Configure **logging synchronous** to prevent console messages from interrupting command entry.

   f. Configure the IP address listed in the Addressing Table for all interfaces.

Note: Do NOT configure the loopback interfaces at this time.

---

   g. Copy the running configuration to the startup configuration.

Part 2: Configure EIGRP and Verify Connectivity

In Part 2, you will configure basic EIGRP for the topology and set bandwidths for the serial interfaces.

Note: This lab provides minimal assistance with the actual commands necessary to configure EIGRP. However, the required commands are provided in Appendix A. Test your knowledge by trying to configure the devices without referring to the appendix.

Step 1. Configure EIGRP.

   a. On R1, configure EIGRP routing with an autonomous system (AS) ID of 1 for all directly connected networks. Write the commands used in the space below.

   _____

   _____

   _____

   _____

b. For the LAN interface on R1, disable the transmission of EIGRP hello packets. Write the command used in the space below.

_____

c. On R1, configure the bandwidth for S0/0/0 to 1024 Kb/s and the bandwidth for S0/0/1 to 64 Kb/s. Write the commands used in the space below. The **bandwidth** command only affects the EIGRP metric calculation, not the actual bandwidth of the serial link.

_____

_____

_____

_____

d. On R2, configure EIGRP routing with an AS ID of 1 for all networks, disable the transmission of EIGRP hello packets for the LAN interface, and configure the bandwidth for S0/0/0 to 1024 Kb/s.

e. On R3, configure EIGRP routing with an AS ID of 1 for all networks, disable the transmission of EIGRP hello packets for the LAN interface, and configure the bandwidth for S0/0/0 to 64 Kb/s.

Step 2. Test connectivity.

All PCs should be able to ping one another. Verify and troubleshoot if necessary.

_____

Note. It may be necessary to disable the PC firewall to ping between PCs.

_____

Part 3: Configure EIGRP for Automatic Summarization

In Part 3, you will add loopback interfaces and enable EIGRP automatic summarization on R1 and R3. You will also observe the effects on the routing table of R2.

Step 1. Configure EIGRP for automatic summarization.

a. Issue the **show ip protocols** command on R1. What is the default status of automatic summarization in EIGRP?

_____

b. Configure the loopback addresses on R1.

c. Add the appropriate network statements to the EIGRP process on R1. Record the commands used in the space below.

_____

_____

_____

_____

d. On R2, issue the **show ip route eigrp** command. How are the loopback networks represented in the output?

_____

e. On R1, issue the **auto-summary** command inside the EIGRP process.

```
R1(config)# router eigrp 1
R1(config-router)# auto-summary
R1(config-router)#
*Apr 14 01:14:55.463: %DUAL-5-NBRCHANGE: EIGRP-IPv4 1: Neighbor 192.168.13.2
(Serial0/0/1) is resync: summary configured
*Apr 14 01:14:55.463: %DUAL-5-NBRCHANGE: EIGRP-IPv4 1: Neighbor 192.168.12.2
(Serial0/0/0) is resync: summary configured
*Apr 14 01:14:55.463: %DUAL-5-NBRCHANGE: EIGRP-IPv4 1: Neighbor 192.168.13.2
(Serial0/0/1) is resync: summary up, remove components
R1(config-router)#67: %DUAL-5-NBRCHANGE: EIGRP-IPv4 1: Neighbor 192.168.12.2
(Serial0/0/0) is resync: summary up, remove components
*Apr 14 01:14:55.467: %DUAL-5-NBRCHANGE: EIGRP-IPv4 1: Neighbor 192.168.12.2
(Serial0/0/0) is resync: summary up, remove components
*Apr 14 01:14:55.467: %DUAL-5-NBRCHANGE: EIGRP-IPv4 1: Neighbor 192.168.13.2
(Serial0/0/1) is resync: summary up, remove components
```

How does the routing table on R2 change?

_____

f. Repeat substeps b through e by adding loopback interfaces, adding EIGRP process networks and auto-summary on R3.

Part 4: Configure and Propagate a Default Static Route

In Part 4, you will configure a default static route on R2 and propagate the route to all other routers.

a. Configure the loopback address on R2.

b. Configure a default static route with an exit interface of Lo1.

```
R2(config)# ip route 0.0.0.0 0.0.0.0 Lo1
```

c. Use the **redistribute static** command within the EIGRP process to propagate the default static route to other participating routers.

```
R2(config)# router eigrp 1
R2(config-router)# redistribute static
```

d. Use the **show ip protocols** command on R2 to verify the static route is being distributed.

```
R2# show ip protocols
*** IP Routing is NSF aware ***
<output omitted>
Routing Protocol is "eigrp 1"
  Outgoing update filter list for all interfaces is not set
  Incoming update filter list for all interfaces is not set
  Default networks flagged in outgoing updates
  Default networks accepted from incoming updates
  Redistributing: static
  EIGRP-IPv4 Protocol for AS(1)
    Metric weight K1=1, K2=0, K3=1, K4=0, K5=0
    NSF-aware route hold timer is 240
    Router-ID: 192.168.23.1
    Topology : 0 (base)
      Active Timer: 3 min
```

```
            Distance: internal 90 external 170
            Maximum path: 4
            Maximum hopcount 100
            Maximum metric variance 1

         Automatic Summarization: disabled
         Maximum path: 4
         Routing for Networks:
           192.168.2.0
           192.168.12.0/30
           192.168.23.0/30
         Passive Interface(s):
           GigabitEthernet0/0
         Routing Information Sources:
           Gateway         Distance      Last Update
           192.168.12.1          90      00:13:20
           192.168.23.2          90      00:13:20
         Distance: internal 90 external 170
```

    e. On R1, issue the **show ip route eigrp | include 0.0.0.0** command to view statements specific to the default route. How is the static default route represented in the output? What is the administrative distance (AD) for the propagated route?

Part 5: Fine-Tune EIGRP

In Part 5, you will configure the percentage of bandwidth that can be used for EIGRP traffic on an interface and change the hello interval and hold timers for EIGRP interfaces.

Step 1. Configure bandwidth utilization for EIGRP.

    a. Configure the serial link between R1 and R2 to allow only 75 percent of the link bandwidth for EIGRP traffic.

```
R1(config)# interface s0/0/0
R1(config-if)# ip bandwidth-percent eigrp 1 75
R2(config)# interface s0/0/0
R2(config-if)# ip bandwidth-percent eigrp 1 75
```

    b. Configure the serial link between R1 and R3 to allow 40 percent of the link bandwidth for EIGRP traffic.

Step 2. Configure the hello interval and hold timer for EIGRP.

    a. On R2, use the **show ip eigrp interfaces detail** command to view the hello interval and hold timer for EIGRP.

```
R2# show ip eigrp interfaces detail
EIGRP-IPv4 Interfaces for AS(1)
                  Xmit Queue    PeerQ       Mean  Pacing Time  Multicast   Pending
Interface Peers   Un/Reliable   Un/Reliable SRTT  Un/Reliable  Flow Timer  Routes
Se0/0/0      1    0/0           0/0         1     0/15         50          0
   Hello-interval is 5, Hold-time is 15
```

```
              Split-horizon is enabled
              Next xmit serial <none>
              Packetized sent/expedited: 29/1
              Hello's sent/expedited: 390/2
              Un/reliable mcasts: 0/0  Un/reliable ucasts: 35/39
              Mcast exceptions: 0  CR packets: 0  ACKs suppressed: 0
              Retransmissions sent: 0  Out-of-sequence rcvd: 0
              Topology-ids on interface - 0
              Interface BW percentage is 75
              Authentication mode is not set
Se0/0/1      1         0/0        0/0          1      0/16       50        0
              Hello-interval is 5, Hold-time is 15
              Split-horizon is enabled
              Next xmit serial <none>
              Packetized sent/expedited: 34/5
              Hello's sent/expedited: 382/2
              Un/reliable mcasts: 0/0  Un/reliable ucasts: 31/42
              Mcast exceptions: 0  CR packets: 0  ACKs suppressed: 2
              Retransmissions sent: 0  Out-of-sequence rcvd: 0
              Topology-ids on interface - 0
              Authentication mode is not set
```

What is the default value for hello time? _____

What is the default value for hold time? _____

b. Configure S0/0/0 and S0/0/1 interfaces on R1 to use a hello interval of 60 seconds and a hold time of 180 seconds in that specific order.

```
R1(config)# interface s0/0/0
R1(config-if)# ip hello-interval eigrp 1 60
R1(config-if)# ip hold-time eigrp 1 180
R1(config)# interface s0/0/1
R1(config-if)# ip hello-interval eigrp 1 60
R1(config-if)# ip hold-time eigrp 1 180
```

c. Configure the serial interfaces on R2 and R3 to use a hello interval of 60 seconds and a hold time of 180 seconds.

d. Use the **show ip eigrp interfaces detail** command on R2 to verify configuration.

Reflection

1. What are the benefits of summarizing routes?

_____

_____

2. When setting EIGRP timers, why is it important to make the hold time value equal to or greater than the hello interval?

_____

_____

Router Interface Summary Table

Router Interface Summary			
Router Model	Ethernet Interface #1	Ethernet Interface #2	Serial Interface #1	Serial Interface #2
---	---	---	---	---
1800	Fast Ethernet 0/0 (F0/0)	Fast Ethernet 0/1 (F0/1)	Serial 0/0/0 (S0/0/0)	Serial 0/0/1 (S0/0/1)
1900	Gigabit Ethernet 0/0 (G0/0)	Gigabit Ethernet 0/1 (G0/1)	Serial 0/0/0 (S0/0/0)	Serial 0/0/1 (S0/0/1)
2801	Fast Ethernet 0/0 (F0/0)	Fast Ethernet 0/1 (F0/1)	Serial 0/1/0 (S0/1/0)	Serial 0/1/1 (S0/1/1)
2811	Fast Ethernet 0/0 (F0/0)	Fast Ethernet 0/1 (F0/1)	Serial 0/0/0 (S0/0/0)	Serial 0/0/1 (S0/0/1)
2900	Gigabit Ethernet 0/0 (G0/0)	Gigabit Ethernet 0/1 (G0/1)	Serial 0/0/0 (S0/0/0)	Serial 0/0/1 (S0/0/1)

Note: To find out how the router is configured, look at the interfaces to identify the type of router and how many interfaces the router has. There is no way to effectively list all the combinations of configurations for each router class. This table includes identifiers for the possible combinations of Ethernet and Serial interfaces in the device. The table does not include any other type of interface, even though a specific router may contain one. An example of this might be an ISDN BRI interface. The string in parentheses is the legal abbreviation that can be used in Cisco IOS commands to represent the interface.

Appendix A: Configuration Commands

Router R1

```
R1(config)# router eigrp 1
R1(config-router)# network 192.168.1.0
R1(config-router)# network 192.168.12.0 0.0.0.3
R1(config-router)# network 192.168.13.0 0.0.0.3
R1(config-router)# network 192.168.11.0 0.0.0.3
R1(config-router)# network 192.168.11.4 0.0.0.3
R1(config-router)# network 192.168.11.8 0.0.0.3
R1(config-router)# network 192.168.11.12 0.0.0.3
R1(config-router)# passive-interface g0/0
R1(config-router)# auto-summary
R1(config)# int s0/0/0
R1(config-if)# bandwidth 1024
R1(config-if)# ip bandwidth-percent eigrp 1 75
R1(config-if)# ip hello-interval eigrp 1 60
R1(config-if)# ip hold-time eigrp 1 180
R1(config-if)# int s0/0/1
R1(config-if)# bandwidth 64
R1(config-if)# ip bandwidth-percent eigrp 1 40
R1(config-if)# ip hello-interval eigrp 1 60
R1(config-if)# ip hold-time eigrp 1 180
```

Router R2

```
R2(config)# router eigrp 1
R2(config-router)# network 192.168.2.0
R2(config-router)# network 192.168.12.0 0.0.0.3
R2(config-router)# network 192.168.23.0 0.0.0.3
R2(config-router)# passive-interface g0/0
R2(config-router)# redistribute static
R2(config)# int s0/0/0
R2(config-if)# bandwidth 1024
R2(config-if)# ip bandwidth-percent eigrp 1 75
R2(config-if)# ip hello-interval eigrp 1 60
R2(config-if)# ip hold-time eigrp 1 180
R2(config-if)# int s0/0/1
R2(config-if)# ip hello-interval eigrp 1 60
R2(config-if)# ip hold-time eigrp 1 180
```

Router R3

```
R3(config)# router eigrp 1
R3(config-router)# network 192.168.3.0
R3(config-router)# network 192.168.13.0 0.0.0.3
R3(config-router)# network 192.168.23.0 0.0.0.3
R3(config-router)# network 192.168.33.0 0.0.0.3
R3(config-router)# network 192.168.33.4 0.0.0.3
R3(config-router)# network 192.168.33.8 0.0.0.3
R3(config-router)# network 192.168.33.12 0.0.0.3
R3(config-router)# passive-interface g0/0
R3(config-router)# auto-summary
R3(config)# int s0/0/0
R3(config-if)# bandwidth 64
R3(config-if)# ip bandwidth-percent eigrp 1 40
R3(config-if)# ip hello-interval eigrp 1 60
R3(config-if)# ip hold-time eigrp 1 180
R3(config-if)# int s0/0/1
R3(config-if)# ip hello-interval eigrp 1 60
R3(config-if)# ip hold-time eigrp 1 180
```

7.2.3.5 Packet Tracer–Troubleshooting EIGRP for IPv4

Topology

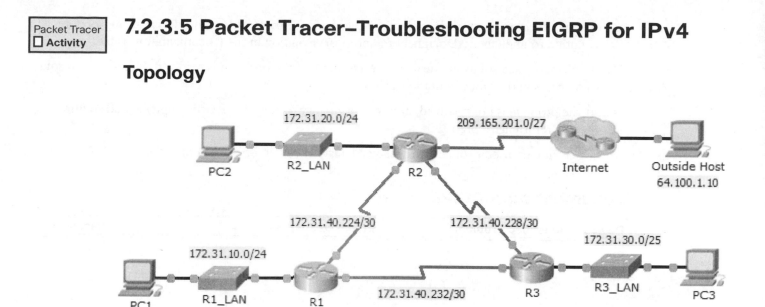

Addressing Table

Device	Interface	IP Address	Subnet Mask	Default Gateway
R1	G0/0	172.31.10.1	255.255.255.0	N/A
	S0/0/0	172.31.40.225	255.255.255.252	N/A
	S0/0/1	172.31.40.233	255.255.255.252	N/A
R2	G0/0	172.31.20.1	255.255.255.0	N/A
	S0/0/0	172.31.40.226	255.255.255.252	N/A
	S0/0/1	172.31.40.229	255.255.255.252	N/A
	S0/1/0	209.165.201.1	255.255.255.224	N/A
R3	G0/0	172.31.30.1	255.255.255.0	N/A
	S0/0/0	172.31.40.234	255.255.255.252	N/A
	S0/0/1	172.31.40.230	255.255.255.252	N/A
PC1	NIC	172.31.10.10	255.255.255.0	172.31.10.1
PC2	NIC	172.31.20.10	255.255.255.0	172.31.20.1
PC3	NIC	172.31.30.10	255.255.255.0	172.31.30.1

Scenario

In this activity, you will troubleshoot EIGRP neighbor issues. Use show commands to identify errors in the network configuration. Then, you will document the errors you discover and implement an appropriate solution. Finally, you will verify full end-to-end connectivity is restored.

Troubleshooting Process

1. Use testing commands to discover connectivity problems in the network and document the problem in the Documentation Table.

2. Use verification commands to discover the source of the problem and devise an appropriate solution to implement. Document the proposed solution in the Documentation Table.

3. Implement each solution one at a time and verify if the problem is resolved. Indicate the resolution status in the Documentation Table.

4. If the problem is not resolved, it may be necessary to first remove the implemented solution before returning to Step 2.

5. Once all identified problems are resolved, test for full end-to-end connectivity.

Documentation Table

Device	Identified Problem	Proposed Solution	Resolved?

7.2.3.6 Lab–Troubleshooting Basic EIGRP for IPv4 and IPv6

Topology

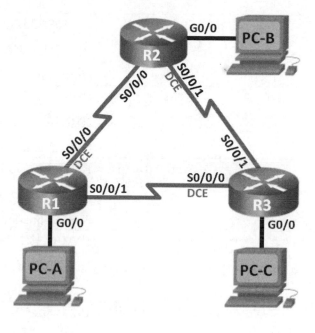

Addressing Table

Device	EIGRP Router ID	Interface	IP Address	Default Gateway
R1	1.1.1.1	G0/0	192.168.1.1/24	N/A
			2001:DB8:ACAD:A::1/64	
			FE80::1 link-local	
		S0/0/0 (DCE)	192.168.12.1/30	N/A
			2001:DB8:ACAD:12::1/64	
			FE80::1 link-local	
		S0/0/1	192.18.13.1/30	N/A
			2001:DB8:ACAD:13::1/64	
			FE80::1 link-local	
R2	2.2.2.2	G0/0	192.168.2.1/24	N/A
			2001:DB8:ACAD:B::2/64	
			FE80::2 link-local	

Device	EIGRP Router ID	Interface	IP Address	Default Gateway
		S0/0/0	192.168.12.2/30	N/A
			2001:DB8:ACAD:12::2/64	
			FE80::2 link-local	
		S0/0/1 (DCE)	192.168.23.1/30	N/A
			2001:DB8:ACAD:23::2/64	
			FE80::2 link-local	
R3	3.3.3.3	G0/0	192.168.3.1/24	N/A
			2001:DB8:ACAD:C::3/64	
			FE80::3 link-local	
		S0/0/0 (DCE)	192.168.13.2/30	N/A
			2001:DB8:ACAD:13::3/64	
			FE80::3 link-local	
		S0/0/1	192.168.23.2/30	N/A
			2001:DB8:ACAD:23::3/64	
			FE80::3 link-local	
PC-A		NIC	192.168.1.3/24	192.168.1.1
			2001:DB8:ACAD:A::A/64	FE80::1
PC-B		NIC	192.168.2.3/24	192.168.2.1
			2001:DB8:ACAD:B::B/64	FE80::2
PC-C		NIC	192.168.3.3/24	192.168.3.1
			2001:DB8:ACAD:C::C/64	FE80::3

Objectives

Part 1: Build the Network and Load Device Configurations

Part 2: Troubleshoot Layer 3 Connectivity

Part 3: Troubleshoot EIGRP for IPv4

Part 4: Troubleshoot EIGRP for IPv6

Background/Scenario

The Enhanced Interior Gateway Routing Protocol (EIGRP) is an advanced distance vector routing protocol developed by Cisco Systems. EIGRP routers discover neighbors and establish and maintain adjacencies with neighbor routers using Hello packets. An EIGRP router assumes that as long as it is receiving Hello packets from a neighboring router, that neighbor is up and its routes remain viable.

EIGRP for IPv4 runs over the IPv4 network layer, communicating with other EIGRP IPv4 peers, and advertising only IPv4 routes. EIGRP for IPv6 has the same functionality as EIGRP for IPv4 but uses

IPv6 as the network layer protocol, communicating with EIGRP for IPv6 peers and advertising IPv6 routes.

In this lab, you will troubleshoot a network that runs EIGRP for IPv4 and EIGRP for IPv6 routing protocols. This network is experiencing problems and you are tasked with finding the problems and correcting them.

Note: The routers used with CCNA hands-on labs are Cisco 1941 Integrated Services Routers (ISRs) with Cisco IOS Release 15.2(4)M3 (universalk9 image). Other routers and Cisco IOS versions can be used. Depending on the model and Cisco IOS version, the commands available and output produced might vary from what is shown in the labs. Refer to the Router Interface Summary Table at the end of this lab for the correct interface identifiers.

Note: Make sure that the routers have been erased and have no startup configurations. If you are unsure, contact your instructor.

Required Resources

- 3 Routers (Cisco 1941 with Cisco IOS Release 15.2(4)M3 universal image or comparable)

- 3 PCs (Windows 7, Vista, or XP with terminal emulation program, such as Tera Term)

- Console cables to configure the Cisco IOS devices via the console ports

- Ethernet and serial cables as shown in the topology

Part 1: Build the Network and Load Device Configurations

In Part 1, you will set up the network topology and configure basic settings on the PC hosts and routers.

Step 1.   Cable the network as shown in the topology.

Step 2.   Configure PC hosts.

Step 3.   Load router configurations.

Load the following configurations into the appropriate router. All routers have the same passwords. The privileged EXEC password is **class**, and the console and vty password is **cisco**.

Router R1 Configuration:

```
conf t
service password-encryption
hostname R1
enable secret class
no ip domain lookup
ipv6 unicast-routing
interface GigabitEthernet0/0
 ip address 192.168.1.1 255.255.255.0
 duplex auto
 speed auto
 ipv6 address FE80::1 link-local
 ipv6 address 2001:DB8:ACAD:A::1/64
 ipv6 eigrp 1
 no shutdown
interface Serial0/0/0
```

```
   bandwidth 128
   ip address 192.168.21.1 255.255.255.252
   ipv6 address FE80::1 link-local
   ipv6 address 2001:DB8:ACAD:12::1/64
   ipv6 eigrp 1
   clock rate 128000
   no shutdown
 interface Serial0/0/1
   ip address 192.168.13.1 255.255.255.252
   ipv6 address FE80::1 link-local
   ipv6 address 2001:DB8:ACAD:31::1/64
   ipv6 eigrp 1
   no shutdown
 router eigrp 1
   network 192.168.1.0
   network 192.168.12.0 0.0.0.3
   network 192.168.13.0 0.0.0.3
   passive-interface GigabitEthernet0/0
   eigrp router-id 1.1.1.1
 ipv6 router eigrp 1
   no shutdown
 banner motd @
    Unauthorized Access is Prohibited! @
 line con 0
   password cisco
   logging synchronous
 line vty 0 4
   password cisco
 login
   transport input all
 end
```

Router R2 Configuration:

```
conf t
service password-encryption
hostname R2
enable secret class
no ip domain lookup
ipv6 unicast-routing
interface GigabitEthernet0/0
  ip address 192.168.2.1 255.255.255.0
  duplex auto
  speed auto
  ipv6 address FE80::2 link-local
  ipv6 address 2001:DB8:ACAD:B::2/64
  ipv6 eigrp 1
interface Serial0/0/0
  ip address 192.168.12.2 255.255.255.252
  ipv6 address FE80::2 link-local
  ipv6 address 2001:DB8:ACAD:12::2/64
  ipv6 eigrp 1
```

```
 no shutdown
interface Serial0/0/1
 bandwidth 128
 ip address 192.168.23.1 255.255.255.0
 ipv6 address FE80::2 link-local
 ipv6 address 2001:DB8:ACAD:23::2/64
 ipv6 eigrp 1
 clock rate 128000
 no shutdown
router eigrp 1
 network 192.168.12.0 0.0.0.3
 network 192.168.23.0 0.0.0.3
 passive-interface GigabitEthernet0/0
 eigrp router-id 2.2.2.2
ipv6 router eigrp 1
 no shutdown
 passive-interface GigabitEthernet0/0
banner motd @
  Unauthorized Access is Prohibited! @
line con 0
 password cisco
 login
 logging synchronous
line vty 0 4
 password cisco
 login
 transport input all
end
```

Router R3 Configuration:

```
conf t
service password-encryption
hostname R3
enable secret class
no ip domain lookup
interface GigabitEthernet0/0
 ip address 192.168.3.1 255.255.255.0
 duplex auto
 speed auto
 ipv6 address FE80::3 link-local
 ipv6 address 2001:DB8:ACAD:C::3/64
 ipv6 eigrp 1
interface Serial0/0/0
 ip address 192.168.13.2 255.255.255.252
 ipv6 address FE80::3 link-local
 ipv6 address 2001:DB8:ACAD:13::3/64
 ipv6 eigrp 1
 no shutdown
interface Serial0/0/1
 bandwidth 128
 ip address 192.168.23.2 255.255.255.252
```

```
    ipv6 address FE80::3 link-local
    ipv6 address 2001:DB8:ACAD:23::3/64
    ipv6 eigrp 1
    no shutdown
 router eigrp 1
    network 192.168.3.0
    network 192.168.13.0 0.0.0.3
    passive-interface GigabitEthernet0/0
    eigrp router-id 3.3.3.3
 banner motd @
    Unauthorized Access is Prohibited! @
 line con 0
    password cisco
    login
    logging synchronous
 line vty 0 4
    password cisco
    login
    transport input all
 end
```

Step 4.   Save the running configuration for all routers.

Part 2: Troubleshoot Layer 3 Connectivity

In Part 2, you will verify that Layer 3 connectivity is established on all interfaces. You will need to test both IPv4 and IPv6 connectivity for all device interfaces.

Note: All serial interfaces should be set with a bandwidth of 128 Kb/s. The clock rate on the DCE interface should be set to 128000.

Step 1.   Verify that the interfaces listed in the Addressing Table are active and configured with correct IP address information.

   a.   Issue the **show ip interface brief** command on all routers to verify that the interfaces are in an up/up state. Record your findings.

   _____

   _____

   _____

   _____

   b.   Issue the **show run interface** command to verify IP address assignments on all router interfaces. Compare the interface IP addresses against the Addressing Table and verify the subnet mask assignments. For IPv6, verify that the link-local address has been assigned. Record your findings.

   _____

   _____

   _____

   _____

c. Issue the **show interfaces** *interface-id* command to verify bandwidth setting on the serial interfaces. Record your findings.

_____

_____

_____

d. Issue the **show controllers** *interface-id* command to verify that clock rates have been set to 128 Kb/s on all DCE serial interfaces. Issue the **show interfaces** *interface-id* command to verify bandwidth setting on the serial interfaces. Record your findings.

_____

_____

_____

e. Resolve all problems found. Record the commands used to correct the issues.

_____

_____

_____

_____

_____

_____

_____

_____

_____

_____

_____

_____

_____

_____

_____

Step 2. Verify Layer 3 connectivity.

Use the **ping** command and verify that each router has network connectivity with the serial interfaces on the neighbor routers. Verify that the PCs can ping their default gateways. If problems still exist, continue troubleshooting Layer 3 issues.

Part 3: Troubleshoot EIGRP for IPv4

In Part 3, you will troubleshoot EIGRP for IPv4 problems and make the necessary changes needed to establish EIGRP for IPv4 routes and end-to-end IPv4 connectivity.

Note: LAN (G0/0) interfaces should not advertise EIGRP routing information, but routes to these networks should be contained in the routing tables.

Step 1. Test IPv4 end-to-end connectivity.

From each PC host, ping the other PC hosts in the topology to verify end-to-end connectivity.

Note: It may be necessary to disable the PC firewall before testing, to ping between PCs.

a. Ping from PC-A to PC-B. Were the pings successful? _____

b. Ping from PC-A to PC-C. Were the pings successful? _____

c. Ping from PC-B to PC-C. Were the pings successful? _____

Step 2. Verify that all interfaces are assigned to EIGRP for IPv4.

a. Issue the **show ip protocols** command to verify that EIGRP is running and that all networks are advertised. This command also allows you to verify that the router ID is set correctly, and that the LAN interfaces are set as passive interfaces. Record your findings.

_____

_____

_____

b. Make the necessary changes based on the output from the **show ip protocols** command. Record the commands that were used to correct the issues.

_____

_____

_____

c. Re-issue the **show ip protocols** command to verify that your changes had the desired effect.

Step 3. Verify EIGRP neighbor information.

a. Issue the **show ip eigrp neighbor** command to verify that EIGRP adjacencies have been established between the neighboring routers.

b. Resolve any outstanding problems that were discovered.

Step 4.   Verify EIGRP for IPv4 routing information.

    a.   Issue the **show ip route eigrp** command to verify that each router has EIGRP for IPv4 routes to all non-adjoining networks.

       Are all EIGRP routes available? _____

       If any EIGRP for IPv4 routes are missing, what is missing?

       _____

    b.   If any routing information is missing, resolve these issues.

Step 5.   Verify IPv4 end-to-end connectivity.

From each PC, verify that IPv4 end-to-end connectivity exists. PCs should be able to ping the other PC hosts in the topology. If IPv4 end-to-end connectivity does not exist, then continue troubleshooting to resolve remaining issues.

Note: It may be necessary to disable the PCs firewall.

Part 4: Troubleshoot EIGRP for IPv6

In Part 4, you will troubleshoot EIGRP for IPv6 problems and make the necessary changes needed to establish EIGRP for IPv6 routes and end-to-end IPv6 connectivity.

Note: LAN (G0/0) interfaces should not advertise EIGRP routing information, but routes to these networks should be contained in the routing tables.

Step 1.   Test IPv6 end-to-end connectivity.

From each PC host, ping the IPv6 addresses of the other PC hosts in the topology to verify end-to-end connectivity.

Step 2.   Verify that IPv6 unicast routing has been enabled on all routers.

    a.   An easy way to verify that IPv6 routing has been enabled on a router is to use the **show run | section ipv6 unicast** command. By adding this pipe to the **show run** command, the **ipv6 unicast-routing** command is displayed if IPv6 routing has been enabled.

Note: The **show run** command can also be issued without any pipe, and then a manual search for the **ipv6 unicast-routing** command can be done.

       Issue the command on each router. Record your findings.

       _____

       _____

       _____

    b.   If IPv6 unicast routing is not enabled on one or more routers, enable it now. Record the commands that were used to correct the issues.

       _____

       _____

Step 3.   Verify that all interfaces are assigned to EIGRP for IPv6.

   a.   Issue the **show ipv6 protocols** command and verify that the router ID is correct. This command also allows you to verify that the LAN interfaces are set as passive interfaces.

Note: If no output is generated from this command, then the EIGRP for IPv6 process has not been configured.

Record your findings.

_____

_____

_____

   b.   Make the necessary configuration changes. Record the commands used to correct the issues.

_____

_____

_____

_____

_____

_____

_____

_____

_____

_____

_____

_____

_____

_____

_____

_____

   c.   Re-issue the **show ipv6 protocols** command to verify that your changes are correct.

Step 4.   Verify that all routers have correct neighbor adjacency information.

   a.   Issue the **show ipv6 eigrp neighbor** command to verify that adjacencies have formed between neighboring routers.

   b.   Resolve any EIGRP adjacency issues that still exist.

Step 5.   Verify EIGRP for IPv6 routing information.

      a.   Issue the **show ipv6 route eigrp** command, and verify that EIGRP for IPv6 routes exist to all non-adjoining networks.

          Are all EIGRP routes available? _____

          If any EIGRP for IPv6 routes are missing, what is missing?

          _____

      b.   Resolve any routing issues that still exist.

Step 6.   Test IPv6 end-to-end connectivity.

      From each PC, verify that IPv6 end-to-end connectivity exists. PCs should be able to ping the other PC hosts in the topology. If IPv6 end-to-end connectivity does not exist, then continue troubleshooting to resolve remaining issues.

Note: It may be necessary to disable the PCs firewall.

Reflection

Why would you troubleshoot EIGRP for IPv4 and EIGRP for IPv6 separately?

_____

_____

Router Interface Summary Table

Router Interface Summary				
Router Model	**Ethernet Interface #1**	**Ethernet Interface #2**	**Serial Interface #1**	**Serial Interface #2**
1800	Fast Ethernet 0/0 (F0/0)	Fast Ethernet 0/1 (F0/1)	Serial 0/0/0 (S0/0/0)	Serial 0/0/1 (S0/0/1)
1900	Gigabit Ethernet 0/0 (G0/0)	Gigabit Ethernet 0/1 (G0/1)	Serial 0/0/0 (S0/0/0)	Serial 0/0/1 (S0/0/1)
2801	Fast Ethernet 0/0 (F0/0)	Fast Ethernet 0/1 (F0/1)	Serial 0/1/0 (S0/1/0)	Serial 0/1/1 (S0/1/1)
2811	Fast Ethernet 0/0 (F0/0)	Fast Ethernet 0/1 (F0/1)	Serial 0/0/0 (S0/0/0)	Serial 0/0/1 (S0/0/1)
2900	Gigabit Ethernet 0/0 (G0/0)	Gigabit Ethernet 0/1 (G0/1)	Serial 0/0/0 (S0/0/0)	Serial 0/0/1 (S0/0/1)

Note: To find out how the router is configured, look at the interfaces to identify the type of router and how many interfaces the router has. There is no way to effectively list all the combinations of configurations for each router class. This table includes identifiers for the possible combinations of Ethernet and Serial interfaces in the device. The table does not include any other type of interface, even though a specific router may contain one. An example of this might be an ISDN BRI interface. The string in parentheses is the legal abbreviation that can be used in Cisco IOS commands to represent the interface.

7.2.3.7 Lab–Troubleshooting Advanced EIGRP

Topology

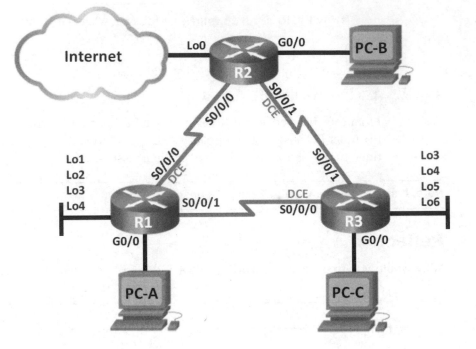

Addressing Table

Device	Interface	IP Address	Subnet Mask	Default Gateway
R1	G0/0	192.168.1.1	255.255.255.0	N/A
	Lo1	172.16.11.1	255.255.255.0	N/A
	Lo2	172.16.12.1	255.255.255.0	N/A
	Lo3	172.16.13.1	255.255.255.0	N/A
	Lo4	172.16.14.1	255.255.255.0	N/A
	S0/0/0 (DCE)	192.168.12.1	255.255.255.252	N/A
	S0/0/1	192.168.13.1	255.255.255.252	N/A
R2	G0/0	192.168.2.1	255.255.255.0	N/A
	Lo0	209.165.200.225	255.255.255.252	N/A
	S0/0/0	192.168.12.2	255.255.255.252	N/A
	S0/0/1 (DCE)	192.168.23.1	255.255.255.252	N/A

Device	Interface	IP Address	Subnet Mask	Default Gateway
R3	G0/0	192.168.3.1	255.255.255.0	N/A
	Lo3	172.16.33.1	255.255.255.0	N/A
	Lo4	172.16.34.1	255.255.255.0	N/A
	Lo5	172.16.35.1	255.255.255.0	N/A
	Lo6	172.16.36.1	255.255.255.0	N/A
	S0/0/0 (DCE)	192.168.13.2	255.255.255.252	N/A
	S0/0/1	192.168.23.2	255.255.255.252	N/A
PC-A	NIC	192.168.1.3	255.255.255.0	192.168.1.1
PC-B	NIC	192.168.2.3	255.255.255.0	192.168.2.1
PC-C	NIC	192.168.3.3	255.255.255.0	192.168.3.1

Objectives

Part 1: Build the Network and Load Device Configurations

Part 2: Troubleshoot EIGRP

Background/Scenario

The Enhanced Interior Gateway Routing Protocol (EIGRP) has advanced features to allow changes related to summarization, default route propagation, bandwidth utilization, metrics, and security.

In this lab, you will troubleshoot a network that is running EIGRP. Advanced EIGRP features have been implemented, but the network is now experiencing problems. You must find and correct the network issues.

Note: The routers used with CCNA hands-on labs are Cisco 1941 Integrated Services Routers (ISRs) with Cisco IOS, Release 15.2(4)M3 (universalk9 image). Other routers and Cisco IOS versions can be used. Depending on the model and Cisco IOS version, the commands available and output produced might vary from what is shown in the labs. Refer to the Router Interface Summary Table at the end of this lab for the correct interface identifiers.

Note: Ensure that the routers have been erased and have no startup configurations. If you are unsure, contact your instructor.

Required Resources

- 3 Routers (Cisco 1941 with Cisco IOS Release 15.2(4)M3 universal image or comparable)
- 3 PCs (Windows with terminal emulation program, such as Tera Term)
- Console cables to configure the Cisco IOS devices via the console ports
- Ethernet cables as shown in the topology

Part 1: Build the Network and Load Device Configurations

Step 1. Cable the network as shown in the topology.

Step 2. Configure PC hosts.

Step 3. Load router configurations.

Load the following configurations into the appropriate router. All routers have the same passwords. The privileged EXEC password is **class**, and **cisco** is the console and vty password.

Router R1 Configuration:

```
conf t
hostname R1
enable secret class
no ip domain lookup
line con 0
 password cisco
 login
 logging synchronous
line vty 0 4
 password cisco
 login
banner motd @
  Unauthorized Access is Prohibited! @
interface lo1
 description Connection to Branch 11
 ip add 172.16.11.1 255.255.255.0
interface lo2
 description Connection to Branch 12
 ip add 172.16.12.1 255.255.255.0
interface lo3
 description Connection to Branch 13
 ip add 172.16.13.1 255.255.255.0
interface lo4
 description Connection to Branch 14
 ip add 172.16.14.1 255.255.255.0
interface g0/0
 description R1 LAN Connection
 ip add 192.168.1.1 255.255.255.0
 no shutdown
interface s0/0/0
 description Serial Link to R2
 ip add 192.168.12.1 255.255.255.252
no shutdown
interface s0/0/1
 description Serial Link to R3
 ip add 192.168.13.1 255.255.255.252
no shutdown
 router eigrp 1
  router-id 1.1.1.1
  network 192.168.1.0 0.0.0.255
  network 192.168.12.0 0.0.0.3
```

```
    network 192.168.13.0 0.0.0.3
    network 172.16.11.0 0.0.0.255
    network 172.16.12.0 0.0.0.255
    network 172.16.13.0 0.0.0.255
    network 172.16.14.0 0.0.0.255
    passive-interface g0/0
end
```

Router R2 Configuration:

```
conf t
hostname R2
enable secret class
no ip domain lookup
line con 0
 password cisco
 login
 logging synchronous
line vty 0 4
 password cisco
 login
banner motd @
  Unauthorized Access is Prohibited! @
interface g0/0
 description R2 LAN Connection
 ip add 192.168.2.1 255.255.255.0
 no shutdown
interface s0/0/0
 description Serial Link to R1
 ip add 192.168.12.2 255.255.255.252
 no shutdown
interface s0/0/1
 description Serial Link to R3
 ip add 192.168.23.1 255.255.255.252
 no shutdown
interface lo0
 ip add 209.165.200.225 255.255.255.252
 description Connection to ISP
router eigrp 1
 router-id 2.2.2.2
 network 192.168.2.0 0.0.0.255
 network 192.168.12.0 0.0.0.3
 network 192.168.23.0 0.0.0.3
 passive-interface g0/0
ip route 0.0.0.0 0.0.0.0 lo0
end
```

Router R3 Configuration:

```
conf t
hostname R3
enable secret class
no ip domain lookup
line con 0
```

```
 password cisco
 login
 logging synchronous
line vty 0 4
 password cisco
 login
banner motd @
  Unauthorized Access is Prohibited! @
interface lo3
 description Connection to Branch 33
 ip add 172.16.33.1 255.255.255.0
interface lo4
 description Connection to Branch 34
 ip add 172.16.34.1 255.255.255.0
interface lo5
 description Connection to Branch 35
 ip add 172.16.35.1 255.255.255.0
interface lo6
 description Connection to Branch 36
 ip add 172.16.36.1 255.255.255.0
interface g0/0
 description R3 LAN Connection
 ip add 192.168.3.1 255.255.255.0
 no shutdown
interface s0/0/0
 description Serial Link to R1
 ip add 192.168.13.2 255.255.255.252
 no shutdown
interface s0/0/1
 description Serial Link to R2
 ip add 192.168.23.2 255.255.255.252
no shutdown
router eigrp 1
 router-id 3.3.3.3
 network 192.168.3.0 0.0.0.255
 network 192.168.13.0 0.0.0.3
 network 192.168.23.0 0.0.0.3
 network 172.16.33.0 0.0.0.255
 network 172.16.34.0 0.0.0.255
 network 172.16.35.0 0.0.0.255
 network 172.16.36.0 0.0.0.255
 passive-interface g0/0
end
```

Step 4.   Verify end-to-end connectivity.

Note: It may be necessary to disable the PC firewall to ping between PCs.

Step 5.   Save the configuration on all routers.

Part 2: Troubleshoot EIGRP

In Part 2, verify that all routers have established neighbor adjacencies, and that all network routes are available.

Additional EIGRP Requirements:

- All serial interface clock rates should be set at 128 Kb/s and a matching bandwidth setting should be available to allow EIGRP cost metrics to be calculated correctly.

- Automatic route summarization of the branch networks.

- EIGRP should redistribute the static default route to the Internet. This is simulated by using Loopback 0 interface on R2.

- EIGRP should be configured to use no more than **40** percent of the available bandwidth on the serial interfaces.

- EIGRP Hello/Hold timer intervals should be set to **30/90** on all serial interfaces.

List the commands used during your EIGRP troubleshooting process:

_____

_____

_____

_____

List the changes made to resolve the EIGRP issues. If no problems were found on the device, then respond with "no problems were found."

R1 Router:

_____

_____

_____

_____

_____

_____

_____

_____

_____

_____

_____

R2 Router:

_____

_____

_____

_____

_____

_____

_____

_____

_____

_____

_____

_____

R3 Router:

_____

_____

_____

_____

_____

_____

_____

_____

_____

_____

_____

_____

_____

Reflection

1. How can the **auto-summary** command create routing issues in EIGRP?

   _____

   _____

   _____

   _____

2. Why would you want to change the EIGRP hello and hold time intervals on an interface?

   _____

   _____

Router Interface Summary Table

Router Interface Summary			
Router Model	**Ethernet Interface #1**	**Ethernet Interface #2**	**Serial Interface #1**	**Serial Interface #2**
1800	Fast Ethernet 0/0 (F0/0)	Fast Ethernet 0/1 (F0/1)	Serial 0/0/0 (S0/0/0)	Serial 0/0/1 (S0/0/1)
1900	Gigabit Ethernet 0/0 (G0/0)	Gigabit Ethernet 0/1 (G0/1)	Serial 0/0/0 (S0/0/0)	Serial 0/0/1 (S0/0/1)
2801	Fast Ethernet 0/0 (F0/0)	Fast Ethernet 0/1 (F0/1)	Serial 0/1/0 (S0/1/0)	Serial 0/1/1 (S0/1/1)
2811	Fast Ethernet 0/0 (F0/0)	Fast Ethernet 0/1 (F0/1)	Serial 0/0/0 (S0/0/0)	Serial 0/0/1 (S0/0/1)
2900	Gigabit Ethernet 0/0 (G0/0)	Gigabit Ethernet 0/1 (G0/1)	Serial 0/0/0 (S0/0/0)	Serial 0/0/1 (S0/0/1)

Note: To find out how the router is configured, look at the interfaces to identify the type of router and how many interfaces the router has. There is no way to effectively list all the combinations of configurations for each router class. This table includes identifiers for the possible combinations of Ethernet and Serial interfaces in the device. The table does not include any other type of interface, even though a specific router may contain one. An example of this might be an ISDN BRI interface. The string in parentheses is the legal abbreviation that can be used in Cisco IOS commands to represent the interface.

7.3.1.1 Class Activity–Tuning EIGRP

Objectives

Implement advanced EIGRP features to enhance operation in a small- to medium-sized business network.

This chapter will focus on some advanced methods to tune EIGRP network configurations. This modeling activity will prove your mastery of some of these concepts.

Scenario

The purpose of this activity is to review EIGRP routing protocol tuning concepts.

You will work with a partner to design one EIGRP topology. This topology will be the basis for two parts of the activity. The first will use default settings for all configurations and the second will incorporate at least three of the following EIGRP tuning options:

- Default routes
- Default routes propagation
- Hello interval timer settings
- EIGRP bandwidth percent utilization

Refer to the labs, Packet Tracer activities, and interactive activities to help you as you progress through this modeling activity.

Directions are listed on the PDF file for this activity. Share your completed work with another group. You may wish to save a copy of this activity to a portfolio.

Resources

- Packet Tracer software or physical network lab equipment
- Word processing program

Directions

Step 1. Design a WAN and LAN topology.

    a. Use Packet Tracer to design a network with two routers (1941 model, suggested). If necessary, add NICs to the routers to provide connectivity to the routers for at least two LANs for each router. Add at least one PC to each LAN.

    b. Address the networks using either an IPv4 or IPv6 addressing scheme. VLSM may be used per group discretion. A fully VLSM-addressed network will work with EIGRP because auto-summarization is turned off by default.

    c. Configure the topology using basic EIGRP default settings.

    d. Make sure all PCs can ping each other, to prove connectivity.

    e. Save your work.

Step 2.   Copy the topology.

   a.   Using your cursor, highlight the entire EIGRP-configured topology.

   b.   Press **Ctrl+C** to copy the highlighted topology.

   c.   Use **Ctrl+V** to paste a full copy of the topology to the Packet Tracer desktop. There should be two EIGRP-configured topologies displayed. You will use the topology copy to tune the network.

   d.   While highlighted, move the copied topology to a different location on the Packet Tracer desktop to create room between the two for configuration purposes.

Step 3.   Configure tuning features on the copied topology.

   a.   Choose three of the bulleted items from the Scenario section of this activity. Configure your changes on the copied topology.

Note: By changing the hello interval times, network instability may occur; however, you should be able to troubleshoot it. Make sure to notice adjacency status changes if you choose the hello interval configuration option.

---

   b.   Save your work to avoid losing your configuration.

Step 4.   Use verification commands to compare and contrast the default configuration and the tuned configuration.

   a.   Use at least three output commands to compare and contrast the two topologies, and copy them to a word processing software program. For example, some useful commands include:

   ■   `show ip route`

   ■   `show running-configuration`

   ■   `show ip protocols, show ip eigrp neighbors`

   b.   Share your work with another group. Explain how you changed the second topology from the first configured example. Justify what happened when you configured the three EIGRP tuning options.

7.3.1.2 Packet Tracer–Skills Integration Challenge

Topology

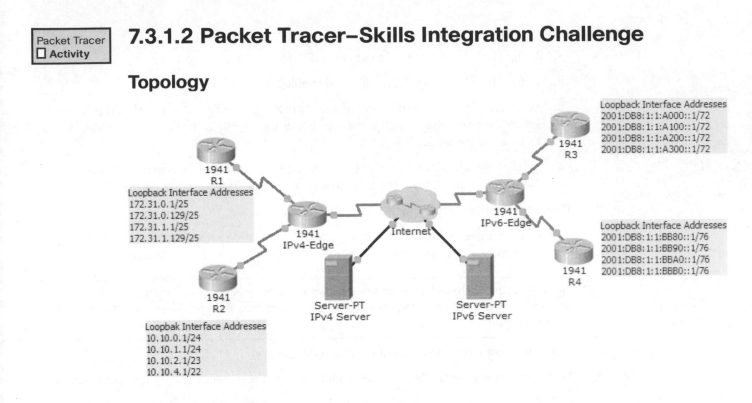

Addressing Table

Device	Interface	IPv4 Address	Subnet Mask
		IPv6 Address/Prefix	
IPv4-Edge	S0/0/0	172.31.6.1	255.255.255.252
	S0/0/1	10.10.8.1	255.255.255.252
	S0/1/0	209.165.200.226	255.255.255.224
R1	S0/0/0	172.31.6.2	255.255.255.252
	Lo8	172.31.0.1	255.255.255.128
	Lo9	172.31.0.129	255.255.255.128
	Lo10	172.31.1.1	255.255.255.128
	Lo11	172.31.1.129	255.255.255.128
R2	S0/0/1	10.10.8.2	255.255.255.252
	Lo1	10.10.0.1	255.255.255.0
	Lo2	10.10.1.1	255.255.255.0
	Lo3	10.10.2.1	255.255.254.0
	Lo4	10.10.4.1	255.255.252.0
IPv6-Edge	S0/0/0	2001:DB8:A001:6::1/64	
	S0/0/1	2001:DB8:A001:7::1/64	
	S0/1/0	2001:DB8:CAFE:1::2/64	
R3	S0/0/0	2001:DB8:A001:7::2/64	
R4	S0/0/1	2001:DB8:A001:6::2/64	

Scenario

In this activity, you must implement EIGRP for IPv4 and IPv6 on two separate networks. Your task includes enabling EIGRP, assigning router IDs, changing the hello timers, and limiting EIGRP advertisements.

Requirements

EIGRP for IPv4

- Implement EIGRP on IPv4-enabled routers using Autonomous System 1.
    - Use a single classful network address to advertise the loopback interfaces.
    - Use the wildcard mask to advertise the /30 networks between **R1**, **R2**, and **IPv4-Edge**.
    - Use the **default** passive interface method and only allow EIGRP updates out the active EIGRP serial interfaces.
- Configure a directly attached default route on **IPv4-Edge** and propagate it in EIGRP updates.
- Configure the serial interfaces between **R1**, **R2**, and **IPv4-Edge** to send hellos every 10 seconds.
- **R1** and **R2** should have a default route in the routing table (D*EX).
- Verify **R1** and **R2** can ping the **IPv4 Server. IPv4 Server** should also be able to ping every loopback address on **R1** and **R2**.

EIGRP for IPv6

- Implement EIGRP for IPv6 on the IPv6-enabled routers using Autonomous System 1.
    - Assign **IPv6-Edge** with the router ID of 1.1.1.1
    - Assign **R3** with the router ID of 3.3.3.3
    - Assign **R4** with the router ID of 4.4.4.4
- Configure a directly attached default route on **IPv6-Edge** and propagate it in EIGRP updates.
- **R3** and **R4** should show a default external route in the routing table.
- Verify **R3** and **R4** can ping the **IPv6 Server. IPv6 Server** should also be able to ping every loopback address on **R3** and **R4**.

Suggested Scoring Rubric

Note: Packet Tracer does not currently grade EIGRP for IPv6 summary routes. Therefore, part of your grade depends on routing table verification by your instructor.

Scored Work	Possible Points	Earned Points
IPv6-Edge Routing Table	10	
Packet Tracer Score	90	
Total Score	100	

CHAPTER 8

Single-Area OSPF

Open Shortest Path First (OSPF) is a link-state routing protocol that was developed as a replacement for the distance vector routing protocol RIP. RIP was an acceptable routing protocol in the early days of networking and the Internet. However, RIP's reliance on hop count as the only metric for determining best route quickly became problematic. Using hop count does not scale well in larger networks with multiple paths of varying speeds. OSPF has significant advantages over RIP in that it offers faster convergence and scales to much larger network implementations.

Study Guide

Characteristics of OSPF

In 1991, OSPFv2 was introduced in RFC 1247 by John Moy. OSPFv2 offered significant technical improvements over OSPFv1. It is classless by design; therefore, it supports VLSM and CIDR.

OSPF Terminology

OSPF introduces many new terms to our discussion of networking. Match the definition on the left with a term on the right.

Definitions

a. Responsible for updating all other OSPF routers when a change occurs in the multiaccess network.

b. OSPF packet used to reply to LSRs as well as to announce new information.

c. Attaches to multiple areas, maintains separate link-state databases for each area it is connected to, and routes traffic destined for or arriving from other areas.

d. Describes the details of OSPF link-state concepts and operations.

e. Sent by an OSPF router to confirm receipt of an LSU.

f. Monitors the DR and takes over as DR if the current DR fails.

g. When a failure occurs in the network, such as when a neighbor becomes unreachable, these are flooded throughout an area.

h. An open standard, link-state routing protocol designed to address the limitations of RIP.

i. An OSPF router that is neither DR or BDR but participates in the OSPF process on a multiaccess network.

j. A network that cycles between an up state and a down state.

k. Connects to an external routing domain that uses a different routing policy.

l. Contains an abbreviated list of the sending router's link-state database and is used by receiving routers to check against the local link-state database.

m. When this is not equal, the router with the highest number will be the DR regardless of router ID values.

n. This is the router ID for an OSPF router if no loopbacks are configured.

o. Asks for more information about any entry in the DBD.

Terms

___ Area Border Router (ABR)

___ Autonomous System Boundary Router (ASBR)

___ Backup Designated Router (BDR)

___ database description (DBD)

___ Designated Router (DR)

___ DRothers

___ flapping link

___ highest IP address

___ link-state acknowledgment (LSAck)

___ link-state advertisement (LSA)

___ link-state request (LSR)

___ link-state update (LSU)

___ Open Shortest Path First (OSPF)

___ RFC 2328

___ router priority

OSPF Concepts

The initial development of OSPF began in 1987 by the _____ OSPF Working Group. At that time, the Internet was largely an academic and research network funded by the U.S. government.

In 1998, the OSPFv2 specification was updated to the current version reflected in RFC _____. Because OSPF is an open standard, you can easily find the RFC online. List one website where the OSPF RFC can be found.

_____

The data portion of an OSPF message is encapsulated in a packet. This data field can include one of five OSPF packet types. Figure 8-1 shows an example of an encapsulated OSPF message. Fill in the missing field contents.

Figure 8-1   Encapsulated OSPF Message

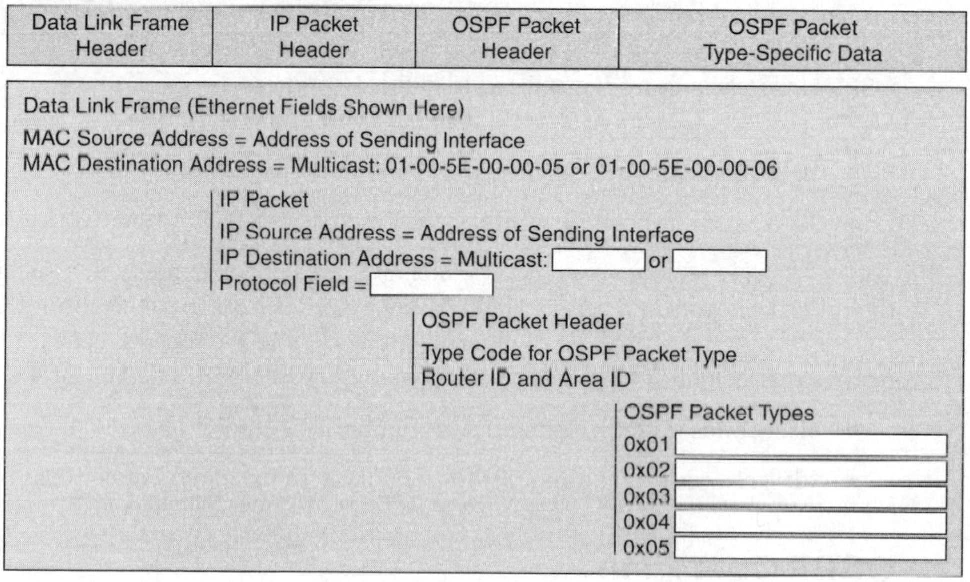

The following list describes the five different types of OSPF LSPs. Each packet serves a specific purpose in the OSPF routing process. Fill in the name for each packet type.

1. _____: Used to establish and maintain adjacency with other OSPF routers

2. _____: Contains an abbreviated list of the sending router's link-state database and is used by receiving routers to check against the local link-state database

3. _____: A request for more information about any entry in the DBD

4. _____: Used to reply to LSRs as well as to announce new information

5. _____: Confirms receipt of an LSU

Every OSPF message includes the header, as shown in Figure 8-2. Also shown in the figure are the fields of the OSPF Hello packet. Fill in the missing field contents.

Figure 8-2   OSPF Message Format

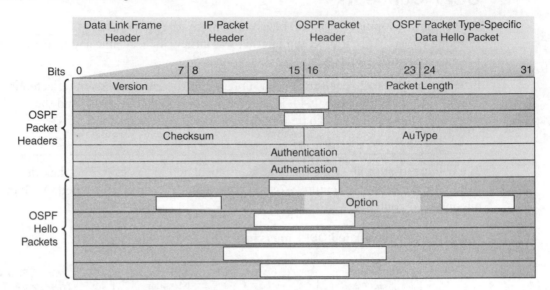

OSPF Hello packets are transmitted to multicast address _____ in IPv4 and _____ in IPv6 (all OSPF routers) every

- 10 seconds (default on multiaccess and point-to-point networks)
- 30 seconds (default on nonbroadcast multiaccess [NBMA] networks; for example, Frame Relay)

The _____ interval is the period, expressed in seconds, that the router will wait to receive a Hello packet before declaring the neighbor down. If the _____ interval expires before the routers receive a Hello packet, OSPF will remove that neighbor from its link-state database. Cisco uses a default of 4 times the Hello interval:

- 40 seconds (default on multiaccess and point-to-point networks)
- 120 seconds (default on NBMA networks; for example, Frame Relay)

OSPF Operation

Receiving an OSPF Hello packet on an interface confirms for a router that there is another OSPF router on this link. OSPF then begins the process of establishing adjacency with the neighbor.

Routers initially exchange Type _____ packets, which is an abbreviated list of the sending router's LSDB and is used by receiving routers to check against the local LSDB.

A Type _____ packet is used by the receiving routers to request more information about an entry in the DBD.

The Type _____ packet is used to reply to an LSR packet.

Then, a Type _____ packet is sent to acknowledge receipt of the LSU.

In Table 8-1, indicate which OSPF packet type matches the LSA purpose.

Table 8-1   Identify OSPF Packet Types

LSA Purpose	OSPF Packet Type				
	Hello	DBD	LSR	LSU	LSAck
Discovers neighbors and builds adjacencies between them.					
Data field is empty.					
Asks for specific link-state records from router to router.					
Sends specifically requested link-state records.					
Contains list of sending router's LSDB.					
Can contain seven different types of LSAs.					
Checks for database synchronization between routers.					
Confirms receipt of a link-state update packet.					
Maintains adjacency with other OSPF routers.					

In Figure 8-3, record the five states that occur between the *down state* and the *full state*.

Figure 8-3   Transitioning Through the OSPF States

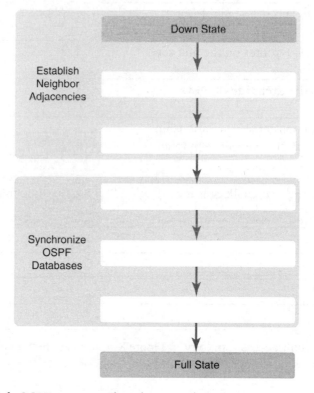

In Table 8-2, indicate which OSPF state matches the state description.

Table 8-2 Identify the OSPF States

State Description	OSPF States						
	Down	Init	Two-Way	Ex-Start	Exchange	Loading	Full
Routes are processed using the SPF algorithm.							
A neighbor responds to a Hello.							
Hello packets are received from neighbors, containing the sending router ID.							
On Ethernet links, elect a Designated Router (DR) and a Backup Designated Router (BDR).							
No Hello packets received.							
Router requests more information about a specific DBD entry.							
Routers exchange DBD packets.							
Routers have converged.							
The LSDB and routing tables are complete.							
A new OSPF router on the link sends first Hello.							
Initiates the exchange of DBD packets.							
Negotiate master/slave relationship and DBD packet sequence number.							

Describe the two challenges regarding OSPF LSA flooding in multiaccess networks.

_____

_____

_____

_____

For each multiaccess topology in Figure 8-4, indicate how many adjacencies would be formed if the DB/BDR process wasn't part of OSPF operations.

Figure 8-4   Multiaccess Topologies

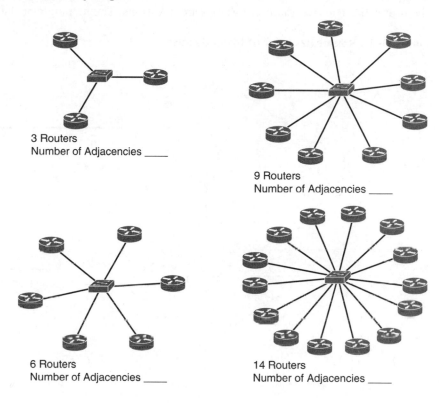

3 Routers
Number of Adjacencies _____

9 Routers
Number of Adjacencies _____

6 Routers
Number of Adjacencies _____

14 Routers
Number of Adjacencies _____

Briefly describe the DR/BDR election process.

Configuring Single-Area OSPFv2

Now that you have a good understanding of how OSPF works, it is time to learn the configuration commands we use for OSPF as well as how to verify OSPF is operating as expected.

The Router ID

Every router requires a router ID to participate in an OSPF domain. The router ID can be defined by an administrator or automatically assigned by the router. The router ID is used by other OSPF routers to uniquely identify neighbors.

Explain the role of the router ID in multiaccess networks.

Complete the flowchart in Figure 8-5 to indicate the order of precedence used by the router to choose the router ID. The two diamond shapes are questions. The rectangle at the bottom is a decision.

Figure 8-5   Router ID Order of Precedence

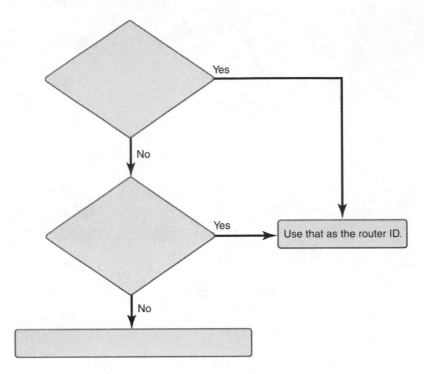

Record the router prompt and command syntax to configure the router ID.

_____

When would it be appropriate to configure a loopback interface to serves as a router ID?

_____

_____

Single-Area OSPFv2 Basic Configuration Scenario

Figure 8-6 shows the topology that we will use to configure OSPFv2 and OSPFv3. This first topology shows IPv4 network addresses. The IPv4 addressing scheme is in Table 8-3.

Figure 8-6   OSPFv2 Topology with IPv4 Network Addresses

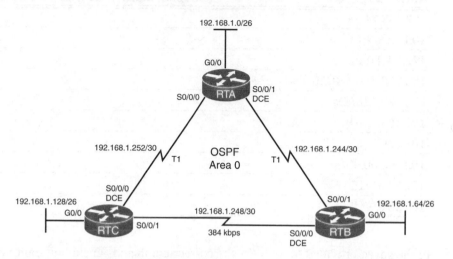

Table 8-3   IPv4 Addressing Scheme for OSPFv2

Device	Interface	IPv4 Address	Subnet Mask
RTA	G0/0	192.168.1.1	255.255.255.192
	S0/0/0	192.168.1.253	255.255.255.252
	S0/0/1	192.168.1.245	255.255.255.252
	Router ID	1.1.1.1	
RTB	G0/0	192.168.1.65	255.255.255.192
	S0/0/0	192.168.1.249	255.255.255.252
	S0/0/1	192.168.1.246	255.255.255.252
	Router ID	2.2.2.2	
RTC	G0/0	192.168.1.129	255.255.255.192
	S0/0/0	192.168.1.254	255.255.255.252
	S0/0/1	192.168.1.250	255.255.255.252
	Router ID	3.3.3.3	

Record the command syntax, including router prompt, to configure the OSPF routing process.

_____

The value for *process-id* can be any number between _____ and _____.

The command syntax, including router prompt, for adding network statements to the OSPF routing process is as follows:

_____

For single area OSPF configurations, the *area-id* is normally set to 0.

The *wildcard-mask* argument is simply the inverse of the subnet mask. For example, the bit pattern for 11110000 (240) becomes 00001111 (15). List the subnet mask and corresponding wildcard mask for each of the following network addresses.

Network Address	Subnet Mask	Wildcard Mask
192.168.14.64/26		
10.1.1.16/28		
172.24.4.0/23		
192.168.200.128/20		
172.17.2.128/25		
192.168.226.96/27		
10.0.0.0/8		
10.100.200.48/30		
172.18.0.0/15		
10.128.0.0/10		

In the space provided, document the correct commands, including router prompt, to configure the routers in Figure 8-6 with OSPFv2. Include commands to configure the router ID and disable updates on the LAN interface.

_____

_____

_____

_____

_____

_____

_____

_____

_____

_____

_____

_____

_____

_____

_____

_____

_____

Adjusting OSPF Cost

The OSPF metric is called cost. From RFC 2328:

> *A cost is associated with the output side of each router interface. This cost is configurable by the system administrator. The lower the cost, the more likely the interface is to be used to forward data traffic.*

Notice that RFC 2328 does not specify which values should be used to determine the cost. So the implementation of the cost metric is up to the operating system that is running OSPF.

The Reference Bandwidth

What is the formula used to calculate OSPF cost in the Cisco IOS?

_____

What is the default value for the reference bandwidth?

_____

In Table 8-4, record the Cisco IOS Cost for each of the interface types.

Table 8-4   Cisco ISO Default OSPF Cost Values

Interface Type	Reference Bandwidth / Default Interface Bandwidth	Cost
10GE	100,000,000 / 10,000,000,000	
Gigabit Ethernet	100,000,000 / 1,000,000,000	
Fast Ethernet	100,000,000 / 100,000,000	
Ethernet	100,000,000 / 10,000,000	
Serial 1.544 Mbps	100,000,000 / 1,544,000	
Serial 128 Kbps	100,000,000 / 128,000	
Serial 64 Kbps	100,000,000 / 64,000	

If you did the calculations right you can see that, by default, 10GE, Gigabit Ethernet, and Fast Ethernet all have the same cost value. The IOS rounds to the nearest integer, so the cost value cannot be less than 1.

What is the router prompt and command syntax to change the reference bandwidth to a higher value so that 10 GigE, Gigabit Ethernet, and Fast Ethernet will all have different values?

_____

The value is entered in M/bs, so what is a good value to enter to change the resulting cost values?

_____

_____

Record the command to set the reference bandwidth on RTA. All three routers would then be configured with the same value.

_____

```
% OSPF: Reference bandwidth is changed.

    Please ensure reference bandwidth is consistent across all routers.
```

The Default Interface Bandwidth

Adjusting the reference bandwidth may not be enough to ensure that OSPF is accurately advertising the cost of its links. Table 8-4 shows the default interface bandwidth that the Cisco IOS uses to calculate the OSPF cost. But these interface bandwidths may not reflect the actual bandwidth for serial interfaces since bandwidth is determined by the agreed-upon rate with the ISP.

What is the router prompt and command syntax to change the interface bandwidth value used by OSPF to calculate cost?

_____

In Figure 8-6, RTC and RTB share a link that is contracted at the rate of 384 kbps. Record the command to change the bandwidth.

_____

_____

_____

_____

_____

Modifying the OSPF Cost Metric

Instead of configuring the bandwidth, you could configure the cost directly. This would allow the IOS to bypass the metric calculation.

What is the router prompt and command syntax to manually configure the cost value?

_____

In what situation is this command useful?

_____

_____

Record the commands to configure the link between RTB and RTC with the actual cost. Remember to take into account the new reference bandwidth value you configured earlier.

_____

_____

_____

_____

_____

Verify the OSPF Configuration

Fill in the missing command to complete the following sentences:

The _____ command can be used to verify and troubleshoot OSPF neighbor relationships.

The _____ command is a quick way to verify vital OSPF configuration information, including the OSPF process ID; the router ID; networks the router is advertising; the neighbors the router is receiving updates from; and the default administrative distance, which is 110 for OSPF.

The _____ command can also be used to examine the OSPF process ID and router ID. In addition, this command displays the OSPF area information as well as the last time the SPF algorithm was calculated.

The quickest way to verify Hello and Dead intervals is to use the _____ command.

The quickest way to verify OSPF convergence is to use the _____ command to view the routing table for each router in the topology.

Configure Single-Area OSPFv3

OSPFv3 is the OSPFv2 equivalent for exchanging IPv6 prefixes. Recall that in IPv6, the network address is referred to as the prefix and the subnet mask is called the prefix-length. Similar to its IPv4 counterpart, OSPFv3 exchanges routing information to populate the IPv6 routing table with remote prefixes.

Comparing OSPFv2 and OSPFv3

As with all IPv6 routing protocols, OSPFv3 has separate processes from its IPv4 counterpart. The processes and operations are basically the same as in the IPv4 routing protocol but run independently. OSPFv2 and OSPFv3 each have separate adjacency tables, OSPF topology tables, and IP routing tables.

In Table 8-5, indicate whether a function or feature belongs to OSPFv2, OSPFv3, or both.

Table 8-5   Compare OSPFv2 and OSPFv3

Function or Feature	OSPFv2	OSPFv3	Both
Uses the SPF algorithm to calculate best paths.			
Uses 5 basic packet types.			
Uses 224.0.0.6 for DR and BDR multicasts.			
Uses cost as its metric.			
Uses IPsec for authentication.			
Link-State Routing Protocol.			
Unicast routing enabled by default.			
Dynamic Routing Protocol.			
Uses FF02::6 for DR and BDR multicasts.			
Uses MD5 or plain-text authentication.			
Elects a DR and a BDR.			
IP unicast routing must be enabled.			

Configuring OSPFv3

Figure 8-7 shows the same topology we used for OSPFv2, but with IPv6 network addresses. Table 8-6 shows the IPv6 addressing scheme.

Figure 8-7   OSPFv3 Topology with IPv6 Network Addresses

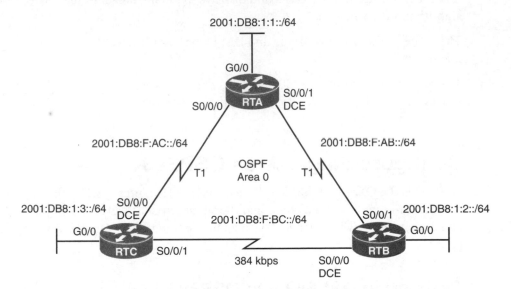

Table 8-6   IPv6 Addressing Scheme for OSPFv3

Device	Interface	IPv6 Address/Prefix
RTA	G0/0	2001:DB8:1:1::1/64
	S0/0/0	2001:DB8:F:AC::1/64
	S0/0/1	2001:DB8:F:AB::1/64
	Link local	FE80::A
	Router ID	1.1.1.1
RTB	G0/0	2001:DB8:1:2::1/64
	S0/0/0	2001:DB8:F:BC::1/64
	S0/0/1	2001:DB8:F:AB::2/64
	Link local	FE80::B
	Router ID	2.2.2.2
RTC	G0/0	2001:DB8:1:3::1/64
	S0/0/0	2001:DB8:F:AC::2/64
	S0/0/1	2001:DB8:F:BC::2/64
	Link local	FE80::C
	Router ID	3.3.3.3

The routers are already configured with interface addressing. Record the correct commands, including router prompt, to configure the routers with OSPFv3. Include commands to enable IPv6 routing, configure the router ID, change the reference bandwidth to 10000, and disable updates on the LAN interface. Except for the router ID, the commands are the same for all three routers, so you only need to document one router.

_____

_____

_____

_____

_____

_____

_____

_____

_____

_____

Verifying OSPFv3

Fill in the missing command to complete the following sentences:

The _____ command can be used to verify and troubleshoot OSPF neighbor relationships.

The _____ command is a quick way to verify vital OSPF configuration information, including the OSPF process ID, the router ID, and interfaces the router is advertising.

The _____ command can also be used to examine the OSPF process ID and router ID. In addition, this command displays the OSPF area information as well as the last time the SPF algorithm was calculated.

To view a quick summary of OSPFv3-enabled interfaces, use the _____ command. However, the quickest way to verify Hello and Dead intervals is to use the _____ command.

The quickest way to verify OSPF convergence is to use the _____ command to view the routing table for each router in the topology.

Packet Tracer Exercise 8-1: Implement Dual-Stacked OSPF

Now you are ready to use Packet Tracer to apply your documented configuration. Download and open the file LSG03-0801.pka found at the companion website for this book. Refer to the Introduction of this book for specifics on accessing files.

Note: The following instructions are also contained within the Packet Tracer Exercise.

In this Packet Tracer activity, you will configure the routers for OSPFv2 and OSPFv3 routing. You will then verify that PCs can ping each other using IPv4 and IPv6 addresses. Use the addressing table and the commands you documented in this chapter.

Requirements

Configure each router with the following:

- Router ID.

- Use OSPF process ID 1.

- Set the reference bandwidth for OSPFv3 to 10000.

- Set the LAN interfaces as passive.

- Verify IPv4 and IPv6 connectivity between the PCs.

Your completion percentage should be 100%. All the connectivity tests should show a status of "successful." If not, click **Check Results** to see which required components are not yet completed.

Labs and Activities

Command Reference

In Table 8-7, record the command, including the correct router or switch prompt, that fits the description. Fill in any blanks with the appropriate missing information.

Table 8-7   Commands for Chapter 8, Single-Area OSPF

Command	Description
	Configure R1 for OSPFv2 routing using process ID 20.
	Configure R1 to advertise network 10.10.10.128/27.
	Configure the R1 OSPFv2 routing process to use a reference bandwidth of 10000.
	List the command you can use to verify and troubleshoot OSPFv2 adjacencies.
	List the command you can use to verify the OSPFv2 SPF information.
	List the command that you can use to verify the OSPFv3 Hello and Dead intervals.
	Configure the OSPFv2 interface cost of 26041.
	Configure R1 for OSPFv3 routing using process ID 20.
	Configure the R1 OSPFv3 routing process to use a reference bandwidth of 10000.
	List the command you can use to verify and troubleshoot OSPFv3 adjacencies.
	List the command you can use to verify the OSPFv3 SPF information.
	List the command that you can use to verify the OSPFv3 Hello and Dead intervals.

8.0.1.2 Class Activity–Can Submarines Swim?

Objectives

Explain the process by which link-state routers learn about other networks.

Scenario

Edsger Wybe Dijkstra was a famous computer programmer and theoretical physicist. One of his most famous quotes was: "The question of whether computers can think is like the question of whether submarines can swim." Dijkstra's work has been to routing protocols, among other things. He created the shortest path first (SPF) algorithm for network routing.

- Visit the Association for Computing Machinery's (ACM) website at http://amturing.acm.org/award_winners/dijkstra_1053701.cfm. Read the article about the life of Dijkstra. List five facts from the article you found interesting about him and his work.

- Next, view Dijkstra's animation of how to find the shortest path first located at http://upload.wikimedia.org/wikipedia/commons/5/57/Dijkstra_Animation.gif. While viewing the animation, pay close attention to what is occurring in it. Note three observations about the animation.

- Lastly, view the graphic located at http://upload.wikimedia.org/wikipedia/commons/3/37/Ricerca_operativa_percorso_minimo_01.gif. Take a few moments to view the visual and notate three observations you have made about the visual. (Note: Use a web translator if you do not know the Italian words "Casa" and "Ufficio.")

Now, open the PDF provided with this activity and answer the reflection questions. Save your work.

Get together with two of your classmates to compare your answers.

Resources

- Internet connection
- Internet browser

Reflection

1. List five facts you found interesting about Edsger Wybe Dijkstra's life.

   _____

   _____

   _____

   _____

   _____

   _____

2. List three observations about the animation found at http://upload.wikimedia.org/wikipedia/commons/5/57/Dijkstra_Animation.gif.

_____

_____

_____

_____

_____

_____

3. List three observations about the visual shown at http://commons.wikimedia.org/wiki/File:Ricerca_operativa_percorso_minimo_01.gif.

_____

_____

_____

_____

_____

4. Distance vector routing protocols basically depend on number of hops to find the best route from source to destination. If you apply the information you learned from this introductory activity to routing, would hops be the main factor in finding the best path from source to destination? If compared to network communication, could it possibly be better to find the best path using a different metric than hop count? Justify your answer.

_____

_____

_____

_____

_____

_____

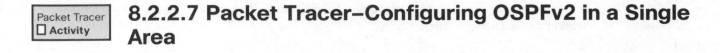

8.2.2.7 Packet Tracer–Configuring OSPFv2 in a Single Area

Topology

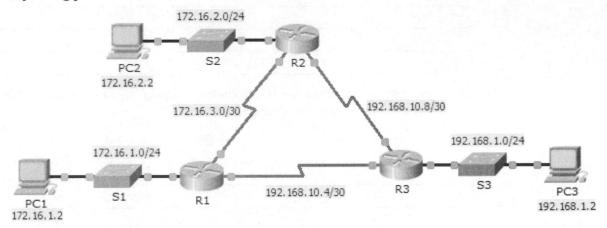

Addressing Table

Device	Interface	IP Address	Subnet Mask	Default Gateway
R1	G0/0	172.16.1.1	255.255.255.0	N/A
	S0/0/0	172.16.3.1	255.255.255.252	N/A
	S0/0/1	192.168.10.5	255.255.255.252	N/A
R2	G0/0	172.16.2.1	255.255.255.0	N/A
	S0/0/0	172.16.3.2	255.255.255.252	N/A
	S0/0/1	192.168.10.9	255.255.255.252	N/A
R3	G0/0	192.168.1.1	255.255.255.0	N/A
	S0/0/0	192.168.10.6	255.255.255.252	N/A
	S0/0/1	192.168.10.10	255.255.255.252	N/A
PC1	NIC	172.16.1.2	255.255.255.0	172.16.1.1
PC2	NIC	172.16.2.2	255.255.255.0	172.16.2.1
PC3	NIC	192.168.1.2	255.255.255.0	192.168.1.1

Objectives

Part 1: Configure OSPFv2 Routing

Part 2: Verify the Configurations

Background

In this activity, the IP addressing is already configured. You are responsible for configuring the three router topologies with basic single area OSPFv2 and then verifying connectivity between end devices.

Part 1: Configure OSPFv2 Routing

Step 1.   Configure OSPF on R1, R2, and R3.

Use the following requirements to configure OSPF routing on all three routers:

- Process ID 10

- Router ID for each router: R1 = 1.1.1.1; R2 = 2.2.2.2; R3 = 3.3.3.3

- Network address for each interface

- LAN interface set to passive (do not use the **default** keyword)

Step 2.   Verify OSPF routing is operational.

On each router, the routing table should now have a route to every network in the topology.

Part 2: Verify the Configurations

Each PC should be able to ping the other two PCs. If not, check your configurations.

8.2.4.5 Lab–Configuring Basic Single-Area OSPFv2

Topology

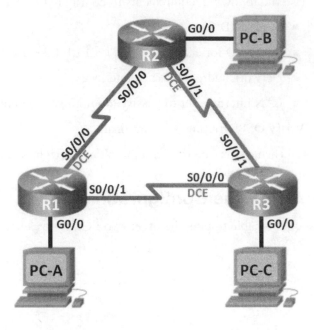

Addressing Table

Device	Interface	IP Address	Subnet Mask	Default Gateway
R1	G0/0	192.168.1.1	255.255.255.0	N/A
	S0/0/0 (DCE)	192.168.12.1	255.255.255.252	N/A
	S0/0/1	192.168.13.1	255.255.255.252	N/A
R2	G0/0	192.168.2.1	255.255.255.0	N/A
	S0/0/0	192.168.12.2	255.255.255.252	N/A
	S0/0/1 (DCE)	192.168.23.1	255.255.255.252	N/A
R3	G0/0	192.168.3.1	255.255.255.0	N/A
	S0/0/0 (DCE)	192.168.13.2	255.255.255.252	N/A
	S0/0/1	192.168.23.2	255.255.255.252	N/A
PC-A	NIC	192.168.1.3	255.255.255.0	192.168.1.1
PC-B	NIC	192.168.2.3	255.255.255.0	192.168.2.1
PC-C	NIC	192.168.3.3	255.255.255.0	192.168.3.1

Objectives

Part 1: Build the Network and Configure Basic Device Settings

Part 2: Configure and Verify OSPF Routing

Part 3: Change Router ID Assignments

Part 4: Configure OSPF Passive Interfaces

Part 5: Change OSPF Metrics

Background/Scenario

Open Shortest Path First (OSPF) is a link-state routing protocol for IP networks. OSPFv2 is defined for IPv4 networks, and OSPFv3 is defined for IPv6 networks. OSPF detects changes in the topology, such as link failures, and converges on a new loop-free routing structure very quickly. It computes each route using Dijkstra's algorithm, a shortest path first algorithm.

In this lab, you will configure the network topology with OSPFv2 routing, change the router ID assignments, configure passive interfaces, adjust OSPF metrics, and use a number of CLI commands to display and verify OSPF routing information.

Note: The routers used with CCNA hands-on labs are Cisco 1941 Integrated Services Routers (ISRs) with Cisco IOS Release 15.2(4)M3 (universalk9 image). Other routers and Cisco IOS versions can be used. Depending on the model and Cisco IOS version, the commands available and output produced might vary from what is shown in the labs. Refer to the Router Interface Summary Table at the end of this lab for the correct interface identifiers.

Note: Make sure that the routers have been erased and have no startup configurations. If you are unsure, contact your instructor.

Required Resources

- 3 Routers (Cisco 1941 with Cisco IOS Release 15.2(4)M3 universal image or comparable)
- 3 PCs (Windows 7, Vista, or XP with terminal emulation program, such as Tera Term)
- Console cables to configure the Cisco IOS devices via the console ports
- Ethernet and serial cables as shown in the topology

Part 1: Build the Network and Configure Basic Device Settings

In Part 1, you set up the network topology and configure basic settings on the PC hosts and routers.

Step 1.   Cable the network as shown in the topology.

Step 2.   Initialize and reload the routers as necessary.

Step 3.   Configure basic settings for each router.

    a.   Disable DNS lookup.

    b.   Configure device name as shown in the topology.

    c.   Assign **class** as the privileged EXEC password.

    d.   Assign **cisco** as the console and vty passwords.

    e.   Configure a message of the day (MOTD) banner to warn users that unauthorized access is prohibited.

    f.   Configure **logging synchronous** for the console line.

    g.   Configure the IP address listed in the Addressing Table for all interfaces.

    h.   Set the clock rate for all DCE serial interfaces at **128000**.

    i.   Copy the running configuration to the startup configuration.

Step 4.   Configure PC hosts.

Step 5.   Test connectivity.

The routers should be able to ping one another, and each PC should be able to ping its default gateway. The PCs are unable to ping other PCs until OSPF routing is configured. Verify and troubleshoot if necessary.

Part 2: Configure and Verify OSPF Routing

In Part 2, you will configure OSPFv2 routing on all routers in the network and then verify that routing tables are updated correctly. After OSPF has been verified, you will configure OSPF authentication on the links for added security.

Step 1.   Configure OSPF on R1.

    a.   Use the **router ospf** command in global configuration mode to enable OSPF on R1.

```
R1(config)# router ospf 1
```

Note: The OSPF process id is kept locally and has no meaning to other routers on the network.

---

    b.   Configure the **network** statements for the networks on R1. Use an area ID of 0.

```
R1(config-router)# network 192.168.1.0 0.0.0.255 area 0
R1(config-router)# network 192.168.12.0 0.0.0.3 area 0
R1(config-router)# network 192.168.13.0 0.0.0.3 area 0
```

Step 2.   Configure OSPF on R2 and R3.

Use the **router ospf** command and add the **network** statements for the networks on R2 and R3. Neighbor adjacency messages display on R1 when OSPF routing is configured on R2 and R3.

```
R1#
00:22:29: %OSPF-5-ADJCHG: Process 1, Nbr 192.168.23.1 on Serial0/0/0 from LOADING to
FULL, Loading Done
R1#
00:23:14: %OSPF-5-ADJCHG: Process 1, Nbr 192.168.23.2 on Serial0/0/1 from LOADING to
FULL, Loading Done
R1#
```

Step 3.   Verify OSPF neighbors and routing information.

    a.   Issue the **show ip ospf neighbor** command to verify that each router lists the other routers in the network as neighbors.

```
R1# show ip ospf neighbor

Neighbor ID     Pri   State       Dead Time   Address        Interface
192.168.23.2      0   FULL/  -    00:00:33    192.168.13.2   Serial0/0/1
192.168.23.1      0   FULL/  -    00:00:30    192.168.12.2   Serial0/0/0
```

    b.   Issue the **show ip route** command to verify that all networks display in the routing table on all routers.

```
R1# show ip route
Codes: L - local, C - connected, S - static, R - RIP, M - mobile, B - BGP
       D - EIGRP, EX - EIGRP external, O - OSPF, IA - OSPF inter area
       N1 - OSPF NSSA external type 1, N2 - OSPF NSSA external type 2
       E1 - OSPF external type 1, E2 - OSPF external type 2, E - EGP
```

```
          i - IS-IS, L1 - IS-IS level-1, L2 - IS-IS level-2, ia - IS-IS inter area
          * - candidate default, U - per-user static route, o - ODR
          P - periodic downloaded static route

   Gateway of last resort is not set

          192.168.1.0/24 is variably subnetted, 2 subnets, 2 masks
   C          192.168.1.0/24 is directly connected, GigabitEthernet0/0
   L          192.168.1.1/32 is directly connected, GigabitEthernet0/0
   O       192.168.2.0/24 [110/65] via 192.168.12.2, 00:32:33, Serial0/0/0
   O       192.168.3.0/24 [110/65] via 192.168.13.2, 00:31:48, Serial0/0/1
          192.168.12.0/24 is variably subnetted, 2 subnets, 2 masks
   C          192.168.12.0/30 is directly connected, Serial0/0/0
   L          192.168.12.1/32 is directly connected, Serial0/0/0
          192.168.13.0/24 is variably subnetted, 2 subnets, 2 masks
   C          192.168.13.0/30 is directly connected, Serial0/0/1
   L          192.168.13.1/32 is directly connected, Serial0/0/1
          192.168.23.0/30 is subnetted, 1 subnets
   O       192.168.23.0/30 [110/128] via 192.168.12.2, 00:31:38, Serial0/0/0
                           [110/128] via 192.168.13.2, 00:31:38, Serial0/0/1
```

What command would you use to only see the OSPF routes in the routing table?

Step 4. Verify OSPF protocol settings.

The **show ip protocols** command is a quick way to verify vital OSPF configuration information. This information includes the OSPF process ID, the router ID, networks the router is advertising, the neighbors the router is receiving updates from, and the default administrative distance, which is 110 for OSPF.

```
R1# show ip protocols
*** IP Routing is NSF aware ***

Routing Protocol is "ospf 1"
  Outgoing update filter list for all interfaces is not set
  Incoming update filter list for all interfaces is not set
  Router ID 192.168.13.1
  Number of areas in this router is 1. 1 normal 0 stub 0 nssa
  Maximum path: 4
  Routing for Networks:
    192.168.1.0 0.0.0.255 area 0
    192.168.12.0 0.0.0.3 area 0
    192.168.13.0 0.0.0.3 area 0
  Routing Information Sources:
    Gateway         Distance      Last Update
    192.168.23.2      110         00:19:16
    192.168.23.1      110         00:20:03
  Distance: (default is 110)
```

Step 5.   Verify OSPF process information.

Use the **show ip ospf** command to examine the OSPF process ID and router ID. This command displays the OSPF area information, as well as the last time the SPF algorithm was calculated.

```
R1# show ip ospf
 Routing Process "ospf 1" with ID 192.168.13.1
 Start time: 00:20:23.260, Time elapsed: 00:25:08.296
 Supports only single TOS(TOS0) routes
 Supports opaque LSA
 Supports Link-local Signaling (LLS)
 Supports area transit capability
 Supports NSSA (compatible with RFC 3101)
 Event-log enabled, Maximum number of events: 1000, Mode: cyclic
 Router is not originating router-LSAs with maximum metric
 Initial SPF schedule delay 5000 msecs
 Minimum hold time between two consecutive SPFs 10000 msecs
 Maximum wait time between two consecutive SPFs 10000 msecs
 Incremental-SPF disabled
 Minimum LSA interval 5 secs
 Minimum LSA arrival 1000 msecs
 LSA group pacing timer 240 secs
 Interface flood pacing timer 33 msecs
 Retransmission pacing timer 66 msecs
 Number of external LSA 0. Checksum Sum 0x000000
 Number of opaque AS LSA 0. Checksum Sum 0x000000
 Number of DCbitless external and opaque AS LSA 0
 Number of DoNotAge external and opaque AS LSA 0
 Number of areas in this router is 1. 1 normal 0 stub 0 nssa
 Number of areas transit capable is 0
 External flood list length 0
 IETF NSF helper support enabled
 Cisco NSF helper support enabled
 Reference bandwidth unit is 100 mbps
    Area BACKBONE(0)
        Number of interfaces in this area is 3
        Area has no authentication
        SPF algorithm last executed 00:22:53.756 ago
        SPF algorithm executed 7 times
        Area ranges are
        Number of LSA 3. Checksum Sum 0x019A61
        Number of opaque link LSA 0. Checksum Sum 0x000000
        Number of DCbitless LSA 0
        Number of indication LSA 0
        Number of DoNotAge LSA 0
        Flood list length 0
```

Step 6.   Verify OSPF interface settings.

    a.   Issue the **show ip ospf interface brief** command to display a summary of OSPF-enabled interfaces.

```
R1# show ip ospf interface brief
Interface   PID   Area            IP Address/Mask      Cost   State  Nbrs F/C
Se0/0/1     1     0               192.168.13.1/30      64     P2P    1/1
Se0/0/0     1     0               192.168.12.1/30      64     P2P    1/1
Gi0/0       1     0               192.168.1.1/24       1      DR     0/0
```

    b.   For a more detailed list of every OSPF-enabled interface, issue the **show ip ospf interface** command.

```
R1# show ip ospf interface
Serial0/0/1 is up, line protocol is up
  Internet Address 192.168.13.1/30, Area 0, Attached via Network Statement
  Process ID 1, Router ID 192.168.13.1, Network Type POINT_TO_POINT, Cost: 64
  Topology-MTID    Cost    Disabled    Shutdown    Topology Name
        0          64         no          no          Base
  Transmit Delay is 1 sec, State POINT_TO_POINT
  Timer intervals configured, Hello 10, Dead 40, Wait 40, Retransmit 5
    oob-resync timeout 40
    Hello due in 00:00:01
  Supports Link-local Signaling (LLS)
  Cisco NSF helper support enabled
  IETF NSF helper support enabled
  Index 3/3, flood queue length 0
  Next 0x0(0)/0x0(0)
  Last flood scan length is 1, maximum is 1
  Last flood scan time is 0 msec, maximum is 0 msec
  Neighbor Count is 1, Adjacent neighbor count is 1
    Adjacent with neighbor 192.168.23.2
  Suppress hello for 0 neighbor(s)
 Serial0/0/0 is up, line protocol is up
  Internet Address 192.168.12.1/30, Area 0, Attached via Network Statement
  Process ID 1, Router ID 192.168.13.1, Network Type POINT_TO_POINT, Cost: 64
  Topology-MTID    Cost    Disabled    Shutdown    Topology Name
        0          64         no          no          Base
  Transmit Delay is 1 sec, State POINT_TO_POINT
  Timer intervals configured, Hello 10, Dead 40, Wait 40, Retransmit 5
    oob-resync timeout 40
    Hello due in 00:00:03
  Supports Link-local Signaling (LLS)
  Cisco NSF helper support enabled
  IETF NSF helper support enabled
  Index 2/2, flood queue length 0
  Next 0x0(0)/0x0(0)
  Last flood scan length is 1, maximum is 1
  Last flood scan time is 0 msec, maximum is 0 msec
  Neighbor Count is 1, Adjacent neighbor count is 1
    Adjacent with neighbor 192.168.23.1
  Suppress hello for 0 neighbor(s)
```

```
GigabitEthernet0/0 is up, line protocol is up
   Internet Address 192.168.1.1/24, Area 0, Attached via Network Statement
   Process ID 1, Router ID 192.168.13.1, Network Type BROADCAST, Cost: 1
   Topology-MTID    Cost    Disabled    Shutdown      Topology Name
        0             1         no          no           Base
   Transmit Delay is 1 sec, State DR, Priority 1
   Designated Router (ID) 192.168.13.1, Interface address 192.168.1.1
   No backup designated router on this network
   Timer intervals configured, Hello 10, Dead 40, Wait 40, Retransmit 5
     oob-resync timeout 40
     Hello due in 00:00:01
   Supports Link-local Signaling (LLS)
   Cisco NSF helper support enabled
   IETF NSF helper support enabled
   Index 1/1, flood queue length 0
   Next 0x0(0)/0x0(0)
   Last flood scan length is 0, maximum is 0
   Last flood scan time is 0 msec, maximum is 0 msec
   Neighbor Count is 0, Adjacent neighbor count is 0
   Suppress hello for 0 neighbor(s)
```

Step 7.   Verify end-to-end connectivity.

Each PC should be able to ping the other PCs in the topology. Verify and troubleshoot if necessary.

Note: It may be necessary to disable the PC firewall to ping between PCs.

Part 3: Change Router ID Assignments

The OSPF router ID is used to uniquely identify the router in the OSPF routing domain. Cisco routers derive the router ID in one of three ways and with the following precedence:

1. IP address configured with the OSPF **router-id** command, if present

2. Highest IP address of any of the router's loopback addresses, if present

3. Highest active IP address on any of the router's physical interfaces

Because no router IDs or loopback interfaces have been configured on the three routers, the router ID for each router is determined by the highest IP address of any active interface.

In Part 3, you will change the OSPF router ID assignment using loopback addresses. You will also use the **router-id** command to change the router ID.

Step 1.   Change router IDs using loopback addresses.

a.   Assign an IP address to loopback 0 on R1.

```
R1(config)# interface lo0
R1(config-if)# ip address 1.1.1.1 255.255.255.255
R1(config-if)# end
```

b.   Assign IP addresses to Loopback 0 on R2 and R3. Use IP address 2.2.2.2/32 for R2 and 3.3.3.3/32 for R3.

c.   Save the running configuration to the startup configuration on all three routers.

d. You must reload the routers in order to reset the router ID to the loopback address. Issue the **reload** command on all three routers. Press Enter to confirm the reload.

e. After the router completes the reload process, issue the **show ip protocols** command to view the new router ID.

```
R1# show ip protocols
*** IP Routing is NSF aware ***

Routing Protocol is "ospf 1"
  Outgoing update filter list for all interfaces is not set
  Incoming update filter list for all interfaces is not set
  Router ID 1.1.1.1
  Number of areas in this router is 1. 1 normal 0 stub 0 nssa
  Maximum path: 4
  Routing for Networks:
    192.168.1.0 0.0.0.255 area 0
    192.168.12.0 0.0.0.3 area 0
    192.168.13.0 0.0.0.3 area 0
  Routing Information Sources:
    Gateway         Distance      Last Update
    3.3.3.3              110      00:01:00
    2.2.2.2              110      00:01:14
  Distance: (default is 110)
```

f. Issue the **show ip ospf neighbor** command to display the router ID changes for the neighboring routers.

```
R1# show ip ospf neighbor

Neighbor ID     Pri   State         Dead Time   Address        Interface
3.3.3.3           0   FULL/  -      00:00:35    192.168.13.2   Serial0/0/1
2.2.2.2           0   FULL/  -      00:00:32    192.168.12.2   Serial0/0/0
R1#
```

Step 2. Change the router ID on R1 using the **router-id** command.

The preferred method for setting the router ID is with the **router-id** command.

a. Issue the **router-id 11.11.11.11** command on R1 to reassign the router ID. Notice the informational message that appears when issuing the **router-id** command.

```
R1(config)# router ospf 1
R1(config-router)# router-id 11.11.11.11
Reload or use "clear ip ospf process" command, for this to take effect
R1(config)# end
```

b. You will receive an informational message telling you that you must either reload the router or use the **clear ip ospf process** command for the change to take effect. Issue the **clear ip ospf process** command on all three routers. Type **yes** to reply to the reset verification message, and press ENTER.

c. Set the router ID for R2 to **22.22.22.22** and the router ID for R3 to **33.33.33.33**. Then use the **clear ip ospf process** command to reset ospf routing process.

d. Issue the **show ip protocols** command to verify that the router ID changed on R1.

```
R1# show ip protocols
*** IP Routing is NSF aware ***

Routing Protocol is "ospf 1"
  Outgoing update filter list for all interfaces is not set
  Incoming update filter list for all interfaces is not set
  Router ID 11.11.11.11
  Number of areas in this router is 1. 1 normal 0 stub 0 nssa
  Maximum path: 4
  Routing for Networks:
    192.168.1.0 0.0.0.255 area 0
    192.168.12.0 0.0.0.3 area 0
    192.168.13.0 0.0.0.3 area 0
  Passive Interface(s):
    GigabitEthernet0/1
  Routing Information Sources:
    Gateway         Distance      Last Update
    33.33.33.33          110      00:00:19
    22.22.22.22          110      00:00:31
    3.3.3.3              110      00:00:41
    2.2.2.2              110      00:00:41
  Distance: (default is 110)
```

e. Issue the **show ip ospf neighbor** command on R1 to verify that new router ID for R2 and R3 is listed.

```
R1# show ip ospf neighbor

Neighbor ID     Pri   State         Dead Time   Address         Interface
33.33.33.33       0   FULL/  -      00:00:36    192.168.13.2    Serial0/0/1
22.22.22.22       0   FULL/  -      00:00:32    192.168.12.2    Serial0/0/0
```

Part 4: Configure OSPF Passive Interfaces

The **passive-interface** command prevents routing updates from being sent through the specified router interface. This is commonly done to reduce traffic on the LANs as they do not need to receive dynamic routing protocol communication. In Part 4, you will use the **passive-interface** command to configure a single interface as passive. You will also configure OSPF so that all interfaces on the router are passive by default, and then enable OSPF routing advertisements on selected interfaces.

Step 1. Configure a passive interface.

a. Issue the **show ip ospf interface g0/0** command on R1. Notice the timer indicating when the next Hello packet is expected. Hello packets are sent every 10 seconds and are used between OSPF routers to verify that their neighbors are up.

```
R1# show ip ospf interface g0/0
GigabitEthernet0/0 is up, line protocol is up
  Internet Address 192.168.1.1/24, Area 0, Attached via Network Statement
  Process ID 1, Router ID 11.11.11.11, Network Type BROADCAST, Cost: 1
  Topology-MTID    Cost    Disabled    Shutdown    Topology Name
        0           1         no          no          Base
  Transmit Delay is 1 sec, State DR, Priority 1
```

```
         Designated Router (ID) 11.11.11.11, Interface address 192.168.1.1
         No backup designated router on this network
         Timer intervals configured, Hello 10, Dead 40, Wait 40, Retransmit 5
           oob-resync timeout 40
           Hello due in 00:00:02
         Supports Link-local Signaling (LLS)
         Cisco NSF helper support enabled
         IETF NSF helper support enabled
         Index 1/1, flood queue length 0
         Next 0x0(0)/0x0(0)
         Last flood scan length is 0, maximum is 0
         Last flood scan time is 0 msec, maximum is 0 msec
         Neighbor Count is 0, Adjacent neighbor count is 0
         Suppress hello for 0 neighbor(s)
```

b. Issue the **passive-interface** command to change the G0/0 interface on R1 to passive.

```
R1(config)# router ospf 1
R1(config-router)# passive-interface g0/0
```

c. Re-issue the **show ip ospf interface g0/0** command to verify that G0/0 is now passive.

```
R1# show ip ospf interface g0/0
GigabitEthernet0/0 is up, line protocol is up
   Internet Address 192.168.1.1/24, Area 0, Attached via Network Statement
   Process ID 1, Router ID 11.11.11.11, Network Type BROADCAST, Cost: 1
   Topology-MTID    Cost    Disabled    Shutdown      Topology Name
         0           1         no          no            Base
   Transmit Delay is 1 sec, State DR, Priority 1
   Designated Router (ID) 11.11.11.11, Interface address 192.168.1.1
   No backup designated router on this network
   Timer intervals configured, Hello 10, Dead 40, Wait 40, Retransmit 5
     oob-resync timeout 40
     No Hellos (Passive interface)
   Supports Link-local Signaling (LLS)
   Cisco NSF helper support enabled
   IETF NSF helper support enabled
   Index 1/1, flood queue length 0
   Next 0x0(0)/0x0(0)
   Last flood scan length is 0, maximum is 0
   Last flood scan time is 0 msec, maximum is 0 msec
   Neighbor Count is 0, Adjacent neighbor count is 0
   Suppress hello for 0 neighbor(s)
```

d. Issue the **show ip route** command on R2 and R3 to verify that a route to the 192.168.1.0/24 network is still available.

```
R2# show ip route
Codes: L - local, C - connected, S - static, R - RIP, M - mobile, B - BGP
       D - EIGRP, EX - EIGRP external, O - OSPF, IA - OSPF inter area
       N1 - OSPF NSSA external type 1, N2 - OSPF NSSA external type 2
       E1 - OSPF external type 1, E2 - OSPF external type 2
       i - IS-IS, su - IS-IS summary, L1 - IS-IS level-1, L2 - IS-IS level-2
       ia - IS-IS inter area, * - candidate default, U - per-user static route
       o - ODR, P - periodic downloaded static route, H - NHRP, l - LISP
```

```
                    + - replicated route, % - next hop override

         Gateway of last resort is not set

                2.0.0.0/32 is subnetted, 1 subnets
         C         2.2.2.2 is directly connected, Loopback0
         O        192.168.1.0/24 [110/65] via 192.168.12.1, 00:58:32, Serial0/0/0
                192.168.2.0/24 is variably subnetted, 2 subnets, 2 masks
         C        192.168.2.0/24 is directly connected, GigabitEthernet0/0
         L        192.168.2.1/32 is directly connected, GigabitEthernet0/0
         O        192.168.3.0/24 [110/65] via 192.168.23.2, 00:58:19, Serial0/0/1
                192.168.12.0/24 is variably subnetted, 2 subnets, 2 masks
         C        192.168.12.0/30 is directly connected, Serial0/0/0
         L        192.168.12.2/32 is directly connected, Serial0/0/0
                192.168.13.0/30 is subnetted, 1 subnets
         O        192.168.13.0 [110/128] via 192.168.23.2, 00:58:19, Serial0/0/1
                                [110/128] via 192.168.12.1, 00:58:32, Serial0/0/0
                192.168.23.0/24 is variably subnetted, 2 subnets, 2 masks
         C        192.168.23.0/30 is directly connected, Serial0/0/1
         L        192.168.23.1/32 is directly connected, Serial0/0/1
```

Step 2. Set passive interface as the default on a router.

a. Issue the **show ip ospf neighbor** command on R1 to verify that R2 is listed as an OSPF neighbor.

```
R1# show ip ospf neighbor

Neighbor ID     Pri   State           Dead Time   Address         Interface
33.33.33.33       0   FULL/  -        00:00:31    192.168.13.2    Serial0/0/1
22.22.22.22       0   FULL/  -        00:00:32    192.168.12.2    Serial0/0/0
```

b. Issue the **passive-interface default** command on R2 to set the default for all OSPF interfaces as passive.

```
R2(config)# router ospf 1
R2(config-router)# passive-interface default
R2(config-router)#
*Apr  3 00:03:00.979: %OSPF-5-ADJCHG: Process 1, Nbr 11.11.11.11 on Serial0/0/0
from FULL to DOWN, Neighbor Down: Interface down or detached
*Apr  3 00:03:00.979: %OSPF-5-ADJCHG: Process 1, Nbr 33.33.33.33 on Serial0/0/1
from FULL to DOWN, Neighbor Down: Interface down or detached
```

c. Re-issue the **show ip ospf neighbor** command on R1. After the dead timer expires, R2 will no longer be listed as an OSPF neighbor.

```
R1# show ip ospf neighbor

Neighbor ID     Pri   State           Dead Time   Address         Interface
33.33.33.33       0   FULL/  -        00:00:34    192.168.13.2    Serial0/0/1
```

d. Issue the **show ip ospf interface S0/0/0** command on R2 to view the OSPF status of interface S0/0/0.

```
R2# show ip ospf interface s0/0/0
Serial0/0/0 is up, line protocol is up
   Internet Address 192.168.12.2/30, Area 0, Attached via Network Statement
   Process ID 1, Router ID 22.22.22.22, Network Type POINT_TO_POINT, Cost: 64
```

```
Topology-MTID    Cost    Disabled    Shutdown    Topology Name
       0          64       no          no            Base
Transmit Delay is 1 sec, State POINT_TO_POINT
Timer intervals configured, Hello 10, Dead 40, Wait 40, Retransmit 5
   oob-resync timeout 40
   No Hellos (Passive interface)
Supports Link-local Signaling (LLS)
Cisco NSF helper support enabled
IETF NSF helper support enabled
Index 2/2, flood queue length 0
Next 0x0(0)/0x0(0)
Last flood scan length is 0, maximum is 0
Last flood scan time is 0 msec, maximum is 0 msec
Neighbor Count is 0, Adjacent neighbor count is 0
Suppress hello for 0 neighbor(s)
```

e. If all interfaces on R2 are passive, then no routing information is being advertised. In this case, R1 and R3 should no longer have a route to the 192.168.2.0/24 network. You can verify this by using the **show ip route** command.

f. On R2, issue the **no passive-interface** command so the router will send and receive OSPF routing updates. After entering this command, you will see an informational message that a neighbor adjacency has been established with R1.

```
R2(config)# router ospf 1
R2(config-router)# no passive-interface s0/0/0
R2(config-router)#
*Apr  3 00:18:03.463: %OSPF-5-ADJCHG: Process 1, Nbr 11.11.11.11 on Serial0/0/0
from LOADING to FULL, Loading Done
```

g. Re-issue the **show ip route** and **show ip ospf neighbor** commands on R1 and R3, and look for a route to the 192.168.2.0/24 network.

_____

_____

_____

_____

What interface is R3 using to route to the 192.168.2.0/24 network? _____

What is the accumulated cost metric for the 192.168.2.0/24 network on R3? _____

Does R2 show up as an OSPF neighbor on R1? _____

Does R2 show up as an OSPF neighbor on R3? _____

What does this information tell you?

_____

_____

_____

_____

h. Change interface S0/0/1 on R2 to allow it to advertise OSPF routes. Record the commands used below.

_____

_____

i. Re-issue the **show ip route** command on R3.

_____

What interface is R3 using to route to the 192.168.2.0/24 network? _____

What is the accumulated cost metric for the 192.168.2.0/24 network on R3 now and how is this calculated?

_____

Is R2 listed as an OSPF neighbor to R3? _____

Part 5: Change OSPF Metrics

In Part 5, you will change OSPF metrics using the **auto-cost reference-bandwidth** command, the **bandwidth** command, and the **ip ospf cost** command.

Note: All DCE interfaces should have been configured with a clocking rate of 128000 in Part 1.

Step 1. Change the reference bandwidth on the routers.

The default reference bandwidth for OSPF is 100Mb/s (Fast Ethernet speed). However, most modern infrastructure devices have links that are faster than 100Mb/s. Because the OSPF cost metric must be an integer, all links with transmission speeds of 100Mb/s or higher have a cost of 1. This results in Fast Ethernet, Gigabit Ethernet, and 10G Ethernet interfaces all having the same cost. Therefore, the reference bandwidth must be changed to a higher value to accommodate networks with links faster that 100Mb/s.

a. Issue the **show interface** command on R1 to view the default bandwidth setting for the G0/0 interface.

```
R1# show interface g0/0
GigabitEthernet0/0 is up, line protocol is up
  Hardware is CN Gigabit Ethernet, address is c471.fe45.7520 (bia c471.
fe45.7520)
  MTU 1500 bytes, BW 1000000 Kbit/sec, DLY 100 usec,
     reliability 255/255, txload 1/255, rxload 1/255
  Encapsulation ARPA, loopback not set
  Keepalive set (10 sec)
  Full Duplex, 100Mbps, media type is RJ45
  output flow-control is unsupported, input flow-control is unsupported
  ARP type: ARPA, ARP Timeout 04:00:00
  Last input never, output 00:17:31, output hang never
  Last clearing of "show interface" counters never
  Input queue: 0/75/0/0 (size/max/drops/flushes); Total output drops: 0
  Queueing strategy: fifo
  Output queue: 0/40 (size/max)
  5 minute input rate 0 bits/sec, 0 packets/sec
  5 minute output rate 0 bits/sec, 0 packets/sec
```

```
0 packets input, 0 bytes, 0 no buffer
Received 0 broadcasts (0 IP multicasts)
0 runts, 0 giants, 0 throttles
0 input errors, 0 CRC, 0 frame, 0 overrun, 0 ignored
0 watchdog, 0 multicast, 0 pause input
279 packets output, 89865 bytes, 0 underruns
0 output errors, 0 collisions, 1 interface resets
0 unknown protocol drops
0 babbles, 0 late collision, 0 deferred
1 lost carrier, 0 no carrier, 0 pause output
0 output buffer failures, 0 output buffers swapped out
```

Note: The bandwidth setting on G0/0 may differ from what is shown above if the PC host interface can only support Fast Ethernet speed. If the PC host interface is not capable of supporting gigabit speed, then the bandwidth will most likely be displayed as 100000 Kbit/sec.

b. Issue the **show ip route ospf** command on R1 to determine the route to the 192.168.3.0/24 network.

```
R1# show ip route ospf
Codes: L - local, C - connected, S - static, R - RIP, M - mobile, B - BGP
       D - EIGRP, EX - EIGRP external, O - OSPF, IA - OSPF inter area
       N1 - OSPF NSSA external type 1, N2 - OSPF NSSA external type 2
       E1 - OSPF external type 1, E2 - OSPF external type 2
       i - IS-IS, su - IS-IS summary, L1 - IS-IS level-1, L2 - IS-IS level-2
       ia - IS-IS inter area, * - candidate default, U - per-user static route
       o - ODR, P - periodic downloaded static route, H - NHRP, l - LISP
       + - replicated route, % - next hop override


Gateway of last resort is not set

O      192.168.2.0/24 [110/65] via 192.168.12.2, 00:01:08, Serial0/0/0
O      192.168.3.0/24 [110/65] via 192.168.13.2, 00:00:57, Serial0/0/1
       192.168.23.0/30 is subnetted, 1 subnets
O         192.168.23.0 [110/128] via 192.168.13.2, 00:00:57, Serial0/0/1
                       [110/128] via 192.168.12.2, 00:01:08, Serial0/0/0
```

Note: The accumulated cost to the 192.168.3.0/24 network from R1 is 65.

c. Issue the **show ip ospf interface** command on R3 to determine the routing cost for G0/0.

```
R3# show ip ospf interface g0/0
GigabitEthernet0/0 is up, line protocol is up
  Internet Address 192.168.3.1/24, Area 0, Attached via Network Statement
  Process ID 1, Router ID 3.3.3.3, Network Type BROADCAST, Cost: 1
  Topology-MTID    Cost    Disabled    Shutdown      Topology Name
        0            1        no          no             Base
  Transmit Delay is 1 sec, State DR, Priority 1
  Designated Router (ID) 192.168.23.2, Interface address 192.168.3.1
  No backup designated router on this network
  Timer intervals configured, Hello 10, Dead 40, Wait 40, Retransmit 5
    oob-resync timeout 40
```

```
     Hello due in 00:00:05
  Supports Link-local Signaling (LLS)
  Cisco NSF helper support enabled
  IETF NSF helper support enabled
  Index 1/1, flood queue length 0
  Next 0x0(0)/0x0(0)
  Last flood scan length is 0, maximum is 0
  Last flood scan time is 0 msec, maximum is 0 msec
  Neighbor Count is 0, Adjacent neighbor count is 0
  Suppress hello for 0 neighbor(s)
```

d. Issue the **show ip ospf interface s0/0/1** command on R1 to view the routing cost for S0/0/1.

```
R1# show ip ospf interface s0/0/1
Serial0/0/1 is up, line protocol is up
  Internet Address 192.168.13.1/30, Area 0, Attached via Network Statement
  Process ID 1, Router ID 1.1.1.1, Network Type POINT_TO_POINT, Cost: 64
  Topology-MTID    Cost    Disabled    Shutdown      Topology Name
        0           64       no          no             Base
  Transmit Delay is 1 sec, State POINT_TO_POINT
  Timer intervals configured, Hello 10, Dead 40, Wait 40, Retransmit 5
    oob-resync timeout 40
    Hello due in 00:00:04
  Supports Link-local Signaling (LLS)
  Cisco NSF helper support enabled
  IETF NSF helper support enabled
  Index 3/3, flood queue length 0
  Next 0x0(0)/0x0(0)
  Last flood scan length is 1, maximum is 1
  Last flood scan time is 0 msec, maximum is 0 msec
  Neighbor Count is 1, Adjacent neighbor count is 1
    Adjacent with neighbor 192.168.23.2
  Suppress hello for 0 neighbor(s)
```

The sum of the costs of these two interfaces is the accumulated cost for the route to the 192.168.3.0/24 network on R3 (1 + 64 = 65), as can be seen in the output from the **show ip route** command.

e. Issue the **auto-cost reference-bandwidth 10000** command on R1 to change the default reference bandwidth setting. With this setting, 10Gb/s interfaces will have a cost of 1, 1 Gb/s interfaces will have a cost of 10, and 100Mb/s interfaces will have a cost of 100.

```
R1(config)# router ospf 1
R1(config-router)# auto-cost reference-bandwidth 10000
% OSPF: Reference bandwidth is changed.
        Please ensure reference bandwidth is consistent across all routers.
```

f. Issue the **auto-cost reference-bandwidth 10000** command on routers R2 and R3.

g. Re-issue the **show ip ospf interface** command to view the new cost of G0/0 on R3, and S0/0/1 on R1.

```
R3# show ip ospf interface g0/0
GigabitEthernet0/0 is up, line protocol is up
  Internet Address 192.168.3.1/24, Area 0, Attached via Network Statement
```

```
               Process ID 1, Router ID 3.3.3.3, Network Type BROADCAST, Cost: 10
               Topology-MTID    Cost    Disabled    Shutdown     Topology Name
                     0            10        no          no           Base
               Transmit Delay is 1 sec, State DR, Priority 1
               Designated Router (ID) 192.168.23.2, Interface address 192.168.3.1
               No backup designated router on this network
               Timer intervals configured, Hello 10, Dead 40, Wait 40, Retransmit 5
                 oob-resync timeout 40
                 Hello due in 00:00:02
               Supports Link-local Signaling (LLS)
               Cisco NSF helper support enabled
               IETF NSF helper support enabled
               Index 1/1, flood queue length 0
               Next 0x0(0)/0x0(0)
               Last flood scan length is 0, maximum is 0
               Last flood scan time is 0 msec, maximum is 0 msec
               Neighbor Count is 0, Adjacent neighbor count is 0
               Suppress hello for 0 neighbor(s)
```

Note: If the device connected to the G0/0 interface does not support Gigabit Ethernet speed, the cost will be different than the output display. For example, the cost will be 100 for Fast Ethernet speed (100Mb/s).

```
     R1# show ip ospf interface s0/0/1
     Serial0/0/1 is up, line protocol is up
        Internet Address 192.168.13.1/30, Area 0, Attached via Network Statement
        Process ID 1, Router ID 1.1.1.1, Network Type POINT_TO_POINT, Cost: 6476
        Topology-MTID    Cost    Disabled    Shutdown     Topology Name
              0           6476      no          no           Base
        Transmit Delay is 1 sec, State POINT_TO_POINT
        Timer intervals configured, Hello 10, Dead 40, Wait 40, Retransmit 5
          oob-resync timeout 40
          Hello due in 00:00:05
        Supports Link-local Signaling (LLS)
        Cisco NSF helper support enabled
        IETF NSF helper support enabled
        Index 3/3, flood queue length 0
        Next 0x0(0)/0x0(0)
        Last flood scan length is 1, maximum is 1
        Last flood scan time is 0 msec, maximum is 0 msec
        Neighbor Count is 1, Adjacent neighbor count is 1
          Adjacent with neighbor 192.168.23.2
        Suppress hello for 0 neighbor(s)
```

h. Re-issue the **show ip route ospf** command to view the new accumulated cost for the 192.168.3.0/24 route (10 + 6476 = 6486).

Note: If the device connected to the G0/0 interface does not support Gigabit Ethernet speed, the total cost will be different than the output display. For example, the accumulated cost will be 6576 if G0/0 is operating at Fast Ethernet speed (100Mb/s).

```
     R1# show ip route ospf
     Codes: L - local, C - connected, S - static, R - RIP, M - mobile, B - BGP
```

```
              D - EIGRP, EX - EIGRP external, O - OSPF, IA - OSPF inter area
              N1 - OSPF NSSA external type 1, N2 - OSPF NSSA external type 2
              E1 - OSPF external type 1, E2 - OSPF external type 2
              i - IS-IS, su - IS-IS summary, L1 - IS-IS level-1, L2 - IS-IS level-2
              ia - IS-IS inter area, * - candidate default, U - per-user static route
              o - ODR, P - periodic downloaded static route, H - NHRP, l - LISP
              + - replicated route, % - next hop override

      Gateway of last resort is not set

      O     192.168.2.0/24 [110/6486] via 192.168.12.2, 00:05:40, Serial0/0/0
      O     192.168.3.0/24 [110/6486] via 192.168.13.2, 00:01:08, Serial0/0/1
            192.168.23.0/30 is subnetted, 1 subnets
      O        192.168.23.0 [110/12952] via 192.168.13.2, 00:05:17, Serial0/0/1
                            [110/12952] via 192.168.12.2, 00:05:17, Serial0/0/
```

Note: Changing the default reference-bandwidth on the routers from 100 to 10,000 in effect changed the accumulated costs of all routes by a factor of 100, but the cost of each interface link and route is now more accurately reflected.

    i. To reset the reference-bandwidth back to its default value, issue the **auto-cost reference-bandwidth 100** command on all three routers.

```
R1(config)# router ospf 1
R1(config-router)# auto-cost reference-bandwidth 100
% OSPF: Reference bandwidth is changed.
        Please ensure reference bandwidth is consistent across all routers.
```

Why would you want to change the OSPF default reference-bandwidth?

_____

_____

Step 2.   Change the bandwidth for an interface.

On most serial links, the bandwidth metric will default to 1544 Kbits (that of a T1). If this is not the actual speed of the serial link, the bandwidth setting will need to be changed to match the actual speed to allow the route cost to be calculated correctly in OSPF. Use the **bandwidth** command to adjust the bandwidth setting on an interface.

Note: A common misconception is to assume that the **bandwidth** command will change the physical bandwidth, or speed, of the link. The command modifies the bandwidth metric used by OSPF to calculate routing costs, and does not modify the actual bandwidth (speed) of the link.

    a. Issue the **show interface s0/0/0** command on R1 to view the current bandwidth setting on S0/0/0. Even though the clock rate, link speed on this interface was set to 128Kb/s, the bandwidth is still showing 1544Kb/s.

```
R1# show interface s0/0/0
Serial0/0/0 is up, line protocol is up
  Hardware is WIC MBRD Serial
  Internet address is 192.168.12.1/30
  MTU 1500 bytes, BW 1544 Kbit/sec, DLY 20000 usec,
     reliability 255/255, txload 1/255, rxload 1/255
  Encapsulation HDLC, loopback not set
```

```
        Keepalive set (10 sec)
    <Output omitted>
```

b. Issue the **show ip route ospf** command on R1 to view the accumulated cost for the route to network 192.168.23.0/24 using S0/0/0. Note that there are two equal-cost (128) routes to the 192.168.23.0/24 network, one via S0/0/0 and one via S0/0/1.

```
R1# show ip route ospf
Codes: L - local, C - connected, S - static, R - RIP, M - mobile, B - BGP
       D - EIGRP, EX - EIGRP external, O - OSPF, IA - OSPF inter area
       N1 - OSPF NSSA external type 1, N2 - OSPF NSSA external type 2
       E1 - OSPF external type 1, E2 - OSPF external type 2
       i - IS-IS, su - IS-IS summary, L1 - IS-IS level-1, L2 - IS-IS level-2
       ia - IS-IS inter area, * - candidate default, U - per-user static route
       o - ODR, P - periodic downloaded static route, H - NHRP, l - LISP
       + - replicated route, % - next hop override


Gateway of last resort is not set

O     192.168.2.0/24 [110/65] via 192.168.12.2, 00:00:26, Serial0/0/0
O     192.168.3.0/24 [110/65] via 192.168.13.2, 00:00:26, Serial0/0/1
      192.168.23.0/30 is subnetted, 1 subnets
O        192.168.23.0 [110/128] via 192.168.13.2, 00:00:26, Serial0/0/1
                      [110/128] via 192.168.12.2, 00:00:26, Serial0/0/0
```

c. Issue the **bandwidth 128** command to set the bandwidth on S0/0/0 to 128Kb/s.

```
R1(config)# interface s0/0/0
R1(config-if)# bandwidth 128
```

d. Re-issue the **show ip route ospf** command. The routing table no longer displays the route to the 192.168.23.0/24 network over the S0/0/0 interface. This is because the best route, the one with the lowest cost, is now via S0/0/1.

```
R1# show ip route ospf
Codes: L - local, C - connected, S - static, R - RIP, M - mobile, B - BGP
       D - EIGRP, EX - EIGRP external, O - OSPF, IA - OSPF inter area
       N1 - OSPF NSSA external type 1, N2 - OSPF NSSA external type 2
       E1 - OSPF external type 1, E2 - OSPF external type 2
       i - IS-IS, su - IS-IS summary, L1 - IS-IS level-1, L2 - IS-IS level-2
       ia - IS-IS inter area, * - candidate default, U - per-user static route
       o - ODR, P - periodic downloaded static route, H - NHRP, l - LISP
       + - replicated route, % - next hop override


Gateway of last resort is not set

O     192.168.2.0/24 [110/129] via 192.168.12.2, 00:01:47, Serial0/0/0
O     192.168.3.0/24 [110/65] via 192.168.13.2, 00:04:51, Serial0/0/1
      192.168.23.0/30 is subnetted, 1 subnets
O        192.168.23.0 [110/128] via 192.168.13.2, 00:04:51, Serial0/0/1
```

e. Issue the **show ip ospf interface brief** command. The cost for S0/0/0 has changed from 64 to 781, which is an accurate cost representation of the link speed.

```
R1# show ip ospf interface brief
Interface   PID   Area         IP Address/Mask    Cost  State Nbrs F/C
Se0/0/1     1     0            192.168.13.1/30    64    P2P   1/1
Se0/0/0     1     0            192.168.12.1/30    781   P2P   1/1
Gi0/0       1     0            192.168.1.1/24     1     DR    0/0
```

f. Change the bandwidth for interface S0/0/1 to the same setting as S0/0/0 on R1.

_____

_____

g. Re-issue the **show ip route ospf** command to view the accumulated cost of both routes to the 192.168.23.0/24 network. Note that there are again two equal-cost (845) routes to the 192.168.23.0/24 network, one via S0/0/0 and one via S0/0/1.

```
R1# show ip route ospf
Codes: L - local, C - connected, S - static, R - RIP, M - mobile, B - BGP
       D - EIGRP, EX - EIGRP external, O - OSPF, IA - OSPF inter area
       N1 - OSPF NSSA external type 1, N2 - OSPF NSSA external type 2
       E1 - OSPF external type 1, E2 - OSPF external type 2
       i - IS-IS, su - IS-IS summary, L1 - IS-IS level-1, L2 - IS-IS level-2
       ia - IS-IS inter area, * - candidate default, U - per-user static route
       o - ODR, P - periodic downloaded static route, H - NHRP, l - LISP
       + - replicated route, % - next hop override


Gateway of last resort is not set

O     192.168.2.0/24 [110/782] via 192.168.12.2, 00:00:09, Serial0/0/0
O     192.168.3.0/24 [110/782] via 192.168.13.2, 00:00:09, Serial0/0/1
      192.168.23.0/30 is subnetted, 1 subnets
O        192.168.23.0 [110/845] via 192.168.13.2, 00:00:09, Serial0/0/1
                      [110/845] via 192.168.12.2, 00:00:09, Serial0/0/0
```

Explain how the costs to the 192.168.3.0/24 and 192.168.23.0/30 networks from R1 were calculated.

_____

_____

h. Issue the **show ip route ospf** command on R3. The accumulated cost of the 192.168.1.0/24 is still showing as 65. Unlike the **clock rate** command, the **bandwidth** command needs to be applied on each side of a serial link.

```
R3# show ip route ospf
Codes: L - local, C - connected, S - static, R - RIP, M - mobile, B - BGP
       D - EIGRP, EX - EIGRP external, O - OSPF, IA - OSPF inter area
       N1 - OSPF NSSA external type 1, N2 - OSPF NSSA external type 2
       E1 - OSPF external type 1, E2 - OSPF external type 2
       i - IS-IS, su - IS-IS summary, L1 - IS-IS level-1, L2 - IS-IS level-2
       ia - IS-IS inter area, * - candidate default, U - per-user static route
       o - ODR, P - periodic downloaded static route, H - NHRP, l - LISP
```

— nothing here —

```
          + - replicated route, % - next hop override

Gateway of last resort is not set

O    192.168.1.0/24 [110/65] via 192.168.13.1, 00:30:58, Serial0/0/0
O    192.168.2.0/24 [110/65] via 192.168.23.1, 00:30:58, Serial0/0/1
     192.168.12.0/30 is subnetted, 1 subnets
O       192.168.12.0 [110/128] via 192.168.23.1, 00:30:58, Serial0/0/1
                     [110/128] via 192.168.13.1, 00:30:58, Serial0/0/0
```

i. Issue the **bandwidth 128** command on all remaining serial interfaces in the topology.

What is the new accumulated cost to the 192.168.23.0/24 network on R1? Why?

Step 3. Change the route cost.

OSPF uses the bandwidth setting to calculate the cost for a link by default. However, you can override this calculation by manually setting the cost of a link using the **ip ospf cost** command. Like the **bandwidth** command, the **ip ospf cost** command only affects the side of the link where it was applied.

a. Issue the **show ip route ospf** on R1.

```
R1# show ip route ospf
Codes: L - local, C - connected, S - static, R - RIP, M - mobile, B - BGP
       D - EIGRP, EX - EIGRP external, O - OSPF, IA - OSPF inter area
       N1 - OSPF NSSA external type 1, N2 - OSPF NSSA external type 2
       E1 - OSPF external type 1, E2 - OSPF external type 2
       i - IS-IS, su - IS-IS summary, L1 - IS-IS level-1, L2 - IS-IS level-2
       ia - IS-IS inter area, * - candidate default, U - per-user static route
       o - ODR, P - periodic downloaded static route, H - NHRP, l - LISP
       + - replicated route, % - next hop override

Gateway of last resort is not set

O    192.168.2.0/24 [110/782] via 192.168.12.2, 00:00:26, Serial0/0/0
O    192.168.3.0/24 [110/782] via 192.168.13.2, 00:02:50, Serial0/0/1
     192.168.23.0/30 is subnetted, 1 subnets
O       192.168.23.0 [110/1562] via 192.168.13.2, 00:02:40, Serial0/0/1
                     [110/1562] via 192.168.12.2, 00:02:40, Serial0/0/0
```

b. Apply the **ip ospf cost 1565** command to the S0/0/1 interface on R1. A cost of 1565 is higher than the accumulated cost of the route through R2, which is 1562.

```
R1(config)# interface s0/0/1
R1(config-if)# ip ospf cost 1565
```

c. Re-issue the **show ip route ospf** command on R1 to display the effect this change has made on the routing table. All OSPF routes for R1 are now being routed through R2.

```
R1# show ip route ospf
Codes: L - local, C - connected, S - static, R - RIP, M - mobile, B - BGP
       D - EIGRP, EX - EIGRP external, O - OSPF, IA - OSPF inter area
       N1 - OSPF NSSA external type 1, N2 - OSPF NSSA external type 2
```

```
        E1 - OSPF external type 1, E2 - OSPF external type 2
        i - IS-IS, su - IS-IS summary, L1 - IS-IS level-1, L2 - IS-IS level-2
        ia - IS-IS inter area, * - candidate default, U - per-user static route
        o - ODR, P - periodic downloaded static route, H - NHRP, l - LISP
        + - replicated route, % - next hop override

Gateway of last resort is not set

O       192.168.2.0/24 [110/782] via 192.168.12.2, 00:02:06, Serial0/0/0
O       192.168.3.0/24 [110/1563] via 192.168.12.2, 00:05:31, Serial0/0/0
        192.168.23.0/30 is subnetted, 1 subnets
O          192.168.23.0 [110/1562] via 192.168.12.2, 01:14:02, Serial0/0/0
```

Note: Manipulating link costs using the **ip ospf cost** command is the easiest and preferred method for changing OSPF route costs. In addition to changing the cost based on bandwidth, a network administrator may have other reasons for changing the cost of a route, such as preference for a particular service provider or the actual monetary cost of a link or route.

Explain why the route to the 192.168.3.0/24 network on R1 is now going through R2?

_____

_____

_____

Reflection

1. Why is it important to control the router ID assignment when using the OSPF protocol?

_____

_____

_____

2. Why is the DR/BDR election process not a concern in this lab?

_____

_____

_____

3. Why would you want to set an OSPF interface to passive?

_____

_____

_____

Router Interface Summary Table

	Router Interface Summary			
Router Model	Ethernet Interface #1	Ethernet Interface #2	Serial Interface #1	Serial Interface #2
1800	Fast Ethernet 0/0 (F0/0)	Fast Ethernet 0/1 (F0/1)	Serial 0/0/0 (S0/0/0)	Serial 0/0/1 (S0/0/1)
1900	Gigabit Ethernet 0/0 (G0/0)	Gigabit Ethernet 0/1 (G0/1)	Serial 0/0/0 (S0/0/0)	Serial 0/0/1 (S0/0/1)
2801	Fast Ethernet 0/0 (F0/0)	Fast Ethernet 0/1 (F0/1)	Serial 0/1/0 (S0/1/0)	Serial 0/1/1 (S0/1/1)
2811	Fast Ethernet 0/0 (F0/0)	Fast Ethernet 0/1 (F0/1)	Serial 0/0/0 (S0/0/0)	Serial 0/0/1 (S0/0/1)
2900	Gigabit Ethernet 0/0 (G0/0)	Gigabit Ethernet 0/1 (G0/1)	Serial 0/0/0 (S0/0/0)	Serial 0/0/1 (S0/0/1)

Note: To find out how the router is configured, look at the interfaces to identify the type of router and how many interfaces the router has. There is no way to effectively list all the combinations of configurations for each router class. This table includes identifiers for the possible combinations of Ethernet and Serial interfaces in the device. The table does not include any other type of interface, even though a specific router may contain one. An example of this might be an ISDN BRI interface. The string in parentheses is the legal abbreviation that can be used in Cisco IOS commands to represent the interface.

Packet Tracer
☐ Activity

8.3.3.5 Packet Tracer–Configuring Basic OSPFv3 in a Single Area

Topology

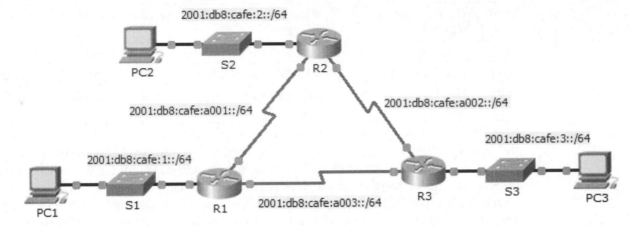

Addressing Table

Device	Interface	IPv6 Address/Prefix	Default Gateway
R1	G0/0	2001:db8:cafe:1::1/64	N/A
	S0/0/0	2001:db8:cafe:a001::1/64	N/A
	S0/0/1	2001:db8:cafe:a003::1/64	N/A
R2	G0/0	2001:db8:cafe:2::1/64	N/A
	S0/0/0	2001:db8:cafe:a001::2/64	N/A
	S0/0/1	2001:db8:cafe:a002::1/64	N/A
R3	G0/0	2001:db8:cafe:3::1/64	N/A
	S0/0/0	2001:db8:cafe:a003::264	N/A
	S0/0/1	2001:db8:cafe:a002::2/64	N/A
PC1	NIC	2001:db8:cafe:1::10/64	fe80::1
PC2	NIC	2001:db8:cafe:2::10/64	fe80::2
PC3	NIC	2001:db8:cafe:3::10/64	fe80::3

Objectives

Part 1: Configure OSPFv3 Routing

Part 2: Verify Connectivity

Background

In this activity, the IPv6 addressing is already configured. You are responsible for configuring the three router topology with basic single area OSPFv3 and then verifying connectivity between end devices.

Part 1: Configure OSPFv3 Routing

Step 1.   Configure OSPFv3 on R1, R2, and R3.

Use the following requirements to configure OSPF routing on all three routers:

- Enable IPv6 routing
- Process ID 10
- Router ID for each router: R1 = 1.1.1.1; R2 = 2.2.2.2; R3 = 3.3.3.3
- Enable OSPFv3 on each interface

Note: Packet Trace version 6.0.1 does not support the **auto-cost reference-bandwidth** command, so you will not be adjusting bandwidth costs in this activity.

Step 2.   Verify OSPF routing is operational.

Verify each router has established adjacency with the other two routers. Verify the routing table has a route to every network in the topology.

Part 2: Verify Connectivity

Each PC should be able to ping the other two PCs. If not, check your configurations.

Note: This activity is graded using only connectivity tests. The instructions window will not show your score. To see your score, click **Check Results > Assessment Items.** To see the results of a specific connectivity test, click **Check Results > Connectivity Tests.**

8.3.3.6 Lab–Configuring Basic Single-Area OSPFv3

Topology

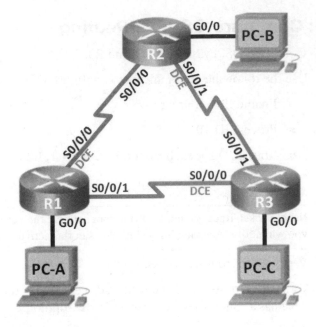

Addressing Table

Device	Interface	IPv6 Address	Default Gateway
R1	G0/0	2001:DB8:ACAD:A::1/64	N/A
		FE80::1 link-local	
	S0/0/0 (DCE)	2001:DB8:ACAD:12::1/64	N/A
		FE80::1 link-local	
	S0/0/1	2001:DB8:ACAD:13::1/64	N/A
		FE80::1 link-local	
R2	G0/0	2001:DB8:ACAD:B::2/64	N/A
		FE80::2 link-local	
	S0/0/0	2001:DB8:ACAD:12::2/64	N/A
		FE80::2 link-local	
	S0/0/1 (DCE)	2001:DB8:ACAD:23::2/64	N/A
		FE80::2 link-local	
R3	G0/0	2001:DB8:ACAD:C::3/64	N/A
		FE80::3 link-local	
	S0/0/0 (DCE)	2001:DB8:ACAD:13::3/64	N/A
		FE80::3 link-local	
	S0/0/1	2001:DB8:ACAD:23::3/64	N/A
		FE80::3 link-local	

Device	Interface	IPv6 Address	Default Gateway
PC-A	NIC	2001:DB8:ACAD:A::A/64	FE80::1
PC-B	NIC	2001:DB8:ACAD:B::B/64	FE80::2
PC-C	NIC	2001:DB8:ACAD:C::C/64	FE80::3

Objectives

Part 1: Build the Network and Configure Basic Device Settings

Part 2: Configure and Verify OSPFv3 Routing

Part 3: Configure OSPFv3 Passive Interfaces

Background/Scenario

Open Shortest Path First (OSPF) is a link-state routing protocol for IP networks. OSPFv2 is defined for IPv4 networks, and OSPFv3 is defined for IPv6 networks.

In this lab, you will configure the network topology with OSPFv3 routing, assign router IDs, configure passive interfaces, and use a number of CLI commands to display and verify OSPFv3 routing information.

Note: The routers used with CCNA hands-on labs are Cisco 1941 Integrated Services Routers (ISRs) with Cisco IOS Release 15.2(4)M3 (universalk9 image). Other routers and Cisco IOS versions can be used. Depending on the model and Cisco IOS version, the commands available and output produced might vary from what is shown in the labs. Refer to the Router Interface Summary Table at the end of this lab for the correct interface identifiers.

Note: Make sure that the routers have been erased and have no startup configurations. If you are unsure, contact your instructor.

Required Resources

- 3 Routers (Cisco 1941 with Cisco IOS Release 15.2(4)M3 universal image or comparable)

- 3 PCs (Windows 7, Vista, or XP with terminal emulation program, such as Tera Term)

- Console cables to configure the Cisco IOS devices via the console ports

- Ethernet and serial cables as shown in the topology

Part 1: Build the Network and Configure Basic Device Settings

In Part 1, you will set up the network topology and configure basic settings on the PC hosts and routers.

Step 1.   Cable the network as shown in the topology.

Step 2.   Initialize and reload the routers as necessary.

Step 3.   Configure basic settings for each router.

    a.   Disable DNS lookup.

    b.   Configure device name as shown in the topology.

c. Assign **class** as the privileged EXEC password.

d. Assign **cisco** as the vty password.

e. Configure a MOTD banner to warn users that unauthorized access is prohibited.

f. Configure **logging synchronous** for the console line.

g. Encrypt plain text passwords.

h. Configure the IPv6 unicast and link-local addresses listed in the Addressing Table for all interfaces.

i. Enable IPv6 unicast routing on each router.

j. Copy the running configuration to the startup configuration.

Step 4. Configure PC hosts.

Step 5. Test connectivity.

The routers should be able to ping one another, and each PC should be able to ping its default gateway. The PCs are unable to ping other PCs until OSPFv3 routing is configured. Verify and troubleshoot if necessary.

Part 2: Configure OSPFv3 Routing

In Part 2, you will configure OSPFv3 routing on all routers in the network and then verify that routing tables are updated correctly.

Step 1. Assign router IDs.

OSPFv3 continues to use a 32 bit address for the router ID. Because there are no IPv4 addresses configured on the routers, you will manually assign the router ID using the **router-id** command.

a. Issue the **ipv6 router ospf** command to start an OSPFv3 process to the router.

```
R1(config)# ipv6 router ospf 1
```

Note: The OSPF process ID is kept locally and has no meaning to other routers on the network.

---

b. Assign the OSPFv3 router ID **1.1.1.1** to R1.

```
R1(config-rtr)# router-id 1.1.1.1
```

c. Start the OSPFv3 routing process and assign a router ID of **2.2.2.2** to R2 and a router ID of **3.3.3.3** to R3.

d. Issue the **show ipv6 ospf** command to verify the router IDs on all routers.

```
R2# show ipv6 ospf
Routing Process "ospfv3 1" with ID 2.2.2.2
Event-log enabled, Maximum number of events: 1000, Mode: cyclic
Router is not originating router-LSAs with maximum metric
<output omitted>
```

Step 2.   Configure OSPFv6 on R1.

With IPv6, it is common to have multiple IPv6 addresses configured on an interface. The network statement has been eliminated in OSPFv3. OSPFv3 routing is enabled at the interface level instead.

a.   Issue the **ipv6 ospf 1 area 0** command for each interface on R1 that is to participate in OSPFv3 routing.

```
R1(config)# interface g0/0
R1(config-if)# ipv6 ospf 1 area 0
R1(config-if)# interface s0/0/0
R1(config-if)# ipv6 ospf 1 area 0
R1(config-if)# interface s0/0/1
R1(config-if)# ipv6 ospf 1 area 0
```

Note: The process ID must match the process ID you used in Step 1a.

b.   Assign the interfaces on R2 and R3 to OSPFv3 area 0. You should see neighbor adjacency messages display when adding the interfaces to area 0.

```
R1#
*Mar 19 22:14:43.251: %OSPFv3-5-ADJCHG: Process 1, Nbr 2.2.2.2 on Serial0/0/0
from LOADING to FULL, Loading Done
R1#
*Mar 19 22:14:46.763: %OSPFv3-5-ADJCHG: Process 1, Nbr 3.3.3.3 on Serial0/0/1
from LOADING to FULL, Loading Done
```

Step 3.   Verify OSPFv3 neighbors.

Issue the **show ipv6 ospf neighbor** command to verify that the router has formed an adjacency with its neighboring routers. If the router ID of the neighboring router is not displayed, or if its state does not show as FULL, the two routers have not formed an OSPF adjacency.

```
R1# show ipv6 ospf neighbor


          OSPFv3 Router with ID (1.1.1.1) (Process ID 1)


Neighbor ID     Pri   State           Dead Time   Interface ID   Interface
3.3.3.3           0   FULL/  -        00:00:39    6              Serial0/0/1
2.2.2.2           0   FULL/  -        00:00:36    6              Serial0/0/0
```

Step 4.   Verify OSPFv3 protocol settings.

The **show ipv6 protocols** command is a quick way to verify vital OSPFv3 configuration information, including the OSPF process ID, the router ID, and the interfaces enabled for OSPFv3.

```
R1# show ipv6 protocols
IPv6 Routing Protocol is "connected"
IPv6 Routing Protocol is "ND"
IPv6 Routing Protocol is "ospf 1"
  Router ID 1.1.1.1
  Number of areas: 1 normal, 0 stub, 0 nssa
  Interfaces (Area 0):
    Serial0/0/1
```

```
        Serial0/0/0
        GigabitEthernet0/0
     Redistribution:
        None
```

Step 5.   Verify OSPFv3 interfaces.

    a.   Issue the **show ipv6 ospf interface** command to display a detailed list for every OSPF-enabled interface.

```
R1# show ipv6 ospf interface
Serial0/0/1 is up, line protocol is up
  Link Local Address FE80::1, Interface ID 7
  Area 0, Process ID 1, Instance ID 0, Router ID 1.1.1.1
  Network Type POINT_TO_POINT, Cost: 64
  Transmit Delay is 1 sec, State POINT_TO_POINT
  Timer intervals configured, Hello 10, Dead 40, Wait 40, Retransmit 5
    Hello due in 00:00:05
  Graceful restart helper support enabled
  Index 1/3/3, flood queue length 0
  Next 0x0(0)/0x0(0)/0x0(0)
  Last flood scan length is 1, maximum is 1
  Last flood scan time is 0 msec, maximum is 0 msec
  Neighbor Count is 1, Adjacent neighbor count is 1
    Adjacent with neighbor 3.3.3.3
  Suppress hello for 0 neighbor(s)
Serial0/0/0 is up, line protocol is up
  Link Local Address FE80::1, Interface ID 6
  Area 0, Process ID 1, Instance ID 0, Router ID 1.1.1.1
  Network Type POINT_TO_POINT, Cost: 64
  Transmit Delay is 1 sec, State POINT_TO_POINT
  Timer intervals configured, Hello 10, Dead 40, Wait 40, Retransmit 5
    Hello due in 00:00:00
  Graceful restart helper support enabled
  Index 1/2/2, flood queue length 0
  Next 0x0(0)/0x0(0)/0x0(0)
  Last flood scan length is 1, maximum is 2
  Last flood scan time is 0 msec, maximum is 0 msec
  Neighbor Count is 1, Adjacent neighbor count is 1
    Adjacent with neighbor 2.2.2.2
  Suppress hello for 0 neighbor(s)
GigabitEthernet0/0 is up, line protocol is up
  Link Local Address FE80::1, Interface ID 3
  Area 0, Process ID 1, Instance ID 0, Router ID 1.1.1.1
  Network Type BROADCAST, Cost: 1
  Transmit Delay is 1 sec, State DR, Priority 1
  Designated Router (ID) 1.1.1.1, local address FE80::1
  No backup designated router on this network
  Timer intervals configured, Hello 10, Dead 40, Wait 40, Retransmit 5
    Hello due in 00:00:03
  Graceful restart helper support enabled
  Index 1/1/1, flood queue length 0
  Next 0x0(0)/0x0(0)/0x0(0)
```

```
Last flood scan length is 0, maximum is 0
Last flood scan time is 0 msec, maximum is 0 msec
Neighbor Count is 0, Adjacent neighbor count is 0
Suppress hello for 0 neighbor(s)
```

b. To display a summary of OSPFv3-enabled interfaces, issue the **show ipv6 ospf interface brief** command.

```
R1# show ipv6 ospf interface brief
Interface   PID   Area        Intf ID   Cost   State Nbrs F/C
Se0/0/1     1     0           7         64     P2P   1/1
Se0/0/0     1     0           6         64     P2P   1/1
Gi0/0       1     0           3         1      DR    0/0
```

Step 6.   Verify the IPv6 routing table.

Issue the **show ipv6 route** command to verify that all networks are appearing in the routing table.

```
R2# show ipv6 route
IPv6 Routing Table - default - 10 entries
Codes: C - Connected, L - Local, S - Static, U - Per-user Static route
       B - BGP, R - RIP, I1 - ISIS L1, I2 - ISIS L2
       IA - ISIS interarea, IS - ISIS summary, D - EIGRP, EX - EIGRP external
       ND - ND Default, NDp - ND Prefix, DCE - Destination, NDr - Redirect
       O - OSPF Intra, OI - OSPF Inter, OE1 - OSPF ext 1, OE2 - OSPF ext 2
       ON1 - OSPF NSSA ext 1, ON2 - OSPF NSSA ext 2
O   2001:DB8:ACAD:A::/64 [110/65]
     via FE80::1, Serial0/0/0
C   2001:DB8:ACAD:B::/64 [0/0]
     via GigabitEthernet0/0, directly connected
L   2001:DB8:ACAD:B::2/128 [0/0]
     via GigabitEthernet0/0, receive
O   2001:DB8:ACAD:C::/64 [110/65]
     via FE80::3, Serial0/0/1
C   2001:DB8:ACAD:12::/64 [0/0]
     via Serial0/0/0, directly connected
L   2001:DB8:ACAD:12::2/128 [0/0]
     via Serial0/0/0, receive
O   2001:DB8:ACAD:13::/64 [110/128]
     via FE80::3, Serial0/0/1
     via FE80::1, Serial0/0/0
C   2001:DB8:ACAD:23::/64 [0/0]
     via Serial0/0/1, directly connected
L   2001:DB8:ACAD:23::2/128 [0/0]
     via Serial0/0/1, receive
L   FF00::/8 [0/0]
     via Null0, receive
```

What command would you use to only see the OSPF routes in the routing table?

Step 7.   Verify end-to-end connectivity.

Each PC should be able to ping the other PCs in the topology. Verify and troubleshoot if necessary.

Note: It may be necessary to disable the PC firewall to ping between PCs.

Part 3: Configure OSPFv3 Passive Interfaces

The **passive-interface** command prevents routing updates from being sent through the specified router interface. This is commonly done to reduce traffic on the LANs as they do not need to receive dynamic routing protocol communication. In Part 3, you will use the **passive-interface** command to configure a single interface as passive. You will also configure OSPFv3 so that all interfaces on the router are passive by default, and then enable OSPF routing advertisements on selected interfaces.

Step 1.   Configure a passive interface.

a.   Issue the **show ipv6 ospf interface g0/0** command on R1. Notice the timer indicating when the next Hello packet is expected. Hello packets are sent every 10 seconds and are used between OSPF routers to verify that their neighbors are up.

```
R1# show ipv6 ospf interface g0/0
GigabitEthernet0/0 is up, line protocol is up
  Link Local Address FE80::1, Interface ID 3
  Area 0, Process ID 1, Instance ID 0, Router ID 1.1.1.1
  Network Type BROADCAST, Cost: 1
  Transmit Delay is 1 sec, State DR, Priority 1
  Designated Router (ID) 1.1.1.1, local address FE80::1
  No backup designated router on this network
  Timer intervals configured, Hello 10, Dead 40, Wait 40, Retransmit 5
    Hello due in 00:00:05
  Graceful restart helper support enabled
  Index 1/1/1, flood queue length 0
  Next 0x0(0)/0x0(0)/0x0(0)
  Last flood scan length is 0, maximum is 0
  Last flood scan time is 0 msec, maximum is 0 msec
  Neighbor Count is 0, Adjacent neighbor count is 0
  Suppress hello for 0 neighbor(s)
```

b.   Issue the **passive-interface** command to change the G0/0 interface on R1 to passive.

```
R1(config)# ipv6 router ospf 1
R1(config-rtr)# passive-interface g0/0
```

c.   Re-issue the **show ipv6 ospf interface g0/0** command to verify that G0/0 is now passive.

```
R1# show ipv6 ospf interface g0/0
GigabitEthernet0/0 is up, line protocol is up
  Link Local Address FE80::1, Interface ID 3
  Area 0, Process ID 1, Instance ID 0, Router ID 1.1.1.1
  Network Type BROADCAST, Cost: 1
  Transmit Delay is 1 sec, State WAITING, Priority 1
  No designated router on this network
  No backup designated router on this network
  Timer intervals configured, Hello 10, Dead 40, Wait 40, Retransmit 5
```

```
No Hellos (Passive interface)
  Wait time before Designated router selection 00:00:34
Graceful restart helper support enabled
Index 1/1/1, flood queue length 0
Next 0x0(0)/0x0(0)/0x0(0)
Last flood scan length is 0, maximum is 0
Last flood scan time is 0 msec, maximum is 0 msec
Neighbor Count is 0, Adjacent neighbor count is 0
Suppress hello for 0 neighbor(s)
```

d. Issue the **show ipv6 route ospf** command on R2 and R3 to verify that a route to the 2001.DB8.ACAD.A../64 network is still available.

```
R2# show ipv6 route ospf
IPv6 Routing Table - default - 10 entries
Codes: C - Connected, L - Local, S - Static, U - Per-user Static route
       B - BGP, R - RIP, I1 - ISIS L1, I2 - ISIS L2
       IA - ISIS interarea, IS - ISIS summary, D - EIGRP, EX - EIGRP external
       ND - ND Default, NDp - ND Prefix, DCE - Destination, NDr - Redirect
       O - OSPF Intra, OI - OSPF Inter, OE1 - OSPF ext 1, OE2 - OSPF ext 2
       ON1 - OSPF NSSA ext 1, ON2 - OSPF NSSA ext 2
O   2001:DB8:ACAD:A::/64 [110/65]
     via FE80::1, Serial0/0/0
O   2001:DB8:ACAD:C::/64 [110/65]
     via FE80::3, Serial0/0/1
O   2001:DB8:ACAD:13::/64 [110/128]
     via FE80::3, Serial0/0/1
     via FE80::1, Serial0/0/0
```

Step 2. Set passive interface as the default on the router.

a. Issue the **passive-interface default** command on R2 to set the default for all OSPFv3 interfaces as passive.

```
R2(config)# ipv6 router ospf 1
R2(config-rtr)# passive-interface default
```

b. Issue the **show ipv6 ospf neighbor** command on R1. After the dead timer expires, R2 is no longer listed as an OSPF neighbor.

```
R1# show ipv6 ospf neighbor

          OSPFv3 Router with ID (1.1.1.1) (Process ID 1)

Neighbor ID     Pri   State           Dead Time   Interface ID    Interface
3.3.3.3           0   FULL/   -       00:00:37    6               Serial0/0/1
```

c. On R2, issue the **show ipv6 ospf interface s0/0/0** command to view the OSPF status of interface S0/0/0.

```
R2# show ipv6 ospf interface s0/0/0
Serial0/0/0 is up, line protocol is up
  Link Local Address FE80::2, Interface ID 6
  Area 0, Process ID 1, Instance ID 0, Router ID 2.2.2.2
  Network Type POINT_TO_POINT, Cost: 64
  Transmit Delay is 1 sec, State POINT_TO_POINT
```

```
Timer intervals configured, Hello 10, Dead 40, Wait 40, Retransmit 5
  No Hellos (Passive interface)
Graceful restart helper support enabled
Index 1/2/2, flood queue length 0
Next 0x0(0)/0x0(0)/0x0(0)
Last flood scan length is 2, maximum is 3
Last flood scan time is 0 msec, maximum is 0 msec
Neighbor Count is 0, Adjacent neighbor count is 0
Suppress hello for 0 neighbor(s)
```

   d. If all OSPFv3 interfaces on R2 are passive, then no routing information is being advertised. If this is the case, then R1 and R3 should no longer have a route to the 2001.DB8.
   ACAD.B../64 network. You can verify this by using the **show ipv6 route** command.

   e. Change S0/0/1 on R2 by issuing the **no passive-interface** command, so that it sends
   and receives OSPFv3 routing updates. After entering this command, an informational
   message displays stating that a neighbor adjacency has been established with R3.

```
R2(config)# ipv6 router ospf 1
R2(config-rtr)# no passive-interface s0/0/1
*Apr  8 19:21:57.939: %OSPFv3-5-ADJCHG: Process 1, Nbr 3.3.3.3 on Serial0/0/1
from LOADING to FULL, Loading Done
```

   f. Re-issue the **show ipv6 route** and **show ipv6 ospf neighbor** commands on R1 and R3,
   and look for a route to the 2001.DB8.ACAD.B../64 network.

   _____

   _____

   What interface is R1 using to route to the 2001:DB8:ACAD:B::/64 network? _____

   What is the accumulated cost metric for the 2001:DB8:ACAD:B::/64 network on R1?

   _____

   Does R2 show up as an OSPFv3 neighbor on R1? _____

   Does R2 show up as an OSPFv3 neighbor on R3? _____

   What does this information tell you?

   _____

   _____

   _____

   g. On R2, issue the **no passive-interface S0/0/0** command to allow OSPFv3 routing
   updates to be advertised on that interface.

   h. Verify that R1 and R2 are now OSPFv3 neighbors.

Reflection

1. If the OSPFv6 configuration for R1 had a process ID of 1, and the OSPFv3 configuration for R2 had a process ID of 2, can routing information be exchanged between the two routers? Why?

_____

_____

2. What may have been the reasoning for removing the network command in OSPFv3?

_____

_____

_____

_____

Router Interface Summary Table

Router Interface Summary				
Router Model	Ethernet Interface #1	Ethernet Interface #2	Serial Interface #1	Serial Interface #2
1800	Fast Ethernet 0/0 (F0/0)	Fast Ethernet 0/1 (F0/1)	Serial 0/0/0 (S0/0/0)	Serial 0/0/1 (S0/0/1)
1900	Gigabit Ethernet 0/0 (G0/0)	Gigabit Ethernet 0/1 (G0/1)	Serial 0/0/0 (S0/0/0)	Serial 0/0/1 (S0/0/1)
2801	Fast Ethernet 0/0 (F0/0)	Fast Ethernet 0/1 (F0/1)	Serial 0/1/0 (S0/1/0)	Serial 0/1/1 (S0/1/1)
2811	Fast Ethernet 0/0 (F0/0)	Fast Ethernet 0/1 (F0/1)	Serial 0/0/0 (S0/0/0)	Serial 0/0/1 (S0/0/1)
2900	Gigabit Ethernet 0/0 (G0/0)	Gigabit Ethernet 0/1 (G0/1)	Serial 0/0/0 (S0/0/0)	Serial 0/0/1 (S0/0/1)

Note: To find out how the router is configured, look at the interfaces to identify the type of router and how many interfaces the router has. There is no way to effectively list all the combinations of configurations for each router class. This table includes identifiers for the possible combinations of Ethernet and Serial interfaces in the device. The table does not include any other type of interface, even though a specific router may contain one. An example of this might be an ISDN BRI interface. The string in parentheses is the legal abbreviation that can be used in Cisco IOS commands to represent the interface.

8.4.1.1 Class Activity–Stepping Through OSPFv3

Objectives

Explain the process by which link-state routers learn about other networks.

Scenario

This class activity is designed for groups of three students. The objective is to review the shortest path first (SPF) routing process.

You will design and address a network, communicate the network address scheme and operation of network links to your group members, and compute the SPF.

Complete the steps as shown on the PDF for this class activity. If you have time, share your network design and Open Shortest Path First (OSPF) process with another group.

Resources

In preparation of this activity, you will need two different IPv6 network and cost numbers. The IPv6 network numbers must be chosen with the following format: 2002:DB8:AAAA:?::0/64, where? is a student-selected network number. You have two choices for *cost* – 10 (Fast Ethernet network), or 1 (Gigabit Ethernet network).

Bring your two IPv6 network and cost numbers to the group setting. One student in your group will act as the recorder, will draw three circles, and connect them on paper. Each circle will represent a student's router and the connecting lines will represent the networks and links to be agreed upon.

Each group member should follow Steps 1 to 4 (below) in the order listed. As the group progresses through the activity, you should keep personal notes about your own router, including information about neighbor adjacency, link-state advertisements, topology table entries, and the SPF algorithm.

Directions

Step 1.

    a. Speak to the classmate to your left. Compare network and cost numbers brought to the group. Agree upon an IPv6 network, links, and cost numbers you would like to use between your two routers. Remember, you may only use 1 (Gigabit Ethernet) or 10 (Fast Ethernet) for cost. When you have agreed upon your network, link numbers, and determined the cost of the route, record the information on the paper graphic created by the recorder.

    b. Complete the same process with the classmate to your right.

    c. After speaking with both of your direct neighbors, you have agreed upon two networks with link addresses and the cost of the route. Record the information you agreed upon on the paper graphic.

Step 2.

    a. Each student will speak only to their direct neighbors. They will share all of their IPv6 network and link numbers and the cost of the networks to which they are connected. Almost immediately, everyone in the group will know about all networks, their links, and the cost of the individual networks between neighbors.

    b. Check with the group members to ascertain all group members have the same information with which to work for Step 3.

Step 3.

    a. On your own paper, create a table listing possible paths to all other networks. Use the formula supplied with this chapter $n(n - 1)/2$. You will have a total of four possible routes to list on your table.

    b. On the table created in the Step 3 a., add a column with the headings, IPv6 Network Number and Cost.

    c. Fill in the table with information you know about the networks on your group's topology.

Step 4.

    a. Go back to the table created in Step 3.

    b. Place a star by the lowest-cost routes to all other routers.

When these four steps are complete, you have established neighbor adjacencies, exchanged link-state advertisements, built a topology table, and created a routing table with the best cost to all other networks within your group or area.

If you have the time, refer to your topology table and build the network on real equipment or Packet Tracer. Use some or all of the commands listed below to prove OSPF's operation:

```
R1# show ipv6 interface brief
R1# show ipv6 protocols
R1# show ip protocols
R1# show ipv6 route
```

Reflection

1. Which OSPFv3 processing step is reviewed in Step 1 of this activity?

_____

2. Which OSPFv3 processing step is reviewed in Step 2 of this activity?

_____

3. Which process for OSPFv3 is reviewed in Step 3 of this activity?

_____

4. Which process step for OSPFv3 is reviewed in Step 4 of this activity?

_____

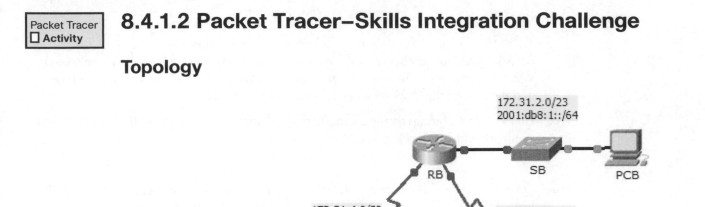

8.4.1.2 Packet Tracer–Skills Integration Challenge

Topology

Addressing Table

Device	Interface	IPv4 Address	Subnet Mask	Default Gateway
		IPv6 Address/Prefix		
RA	G0/0	172.31.0.1	255.255.254.0	N/A
	S0/0/0	172.31.4.1	255.255.255.252	N/A
RB	G0/0	172.31.2.1	255.255.254.0	N/A
		2001:DB8:1::1/64		N/A
	S0/0/0	172.31.4.2	255.255.255.252	N/A
	S0/0/1	2001:DB8:2::1/64		N/A
RC	G0/0	2001:DB8:3::1/64		N/A
	S0/0/0	2001:DB8:2::2/64		N/A
PC-A	NIC			
PC-B	NIC			
PC-C	NIC			

Background

In this Skills Integration Challenge, your focus is OSPFv2 and OSPFv3 configurations. You will configure IP addressing for all devices. Then you will configure OSPFv2 routing for the IPv4 portion of the network and OSPFv3 routing for the IPv6 portion of the network. One router will be configured with both IPv4 and IPv6 configurations. Finally, you will verify your configurations and test connectivity between end devices.

Note: This activity is graded using a combination of assessment items and connectivity tests. The instructions window will not show your score. To see your score, click **Check Results > Assessment Items**. To see the results of a specific connectivity test, click **Check Results > Connectivity Tests**.

Requirements

- Use the following requirements to configure **RA** addressing and OSPFv2 routing:

  - IPv4 addressing according to the Addressing Table

  - Process ID 1

  - Router ID 1.1.1.1

  - Network address for each interface

  - LAN interface set to passive (do not use the **default** keyword)

- Use the following requirements to configure **RB** addressing, OSPFv2 routing, and OSPFv3 routing:

  - IPv4 and IPv6 addressing according to the Addressing Table

    - Set the Gigabit Ethernet 0/0 Link Local address to FE80::1

  - OSPFv2 routing requirements:

    - Process ID 1

    - Router ID 2.2.2.2

    - Network address for each interface

    - LAN interface set to passive (do not use the **default** keyword)

  - OSPFv3 routing requirements:

    - Enable IPv6 routing

    - Process ID 1

    - Router ID 2.2.2.2

    - Enable OSPFv3 on each interface

- Use the following requirements to configure **RC** addressing and OSPFv3 routing:

  - IPv6 addressing according to the Addressing Table

    - Set the Gigabit Ethernet 0/0 Link Local address to FE80::3

  - OSPFv3 routing requirements:

    - Enable IPv6 routing

    - Process ID 1

    - Router ID 3.3.3.3

    - Enable OSPFv3 on each interface

- Configure PCs with appropriate addressing.

  - **PCA** and **PCB** IPv4 addressing must use the last assignable address in the IPv4 subnet.

  - **PCB** and **PCC** IPv6 addressing must use the second assignable address in the IPv6 network and the link-local FE80 address as the default gateway.

  - Finish the Addressing Table documentation

- Verify your configurations and test connectivity
    - OSPF neighbors should be established and routing tables should be complete
    - Pings between PCA and PCB should be successful
    - Pings between PCB and PCC should be successful

Note: If OSPFv3 has not converged, check the status of interfaces using the show ip ospf interface command. Sometimes, the OSPFv3 process needs to be deleted from the configuration and reapplied to force convergence.

CHAPTER 9

Multiarea OSPF

In larger network implementations, single-area OSPF can require a significant amount of CPU and memory resources. As the number of routers grows, network administrators often implement multiarea OSPF to control the size of link-state databases, routing table entries, and the number of SPF calculations. This chapter reviews the concepts and configurations for multiarea OSPFv2 and OSPFv3.

Study Guide

Multiarea OSPF Operation

Multiarea OSPF was specifically designed to address several issues that result from single-area OSPF growing beyond its constraints.

Multiarea OSPF Terminology and Concepts

Briefly describe three issues that arise if an OSPF area becomes too big.

_____

_____

_____

_____

_____

Briefly describe the role of each of the following OSPF router types.

- Internal router:

_____

- Backbone router:

_____

- Area Border Router (ABR):

_____

- Autonomous System Boundary Router (ASBR):

_____

In Table 9-1, indicate the OSPF router type for each router in Figure 9-1. A router can be more than one type.

Figure 9-1   Sample Multiarea OSPF Topology

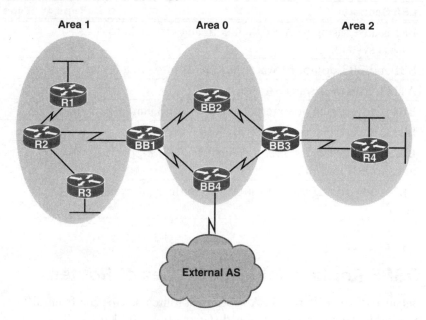

Table 9-1   Identify the OSPF Router Type

OSPF Router Type	BB1	BB2	BB3	BB4	R1	R2	R3	R4
Internal router								
Backbone router								
Area Border Router (ABR)								
Autonomous System Boundary Router (ASBR)								

Multiarea OSPF LSA Operation

Although the RFCs for OSPF specify up to 11 different LSA types, at the CCNA level we are only concerned with the first 5. In Table 9-2, indicate the name for each LSA type.

Table 9-2   Most Common OSPF LSA Types

LSA Type	Description
1	
2	
3 and 4	
5	

Refer to Figure 9-1. In Table 9-3, indicate which LSA type is used in each of the scenarios.

Table 9-3   Determine the LSA Type

LSA Scenario	Type 1	Type 2	Type 3	Type 4	Type 5
BB1 is advertising to Area 1 a link to an external autonomous system.					
BB1 and BB3 do not forward these LSAs into Area 0.					
As DR, R2 sends this LSA type to R3.					
BB4 is advertising an external network to BB3 and BB1.					
BB3 is advertising to Area 2 that BB4 is the ASBR.					
BB2 is advertising its directly connected OSPF-enabled links to BB1 and BB3.					
BB2 is advertising the links in Area 0 to the routers in Area 1.					

OSPF Routing Table and Types of Routes

Because of the different LSA types with routes originating from different areas and from non-OSPF networks, the routing table uses different codes to identify the various types of routes.

Refer to Example 9-1. Briefly describe each of the three OSPF route types shown.

Example 9-1   A Sample Multiarea OSPF Routing Table

```
BB1# show ip route | begin Gateway
Gateway of last resort is 10.0.0.1 to network 0.0.0.0

O*E2  0.0.0.0/0 [110/1] via 10.0.0.1, 00:02:16, Serial0/0/0
      10.0.0.0/8 is variably subnetted, 3 subnets, 2 masks
C        10.0.0.0/30 is directly connected, Serial0/0/0
L        10.0.0.2/32 is directly connected, Serial0/0/0
O        10.0.1.0/30 [110/128] via 10.0.0.1, 00:03:24, Serial0/0/0
      172.16.0.0/16 is variably subnetted, 7 subnets, 4 masks
C        172.16.0.0/23 is directly connected, GigabitEthernet0/0
L        172.16.0.1/32 is directly connected, GigabitEthernet0/0
C        172.16.2.0/23 is directly connected, GigabitEthernet0/1
L        172.16.2.1/32 is directly connected, GigabitEthernet0/1
O        172.16.5.0/24 [110/65] via 10.0.0.1, 00:03:24, Serial0/0/0
O IA     172.16.16.0/21 [110/129] via 10.0.0.1, 00:03:24, Serial0/0/0
O IA     172.16.24.0/21 [110/129] via 10.0.0.1, 00:03:24, Serial0/0/0
BB1#
```

List the steps in order that OSPF uses to calculate the best paths.

_____

_____

_____

Configuring Multiarea OSPF

At the CCNA level, the configuration of multiarea OSPF is rather straightforward if you are already comfortable configuring single-area OSPF. This section reviews configuring and verifying multiarea OSPFv2 and OSPFv3.

Configuring Multiarea OSPF

We will use the topology in Figure 9-2 and the addressing in Table 9-4 to configure a dual-stacked network running multiarea OSPFv2 and OSPFv3.

Figure 9-2   Dual-Stacked Multiarea OSPF Topology

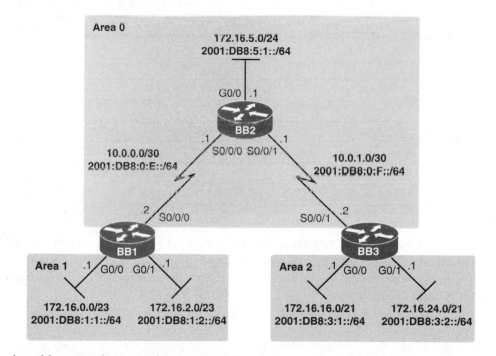

Based on the addressing shown in the topology, finish documenting the addressing scheme in Table 9-4.

Table 9-4   Addressing for the Dual-Stacked Multiarea OSPF Topology

Device	Interface	Addressing Information	
BB1	G0/0	172.16.1.1	255.255.254.0
		2001:DB8:1:1::1/64	
	G0/1	172.16.2.1	255.255.254.0
		2001:DB8:1:2::1/64	
	S0/0/0	10.0.0.2	255.255.255.252
		2001:DB8:0:E::2/64	
	Link-Local	FE80::1	
	Router ID	1.1.1.1	
BB2	G0/0		
	S0/0/0		
	S0/0/1		
	Link-Local		
	Router ID		
BB3	G0/0		
	G0/1		
	S0/0/1		
	Link-Local		
	Router ID		

The only difference between configuring single-area OSPF and multiarea OSPF is assigning the area value. Recall that for OSPFv2, you configure the area as part of the **network** command in OSPF router configuration mode. In OSPFv3, you configure the area as part of the **ipv6 ospf** command in interface configuration mode.

Document the OSPFv2 and OSPFv3 routing configurations for all three routers. Include default routing to the Internet with BB2 redistributing the IPv4 and IPv6 default routes to BB1 and BB2.

Verifying Multiarea OSPF

In Table 9-5, indicate which command or commands will provide the multiarea OSPFv2 verification information.

Table 9-5   Multiarea OSPFv2 Verification Commands

Verification Information	show ip protocols	show ip ospf interface brief	show ip route ospf	show ip ospf database
Process ID				
State of OSPF Interface				
Networks Configured				
Interface Cost				
Router ID				
Administrative Distance				
Number of Areas				
Networks from Other Areas				
All Known Routes				
Total Cost of Route				

Verification commands for multiarea OSPFv3 are almost identical to OSPFv2. In Table 9-6, indicate which command or commands will provide the multiarea OSPFv3 verification information.

Table 9-6   Multiarea OSPFv3 Verification Commands

Verification Information	show ipv6 protocols	show ipv6 ospf interface brief	show ipv6 route ospf	show ipv6 ospf database
Administrative Distance				
All Known Routes				
Interface Cost				
Networks from Other Areas				
Number of Areas				
Process ID				
Router ID				
Passive Interfaces				
State of OSPF Interface				
Total Cost of Route				

Packet Tracer Exercise 9-1: Implement Dual-Stacked Multiarea OSPF

Now you are ready to use Packet Tracer to apply your documented configuration. Download and open the file LSG03-0901.pka found at the companion website for this book. Refer to the Introduction of this book for specifics on accessing files.

Note: The following instructions are also contained within the Packet Tracer Exercise.

In this Packet Tracer activity, you will configure the routers for multiarea OSPFv2 and multiarea OSPFv3 routing. You will then verify that PCs can ping each other using IPv4 and IPv6 addresses. Use the addressing table and the commands you documented in this chapter.

Requirements

Configure each router with the following:

- IPv6 routing and Router ID.
- Use OSPF process ID 10.
- Verify IPv4 and IPv6 connectivity between the PCs.

Your completion percentage should be 100%. All the connectivity tests should show a status of "successful." If not, click **Check Results** to see which required components are not yet completed.

Labs and Activities

Command Reference

In Table 9-7, record the command, including the correct router or switch prompt, which fits the description. Fill in any blanks with the appropriate missing information.

Table 9-7   Commands for Chapter 9, Multiarea OSPF

Command	Description
	Configure R1 to use OSPFv2 to route network 10.10.10.0/24 in area 51.
	Configure R1 to use OSPFv3 to route network 10.10.10.0/24 in area 51 using process ID 20.

9.0.1.2 Class Activity–Leaving on a Jet Plane

Objective

Explain the operation of multiarea OSPF to enable internetworking in a small- to medium-sized business network.

Scenario

You and a classmate are starting a new airline to serve your continent. In addition to your core area or headquarters airport, you will locate and map four intra-continental airport service areas and one trans-continental airport service area that can be used for additional source and destination travel.

Use the blank world map provided to design your airport locations. Additional instructions for completing this activity can be found in the accompanying PDF.

Required Resources

- Blank world map diagram
- Word processing software or alternative graphics software for marking airport locations and their connections

Blank World Map Diagram

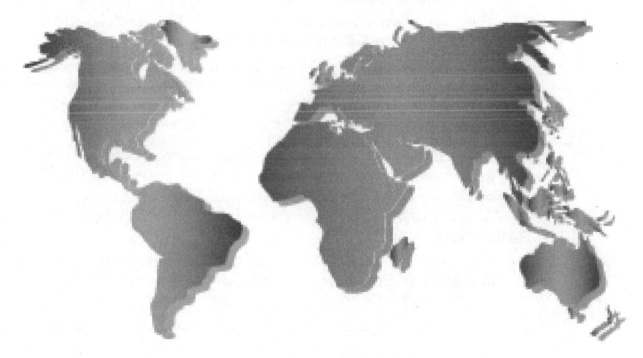

Directions

Step 1.   Design the airport locations.

    a.   Use the blank world map diagram provided.

    b.   On your map, place a star in the center of the continent in which you live. This is now the Airport Core Site and will serve as your core transit location. Label it as Airport Core Site. This is your first area of intra-continental service and all airports will be connected to the Airport Core Site.

Step 2.   Map airports within your continent to serve your passengers.

    a.   Map four airport locations within your continent to connect to the Airport Core Site. Call them North, South, East, and West Airport Sites.

    b.   Place four circles on your continent's map to represent the North, South, East, and West Airport Sites. Some circles may overlap due to the size of the continent and the sites' placement on the map.

    c.   Draw a straight line from each of these airports to the Airport Core Site. These intra-continent locations are your first level of service for your airlines. They are also known as area border airport sites.

Step 3.   Identify another continent your airline will serve.

    a.   On the world map, locate another continent you would like to provide service to and from the Airport Core Site.

    b.   Place a circle in the center of the continent you chose for second-level service. This airport will be called Transcontinental Airport Site.

    c.   Draw a line from your Airport Core Site to the Transcontinental Airport Site. This airport will be known as an autonomous system border router (ASBR) airport site.

Summary

After completing Step 3, you should be able to see that the airport connections resemble a network topology. Complete the reflection questions, save your work, and be prepared to share your answers with the class.

Reflection

    1.   While designing your airline travel routes, did you pay close attention to the headquarters location? Why would it be important to have a core site for airline travel?

_____

_____

_____

_____

_____

2. Would networks incorporate core, border, and ASBRs into area sites? Justify your answer.

_____

_____

_____

_____

_____

3. What is the significance of mapping transcontinental areas?

_____

_____

_____

_____

_____

4. What is the significance of mapping internal airline destination routes? Compare this to a routing topology.

_____

_____

_____

_____

_____

5. Is it possible that the Airport Core Site could serve several functions for your airlines (network)? Explain your answer.

_____

_____

_____

_____

_____

9.2.2.6 Packet Tracer–Configuring Multiarea OSPFv2

Topology

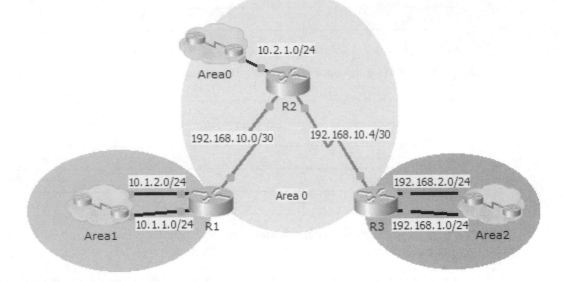

Addressing Table

Device	Interface	IP Address	Subnet Mask	OSPFv2 Area
R1	G0/0	10.1.1.1	255.255.255.0	1
	G0/1	10.1.2.1	255.255.255.0	1
	S0/0/0	192.168.10.2	255.255.255.252	0
R2	G0/0	10.2.1.1	255.255.255.0	0
	S0/0/0	192.168.10.1	255.255.255.252	0
	S0/0/1	192.168.10.5	255.255.255.252	0
R3	G0/0	192.168.2.1	255.255.255.0	2
	G0/1	192.168.1.1	255.255.255.0	2
	S0/0/1	192.168.10.6	255.255.255.252	0

Objectives

Part 1: Configure Multiarea OSPFv2

Part 2: Verify and Examine Multiarea OSPFv2

Background

In this activity, you will configure multiarea OSPFv2. The network is already connected and interfaces are configured with IPv4 addressing. Your job is to enable multiarea OSPFv2, verify connectivity, and examine the operation of multiarea OSPFv2.

Part 1: Configure OSPFv2

Step 1. Configure OSPFv2 on R1.

Configure OSPFv2 on R1 with a process ID of 1 and a router ID of 1.1.1.1.

Step 2. Advertise each directly connected network in OSPFv2 on R1.

Configure each network in OSPFv2 assigning areas according to the **Addressing Table**.

```
R1(config-router)# network 10.1.1.0 0.0.0.255 area 1
R1(config-router)# network 10.1.2.0 0.0.0.255 area 1
R1(config-router)# network 192.168.10.0 0.0.0.3 area 0
```

Step 3. Configure OSPFv2 on R2 and R3.

Repeat the steps above for **R2** and **R3** using a router ID of 2.2.2.2 and 3.3.3.3, respectively.

Part 2: Verify and Examine Multiarea OSPFv2

Step 1. Verify connectivity to each of the OSPFv2 areas.

From R1, ping each of the following remote devices in area 0 and area 2: 192.168.1.2, 192.168.2.2, and 10.2.1.2.

Step 2. Use **show** commands to examine the current OSPFv2 operations.

Use the following commands to gather information about your OSPFv2 multiarea implementation.

```
show ip protocols
show ip route
show ip ospf database
show ip ospf interface
show ip ospf neighbor
```

Reflection Questions

1. Which router(s) are internal routers? _____

2. Which router(s) are backbone routers? _____

3. Which router(s) are area border routers? _____

4. Which router(s) are autonomous system routers? _____

5. Which routers are generating Type 1 LSAs? _____

_____

6. Which routers are generating Type 2 LSAs? _____

_____

7. Which routers are generating Type 3 LSAs? _____

_____

8. Which routers are generating Type 4 and 5 LSAs? _____

_____

9. How many inter-area routes does each router have? _____

10. Why would there usually be an ASBR in this type of network? _____

_____

Suggested Scoring Rubric

Packet Tracer scores 80 points. Each of the Reflection Questions is worth 2 points.

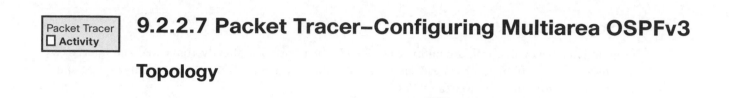

9.2.2.7 Packet Tracer–Configuring Multiarea OSPFv3

Topology

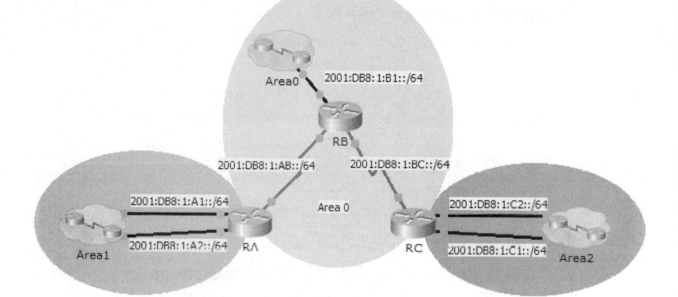

Addressing Table

Device	Interface	IPv6 Address	OSPF Area
RA	G0/0	2001:DB8:1:A1::1/64	1
	G0/1	2001:DB8:1:A2::1/64	1
	S0/0/0	2001:DB8:1:AB::2/64	0
	Link-Local	FE80::A	N/A
RB	G0/0	2001:DB8:1:B1::1/64	0
	S0/0/0	2001:DB8:1:AB::1/64	0
	S0/0/1	2001:DB8:1:BC::1/64	0
	Link-Local	FE80::B	N/A
RC	G0/0	2001:DB8:1:C1::1/64	2
	G0/1	2001:DB8:1:C2::1/64	2
	S0/0/1	2001:DB8:1:BC::2/64	0
	Link-Local	FE80::C	N/A

Objectives

Part 1: Configure OSPFv3

Part 2: Verify Multiarea OSPFv3 Operations

Background

In this activity, you will configure multiarea OSPFv3. The network is already connected and interfaces are configured with IPv6 addressing. Your job is to enable multiarea OSPFv3, verify connectivity, and examine the operation of multiarea OSPFv3.

Part 1: Configure OSPFv3

Step 1.   Enable IPv6 routing and configure OSPFv3 on RA.

    a.   Enable IPv6 routing.

    b.   Configure OSPFv3 on RA with a process ID of 1 and a router ID of 1.1.1.1.

Step 2.   Advertise each directly connected network in OSPFv3 on RA.

Configure each active IPv6 interface with OSPFv3 assigning each to the area listed in the **Addressing Table**.

Step 3.   Configure OSPFv3 on RB and RC

Repeat Steps 1 and 2 for **RB** and **RC**, changing the router ID to 2.2.2.2 and 3.3.3.3 respectively.

Part 2: Verify Multiarea OSPFv3 Operations

Step 1.   Verify connectivity to each of the OSPFv3 areas.

From RA, ping each of the following remote devices in area 0 and area 2: 2001:DB8:1:B1::2, 2001:DB8:1:A1::2, 2001:DB8:1:A2::2, 2001:DB8:1:C1::2, and 2001:DB8:1:C2::2.

Step 2.   Use **show** commands to examine the current OSPFv3 operations.

Use the following commands to gather information about your OSPFv3 multiarea implementation.

```
show ipv6 ospf
show ipv6 route
show ipv6 ospf database
show ipv6 ospf interface
show ipv6 ospf neighbor
```

Note: Packet Tracer output for **show ipv6 protocols** is currently not aligned with IOS 15 output. Refer to the real equipment labs for correct **show** command output.

9.2.2.8 Lab–Configuring Multiarea OSPFv2

Topology

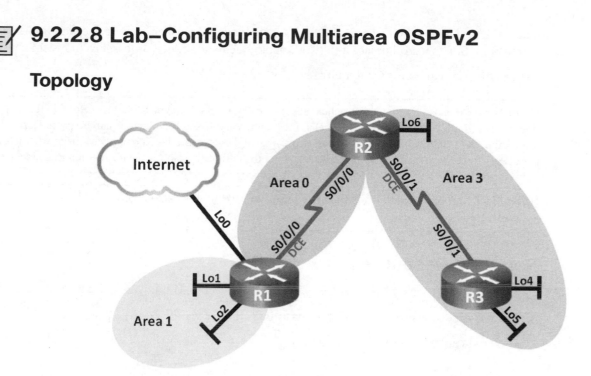

Addressing Table

Device	Interface	IP Address	Subnet Mask
R1	Lo0	209.165.200.225	255.255.255.252
	Lo1	192.168.1.1	255.255.255.0
	Lo2	192.168.2.1	255.255.255.0
	S0/0/0 (DCE)	192.168.12.1	255.255.255.252
R2	Lo6	192.168.6.1	255.255.255.0
	S0/0/0	192.168.12.2	255.255.255.252
	S0/0/1 (DCE)	192.168.23.1	255.255.255.252
R3	Lo4	192.168.4.1	255.255.255.0
	Lo5	192.168.5.1	255.255.255.0
	S0/0/1	192.168.23.2	255.255.255.252

Objectives

Part 1: Build the Network and Configure Basic Device Settings

Part 2: Configure a Multiarea OSPFv2 Network

Background/Scenario

To make OSPF more efficient and scalable, OSPF supports hierarchical routing using the concept of areas. An OSPF area is a group of routers that share the same link-state information in their link-state databases (LSDBs). When a large OSPF area is divided into smaller areas, it is called multiarea OSPF. Multiarea OSPF is useful in larger network deployments to reduce processing and memory overhead.

In this lab, you will configure a multiarea OSPFv2 network.

Note: The routers used with CCNA hands-on labs are Cisco 1941 Integrated Services Routers (ISRs) with Cisco IOS Release 15.2(4)M3 (universalk9 image). Other routers and Cisco IOS versions can be used. Depending on the model and Cisco IOS version, the commands available and output produced might vary from what is shown in the labs. Refer to the Router Interface Summary Table at the end of this lab for the correct interface identifiers.

Note: Make sure that the routers have been erased and have no startup configurations. If you are unsure, contact your instructor.

Required Resources

- 3 Routers (Cisco 1941 with Cisco IOS Release 15.2(4)M3 universal image or comparable)
- Console cables to configure the Cisco IOS devices via the console ports
- Serial cables as shown in the topology

Part 1: Build the Network and Configure Basic Device Settings

In Part 1, you will set up the network topology and configure basic settings on the routers.

Step 1.   Cable the network as shown in the topology.

Step 2.   Initialize and reload the routers as necessary.

Step 3.   Configure basic settings for each router.

    a.   Disable DNS lookup.

    b.   Configure device name, as shown in the topology.

    c.   Assign **class** as the privileged EXEC password.

    d.   Assign **cisco** as the console and vty passwords.

    e.   Configure **logging synchronous** for the console line.

    f.   Configure an MOTD banner to warn users that unauthorized access is prohibited.

    g.   Configure the IP addresses listed in the Addressing Table for all interfaces. DCE interfaces should be configured with a clock rate of 128000. Bandwidth should be set to 128 Kb/s on all serial interfaces.

    h.   Copy the running configuration to the startup configuration.

Step 4.   Verify Layer 3 connectivity.

    Use the **show ip interface brief** command to verify that the IP addressing is correct and that the interfaces are active. Verify that each router can ping their neighbor's serial interface.

Part 2: Configure a Multiarea OSPFv2 Network

In Part 2, you will configure a multiarea OSPFv2 network with a process ID of 1. All LAN loopback interfaces should be passive.

Step 1. Identify the OSPF router types in the topology.

Identify the backbone router(s): _____

Identify the Autonomous System Boundary Router(s) (ASBR): _____

Identify the Area Border Router(s) (ABR): _____

Identify the internal router(s): _____

Step 2. Configure OSPF on R1.

    a. Configure a router ID of 1.1.1.1 with OSPF process ID of 1.

    b. Add the networks for R1 to OSPF.

```
R1(config-router)# network 192.168.1.0 0.0.0.255 area 1
R1(config-router)# network 192.168.2.0 0.0.0.255 area 1
R1(config-router)# network 192.168.12.0 0.0.0.3 area 0
```

    c. Set LAN loopback interfaces, Lo1 and Lo2, as passive.

    d. Create a default route to the Internet using exit interface Lo0.

Note: You may see the "%Default route without gateway, if not a point-to-point interface, may impact performance" message. This is normal behavior if using a Loopback interface to simulate a default route.

---

    e. Configure OSPF to propagate the routes throughout the OSPF areas.

Step 3. Configure OSPF on R2.

    a. Configure a router ID of 2.2.2.2 with OSPF process ID of 1.

    b. Add the networks for R2 to OSPF. Add the networks to the correct area. Write the commands used in the space below.

_____

_____

_____

    c. Set all LAN loopback interfaces as passive.

Step 4. Configure OSPF on R3.

    a. Configure a router ID of 3.3.3.3 with OSPF process ID of 1.

    b. Add the networks for R3 to OSPF. Write the commands used in the space below.

_____

_____

_____

    c. Set all LAN loopback interfaces as passive.

Step 5.   Verify that OSPF settings are correct and adjacencies have been established between routers.

    a.   Issue the **show ip protocols** command to verify OSPF settings on each router. Use this command to identify the OSPF router types and to determine the networks assigned to each area.

```
R1# show ip protocols
*** IP Routing is NSF aware ***


Routing Protocol is "ospf 1"
  Outgoing update filter list for all interfaces is not set
  Incoming update filter list for all interfaces is not set
  Router ID 1.1.1.1
  It is an area border and autonomous system boundary router
 Redistributing External Routes from,
  Number of areas in this router is 2. 2 normal 0 stub 0 nssa
  Maximum path: 4
  Routing for Networks:
    192.168.1.0 0.0.0.255 area 1
    192.168.2.0 0.0.0.255 area 1
    192.168.12.0 0.0.0.3 area 0
  Passive Interface(s):
    Loopback1
    Loopback2
  Routing Information Sources:
    Gateway         Distance      Last Update
    2.2.2.2              110      00:01:45
  Distance: (default is 110)
R2# show ip protocols
*** IP Routing is NSF aware ***


Routing Protocol is "ospf 1"
  Outgoing update filter list for all interfaces is not set
  Incoming update filter list for all interfaces is not set
  Router ID 2.2.2.2
  It is an area border router
  Number of areas in this router is 2. 2 normal 0 stub 0 nssa
  Maximum path: 4
  Routing for Networks:
    192.168.6.0 0.0.0.255 area 3
    192.168.12.0 0.0.0.3 area 0
    192.168.23.0 0.0.0.3 area 3
  Passive Interface(s):
    Loopback6
  Routing Information Sources:
    Gateway         Distance      Last Update
    3.3.3.3              110      00:01:20
    1.1.1.1              110      00:10:12
  Distance: (default is 110)
R3# show ip protocols
*** IP Routing is NSF aware ***
```

```
Routing Protocol is "ospf 1"
  Outgoing update filter list for all interfaces is not set
  Incoming update filter list for all interfaces is not set
  Router ID 3.3.3.3
  Number of areas in this router is 1. 1 normal 0 stub 0 nssa
  Maximum path: 4
  Routing for Networks:
    192.168.4.0 0.0.0.255 area 3
    192.168.5.0 0.0.0.255 area 3
    192.168.23.0 0.0.0.3 area 3
  Passive Interface(s):
    Loopback4
    Loopback5
  Routing Information Sources:
    Gateway          Distance       Last Update
    1.1.1.1              110        00:07:46
    2.2.2.2              110        00:07:46
  Distance: (default is 110)
```

What is the OSPF router type for each router?

R1. _____

R2. _____

R3. _____

b. Issue the **show ip ospf neighbor** command to verify that OSPF adjacencies have been established between routers.

```
R1# show ip ospf neighbor

Neighbor ID      Pri   State        Dead Time    Address        Interface
2.2.2.2            0   FULL/ -      00:00:34     192.168.12.2   Serial0/0/0


R2# show ip ospf neighbor

Neighbor ID      Pri   State        Dead Time    Address        Interface
1.1.1.1            0   FULL/ -      00:00:36     192.168.12.1   Serial0/0/0
3.3.3.3            0   FULL/ -      00:00:36     192.168.23.2   Serial0/0/1


R3# show ip ospf neighbor

Neighbor ID      Pri   State        Dead Time    Address        Interface
2.2.2.2            0   FULL/ -      00:00:38     192.168.23.1   Serial0/0/1
```

c. Issue the **show ip ospf interface brief** command to display a summary of interface route costs.

```
R1# show ip ospf interface brief
Interface   PID   Area        IP Address/Mask      Cost   State Nbrs F/C
Se0/0/0      1     0          192.168.12.1/30      781    P2P   1/1
Lo1          1     1          192.168.1.1/24       1      LOOP  0/0
Lo2          1     1          192.168.2.1/24       1      LOOP  0/0
```

```
R2# show ip ospf interface brief
Interface   PID   Area        IP Address/Mask      Cost   State  Nbrs F/C
Se0/0/0     1     0           192.168.12.2/30      781    P2P    1/1
Lo6         1     3           192.168.6.1/24       1      LOOP   0/0
Se0/0/1     1     3           192.168.23.1/30      781    P2P    1/1

R3# show ip ospf interface brief
Interface   PID   Area        IP Address/Mask      Cost   State  Nbrs F/C
Lo4         1     3           192.168.4.1/24       1      LOOP   0/0
Lo5         1     3           192.168.5.1/24       1      LOOP   0/0
Se0/0/1     1     3           192.168.23.2/30      781    P2P    1/1
```

Reflection

What are three advantages for designing a network with multiarea OSPF?

_____

_____

_____

Router Interface Summary Table

Router Interface Summary				
Router Model	Ethernet Interface #1	Ethernet Interface #2	Serial Interface #1	Serial Interface #2
1800	Fast Ethernet 0/0 (F0/0)	Fast Ethernet 0/1 (F0/1)	Serial 0/0/0 (S0/0/0)	Serial 0/0/1 (S0/0/1)
1900	Gigabit Ethernet 0/0 (G0/0)	Gigabit Ethernet 0/1 (G0/1)	Serial 0/0/0 (S0/0/0)	Serial 0/0/1 (S0/0/1)
2801	Fast Ethernet 0/0 (F0/0)	Fast Ethernet 0/1 (F0/1)	Serial 0/1/0 (S0/1/0)	Serial 0/1/1 (S0/1/1)
2811	Fast Ethernet 0/0 (F0/0)	Fast Ethernet 0/1 (F0/1)	Serial 0/0/0 (S0/0/0)	Serial 0/0/1 (S0/0/1)
2900	Gigabit Ethernet 0/0 (G0/0)	Gigabit Ethernet 0/1 (G0/1)	Serial 0/0/0 (S0/0/0)	Serial 0/0/1 (S0/0/1)

Note: To find out how the router is configured, look at the interfaces to identify the type of router and how many interfaces the router has. There is no way to effectively list all the combinations of configurations for each router class. This table includes identifiers for the possible combinations of Ethernet and Serial interfaces in the device. The table does not include any other type of interface, even though a specific router may contain one. An example of this might be an ISDN BRI interface. The string in parentheses is the legal abbreviation that can be used in Cisco IOS commands to represent the interface.

9.2.2.9 Lab–Configuring Multiarea OSPFv3

Topology

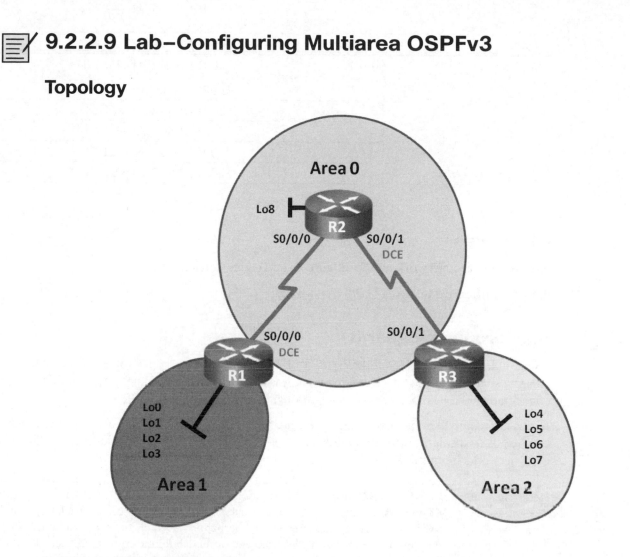

Addressing Table

Device	Interface	IPv6 Address
R1	S0/0/0 (DCE)	2001:DB8:ACAD:12::1/64
		FE80::1 link-local
	Lo0	2001:DB8:ACAD::1/64
	Lo1	2001:DB8:ACAD:1::1/64
	Lo2	2001:DB8:ACAD:2::1/64
	Lo3	2001:DB8:ACAD:3::1/64
R2	S0/0/0	2001:DB8:ACAD:12::2/64
		FE80::2 link-local
	S0/0/1 (DCE)	2001:DB8:ACAD:23::2/64
		FE80::2 link-local
	Lo8	2001:DB8:ACAD:8::1/64

Device	Interface	IPv6 Address
R3	S0/0/1	2001:DB8:ACAD:23::3/64
		FE80::3 link-local
	Lo4	2001:DB8:ACAD:4::1/64
	Lo5	2001:DB8:ACAD:5::1/64
	Lo6	2001:DB8:ACAD:6::1/64
	Lo7	2001:DB8:ACAD:7::1/64

Objectives

Part 1: Build the Network and Configure Basic Device Settings

Part 2: Configure Multiarea OSPFv3 Routing

Background/Scenario

Using multiarea OSPFv3 in large IPv6 network deployments can reduce router processing cycles by creating smaller routing tables and requiring less memory overhead. In multiarea OSPFv3, all areas are connected to the backbone area (area 0) through area border routers (ABRs).

In this lab, you will implement OSPFv3 routing for multiple areas. You will also use a number of **show** commands to display and verify OSPFv3 routing information. This lab uses loopback addresses to simulate networks in multiple OSPFv3 areas.

Note: The routers used with CCNA hands-on labs are Cisco 1941 Integrated Services Routers (ISRs) with Cisco IOS Release 15.2(4)M3 (universalk9 image). Other routers and Cisco IOS versions can be used. Depending on the model and Cisco IOS version, the commands available and output produced might vary from what is shown in the labs. Refer to the Router Interface Summary Table at this end of this lab for the correct interface identifiers.

Note: Make sure that the routers have been erased and have no startup configurations. If you are unsure, contact your instructor.

Required Resources

- 3 Routers (Cisco 1941 with Cisco IOS Release 15.2(4)M3 universal image or comparable)
- 3 PCs (Windows with terminal emulation program, such as Tera Term)
- Console cables to configure the Cisco IOS devices via the console ports
- Serial cables as shown in the topology

Part 1: Build the Network and Configure Basic Device Settings

In Part 1, you will set up the network topology and configure basic settings on the routers.

Step 1.   Cable the network as shown in the topology.

Step 2.   Initialize and reload the routers as necessary.

Step 3.   Configure basic settings for each router.

    a.   Disable DNS lookup.

    b.   Configure device name as shown in the topology.

    c.   Assign **class** as the privileged EXEC password.

    d.   Assign **cisco** as the vty password.

    e.   Configure a MOTD banner to warn users that unauthorized access is prohibited.

    f.   Configure **logging synchronous** for the console line.

    g.   Encrypt plaintext passwords.

    h.   Configure the IPv6 unicast and link-local addresses listed in the Addressing Table for all interfaces.

    i.   Enable IPv6 unicast routing on each router.

    j.   Copy the running configuration to the startup configuration.

Step 4.   Test connectivity.

The routers should be able to ping one another. The routers are unable to ping distant loopbacks until OSPFv3 routing is configured. Verify and troubleshoot if necessary.

Part 2: Configure Multiarea OSPFv3 Routing

In Part 2, you will configure OSPFv3 routing on all routers to separate the network domain into three distinct areas, and then verify that routing tables are updated correctly.

Step 1.   Assign router IDs.

    a.   On R1, issue the **ipv6 router ospf** command to start an OSPFv3 process on the router.

```
R1(config)# ipv6 router ospf 1
```

Note: The OSPF process ID is kept locally and has no meaning to other routers on the network.

    b.   Assign the OSPFv3 router ID **1.1.1.1** to R1.

```
R1(config-rtr)# router-id 1.1.1.1
```

    c.   Start an OSPFv3 process on R2 and R3 and assign a router ID of **2.2.2.2** to R2 and a router ID of **3.3.3.3** to R3.

    d.   Issue the **show ipv6 ospf** command to verify the router IDs on all routers.

```
R2# show ipv6 ospf
Routing Process "ospfv3 1" with ID 2.2.2.2
Event-log enabled, Maximum number of events: 1000, Mode: cyclic
Router is not originating router-LSAs with maximum metric
<output omitted>
```

Step 2.   Configure multiarea OSPFv3.

a.   Issue the **ipv6 ospf 1 area** *area-id* command for each interface on R1 that is to partici-pate in OSPFv3 routing. The loopback interfaces are assigned to area 1 and the serial interface is assigned to area 0. You will change the network type on the loopback inter-faces to ensure that the correct subnet is advertised.

```
R1(config)# interface lo0
R1(config-if)# ipv6 ospf 1 area 1
R1(config-if)# ipv6 ospf network point-to-point
R1(config-if)# interface lo1
R1(config-if)# ipv6 ospf 1 area 1
R1(config-if)# ipv6 ospf network point-to-point
R1(config-if)# interface lo2
R1(config-if)# ipv6 ospf 1 area 1
R1(config-if)# ipv6 ospf network point-to-point
R1(config-if)# interface lo3
R1(config-if)# ipv6 ospf 1 area 1
R1(config-if)# ipv6 ospf network point-to-point
R1(config-if)# interface s0/0/0
R1(config-if)# ipv6 ospf 1 area 0
```

b.   Use the **show ipv6 protocols** command to verify multiarea OSPFv3 status.

```
R1# show ipv6 protocols
IPv6 Routing Protocol is "connected"
IPv6 Routing Protocol is "ND"
IPv6 Routing Protocol is "ospf 1"
  Router ID 1.1.1.1
  Area border router
  Number of areas: 2 normal, 0 stub, 0 nssa
  Interfaces (Area 0):
    Serial0/0/0
  Interfaces (Area 1):
    Loopback0
    Loopback1
    Loopback2
    Loopback3
  Redistribution:
    None
```

c.   Assign all interfaces on R2 to participate in OSPFv3 area 0. For the loopback interface, change the network type to point-to point. Write the commands used in the space below.

_____

_____

_____

_____

_____

_____

d. Use the **show ipv6 ospf interface brief** command to view OSPFv3-enabled interfaces.

```
R2# show ipv6 ospf interface brief
Interface      PID   Area         Intf ID    Cost   State Nbrs F/C
Lo8            1     0            13         1      P2P   0/0
Se0/0/1        1     0            7          64     P2P   1/1
Se0/0/0        1     0            6          64     P2P   1/1
```

e. Assign the loopback interfaces on R3 to participate in OSPFv3 area 2 and change the network type to point-to-point. Assign the serial interface to participate in OSPFv3 area 0. Write the commands used in the space below.

_____

_____

_____

_____

_____

_____

_____

_____

f. Use the **show ipv6 ospf** command to verify configurations.

```
R3# show ipv6 ospf
Routing Process "ospfv3 1" with ID 3.3.3.3
Event-log enabled, Maximum number of events: 1000, Mode: cyclic
It is an area border router
Router is not originating router-LSAs with maximum metric
Initial SPF schedule delay 5000 msecs
Minimum hold time between two consecutive SPFs 10000 msecs
Maximum wait time between two consecutive SPFs 10000 msecs
Minimum LSA interval 5 secs
Minimum LSA arrival 1000 msecs
LSA group pacing timer 240 secs
Interface flood pacing timer 33 msecs
Retransmission pacing timer 66 msecs
Number of external LSA 0. Checksum Sum 0x000000
Number of areas in this router is 2. 2 normal 0 stub 0 nssa
Graceful restart helper support enabled
Reference bandwidth unit is 100 mbps
RFC1583 compatibility enabled
    Area BACKBONE(0)
        Number of interfaces in this area is 1
        SPF algorithm executed 2 times
        Number of LSA 16. Checksum Sum 0x0929F8
        Number of DCbitless LSA 0
        Number of indication LSA 0
        Number of DoNotAge LSA 0
        Flood list length 0
```

```
Area 2
    Number of interfaces in this area is 4
    SPF algorithm executed 2 times
    Number of LSA 13. Checksum Sum 0x048E3C
    Number of DCbitless LSA 0
    Number of indication LSA 0
    Number of DoNotAge LSA 0
    Flood list length 0
```

Step 3. Verify OSPFv3 neighbors and routing information.

a. Issue the **show ipv6 ospf neighbor** command on all routers to verify that each router is listing the correct routers as neighbors.

```
R1# show ipv6 ospf neighbor


        OSPFv3 Router with ID (1.1.1.1) (Process ID 1)


Neighbor ID     Pri   State           Dead Time   Interface ID    Interface
2.2.2.2           0   FULL/  -        00:00:39    6               Serial0/0/0
```

b. Issue the **show ipv6 route ospf** command on all routers to verify that each router has learned routes to all networks in the Addressing Table.

```
R1# show ipv6 route ospf
IPv6 Routing Table - default - 16 entries
Codes: C - Connected, L - Local, S - Static, U - Per-user Static route
       B - BGP, R - RIP, H - NHRP, I1 - ISIS L1
       I2 - ISIS L2, IA - ISIS interarea, IS - ISIS summary, D - EIGRP
       EX - EIGRP external, ND - ND Default, NDp - ND Prefix, DCE - Destination
       NDr - Redirect, O - OSPF Intra, OI - OSPF Inter, OE1 - OSPF ext 1
       OE2 - OSPF ext 2, ON1 - OSPF NSSA ext 1, ON2 - OSPF NSSA ext 2
OI  2001:DB8:ACAD:4::/64 [110/129]
     via FE80::2, Serial0/0/0
OI  2001:DB8:ACAD:5::/64 [110/129]
     via FE80::2, Serial0/0/0
OI  2001:DB8:ACAD:6::/64 [110/129]
     via FE80::2, Serial0/0/0
OI  2001:DB8:ACAD:7::/64 [110/129]
     via FE80::2, Serial0/0/0
O   2001:DB8:ACAD:8::/64 [110/65]
     via FE80::2, Serial0/0/0
O   2001:DB8:ACAD:23::/64 [110/128]
     via FE80::2, Serial0/0/0
```

What does OI stand for? How was the OI route learned?

_____

c. Issue the **show ipv6 ospf database** command on all routers.

```
R1# show ipv6 ospf database


        OSPFv3 Router with ID (1.1.1.1) (Process ID 1)


                Router Link States (Area 0)
```

```
ADV Router          Age         Seq#          Fragment ID  Link count  Bits
1.1.1.1             908         0x80000001    0            1           B
2.2.2.2             898         0x80000003    0            2           None
3.3.3.3             899         0x80000001    0            1           B


           Inter Area Prefix Link States (Area 0)


ADV Router          Age         Seq#          Prefix
1.1.1.1             907         0x80000001    2001:DB8:ACAD::/62
3.3.3.3             898         0x80000001    2001:DB8:ACAD:4::/62


           Link (Type-8) Link States (Area 0)


ADV Router          Age         Seq#          Link ID    Interface
1.1.1.1             908         0x80000001    6          Se0/0/0
2.2.2.2             909         0x80000002    6          Se0/0/0


           Intra Area Prefix Link States (Area 0)


ADV Router          Age         Seq#          Link ID    Ref-lstype   Ref-LSID
1.1.1.1             900         0x80000001    0          0x2001       0
2.2.2.2             898         0x00000003    0          0x2001       0
3.3.3.3             899         0x80000001    0          0x2001       0


           Router Link States (Area 1)


ADV Router          Age         Seq#          Fragment ID  Link count  Bits
1.1.1.1             908         0x80000001    0            0           B


           Inter Area Prefix Link States (Area 1)


ADV Router          Age         Seq#          Prefix
1.1.1.1             907         0x80000001    2001:DB8:ACAD:12::/64
1.1.1.1             907         0x80000001    2001:DB8:ACAD:8::/64
1.1.1.1             888         0x80000001    2001:DB8:ACAD:23::/64
1.1.1.1             888         0x80000001    2001:DB8:ACAD:4::/62


           Link (Type-8) Link States (Area 1)


ADV Router          Age         Seq#          Link ID    Interface
1.1.1.1             908         0x80000001    13         Lo0
1.1.1.1             908         0x80000001    14         Lo1
1.1.1.1             908         0x80000001    15         Lo2
1.1.1.1             908         0x80000001    16         Lo3


           Intra Area Prefix Link States (Area 1)


ADV Router          Age         Seq#          Link ID    Ref-lstype   Ref-LSID
1.1.1.1             908         0x80000001    0          0x2001       0
```

How many link state databases are found on R1? _____

How many link state databases are found on R2? _____

How many link state databases are found on R3? _____

Reflection

1. Why would multiarea OSPFv3 be used?

_____

_____

Router Interface Summary Table

Router Interface Summary				
Router Model	Ethernet Interface #1	Ethernet Interface #2	Serial Interface #1	Serial Interface #2
1800	Fast Ethernet 0/0 (F0/0)	Fast Ethernet 0/1 (F0/1)	Serial 0/0/0 (S0/0/0)	Serial 0/0/1 (S0/0/1)
1900	Gigabit Ethernet 0/0 (G0/0)	Gigabit Ethernet 0/1 (G0/1)	Serial 0/0/0 (S0/0/0)	Serial 0/0/1 (S0/0/1)
2801	Fast Ethernet 0/0 (F0/0)	Fast Ethernet 0/1 (F0/1)	Serial 0/1/0 (S0/1/0)	Serial 0/1/1 (S0/1/1)
2811	Fast Ethernet 0/0 (F0/0)	Fast Ethernet 0/1 (F0/1)	Serial 0/0/0 (S0/0/0)	Serial 0/0/1 (S0/0/1)
2900	Gigabit Ethernet 0/0 (G0/0)	Gigabit Ethernet 0/1 (G0/1)	Serial 0/0/0 (S0/0/0)	Serial 0/0/1 (S0/0/1)

Note: To find out how the router is configured, look at the interfaces to identify the type of router and how many interfaces the router has. There is no way to effectively list all the combinations of configurations for each router class. This table includes identifiers for the possible combinations of Ethernet and Serial interfaces in the device. The table does not include any other type of interface, even though a specific router may contain one. An example of this might be an ISDN BRI interface. The string in parentheses is the legal abbreviation that can be used in Cisco IOS commands to represent the interface.

9.3.1.1 Class Activity–Digital Trolleys

Objective

Use CLI commands to verify operational status of a multiarea OSPF network.

Scenario

Your city has an aging digital trolley system based on a one-area design. All communications within this one area are taking longer to process as trolleys are being added to routes serving the population of your growing city. Trolley departures and arrivals are also taking a little longer, because each trolley must check large routing tables to determine where to pick up and deliver residents from their source and destination streets.

A concerned citizen has come up with the idea of dividing the city into different areas for a more efficient way to determine trolley routing information. It is thought that if the trolley maps are smaller, the system might be improved because of faster and smaller updates to the routing tables.

Your city board approves and implements the new area-based, digital trolley system. But to ensure the new area routes are more efficient, the city board needs data to show the results at the next open board meeting.

Complete the activity directions as stated below.

Save your work and explain the differences between the old, single area and new, multiarea system to another group or the entire class.

Required Resources

- Packet Tracer software
- Word processing software

Directions

Step 1.   Map the single-area city trolley routing topology.

   a.   Use Packet Tracer to map the old routing topology for the city. Cisco 1941 Integrated Services Routers (ISRs) are preferred.

   b.   Create a core area and place one of the routers in the core area.

   c.   Connect at least two routers to the core area router.

   d.   Choose to connect two more routers to the routers from Step 1c or create loopback addresses for the LAN interfaces on the routers from Step 1c.

   e.   Address the connected links or interfaces using IPv4 and VLSM.

   f.   Configure OSPF on each router for area 0 only.

   g.   Ping all routers to ensure full connectivity within the entire area.

Step 2.   Map the multiarea city trolley routing topology.

   a.   Use your cursor to highlight all devices from Step 1, and copy and paste them to another area of the Packet Tracer desktop.

    b. Assign at least three areas to your topology. One must be the backbone (or core area) and the other two areas will be joined to the backbone area using current routers, which will now become area border routers.

    c. Configure the appropriate routers to their new area assignments. Remove old area configuration commands and assign new area commands to the appropriate interfaces.

    d. Save each router's changes as you make changes.

    e. When complete, you should have three areas represented on the topology and all routers should be able to ping each other throughout the network.

    f. Use the drawing tool and identify your areas by drawing circles or rectangles around the three areas.

    g. Save your work.

Step 3.   Verify the network for city council members.

    a. Use at least three commands learned (or used in this chapter) to help the city council prove that the new area, digital trolley routing topology works.

    b. Save a copy of topology graphics and verification commands comparisons in table format to a word processing file.

    c. Share your work with another group or the class. You may also want to add this activity and its files to a portfolio for this course.

CHAPTER 10

OSPF Tuning and Troubleshooting

This chapter focuses on the concepts and configurations to fine-tune the operation of Open Shortest Path First (OSPF), including manipulating the Designated Router/Backup Designated Router (DR/BDR) election, propagating a default router, and fine-tuning OSPF interfaces.

Study Guide

Advanced Single-Area OSPF Configurations

In this section, we review the concepts and configurations to fine-tune the operation of OSPFv2 and OSPFv3.

Identify Network Types

Match the definition on the left with the network type on the right. This is a one-to-one matching exercise.

Definitions	Network Type
___ Connects distant OSPF networks to the backbone area	**a.** Broadcast multiaccess
___ Connects multiple routers using Frame Relay	**b.** Nonbroadcast multiaccess
___ Connects multiple routers in a hub-and-spoke topology	**c.** Point to multipoint
___ Connects two routers directly on a single WAN network	**d.** Point to point
___ Connects multiple routers using Ethernet technology	**e.** Virtual links

In Figure 10-1, label each network type.

Figure 10-1   Network Types

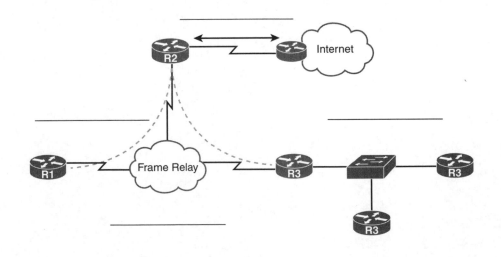

OSPF and Multiaccess Networks

A multiaccess network is a network with more than two devices on the same shared media. Examples of multiaccess networks include Ethernet and Frame Relay. Frame Relay is a WAN technology that is discussed in a later CCNA course. The following exercises cover the concepts of multiaccess networks in OSPF and the DR/BDR election process.

OSPF and Multiaccess Networks Completion Exercise

Complete the missing words or phrases in the following paragraphs.

On multiaccess networks (networks supporting more than two routers) such as Ethernet and Frame Relay networks, the hello protocol elects a _____ (DR) and a _____ (BDR). Among other things, the _____ is responsible for generating LSAs for the entire multiaccess network, which allows a reduction in routing update traffic.

The DR, BDR, and every other router in an OSPF network send out Hellos using _____ as the destination address. If a DRother (a router that is not the DR) needs to send a link-state advertisement (LSA), it will send it using _____ as the destination address. The DR and the BDR will receive LSAs at this address.

The DR/BDR election is based on OSPF _____ and OSPF router _____. By default, all OSPF routers have a _____ of _____. If all OSPF routers have the same _____, the highest router _____ determines the DR and BDR.

If the router _____ is not explicitly configured and a loopback interface is not configured, the _____ IP address on an active interface at the moment of OSPF process startup is used as the router _____.

In Figure 10-2, describe the steps taken to elect the DR.

Figure 10-2   Steps in the DR Election Process

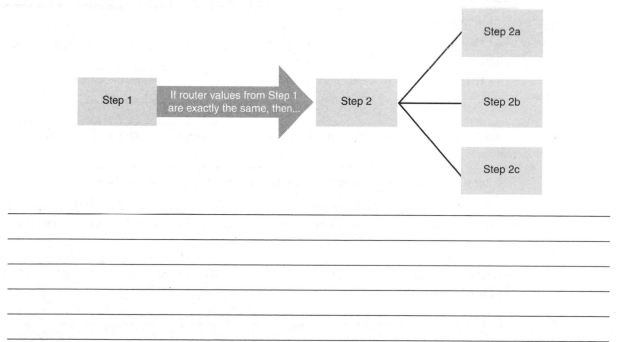

_____

_____

_____

_____

_____

_____

Use the topology in Figure 10-3 to determine the router ID for each router, and then determine which router will be the DR, if applicable.

Figure 10-3   Determine the Router ID

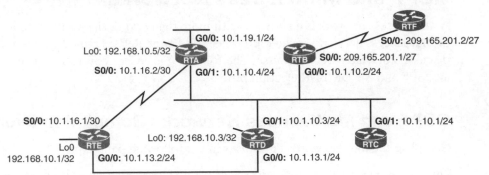

In Table 10-1, record the router ID for each router.

Table 10-1   Listing of Router IDs

Device	Router ID
Router A	
Router B	
Router C	
Router D	
Router E	
Router F	

In Table 10-2, determine whether a DR will be elected for each network and record the DR's hostname. If no DR is elected, indicate so with "none."

Table 10-2   Listing of DRs

Network	DR
209.165.201.0	
10.1.16.0	
10.1.13.0	
10.1.10.0	

Note: Configure your OSPFv2 routers with a router ID to control the DR/BDR election. With OSPFv3, you must configure a router ID.

Setting the priority on the interface is another way to control DR or BDR.

In addition to configuring loopbacks, it is a good idea to configure RTA with an OSPF priority that will ensure it always wins the DR/BDR election. The syntax for configuring OSPF priority is as follows:

Document the commands you use to configure on RTA to make sure that its priority will always win the DR/BDR election.

DR/BDR Election Exercise

In the following exercises, assume that all routers are simultaneously booted and that router priorities are set to the default. Determine the network type, if applicable, and label which router is elected as the DR and which router is elected as the BDR.

Refer to Figure 10-4 and answer the following questions.

Figure 10-4   DR/BDR Election Exercise 1 Topology

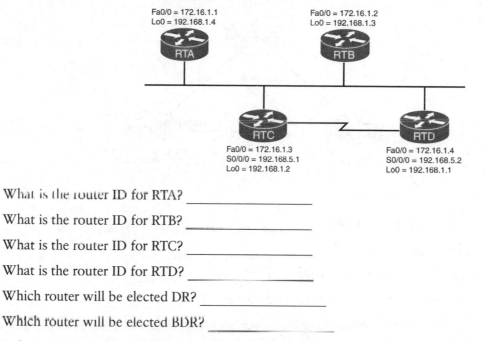

What is the router ID for RTA? _____

What is the router ID for RTB? _____

What is the router ID for RTC? _____

What is the router ID for RTD? _____

Which router will be elected DR? _____

Which router will be elected BDR? _____

Refer to Figure 10-5 and determine whether there will be a DR/BDR election. If applicable, designate which router is DR and which router is BDR.

Figure 10-5   DR/BDR Election Exercise 2 Topology

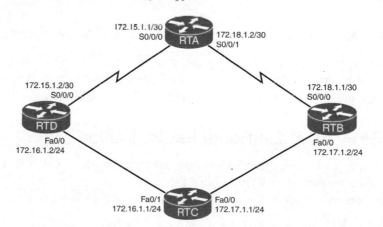

Network	DR/BDR Election?	Which Router Is the DR?	Which Router Is the BDR?
172.15.1.0/30			
172.16.1.0/24			
172.17.1.0/24			
172.18.1.0/30			

Refer to Figure 10-6 and answer the following questions.

Figure 10-6 DR/BDR Election Exercise 3 Topology

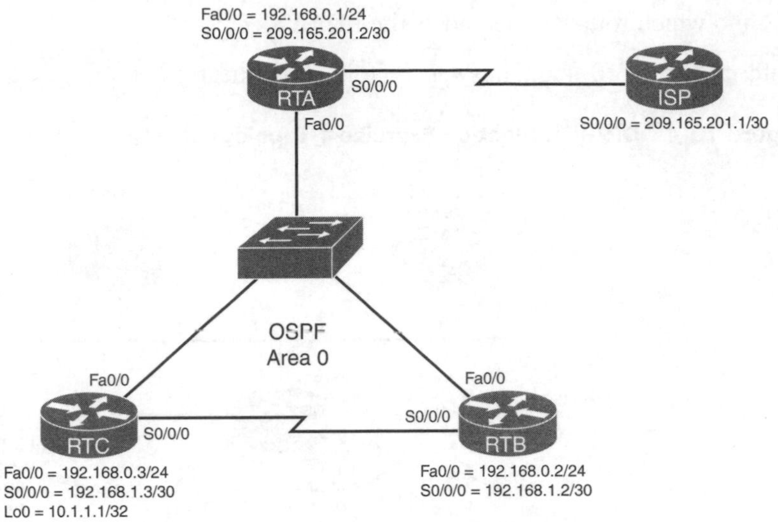

What is the router ID for RTA? _____

What is the router ID for RTB? _____

What is the router ID for RTC? _____

Which router is DR for the 192.168.0.0/24 network? _____

Which router is BDR for the 192.168.0.0/24 network? _____

Now assume a priority of zero on RTA. Which router is DR for the 192.168.1.0/24 network? _____

What will happen if another router, RTD, joins the 192.168.0.0/24 network with a router ID of 209.165.201.9?

Redistributing an OSPF Default Route Exercise

In some topology configurations and routing policy situations, it is desirable to have an Autonomous System Boundary Router (ASBR) redistribute a default route to the OSPF neighbors in the area. This can be quickly accomplished in both OSPFv2 and OSPFv3.

OSPFv2 Default Route Redistribution

In Figure 10-7, notice that RTA is now our gateway router because it provides access outside the area. In OSPF terminology, RTA is called the _____ (ASBR) because it connects to an external routing domain that uses a different routing policy.

Figure 10-7   Propagating a Default Route in OSPFv2

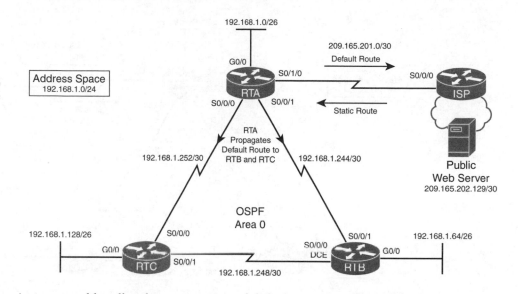

Each routing protocol handles the propagation of default routing information a little differently. For OSPF, the gateway router must be configured with two commands. First, RTA will need a static default route pointing to ISP. Document the command to configure a static default route on RTA using the *exit interface* argument.

Using the *exit interface* argument, document the command necessary to configure ISP with a static route pointing to the 192.168.1.0/24 address space.

At this point, any host on the LAN attached to RTA will be able to access ISP and be able to ping the Public Web Server at 209.165.202.129. However, RTB and RTC still cannot ping outside the 192.168.1.0/24 address space. Why?

Document the command that needs to be configured on RTA to fix this problem.

OSPFv3 Default Route Redistribution

Configuring OSPFv3 to propagate a default route is essentially the same tasks as you do in OSPFv2. Figure 10-8 is an IPv6 version of Figure 10-7.

Figure 10-8   Propagating a Default Route in OSPFv3

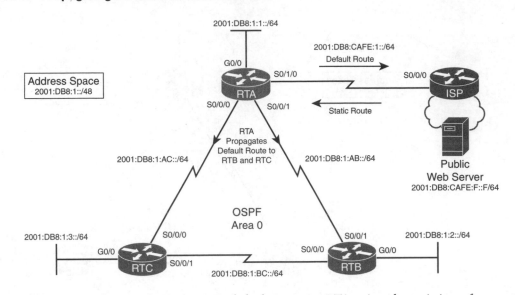

Document the command to configure a static default route on RTA using the *exit interface* argument.

_____

Using the *exit interface* argument, document the command necessary to configure ISP with a static route pointing to the 2001:DB8:1::/48 address space.

_____

Document the command that will cause RTA to propagate the default router to RTB and RTC.

_____

_____

Fine-Tuning OSPF Interfaces

OSPF routers must use matching Hello intervals and Dead intervals on the same link. The default interval values result in efficient OSPF operation and seldom need to be modified. However, you can change them.

Again, refer to Figure 10-7. Assuming that the current intervals are 10 and 40, document the commands necessary to change these OSPFv2 intervals on the link between RTB and RTC to a value four times greater than the current value.

_____

_____

_____

_____

_____

_____

Note that it is not necessary to configure the Dead interval as long as the desired interval is four times the Hello. The IOS will automatically increase the Dead interval to four times the configured Hello interval.

Now refer to Figure 10-8. Assuming that the current intervals are 10 and 40, document the commands necessary to change the OSPFv3 intervals on the link between RTB and RTC to a value four times greater than the current value.

_____

_____

_____

_____

_____

_____

Other than the **show run** command, what commands can you use to verify OSPF timers on an interface for both IPv4 and IPv6?

_____

_____

Packet Tracer Exercise 10-1: Fine-Tune Dual-Stacked OSPF

Now you are ready to use Packet Tracer to apply your documented configuration. Download and open the file LSG03-1001.pka found at the companion website for this book. Refer to the Introduction of this book for specifics on accessing files.

Note: The following instructions are also contained within the Packet Tracer Exercise.

In this Packet Tracer activity, you will configure the RTA router with IPv4 and IPv6 default routes and then propagate them to RTB and RTC. You will then fine-tune the OSPF Hello and Dead intervals. Finally, you will then verify that the PCs can ping the outside Web Server.

Requirements

- Configure RTA with an IPv4 default route using the *exit interface* argument.
- Configure RTA with an IPv6 default route using the *exit interface* argument.
- Configure RTA, RTB, and RTC serial interfaces to use a 40 second hello interval and a 160 second dead interval.
- Verify the PCs can ping the outside Web Server.

Your completion percentage should be 100%. All the connectivity tests should show a status of "successful." If not, click **Check Results** to see which required components are not yet completed.

Troubleshooting Single-Area OSPF Implementations

Troubleshooting single-area OSPF is a required skill for any network professional involved in the implementation and maintenance of an OSPF network. Solid understanding of OSPF operation and the impact of the OSPF configuration commands is essential.

OSPF Adjacency Issues

A common problem in OSPF convergence is a lack of adjacency with OSPF neighbors. List at least four reasons why adjacency might fail to establish.

_____

_____

_____

_____

_____

_____

What are the OSPFv2 and OSPFv3 commands you use to quickly verify adjacency between OSPF routers?

_____

_____

The command will list a state for each known OSPF router. What are the seven states OSPF transitions through on its way to convergence?

_____

_____

Identify OSPFv2 Troubleshooting Commands

The following output is from the topology shown in Figure 10-7. Indicate the command used to generate the output.

```
RTA# _____

Codes: L - local, C - connected, S - static, R - RIP, M - mobile, B - BGP
       D - EIGRP, EX - EIGRP external, O - OSPF, IA - OSPF inter area
       N1 - OSPF NSSA external type 1, N2 - OSPF NSSA external type 2
       E1 - OSPF external type 1, E2 - OSPF external type 2
       i - IS-IS, su - IS-IS summary, L1 - IS-IS level-1, L2 - IS-IS level-2
       ia - IS-IS inter area, * - candidate default, U - per-user static route
       o - ODR, P - periodic downloaded static route, H - NHRP, l - LISP
       + - replicated route, % - next hop override


Gateway of last resort is 0.0.0.0 to network 0.0.0.0


      192.168.1.0/24 is variably subnetted, 9 subnets, 3 masks
O        192.168.1.64/26 [110/65] via 192.168.1.246, 00:19:35, Serial0/0/1
```

```
O        192.168.1.128/26 [110/65] via 192.168.1.254, 00:19:10, Serial0/0/0
O        192.168.1.248/30 [110/128] via 192.168.1.254, 00:19:10, Serial0/0/0
                          [110/128] via 192.168.1.246, 00:19:35, Serial0/0/1
RTA# _____

Neighbor ID    Pri   State        Dead Time   Address         Interface
3.3.3.3          0   FULL/ -      00:00:31    192.168.1.254   Serial0/0/0
2.2.2.2          0   FULL/ -      00:00:32    192.168.1.246   Serial0/0/1
RTA# _____
Serial0/0/0 is up, line protocol is up
  Internet Address 192.168.1.253/30, Area 0, Attached via Network Statement
  Process ID 1, Router ID 1.1.1.1, Network Type POINT_TO_POINT, Cost: 64
  Topology-MTID    Cost    Disabled    Shutdown    Topology Name
        0           64       no          no          Base
  Transmit Delay is 1 sec, State POINT_TO_POINT
  Timer intervals configured, Hello 10, Dead 40, Wait 40, Retransmit 5
    oob-resync timeout 40
    Hello due in 00:00:03
  Supports Link-local Signaling (LLS)
  Cisco NSF helper support enabled
  IETF NSF helper support enabled
  Index 3/3, flood queue length 0
  Next 0x0(0)/0x0(0)
  Last flood scan length is 1, maximum is 1
  Last flood scan time is 0 msec, maximum is 0 msec
  Neighbor Count is 1, Adjacent neighbor count is 1
    Adjacent with neighbor 192.168.1.254
  Suppress hello for 0 neighbor(s)
RTA# _____
*** IP Routing is NSF aware ***

Routing Protocol is "ospf 1"
  Outgoing update filter list for all interfaces is not set
  Incoming update filter list for all interfaces is not set
  Router ID 192.168.1.253
  It is an autonomous system boundary router
 Redistributing External Routes from,
  Number of areas in this router is 1. 1 normal 0 stub 0 nssa
  Maximum path: 4
  Routing for Networks:
    192.168.1.0 0.0.0.63 area 0
    192.168.1.244 0.0.0.3 area 0
    192.168.1.252 0.0.0.3 area 0
  Routing Information Sources:
```

```
    Gateway        Distance     Last Update
    2.2.2.2            110      00:18:13
    3.3.3.3            110      00:17:48
Distance: (default is 110)
```

```
RTA# _____
Routing Process "ospf 1" with ID 1.1.1.1
Start time: 00:44:46.536, Time elapsed: 00:23:27.360
Supports only single TOS(TOS0) routes
Supports opaque LSA
Supports Link-local Signaling (LLS)
Supports area transit capability
Supports NSSA (compatible with RFC 3101)
Event-log enabled, Maximum number of events: 1000, Mode: cyclic
It is an autonomous system boundary router
Redistributing External Routes from,
Router is not originating router-LSAs with maximum metric
Initial SPF schedule delay 5000 msecs
Minimum hold time between two consecutive SPFs 10000 msecs
Maximum wait time between two consecutive SPFs 10000 msecs
Incremental-SPF disabled
Minimum LSA interval 5 secs
Minimum LSA arrival 1000 msecs
LSA group pacing timer 240 secs
Interface flood pacing timer 33 msecs
Retransmission pacing timer 66 msecs
Number of external LSA 1. Checksum Sum 0x003416
Number of opaque AS LSA 0. Checksum Sum 0x000000
Number of DCbitless external and opaque AS LSA 0
Number of DoNotAge external and opaque AS LSA 0
Number of areas in this router is 1. 1 normal 0 stub 0 nssa
Number of areas transit capable is 0
External flood list length 0
IETF NSF helper support enabled
Cisco NSF helper support enabled
Reference bandwidth unit is 100 mbps
    Area BACKBONE(0)
        Number of interfaces in this area is 3
        Area has no authentication
        SPF algorithm last executed 00:16:47.472 ago
        SPF algorithm executed 4 times
        Area ranges are
        Number of LSA 3. Checksum Sum 0x00E037
        Number of opaque link LSA 0. Checksum Sum 0x000000
```

```
        Number of DCbitless LSA 0
        Number of indication LSA 0
        Number of DoNotAge LSA 0
        Flood list length 0
```

Identify OSPFv3 Troubleshooting Commands

The following output is from the topology shown in Figure 10-8. Indicate the command used to generate the output.

```
RTC# _____

IPv6 Routing Protocol is "connected"
IPv6 Routing Protocol is "ND"
IPv6 Routing Protocol is "ospf 1"
  Router ID 3.3.3.3
  Number of areas: 1 normal, 0 stub, 0 nssa
  Interfaces (Area 0):
    GigabitEthernet0/0
    Serial0/0/1
    Serial0/0/0
  Redistribution:
    None
```

```
RTC# _____
```

```
            OSPFv3 Router with ID (3.3.3.3) (Process ID 1)


Neighbor ID     Pri   State         Dead Time    Interface ID   Interface
2.2.2.2          0    FULL/  -      00:00:39     6              Serial0/0/1
1.1.1.1          0    FULL/  -      00:00:31     6              Serial0/0/0
```

```
RTC# _____

Serial0/0/1 is up, line protocol is up
  Link Local Address FE80::C, Interface ID 7
  Area 0, Process ID 1, Instance ID 0, Router ID 3.3.3.3
  Network Type POINT_TO_POINT, Cost: 64
  Transmit Delay is 1 sec, State POINT_TO_POINT
  Timer intervals configured, Hello 10, Dead 40, Wait 40, Retransmit 5
    Hello due in 00:00:06
  Graceful restart helper support enabled
  Index 1/2/2, flood queue length 0
  Next 0x0(0)/0x0(0)/0x0(0)
  Last flood scan length is 2, maximum is 4
  Last flood scan time is 0 msec, maximum is 0 msec
  Neighbor Count is 1, Adjacent neighbor count is 1
    Adjacent with neighbor 2.2.2.2
```

```
  Suppress hello for 0 neighbor(s)
RTC# _____
  Routing Process "ospfv3 1" with ID 3.3.3.3
  Event-log enabled, Maximum number of events: 1000, Mode: cyclic
  Router is not originating router-LSAs with maximum metric
  Initial SPF schedule delay 5000 msecs
  Minimum hold time between two consecutive SPFs 10000 msecs
  Maximum wait time between two consecutive SPFs 10000 msecs
  Minimum LSA interval 5 secs
  Minimum LSA arrival 1000 msecs
  LSA group pacing timer 240 secs
  Interface flood pacing timer 33 msecs
  Retransmission pacing timer 66 msecs
  Number of external LSA 1. Checksum Sum 0x00B657
  Number of areas in this router is 1. 1 normal 0 stub 0 nssa
  Graceful restart helper support enabled
  Reference bandwidth unit is 100 mbps
  RFC1583 compatibility enabled
     Area BACKBONE(0)
        Number of interfaces in this area is 3
        SPF algorithm executed 4 times
        Number of LSA 15. Checksum Sum 0x07E293
        Number of DCbitless LSA 0
        Number of indication LSA 0
        Number of DoNotAge LSA 0
        Flood list length 0
RTC# _____
IPv6 Routing Table - default - 11 entries
Codes: C - Connected, L - Local, S - Static, U - Per-user Static route
       B - BGP, R - RIP, H - NHRP, I1 - ISIS L1
       I2 - ISIS L2, IA - ISIS interarea, IS - ISIS summary, D - EIGRP
       EX - EIGRP external, ND - ND Default, NDp - ND Prefix, DCE - Destination
       NDr - Redirect, O - OSPF Intra, OI - OSPF Inter, OE1 - OSPF ext 1
       OE2 - OSPF ext 2, ON1 - OSPF NSSA ext 1, ON2 - OSPF NSSA ext 2
       a - Application
OE2 ::/0 [110/1], tag 1
     via FE80::A, Serial0/0/0
O    2001:DB8:1:1::/64 [110/6576]
     via FE80::A, Serial0/0/0
O    2001:DB8:1:2::/64 [110/6576]
     via FE80::B, Serial0/0/1
O    2001:DB8:1:AB::/64 [110/12952]
     via FE80::B, Serial0/0/1
     via FE80::A, Serial0/0/0
```

Labs and Activities

Command Reference

In Table 10-3, record the command, including the correct router or switch prompt, that fits the description. Fill in any blanks with the appropriate missing information.

Table 10-3   Commands for Chapter 10, OSPF Tuning and Troubleshooting

Command	Description
	Configure R1's LAN interface to be the DR.
	Configure R1 with an IPv4 default route pointing out the serial 0/1/0 interface.
	Configure R1 with an IPv6 default route pointing out the serial 0/1/0 interface.
	Propagate the default route in OSPFv2.
	Propagate the default route in OSPFv3.
	On R1, set the OSPFv2 hello interval to 60 seconds.
	On R1, set the OSPFv2 dead interval to 240 seconds.
	On R1, set the OSPFv3 hello interval to 60 seconds.
	On R1, set he OSPFv3 dead interval to 240 seconds.

10.0.1.2 Class Activity–DR and BDR Elections

Objectives

Modify the OSPF interface priority to influence the Designated Router (DR) and Backup Designated Router (BDR) election.

Scenario

You are trying to decide how to influence the selection of the Designated Router and Backup Designated Router for your OSPF network. This activity simulates that process.

Three separate Designated Router election scenarios will be presented. The focus is on electing a DR and BDR for your group. Refer to the PDF for this activity for the remaining instructions.

If additional time is available, two groups can be combined to simulate DR and BDR elections.

Required Resources

- Router priorities paper sign example (student developed)
- Router ID paper sign example (student developed)

Directions

This is a group activity with four classmates comprising each group. Before reporting to the group, each student will prepare router priority and router ID signs to bring to the group.

Step 1. Decide the router priority.

    a. Prior to joining your group, use a clean sheet of paper. On one side of the paper, write DEFAULT ROUTER PRIORITY = 1.

    b. On the other side of the same sheet of paper, write ROUTER PRIORITY = (choose a number between 0 and 255).

Step 2. Decide the router ID.

    a. On a second clean sheet of paper, on one side, write ROUTER ID = (any IPv4 number).

    b. On the other side, write ROUTER ID = Loopback (any IPv4) number.

Step 3. Begin DR and BDR elections.

    a. Start the first election process.

        1. Students within the group will show each other the router priority numbers they selected for Step 1b.

        2. After comparing their priority numbers, the student with the highest priority number is elected the DR and the student with the second-highest priority number is elected the BDR. Any student who wrote 0 as their priority number cannot participate in the election.

3. The elected DR student will announce the elections by saying "I am the DR for all of you in this group. Please send me any changes to your networks or interfaces to IP address 224.0.0.6. I will then forward those changes to all of you at IP address 224.0.0.5. Stay tuned for future updates."

4. The BDR's elected student will say, "I am your BDR. Please send all changes to your router interfaces or networks to the DR. If the DR does not announce your changes, I will step in and do that from that point onward."

b. Start the second election process.

1. Students will hold up their DEFAULT ROUTER PRIORITY = 1 sign first. When it is agreed that all of the students have the same router priority, they will put that paper down.

2. Next, students will display their ROUTER ID = Loopback (IPv4) address signs.

3. The student with the highest loopback IPv4 address wins the election and repeats "I am the DR for all of you in this group. Our priorities are the same, but I have the highest loopback address on my router as compared to all of you; therefore, you have elected me as your DR. Please send all changes to your network addresses or interfaces to 224.0.0.6. I will then report any changes to all of you via 224.0.0.5."

4. The BDR will repeat his/her respective phrase from Step 3a, 4).

c. Start the third election process, but this time, all students can choose which sides of their papers to display. The DR/BDR election process uses the highest router priority first, highest loopback router ID second, and highest IPv4 router ID third, and elects a DR and BDR.

1. Elect a DR and BDR.

2. Justify your elections.

3. If you have time, get together with another group and go through the scenario processes again to solidify DR and BDR elections.

10.1.1.12 Packet Tracer–Determining the DR and BDR

Topology

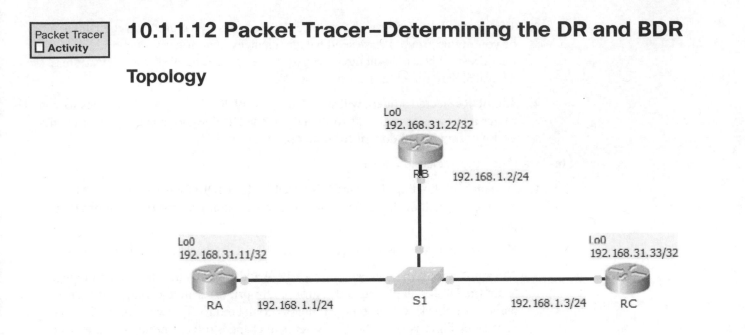

Addressing Table

Device	Interface	IP Address	Subnet Mask
RA	G0/0	192.168.1.1	255.255.255.0
	Lo0	192.168.31.11	255.255.255.255
RB	G0/0	192.168.1.2	255.255.255.0
	Lo0	192.168.31.22	255.255.255.255
RC	G0/0	192.168.1.3	255.255.255.0
	Lo0	192.168.31.33	255.255.255.255

Objectives

Part 1: Examine DR and BDR Changing Roles

Part 2: Modify OSPF Priority and Force Elections

Scenario

In this activity, you will examine DR and BDR roles and watch the roles change when there is a change in the network. You will then modify the priority to control the roles and force a new election. Finally, you will verify routers are filling the desired roles.

Part 1: Examine DR and BDR Changing Roles

Step 1.   Wait until the amber link lights turn green.

When you first open the file in Packet Tracer, you may notice that the link lights for the switch are amber. These link lights will stay amber for 50 seconds while the switch makes sure that one of the routers is not another switch. Alternatively, you can click **Fast Forward Time** to bypass this process.

Step 2.   Verify the current OSPF neighbor states.

    a.   Use the appropriate command on each router to examine the current DR and BDR.

    b.   Which router is the DR? _____

    c.   Which router is the BDR? _____

Step 3.   Turn on IP OSPF adjacency debugging.

    a.   You can monitor the DR and BDR election process with a **debug** command. On **RA** and **RB**, enter the following command.

```
RA# debug ip ospf adj
RB# debug ip ospf adj
```

Step 4.   Disable the Gigabit Ethernet 0/0 interface on RC.

    a.   Disable the link between **RC** and the switch to cause roles to change.

    b.   Wait about 30 seconds for the dead timers to expire on **RA** and **RB**. According to the debug output, which router was elected DR and which router was elected BDR?

    _____

Step 5.   Restore the Gigabit Ethernet 0/0 interface on RC.

    a.   Re-enable the link between **RC** and the switch.

    b.   Wait for the new DR/BDR elections to occur. Did DR and BDR roles change? Why or why not?

    _____

    _____

Step 6.   Disable the Gigabit Ethernet 0/0 interface on RB.

    a.   Disable the link between **RB** and the switch to cause roles to change.

    b.   Wait about 30 seconds for the holddown timers to expire on **RA** and **RC**. According to the debug output on **RA**, which router was elected DR and which router was elected BDR?_____

Step 7.   Restore the Gigabit Ethernet 0/0 interface on RB.

    a.   Re-enable the link between **RB** and the switch.

    b.   Wait for the new DR/BDR elections to occur. Did DR and BDR roles change? Why or why not?

    _____

    _____

Step 8.   Turn off Debugging.

    Enter the command **undebug all** on **RA** and **RB** to disable debugging.

Part 2: Modify OSPF Priority and Force Elections

Step 1.   Configure OSPF priorities on each router.

To change the DR and BDR, configure the Gigabit Ethernet 0/0 port of each router with the following OSPF interface priorities:

- RA: 200

- RB: 100

- RC: 1 (This is the default priority)

Step 2.   Force an election by reloading the switch.

Note: The command **clear ip ospf process** can also be used on the routers to reset the OSPF process.

Step 3.   Verify DR and BDR elections were successful.

a.   Wait long enough for OSPF to converge and for the DR/BDR election to occur. This should take a few minutes. You can click **Fast Forward Time** to speed up the process.

b.   According to output from an appropriate command, which router is now DR and which router is now BDR?_____

Suggested Scoring Rubric

Activity Section	Question Location	Possible Points	Earned Points
Part 1: Examine DR and BDR Changing Roles	Step 2b	10	
	Step 2c	10	
	Step 4b	10	
	Step 5b	10	
	Step 6b	10	
	Step 7b	10	
	Part 1 Total	60	
Part 2: Modify OSPF Priority and Force Elections	Step 3b	10	
	Part 2 Total	10	
	Packet Tracer Score	30	
	Total Score	100	

10.1.1.13 Lab–Configuring OSPFv2 on a Multiaccess Network

Topology

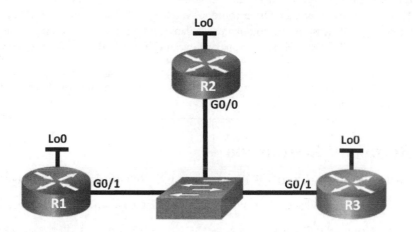

Addressing Table

Device	Interface	IP Address	Subnet Mask
R1	G0/1	192.168.1.1	255.255.255.0
	Lo0	192.168.31.11	255.255.255.255
R2	G0/0	192.168.1.2	255.255.255.0
	Lo0	192.168.31.22	255.255.255.255
R3	G0/1	192.168.1.3	255.255.255.0
	Lo0	192.168.31.33	255.255.255.255

Objectives

Part 1: Build the Network and Configure Basic Device Settings

Part 2: Configure and Verify OSPFv2 on the DR, BDR, and DROther

Part 3: Configure OSPFv2 Interface Priority to Determine the DR and BDR

Background/Scenario

A multiaccess network is a network with more than two devices on the same shared media. Examples include Ethernet and Frame Relay. On multiaccess networks, OSPFv2 elects a Designated Router (DR) to be the collection and distribution point for link-state advertisements (LSAs) that are sent and received. A Backup Designated Router (BDR) is also elected in case the DR fails. All other routers become DROthers as this indicates a router that is neither the DR nor the BDR.

Because the DR acts as a focal point for OSPF routing protocol communication, the router chosen should be capable of supporting a heavier traffic load than other routers in the network. A router with a powerful CPU and adequate DRAM is typically the best choice for the DR.

In this lab, you will configure OSPFv2 on the DR, BDR, and DROther. You will then modify the priority of routers to control the outcome of the DR/BDR election process and ensure that the desired router becomes the DR.

Note: The routers used with CCNA hands-on labs are Cisco 1941 Integrated Services Routers (ISRs) with Cisco IOS Release 15.2(4)M3 (universalk9 image). The switches used are Cisco Catalyst 2960s with Cisco IOS Release 15.0(2) (lanbasek9 image). Other routers, switches, and Cisco IOS versions can be used. Depending on the model and Cisco IOS version, the commands available and output produced might vary from what is shown in the labs. Refer to the Router Interface Summary Table at the end of this lab for the correct interface identifiers.

Note: Make sure that the routers and switches have been erased and have no startup configurations. If you are unsure, contact your instructor.

Required Resources

- 3 Routers (Cisco 1941 with Cisco IOS Release 15.2(4)M3 universal image or comparable)
- 1 Switch (Cisco 2960 with Cisco IOS Release 15.0(2) lanbasek9 image or comparable)
- Console cables to configure the Cisco IOS devices via the console ports
- Ethernet cables as shown in the topology

Part 1: Build the Network and Configure Basic Device Settings

In Part 1, you will set up the network topology and configure basic settings on the routers.

Step 1. Cable the network as shown in the topology.

Attach the devices as shown in the topology diagram, and cable as necessary.

Step 2. Initialize and reload the routers.

Step 3. Configure basic settings for each router.

    a. Disable DNS lookup.

    b. Configure device names as shown in the topology.

    c. Assign **class** as the privileged EXEC password.

    d. Assign **cisco** as the console and vty passwords.

    e. Encrypt the plain text passwords.

    f. Configure a MOTD banner to warn users that unauthorized access is prohibited.

    g. Configure **logging synchronous** for the console line.

    h. Configure the IP addresses listed in the Addressing Table for all interfaces.

    i. Use the **show ip interface brief** command to verify that the IP addressing is correct and that the interfaces are active.

    j. Copy the running configuration to the startup configuration.

Part 2: Configure and Verify OSPFv2 on the DR, BDR, and DROther

In Part 2, you will configure OSPFv2 on the DR, BDR, and DROther. The DR and BDR election process takes place as soon as the first router has its interface enabled on the multiaccess network. This can happen as the routers are powered-on or when the OSPF **network** command for that interface is configured. If a new router enters the network after the DR and BDR have already been elected, it does not become the DR or BDR, even if it has a higher OSPF interface priority or router ID than the current DR or BDR. Configure the OSPF process on the router with the highest router ID first to ensure that this router becomes the DR.

Step 1. Configure OSPF on R3.

Configure the OSPF process on R3 (the router with the highest router ID) to ensure that this router becomes the DR.

  a. Assign 1 as the process ID for the OSPF process. Configure the router to advertise the 192.168.1.0/24 network. Use an area ID of 0 for the OSPF *area-id* parameter in the **network** statement.

  What factor determined that R3 has the highest router ID?

  _____

  b. Verify that OSPF has been configured and R3 is the DR.

  What command would you use to verify that OSPF has been configured correctly and R3 is the DR?

  _____

Step 2. Configure OSPF on R2.

Configure the OSPF process on R2 (the router with the second highest router ID) to ensure that this router becomes the BDR.

  a. Assign 1 as the process ID for the OSPF process. Configure the router to advertise the 192.168.1.0/24 network. Use an area ID of 0 for the OSPF *area-id* parameter in the **network** statement.

  b. Verify that the OSPF has been configured and that R2 is the BDR. Record the command used for verification.

  _____

  c. Issue the **show ip ospf neighbor** command to view information about the other routers in the OSPF area.

```
R2# show ip ospf neighbor
Neighbor ID      Pri   State            Dead Time    Address        Interface
192.168.31.33     1    FULL/DR          00:00:33     192.168.1.3
GigabitEthernet0/0
```

Notice that R3 is the DR.

Step 3.   Configure OSPF on R1.

Configure the OSPF process on R1 (the router with the lowest router ID). This router will be designated as DROther instead of DR or BDR.

a.   Assign 1 as the process ID for the OSPF process. Configure the router to advertise the 192.168.1.0/24 network. Use an area ID of 0 for the OSPF *area-id* parameter in the **network** statement.

b.   Issue the **show ip ospf interface brief** command to verify that OSPF has been configured and R1 is the DROther.

```
R1# show ip ospf interface brief
Interface    PID   Area            IP Address/Mask      Cost  State Nbrs F/C
Gi0/1         1     0              192.168.1.1/24        1     DROTH 2/2
```

c.   Issue the **show ip ospf neighbor** command to view information about the other routers in the OSPF area.

```
R1# show ip ospf neighbor
Neighbor ID      Pri   State     Dead Time   Address       ·  Interface
192.168.31.22     1    FULL/BDR  00:00:35    192.168.1.2      GigabitEthernet0/1
192.168.31.33     1    FULL/DR   00:00:30    192.168.1.3      GigabitEthernet0/1
```

What priority are both the DR and BDR routers? _____

Part 3: Configure OSPFv2 Interface Priority to Determine the DR and BDR

In Part 3, you will configure router interface priority to determine the DR/BDR election, reset the OSPFv2 process, and then verify that the DR and BDR routers have changed. OSPF interface priority overrides all other settings in determining which routers become the DR and BDR.

Step 1.   Configure R1 G0/1 with OSPF priority 255.

A value of 255 is the highest possible interface priority.

```
R1(config)# interface g0/1
R1(config-if)# ip ospf priority 255
R1(config-if)# end
```

Step 2.   Configure R3 G0/1 with OSPF priority 100.

```
R3(config)# interface g0/1
R3(config-if)# ip ospf priority 100
R3(config-if)# end
```

Step 3.   Configure R2 G0/0 with OSPF priority 0.

A priority of 0 causes the router to be ineligible to participate in an OSPF election and does not become a DR or BDR.

```
R2(config)# interface g0/0
R2(config-if)# ip ospf priority 0
R2(config-if)# end
```

Step 4.   Reset the OSPF process.

a.   Issue the **show ip ospf neighbor** command to determine the DR and BDR.

b.   Has the DR designation changed? _____
Which router is the DR? _____

Has the BDR designation changed? _____

Which router is the BDR? _____

What is the role of R2 now? _____

Explain the immediate effects caused by the **ip ospf priority** command.

_____

_____

_____

Note: If the DR and BDR designations did not change, issue the **clear ip ospf 1 process** command on all of the routers to reset the OSPF processes and force a new election.

If the **clear ip ospf process** command does not reset the DR and BDR, issue the **reload** command on all routers after saving the running configuration to the startup configuration.

c. Issue the **show ip ospf interface** command on R1 and R3 to confirm the priority settings and DR/BDR status on the routers.

```
R1# show ip ospf interface
GigabitEthernet0/1 is up, line protocol is up
  Internet Address 192.168.1.1/24, Area 0
  Process ID 1, Router ID 192.168.31.11, Network Type BROADCAST, Cost: 1
  Transmit Delay is 1 sec, State DR, Priority 255
  Designated Router (ID) 192.168.31.11, Interface address 192.168.1.1
  Backup Designated router (ID) 192.168.31.33, Interface address 192.168.1.3
  Timer intervals configured, Hello 10, Dead 40, Wait 40, Retransmit 5
    oob-resync timeout 40
    Hello due in 00:00:00
  Supports Link-local Signaling (LLS)
  Index 1/1, flood queue length 0
  Next 0x0(0)/0x0(0)
  Last flood scan length is 1, maximum is 2
  Last flood scan time is 0 msec, maximum is 0 msec
  Neighbor Count is 2, Adjacent neighbor count is 2
    Adjacent with neighbor 192.168.31.22
    Adjacent with neighbor 192.168.31.33   (Backup Designated Router)
  Suppress hello for 0 neighbor(s)


R3# show ip ospf interface
GigabitEthernet0/1 is up, line protocol is up
  Internet Address 192.168.1.3/24, Area 0
  Process ID 1, Router ID 192.168.31.33, Network Type BROADCAST, Cost: 1
  Transmit Delay is 1 sec, State BDR, Priority 100
  Designated Router (ID) 192.168.31.11, Interface address 192.168.1.1
  Backup Designated router (ID) 192.168.31.33, Interface address 192.168.1.3
  Timer intervals configured, Hello 10, Dead 40, Wait 40, Retransmit 5
    oob-resync timeout 40
    Hello due in 00:00:00
  Supports Link-local Signaling (LLS)
```

```
        Index 1/1, flood queue length 0
        Next 0x0(0)/0x0(0)
        Last flood scan length is 0, maximum is 2
        Last flood scan time is 0 msec, maximum is 0 msec
        Neighbor Count is 2, Adjacent neighbor count is 2
          Adjacent with neighbor 192.168.31.22
          Adjacent with neighbor 192.168.31.11   (Designated Router)
        Suppress hello for 0 neighbor(s)
```

Which router is now the DR? _____

Which router is now the BDR? _____

Did the interface priority override the router ID in determining the DR/BDR?

_____

Reflection

1. List the criteria used from highest to lowest for determining the DR on an OSPF network.

    _____

    _____

    _____

2. What is the significance of a 255 interface priority?

    _____

Router Interface Summary Table

Router Interface Summary				
Router Model	Ethernet Interface #1	Ethernet Interface #2	Serial Interface #1	Serial Interface #2
1800	Fast Ethernet 0/0 (F0/0)	Fast Ethernet 0/1 (F0/1)	Serial 0/0/0 (S0/0/0)	Serial 0/0/1 (S0/0/1)
1900	Gigabit Ethernet 0/0 (G0/0)	Gigabit Ethernet 0/1 (G0/1)	Serial 0/0/0 (S0/0/0)	Serial 0/0/1 (S0/0/1)
2801	Fast Ethernet 0/0 (F0/0)	Fast Ethernet 0/1 (F0/1)	Serial 0/1/0 (S0/1/0)	Serial 0/1/1 (S0/1/1)
2811	Fast Ethernet 0/0 (F0/0)	Fast Ethernet 0/1 (F0/1)	Serial 0/0/0 (S0/0/0)	Serial 0/0/1 (S0/0/1)
2900	Gigabit Ethernet 0/0 (G0/0)	Gigabit Ethernet 0/1 (G0/1)	Serial 0/0/0 (S0/0/0)	Serial 0/0/1 (S0/0/1)

Note: To find out how the router is configured, look at the interfaces to identify the type of router and how many interfaces the router has. There is no way to effectively list all the combinations of configurations for each router class. This table includes identifiers for the possible combinations of Ethernet and Serial interfaces in the device. The table does not include any other type of interface, even though a specific router may contain one. An example of this might be an ISDN BRI interface. The string in parentheses is the legal abbreviation that can be used in Cisco IOS commands to represent the interface.

10.1.2.5 Packet Tracer–Propagating a Default Route in OSPFv2

Topology

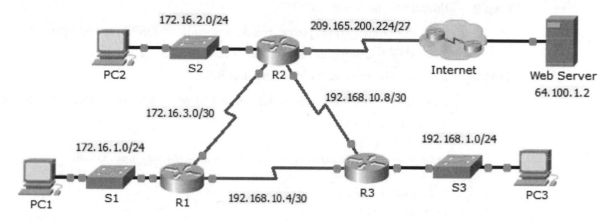

Addressing Table

Device	Interface	IPv4 Address	Subnet Mask	Default Gateway
R1	G0/0	172.16.1.1	255.255.255.0	N/A
	S0/0/0	172.16.3.1	255.255.255.252	N/A
	S0/0/1	192.168.10.5	255.255.255.252	N/A
R2	G0/0	172.16.2.1	255.255.255.0	N/A
	S0/0/0	172.16.3.2	255.255.255.252	N/A
	S0/0/1	192.168.10.9	255.255.255.252	N/A
	S0/1/0	209.165.200.225	255.255.255.224	N/A
R3	G0/0	192.168.1.1	255.255.255.0	N/A
	S0/0/0	192.168.10.6	255.255.255.252	N/A
	S0/0/1	192.168.10.10	255.255.255.252	N/A
PC1	NIC	172.16.1.2	255.255.255.0	172.16.1.1
PC2	NIC	172.16.2.2	255.255.255.0	172.16.2.1
PC3	NIC	192.168.1.2	255.255.255.0	192.168.1.1

Objectives

Part 1: Propagate a Default Route

Part 2: Verify Connectivity

Background

In this activity, you will configure an IPv4 default route to the Internet and propagate that default route to other OSPF routers. You will then verify the default route is in downstream routing tables and that hosts can now access a Web Server on the Internet.

Part 1: Propagate a Default Route

Step 1.   Configure a default route on **R2**.

Configure **R2** with a directly attached default route to the Internet.

```
R2(config)# ip route 0.0.0.0 0.0.0.0 Serial0/1/0
```

Step 2.   Propagate the route in OSPF.

Configure OSPF to propagate the default route in OSPF routing updates.

```
R2(config-router)# default-information originate
```

Step 3.   Examine the routing tables on **R1** and **R3**.

Examine the routing tables of **R1** and **R3** to verify that the route has been propagated.

```
R1> show ip route
<output omitted>
O*E2 0.0.0.0/0 [110/1] via 172.16.3.2, 00:00:08, Serial0/0/0
!-------------------
R3> show ip route
<output omitted>
O*E2 0.0.0.0/0 [110/1] via 192.168.10.9, 00:08:15, Serial0/0/1
```

Part 2: Verify Connectivity

Verify that **PC1**, **PC2**, and **PC3** can ping the Web Server.

Packet Tracer
☐ Activity

10.1.3.4 Packet Tracer–Configuring OSPFv2 Advanced Features

Topology

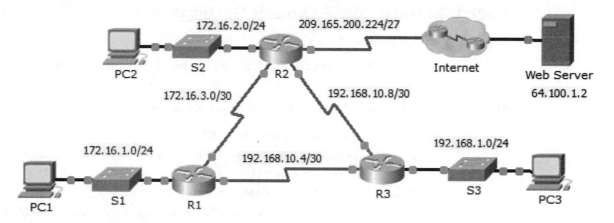

Addressing Table

Device	Interface	IPv4 Address	Subnet Mask	Default Gateway
R1	G0/0	172.16.1.1	255.255.255.0	N/A
	S0/0/0	172.16.3.1	255.255.255.252	N/A
	S0/0/1	192.168.10.5	255.255.255.252	N/A
R2	G0/0	172.16.2.1	255.255.255.0	N/A
	S0/0/0	172.16.3.2	255.255.255.252	N/A
	S0/0/1	192.168.10.9	255.255.255.252	N/A
	S0/1/0	209.165.200.225	255.255.255.224	N/A
R3	G0/0	192.168.1.1	255.255.255.0	N/A
	S0/0/0	192.168.10.6	255.255.255.252	N/A
	S0/0/1	192.168.10.10	255.255.255.252	N/A
PC1	NIC	172.16.1.2	255.255.255.0	172.16.1.1
PC2	NIC	172.16.2.2	255.255.255.0	172.16.2.1
PC3	NIC	192.168.1.2	255.255.255.0	192.168.1.1

Objectives

Part 1: Modify OSPF Default Settings

Part 2: Verify Connectivity

Scenario

In this activity, OSPF is already configured and all end devices currently have full connectivity. You will modify the default OSPF routing configurations by changing the hello and dead timers and adjusting the bandwidth of a link. Then you will verify that full connectivity is restored for all end devices.

Part 1: Modify OSPF Default Settings

Step 1.   Test connectivity between all end devices.

Before modifying the OSPF settings, verify that all PCs can ping the Web Server and each other.

Step 2.   Adjust the hello and dead timers between **R1** and **R2**.

a.   Enter the following commands on **R1**.

```
R1(config)# interface s0/0/0
R1(config-if)# ip ospf hello-interval 15
R1(config-if)# ip ospf dead-interval 60
```

b.   After a short period of time, the OSPF connection with **R2** will fail. **Both sides of the connection need to have the same timers in order for the adjacency to be maintained.** Adjust the timers on **R2**.

Step 3.   Adjust the bandwidth setting on **R1**.

a.   Trace the path between **PC1** and the Web Server located at 64.100.1.2. Notice that the path from **PC1** to 64.100.1.2 is routed through **R2**. OSPF prefers the lower cost path.

b.   On the **R1** Serial 0/0/0 interface, set the bandwidth to 64 Kb/s. This does not change the actual port speed, only the metric that the OSPF process on **R1** will use to calculate best routes.

```
R1(config-if)# bandwidth 64
```

c.   Trace the path between **PC1** and the Web Server located at 64.100.1.2. Notice that the path from **PC1** to 64.100.1.2 is redirected through **R3**. OSPF prefers the lower cost path.

Part 2: Verify Connectivity

Verify all PCs can ping the Web Server and each other.

10.1.3.5 Lab–Configuring OSFPv2 Advanced Features

Topology

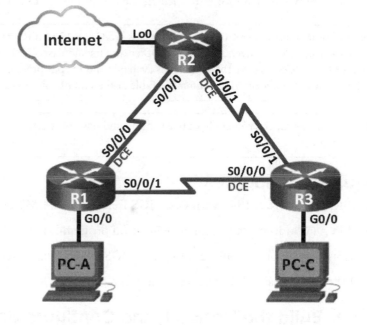

Addressing Table

Device	Interface	IP Address	Subnet Mask	Default Gateway
R1	G0/0	192.168.1.1	255.255.255.0	N/A
	S0/0/0 (DCE)	192.168.12.1	255.255.255.252	N/A
	S0/0/1	192.168.13.1	255.255.255.252	N/A
R2	Lo0	209.165.200.225	255.255.255.252	N/A
	S0/0/0	192.168.12.2	255.255.255.252	N/A
	S0/0/1 (DCE)	192.168.23.1	255.255.255.252	N/A
R3	G0/0	192.168.3.1	255.255.255.0	N/A
	S0/0/0 (DCE)	192.168.13.2	255.255.255.252	N/A
	S0/0/1	192.168.23.2	255.255.255.252	N/A
PC-A	NIC	192.168.1.3	255.255.255.0	192.168.1.1
PC-C	NIC	192.168.3.3	255.255.255.0	192.168.3.1

Objectives

Part 1: Build the Network and Configure Basic Device Settings

Part 2: Configure and Verify OSPF Routing

Part 3: Change OSPF Metrics

Part 4: Configure and Propagate a Static Default Route

Background/Scenario

Open Shortest Path First (OSPF) has advanced features to allow changes to be made to control metrics, default route propagation, and security.

In this lab, you will adjust OSPF metrics on the router interfaces and configure OSPF route propagation.

Note: The routers used with CCNA hands-on labs are Cisco 1941 Integrated Services Routers (ISRs) with Cisco IOS Release 15.2(4)M3 (universalk9 image). Other routers and Cisco IOS versions can be used. Depending on the model and Cisco IOS version, the commands available and output produced might vary from what is shown in the labs. Refer to the Router Interface Summary Table at the end of this lab for the correct interface identifiers.

Note: Make sure that the routers have been erased and have no startup configurations. If you are unsure, contact your instructor.

Required Resources

- 3 Routers (Cisco 1941 with Cisco IOS Release 15.2(4)M3 universal image or comparable)
- 2 PCs (Windows with terminal emulation program, such as Tera Term)
- Console cables to configure the Cisco IOS devices via the console ports
- Ethernet and serial cables as shown in the topology

Part 1: Build the Network and Configure Basic Device Settings

In Part 1, you will set up the network topology and configure basic settings on the PC hosts and routers.

Step 1. Cable the network as shown in the topology.

Step 2. Initialize and reload the routers as necessary.

Step 3. Configure basic settings for each router.

    a. Disable DNS lookup.

    b. Configure device name as shown in the topology.

    c. Assign **class** as the privileged EXEC password.

    d. Assign **cisco** as the console and vty passwords.

    e. Encrypt the plaintext passwords.

    f. Configure a MOTD banner to warn users that unauthorized access is prohibited.

    g. Configure **logging synchronous** for the console line.

    h. Configure the IP addresses listed in the Addressing Table for all interfaces.

    i. Set the clock rate for all DCE serial interfaces at 128000.

    j. Copy the running configuration to the startup configuration.

Step 4. Configure PC hosts.

Refer to the Addressing Table for PC host address information.

Step 5. Test connectivity.

At this point, the PCs are unable to ping each other. However, the routers should be able to ping the directly connected neighbor interfaces, and the PCs should be able to ping their default gateway. Verify and troubleshoot if necessary.

Part 2: Configure and Verify OSPF Routing

In Part 2, you will configure OSPFv2 routing on all routers in the network and then verify that routing tables are updated correctly.

Step 1.   Configure the router ID on all routers.

Assign 1 as the process ID for this OSPF process. Each router should be given the following router ID assignments:

- R1 Router ID: **1.1.1.1**

- R2 Router ID: **2.2.2.2**

- R3 Router ID: **3.3.3.3**

Step 2.   Configure OSPF network information on the routers.

Step 3.   Verify OSPF routing.

    a.   Issue the **show ip ospf neighbor** command to verify that each router is listing the other routers in the network.

    b.   Issue the **show ip route ospf** command to verify that all OSPF networks are present in the routing tables on all routers.

Step 4.   Test end to end connectivity.

Ping PC-C from PC-A to verify end-to-end connectivity. The pings should be successful. If they are not, troubleshoot as necessary.

Note: It may be necessary to disable the PC firewall for the pings to be successful.

Part 3: Change OSPF Metrics

In Part 3, you will change OSPF metrics using the **bandwidth** command, the **auto-cost reference-bandwidth** command, and the **ip ospf cost** command. Making these changes will provide more accurate metrics to OSPF.

Note: All DCE interfaces should have been configured with a clocking rate of 128000 in Part 1, Step 3., substep i.

Step 1.   Change the bandwidth on all serial interfaces to 128Kb/s.

    a.   Issue the **show ip ospf interface brief** command to view the default cost settings on the router interfaces.

```
R1# show ip ospf interface brief
Interface    PID   Area         IP Address/Mask      Cost   State Nbrs F/C
Se0/0/1      1     0            192.168.13.1/30      64     P2P   1/1
Se0/0/0      1     0            192.168.12.1/30      64     P2P   1/1
Gi0/0        1     0            192.168.1.1/24       1      DR    0/0
```

    b.   Use the **bandwidth 128** interface command on all serial interfaces.

c. Issue the **show ip ospf interface brief** command to view the new cost settings.

```
R1# show ip ospf interface brief
Interface   PID   Area        IP Address/Mask     Cost   State Nbrs F/C
Se0/0/1     1     0           192.168.13.1/30     781    P2P   1/1
Se0/0/0     1     0           192.168.12.1/30     781    P2P   1/1
Gi0/0       1     0           192.168.1.1/24      1      DR    0/0
```

Step 2.   Change the reference bandwidth on the routers.

a. Issue the **auto-cost reference-bandwidth 1000** command on the routers to change the default reference bandwidth setting to account for Gigabit Ethernet Interfaces.

b. Re-issue the **show ip ospf interface brief** command to view how this command has changed cost values.

```
R1# show ip ospf interface brief
Interface   PID   Area        IP Address/Mask     Cost   State Nbrs F/C
Se0/0/1     1     0           192.168.13.1/30     7812   P2P   0/0
Se0/0/0     1     0           192.168.12.1/30     7812   P2P   0/0
Gi0/0       1     0           192.168.1.1/24      1      DR    0/0
```

Note: If the router had Fast Ethernet interfaces instead of Gigabit Ethernet interfaces, then the cost would now be 10 on those interfaces.

Step 3.   Change the route cost.

a. Issue the **show ip route ospf** command to display the current OSPF routes on R1. Notice that there are currently two routes in the table that use the S0/0/1 interface.

```
R1# show ip route ospf
Codes: L - local, C - connected, S - static, R - RIP, M - mobile, B - BGP
       D - EIGRP, EX - EIGRP external, O - OSPF, IA - OSPF inter area
       N1 - OSPF NSSA external type 1, N2 - OSPF NSSA external type 2
       E1 - OSPF external type 1, E2 - OSPF external type 2
       i - IS-IS, su - IS-IS summary, L1 - IS-IS level-1, L2 - IS-IS level-2
       ia - IS-IS inter area, * - candidate default, U - per-user static route
       o - ODR, P - periodic downloaded static route, H - NHRP, l - LISP
       + - replicated route, % - next hop override


Gateway of last resort is not set

O       192.168.3.0/24 [110/7822] via 192.168.13.2, 00:00:12, Serial0/0/1
        192.168.23.0/30 is subnetted, 1 subnets
O       192.168.23.0 [110/15624] via 192.168.13.2, 00:00:12, Serial0/0/1
                      [110/15624] via 192.168.12.2, 00:20:03, Serial0/0/0
```

b. Apply the **ip ospf cost 16000** command to the S0/0/1 interface on R1. A cost of 16,000 is higher than the accumulated cost of the route through R2 which is 15,624.

c. Issue the **show ip ospf interface brief** command on R1 to view the cost change to S0/0/1.

```
R1# show ip ospf interface brief
Interface    PID   Area           IP Address/Mask     Cost   State Nbrs F/C
Se0/0/1      1     0              192.168.13.1/30     16000  P2P   1/1
Se0/0/0      1     0              192.168.12.1/30     7812   P2P   1/1
Gi0/0        1     0              192.168.1.1/24      1      DR    0/0
```

d. Re-issue the **show ip route ospf** command on R1 to display the effect this change has made on the routing table. All OSPF routes for R1 are now being routed through R2.

```
R1# show ip route ospf
Codes: L - local, C - connected, S - static, R - RIP, M - mobile, B - BGP
       D - EIGRP, EX - EIGRP external, O - OSPF, IA - OSPF inter area
       N1 - OSPF NSSA external type 1, N2 - OSPF NSSA external type 2
       E1 - OSPF external type 1, E2 - OSPF external type 2
       i - IS-IS, su - IS-IS summary, L1 - IS-IS level-1, L2 - IS-IS level-2
       ia - IS-IS inter area, * - candidate default, U - per-user static route
       o - ODR, P - periodic downloaded static route, H - NHRP, l - LISP
       + - replicated route, % - next hop override


Gateway of last resort is not set

O        192.168.3.0/24 [110/15625] via 192.168.12.2, 00:05:31, Serial0/0/0
         192.168.23.0/30 is subnetted, 1 subnets
O        192.168.23.0 [110/15624] via 192.168.12.2, 01:14:02, Serial0/0/0
```

Explain why the route to the 192.168.3.0/24 network on R1 is now going through R2?

_____

_____

_____

Part 4: Configure and Propagate a Static Default Route

In Part 4, you will use a loopback interface on R2 to simulate an ISP connection to the Internet. You will create a static default route on R2, and then OSPF will propagate that route to the other two routers on the network.

Step 1. Configure a static default route on R2 to loopback 0.

Configure a default route using the loopback interface configured in Part 1, to simulate a connection to an ISP.

Step 2. Have OSPF propagate the default static route.

Issue the **default-information originate** command to include the static default route in the OSPF updates that are sent from R2.

```
R2(config)# router ospf 1
R2(config-router)# default-information originate
```

Step 3. Verify OSPF static route propagation.

    a. Issue the **show ip route static** command on R2.

```
R2# show ip route static
Codes: L - local, C - connected, S - static, R - RIP, M - mobile, B - BGP
       D - EIGRP, EX - EIGRP external, O - OSPF, IA - OSPF inter area
       N1 - OSPF NSSA external type 1, N2 - OSPF NSSA external type 2
       E1 - OSPF external type 1, E2 - OSPF external type 2
       i - IS-IS, su - IS-IS summary, L1 - IS-IS level-1, L2 - IS-IS level-2
       ia - IS-IS inter area, * - candidate default, U - per-user static route
       o - ODR, P - periodic downloaded static route, H - NHRP, l - LISP
       + - replicated route, % - next hop override


Gateway of last resort is 0.0.0.0 to network 0.0.0.0


S*     0.0.0.0/0 is directly connected, Loopback0
```

    b. Issue the **show ip route** command on R1 to verify the propagation of the static route from R2.

```
R1# show ip route
Codes: L - local, C - connected, S - static, R - RIP, M - mobile, B - BGP
       D - EIGRP, EX - EIGRP external, O - OSPF, IA - OSPF inter area
       N1 - OSPF NSSA external type 1, N2 - OSPF NSSA external type 2
       E1 - OSPF external type 1, E2 - OSPF external type 2
       i - IS-IS, su - IS-IS summary, L1 - IS-IS level-1, L2 - IS-IS level-2
       ia - IS-IS inter area, * - candidate default, U - per-user static route
       o - ODR, P - periodic downloaded static route, H - NHRP, l - LISP
       + - replicated route, % - next hop override


Gateway of last resort is 192.168.12.2 to network 0.0.0.0


O*E2  0.0.0.0/0 [110/1] via 192.168.12.2, 00:02:57, Serial0/0/0
      192.168.1.0/24 is variably subnetted, 2 subnets, 2 masks
C        192.168.1.0/24 is directly connected, GigabitEthernet0/0
L        192.168.1.1/32 is directly connected, GigabitEthernet0/0
O     192.168.3.0/24 [110/15634] via 192.168.12.2, 00:03:35, Serial0/0/0
      192.168.12.0/24 is variably subnetted, 2 subnets, 2 masks
C        192.168.12.0/30 is directly connected, Serial0/0/0
L        192.168.12.1/32 is directly connected, Serial0/0/0
      192.168.13.0/24 is variably subnetted, 2 subnets, 2 masks
C        192.168.13.0/30 is directly connected, Serial0/0/1
L        192.168.13.1/32 is directly connected, Serial0/0/1
      192.168.23.0/30 is subnetted, 1 subnets
O        192.168.23.0 [110/15624] via 192.168.12.2, 00:05:18, Serial0/0/0
```

    c. Verify end-to-end connectivity by issuing a ping from PC-A to the ISP interface address 209.165.200.225.

    Were the pings successful? _____

Reflection

1. What is the easiest and preferred method of manipulating OSPF route costs?

_____

_____

2. What does the default-information originate command do for a network using the OSPF routing protocol?

_____

Router Interface Summary Table

Router Interface Summary			
Router Model	Ethernet Interface #1	Ethernet Interface #2	Serial Interface #1	Serial Interface #2
1800	Fast Ethernet 0/0 (F0/0)	Fast Ethernet 0/1 (F0/1)	Serial 0/0/0 (S0/0/0)	Serial 0/0/1 (S0/0/1)
1900	Gigabit Ethernet 0/0 (G0/0)	Gigabit Ethernet 0/1 (G0/1)	Serial 0/0/0 (S0/0/0)	Serial 0/0/1 (S0/0/1)
2801	Fast Ethernet 0/0 (F0/0)	Fast Ethernet 0/1 (F0/1)	Serial 0/1/0 (S0/1/0)	Serial 0/1/1 (S0/1/1)
2811	Fast Ethernet 0/0 (F0/0)	Fast Ethernet 0/1 (F0/1)	Serial 0/0/0 (S0/0/0)	Serial 0/0/1 (S0/0/1)
2900	Gigabit Ethernet 0/0 (G0/0)	Gigabit Ethernet 0/1 (G0/1)	Serial 0/0/0 (S0/0/0)	Serial 0/0/1 (S0/0/1)

Note: To find out how the router is configured, look at the interfaces to identify the type of router and how many interfaces the router has. There is no way to effectively list all the combinations of configurations for each router class. This table includes identifiers for the possible combinations of Ethernet and Serial interfaces in the device. The table does not include any other type of interface, even though a specific router may contain one. An example of this might be an ISDN BRI interface. The string in parentheses is the legal abbreviation that can be used in Cisco IOS commands to represent the interface.

10.2.2.3 Packet Tracer–Troubleshooting Single-Area OSPFv2

Topology

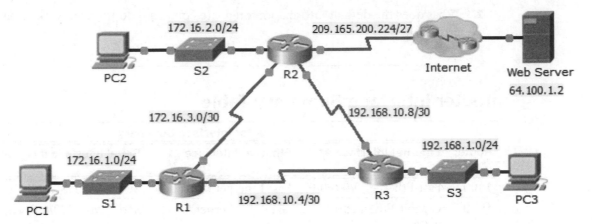

Addressing Table

Device	Interface	IP Address	Subnet Mask	Default Gateway
R1	G0/0	172.16.1.1	255.255.255.0	N/A
	S0/0/0	172.16.3.1	255.255.255.252	N/A
	S0/0/1	192.168.10.5	255.255.255.252	N/A
R2	G0/0	172.16.2.1	255.255.255.0	N/A
	S0/0/0	172.16.3.2	255.255.255.252	N/A
	S0/0/1	192.168.10.9	255.255.255.252	N/A
	S0/1/0	209.165.200.225	255.255.255.224	N/A
R3	G0/0	192.168.1.1	255.255.255.0	N/A
	S0/0/0	192.168.10.6	255.255.255.252	N/A
	S0/0/1	192.168.10.10	255.255.255.252	N/A
PC1	NIC	172.16.1.2	255.255.255.0	172.16.1.1
PC2	NIC	172.16.2.2	255.255.255.0	172.16.2.1
PC3	NIC	192.168.1.2	255.255.255.0	192.168.1.1

Scenario

In this activity, you will troubleshoot OSPF routing issues using **ping** and **show** commands to identify errors in the network configuration. Then, you will document the errors you discover and implement an appropriate solution. Finally, you will verify end-to-end connectivity is restored.

Troubleshooting Process

1. Use testing commands to discover connectivity problems in the network and document the problem in the Documentation Table.

2. Use verification commands to discover the source of the problem and devise an appropriate solution to implement. Document the proposed solution in the Documentation Table.

3. Implement each solution one at a time and verify if the problem is resolved. Indicate the resolution status in the Documentation Table.

4.   If the problem is not resolved, it may be necessary to first remove the implemented solution before returning to Step 2.

5. Once all identified problems are resolved, test for end-to-end connectivity.

Documentation Table

Device	Identified Problem	Proposed Solution	Resolved?

10.2.3.3 Lab–Troubleshooting Basic Single-Area OSPFv2 and OSPFv3

Topology

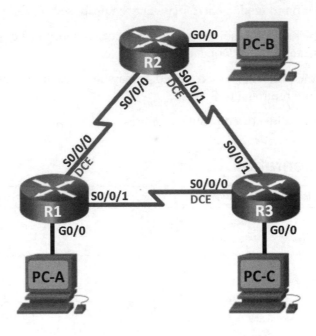

Addressing Table

Device	OSPF Router ID	Interface	IP Address	Default Gateway
R1	1.1.1.1	G0/0	192.168.1.1/24	N/A
			2001:DB8:ACAD:A::1/64	
			FE80::1 link-local	
		S0/0/0	192.168.12.1/30	N/A
			2001:DB8:ACAD:12::1/64	
			FE80::1 link-local	
		S0/0/1	192.18.13.1/30	N/A
			2001:DB8:ACAD:13::1/64	
			FE80::1 link-local	
R2	2.2.2.2	G0/0	192.168.2.1/24	N/A
			2001:DB8:ACAD:B::2/64	
			FE80::2 link-local	

Device	OSPF Router ID	Interface	IP Address	Default Gateway
		S0/0/0	192.168.12.2/30	N/A
			2001:DB8:ACAD:12::2/64	
			FE80::2 link-local	
		S0/0/1	192.168.23.1/30	N/A
			2001:DB8:ACAD:23::2/64	
			FE80::2 link-local	
R3	3.3.3.3	G0/0	192.168.3.1/24	N/A
			2001:DB8:ACAD:C::3/64	
			FE80::3 link-local	
		S0/0/0	192.168.13.2/30	N/A
			2001:DB8:ACAD:13::3/64	
			FE80::3 link-local	
		S0/0/1	192.168.23.2/30	N/A
			2001:DB8:ACAD:23::3/64	
			FE80::3 link-local	
PC-A		NIC	192.168.1.3/24	192.168.1.1
			2001:DB8:ACAD:A::A/64	FE80::1
PC-B		NIC	192.168.2.3/24	192.168.2.1
			2001:DB8:ACAD:B::B/64	FE80::2
PC-C		NIC	192.168.3.3/24	192.168.3.1
			2001:DB8:ACAD:C::C/64	FE80::3

Objectives

Part 1: Build the Network and Load Device Configurations

Part 2: Troubleshoot Layer 3 Connectivity

Part 3: Troubleshoot OSPFv2

Part 4: Troubleshoot OSPFv3

Background/Scenario

Open Shortest Path First (OSPF) is a link-state routing protocol for IP networks. OSPFv2 is defined for IPv4 networks, and OSPFv3 is defined for IPv6 networks. OSPFv2 and OSPFv3 are completely isolated routing protocols, changes in OSPFv2 do not affect OSPFv3 routing, and vice versa.

In this lab, a single-area OSPF network running OSPFv2 and OSPFv3 is experiencing problems. You have been assigned to find the problems with the network and correct them.

Note: The routers used with CCNA hands-on labs are Cisco 1941 Integrated Services Routers (ISRs) with Cisco IOS Release 15.2(4)M3 (universalk9 image). Other routers and Cisco IOS versions can be used. Depending on the model and Cisco IOS version, the commands available and output produced might vary from what is shown in the labs. Refer to the Router Interface Summary Table at the end of this lab for the correct interface identifiers.

Note: Make sure that the routers have been erased and have no startup configurations. If you are unsure, contact your instructor.

Required Resources

- 3 Routers (Cisco 1941 with Cisco IOS Release 15.2(4)M3 universal image or comparable)
- 3 PCs (Windows 7, Vista, or XP with terminal emulation program, such as Tera Term)
- Console cables to configure the Cisco IOS devices via the console ports
- Ethernet and serial cables as shown in the topology

Part 1: Build the Network and Load Device Configurations

In Part 1, you will set up the network topology and configure basic settings on the PC hosts and routers.

Step 1. Cable the network as shown in the topology.

Step 2. Configure PC hosts.

Step 3. Load router configurations.

Load the following configurations into the appropriate router. All routers have the same passwords. The privileged EXEC password is **cisco**. The password for console and vty access is **class**.

Router R1 Configuration:

```
conf t
service password-encryption
no ip domain lookup
hostname R1
enable secret class
line con 0
 logging synchronous
 password cisco
 login
line vty 0
 password cisco
 login
banner motd @Unauthorized Access is Prohibited!@
ipv6 unicast-routing
ipv6 router ospf 1
 router-id 1.1.1.1
 passive-interface g0/0
interface g0/0
 ip address 192.168.1.1 255.255.255.0
 ipv6 address 2001:db8:acad:a::1/64
```

```
 ipv6 address fe80::1 link-local
interface s0/0/0
 clock rate 128000
 ip address 192.168.12.1 255.255.255.0
 ipv6 address 2001:db8:acad:12::1/64
 ipv6 address fe80::1 link-local
 ipv6 ospf 1 area 0
 no shutdown
interface s0/0/1
 ip address 192.168.13.1 255.255.255.0
 ipv6 address 2001:db8:acad:13::1/64
 ipv6 address fe80::1 link-local
 ipv6 ospf 1 area 0
 no shutdown
router ospf 1
 network 192.168.1.0 0.0.0.255 area 0
 network 129.168.12.0 0.0.0.3 area 0
 network 192.168.13.0 0.0.0.3 area 0
 passive-interface g0/0
end
```

Router R2 Configuration:

```
conf t
service password-encryption
no ip domain lookup
hostname R2
enable secret class
line con 0
 logging synchronous
 password cisco
 login
line vty 0
 password cisco
 login
banner motd @Unauthorized Access is Prohibited!@
ipv6 unicast-routing
ipv6 router ospf 1
 router-id 2.2.2.2
interface g0/0
ip address 192.168.2.1 255.255.255.0
 ipv6 address 2001:db8:acad:B::2/64
 ipv6 address fe80::1 link-local
 no shutdown
interface s0/0/0
 ip address 192.168.12.2 255.255.255.252
 ipv6 address 2001:db8:acad:12::2/64
 ipv6 address fe80::2 link-local
 ipv6 ospf 1 area 0
 no shutdown
interface s0/0/1
 clock rate 128000
```

```
      ipv6 address 2001:db8:acad:23::2/64
      ipv6 address fe80::2 link-local
      no shutdown
     router ospf 1
      network 192.168.2.0 0.0.0.255 area 0
      network 192.168.12.0 0.0.0.3 area 0
      network 192.168.23.0 0.0.0.3 area 0
     end
```

Router R3 Configuration:

```
conf t
service password-encryption
no ip domain lookup
enable secret class
hostname R3
line con 0
 logging synchronous
 password cisco
 login
line vty 0
 password cisco
 login
banner motd @Unauthorized Access is Prohibited!@
interface g0/0
 ipv6 address 2001:db8:acad:c::3/64
 ipv6 address fe80::3 link-local
interface s0/0/0
 clock rate 128000
 ip address 192.168.13.1 255.255.255.252
 ipv6 address 2001:db8:acad:13::3/64
 ipv6 address fe80::3 link-local
 no shutdown
interface s0/0/1
 ip address 192.168.23.2 255.255.255.252
 ipv6 address 2001:db8:acad:23::3/64
 ipv6 address fe80::3 link-local
router ospf 1
 network 192.168.3.0 0.0.0.255 area 0
 passive-interface g0/0
end
```

Part 2: Troubleshoot Layer 3 Connectivity

In Part 2, you will verify that Layer 3 connectivity is established on all interfaces. You will need to test both IPv4 and IPv6 connectivity for all device interfaces.

Step 1.   Verify that the interfaces listed in the Addressing Table are active and configured with the correct IP address information.

a. Issue the **show ip interface brief** command on all routers to verify that the interfaces are in an up/up state. Record your findings.

_____

_____

_____

_____

b. Issue the **show run interface** command to verify IP address assignments on all router interfaces. Compare the interface IP addresses against the Addressing Table and verify the subnet mask assignments. For IPv6, verify that the link-local address has been assigned. Record your findings.

_____

_____

_____

_____

c. Resolve all problems that are found. Record the commands used to correct the issues.

_____

_____

_____

_____

_____

_____

_____

_____

_____

_____

_____

_____

_____

_____

_____

_____

    d.   Using the **ping** command, verify that each router has network connectivity with the serial interfaces on the neighbor routers. Verify that the PCs can ping their default gateways. If problems still exist, continue troubleshooting Layer 3 issues.

Part 3: Troubleshoot OSPFv2

In Part 3, you will troubleshoot OSPFv2 problems and make the necessary changes needed to establish OSPFv2 routes and end-to-end IPv4 connectivity.

Note: LAN (G0/0) interfaces should not advertise OSPF routing information, but routes to these networks should be in the routing tables.

Step 1.   Test IPv4 end-to-end connectivity.

From each PC host, ping the other PC hosts in the topology to verify end-to-end connectivity.

    Note: It may be necessary to disable the PC firewall before testing, to ping between PCs.

---

    a.   Ping from PC-A to PC-B. Were the pings successful? _____

    b.   Ping from PC-A to PC-C. Were the pings successful? _____

    c.   Ping from PC-B to PC-C. Were the pings successful? _____

Step 2.   Verify that all interfaces are assigned to OSPFv2 area 0 on R1.

    a.   Issue the **show ip protocols** command to verify that OSPF is running and that all networks are advertised in area 0. Verify that the router ID is set correctly. Record your findings.

          _____

          _____

          _____

    b.   Make the necessary changes to the configuration on R1 based on the output from the **show ip protocols** command. Record the commands used to correct the issues.

          _____

          _____

          _____

    c.   Issue the **clear ip ospf process** command if necessary.

    d.   Re-issue the **show ip protocols** command to verify that your changes had the desired effect.

    e.   Issue the **show ip ospf interface brief** command to verify that all interfaces are listed as OSPF networks assigned to area 0.

    f.   Issue the **show ip ospf interface g0/0** command to verify that G0/0 is a passive interface.

    Note: This information is also in the **show ip protocols** command.

---

g. Resolve any problems discovered on R1. List any additional changes made to R1. If no problems were found on the device, then respond with "no problems were found."

_____

Step 3.   Verify that all interfaces are assigned to OSPFv2 area 0 on R2.

a. Issue the **show ip protocols** command to verify that OSPF is running and that all networks are being advertised in area 0. Verify that the router ID is set correctly. Record your findings.

_____

_____

_____

b. Make the necessary changes to the configuration on R2 based on the output from the **show ip protocols** command. Record the commands used to correct the issues.

_____

_____

_____

c. Issue the **clear ip ospf process** command if necessary.

d. Re-issue the **show ip protocols** command to verify that your changes had the desired effect.

e. Issue the **show ip ospf interface brief** command to verify that all interfaces are listed as OSPF networks assigned to area 0.

f. Issue the **show ip ospf interface g0/0** command to verify that G0/0 is a passive interface.

_____

Note: This information is also available from the **show ip protocols** command.

_____

g. Resolve any problems discovered on R2. List any additional changes made to R2. If no problems were found on the device, then respond with "no problems were found."

_____

Step 4.   Verify that all interfaces are assigned to OSPFv2 area 0 on R3.

a. Issue the **show ip protocols** command to verify that OSPF is running and that all networks are being advertised in area 0. Verify that the router ID is set correctly as well. Record your findings.

_____

_____

_____

b. Make the necessary changes to the configuration on R3 based on the output from the **show ip protocols** command. Record the commands used to correct the issues.

_____

_____

_____

c. Issue the **clear ip ospf process** command if necessary.

d. Re-issue the **show ip protocols** command to verify that your changes had the desired effect.

e. Issue the **show ip ospf interface brief** command to verify that all interfaces are listed as OSPF networks assigned to area 0.

f. Issue the **show ip ospf interface g0/0** command to verify that G0/0 is a passive interface.

Note: This information is also in the **show ip protocols** command.

g. Resolve any problems discovered on R3. List any additional changes made to R3. If no problems were found on the device, then respond with "no problems were found."

_____

Step 5. Verify OSPF neighbor information.

a. Issue the **show ip ospf neighbor** command on all routers to view the OSPF neighbor information.

Step 6. Verify OSPFv2 Routing Information.

a. Issue the **show ip route ospf** command to verify that each router has OSPFv2 routes to all non-adjoining networks.

Are all OSPFv2 routes available? _____

If any OSPFv2 routes are missing, what is missing?

_____

b. If any routing information is missing, resolve these issues.

Step 7. Verify IPv4 end-to-end connectivity.

From each PC, verify that IPv4 end-to-end connectivity exists. PCs should be able to ping the other PC hosts in the topology. If IPv4 end-to-end connectivity does not exist, then continue troubleshooting to resolve any remaining issues.

Note: It may be necessary to disable the PC firewall to ping between PCs.

Part 4: Troubleshoot OSPFv3

In Part 4, you will troubleshoot OSPFv3 problems and make the necessary changes needed to establish OSPFv3 routes and end-to-end IPv6 connectivity.

Note: LAN (G0/0) interfaces should not advertise OSPFv3 routing information, but routes to these networks should be contained in the routing tables.

Step 1.   Test IPv6 end-to-end connectivity.

From each PC host, ping the IPv6 addresses of the other PC hosts in the topology to verify IPv6 end-to-end connectivity.

Note: It may be necessary to disable the PC firewall to ping between PCs.

Step 2.   Verify that IPv6 unicast routing has been enabled on all routers.

    a.   An easy way to verify that IPv6 routing has been enabled on a router is to use the **show run | section ipv6 unicast** command. By adding this pipe (|) section to the **show run** command, the **ipv6 unicast-routing** command displays if IPv6 routing has been enabled.

Note: The **show run** command can also be issued without any pipe, and then a manual search for the **ipv6 unicast-routing** command can be done.

    Issue the command on each router. Record your findings.

    _____

    _____

    _____

    b.   If IPv6 unicast routing is not enabled on one or more routers, enable it now. Record the commands used to correct the issues.

    _____

    _____

Step 3.   Verify that all interfaces are assigned to OSPFv3 area 0 on R1.

    a.   Issue the **show ipv6 protocols** command and verify that the router ID is correct. Also verify that the expected interfaces are displayed under area 0.

Note: If no output is generated from this command, then the OSPFv3 process has not been configured.

    Record your findings.

    _____

    _____

    _____

    b.   Make the necessary configuration changes to R1. Record the commands used to correct the issues.

    _____

    _____

    _____

    c.   Issue the **clear ipv6 ospf process** command if necessary.

    d.   Re-issue the **show ipv6 protocols** command to verify that your changes had the desired effect.

    e.   Issue the **show ipv6 ospf interface brief** command to verify that all interfaces are listed as OSPF networks assigned to area 0.

f. Issue the **show ipv6 ospf interface g0/0** command to verify that this interface is set not to advertise OSPFv3 routes.

g. Resolve any problems discovered on R1. List any additional changes made to R1. If no problems were found on the device, then respond with "no problems were found."

_____

Step 4. Verify that all interfaces are assigned to OSPFv3 area 0 on R2.

a. Issue the **show ipv6 protocols** command and verify the router ID is correct. Also verify that the expected interfaces display under area 0.

Note: If no output is generated from this command, then the OSPFv3 process has not been configured.

Record your findings.

_____

_____

_____

b. Make the necessary configuration changes to R2. Record the commands used to correct the issues.

_____

_____

_____

c. Issue the **clear ipv6 ospf process** command if necessary.

d. Re-issue the **show ipv6 protocols** command to verify that your changes had the desired effect.

e. Issue the **show ipv6 ospf interface brief** command to verify that all interfaces are listed as OSPF networks assigned to area 0.

f. Issue the **show ipv6 ospf interface g0/0** command to verify that this interface is not set to advertise OSPFv3 routes.

g. List any additional changes made to R2. If no problems were found on the device, then respond with "no problems were found."

_____

Step 5. Verify that all interfaces are assigned to OSPFv3 area 0 on R3.

a. Issue the **show ipv6 protocols** command and verify that the router ID is correct. Also verify that the expected interfaces display under area 0.

Note: If no output is generated from this command, then the OSPFv3 process has not been configured.

Record your findings.

_____

_____

_____

b. Make the necessary configuration changes to R3. Record the commands used to correct the issues.

_____

_____

_____

_____

_____

_____

_____

_____

_____

c. Issue the **clear ipv6 ospf process** command if necessary.

d. Re-issue the **show ipv6 protocols** command to verify that your changes had the desired effect.

e. Issue the **show ipv6 ospf interface brief** command to verify that all interfaces are listed as OSPF networks assigned to area 0.

f. Issue the **show ipv6 ospf interface g0/0** command to verify that this interface is set not to advertise OSPFv3 routes.

g. Resolve any problems discovered on R3. List any additional changes made to R3. If no problems were found on the device, then respond with "no problems were found."

_____

Step 6. Verify that all routers have correct neighbor adjacency information.

a. Issue the **show ipv6 ospf neighbor** command to verify that adjacencies have formed between neighboring routers.

b. Resolve any OSPFv3 adjacency issues that still exist.

Step 7. Verify OSPFv3 routing information.

a. Issue the **show ipv6 route ospf** command, and verify that OSPFv3 routes exist to all non-adjoining networks.

Are all OSPFv3 routes available? _____

If any OSPFv3 routes are missing, what is missing?

_____

b. Resolve any routing issues that still exist.

Step 8. Verify IPv6 end-to-end connectivity.

From each PC, verify that IPv6 end-to-end connectivity exists. PCs should be able to ping each interface on the network. If IPv6 end-to-end connectivity does not exist, then continue troubleshooting to resolve remaining issues.

Note: It may be necessary to disable the PC firewall to ping between PCs.

Reflection

Why would you troubleshoot OSPFv2 and OSPFv3 separately?

_____

_____

Router Interface Summary Table

Router Interface Summary				
Router Model	Ethernet Interface #1	Ethernet Interface #2	Serial Interface #1	Serial Interface #2
1800	Fast Ethernet 0/0 (F0/0)	Fast Ethernet 0/1 (F0/1)	Serial 0/0/0 (S0/0/0)	Serial 0/0/1 (S0/0/1)
1900	Gigabit Ethernet 0/0 (G0/0)	Gigabit Ethernet 0/1 (G0/1)	Serial 0/0/0 (S0/0/0)	Serial 0/0/1 (S0/0/1)
2801	Fast Ethernet 0/0 (F0/0)	Fast Ethernet 0/1 (F0/1)	Serial 0/1/0 (S0/1/0)	Serial 0/1/1 (S0/1/1)
2811	Fast Ethernet 0/0 (F0/0)	Fast Ethernet 0/1 (F0/1)	Serial 0/0/0 (S0/0/0)	Serial 0/0/1 (S0/0/1)
2900	Gigabit Ethernet 0/0 (G0/0)	Gigabit Ethernet 0/1 (G0/1)	Serial 0/0/0 (S0/0/0)	Serial 0/0/1 (S0/0/1)

Note: To find out how the router is configured, look at the interfaces to identify the type of router and how many interfaces the router has. There is no way to effectively list all the combinations of configurations for each router class. This table includes identifiers for the possible combinations of Ethernet and Serial interfaces in the device. The table does not include any other type of interface, even though a specific router may contain one. An example of this might be an ISDN BRI interface. The string in parentheses is the legal abbreviation that can be used in Cisco IOS commands to represent the interface.

10.2.3.4 Lab–Troubleshooting Advanced Single-Area OSPFv2

Topology

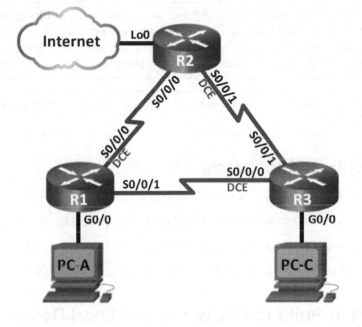

Addressing Table

Devioc	Interface	IP Address	Subnet Mask	Default Gateway
R1	G0/0	192.168.1.1	255.255.255.0	N/A
	S0/0/0 (DCE)	192.168.12.1	255.255.255.252	N/A
	S0/0/1	192.168.13.1	255.255.255.252	N/A
R2	Lo0	209.165.200.225	255.255.255.252	N/A
	S0/0/0	192.168.12.2	255.255.255.252	N/A
	S0/0/1 (DCE)	192.168.23.1	255.255.255.252	N/A
R3	G0/0	192.168.3.1	255.255.255.0	N/A
	S0/0/0 (DCE)	192.168.13.2	255.255.255.252	N/A
	S0/0/1	192.168.23.2	255.255.255.252	N/A
PC-A	NIC	192.168.1.3	255.255.255.0	192.168.1.1
PC-C	NIC	192.168.3.3	255.255.255.0	192.168.3.1

Objectives

Part 1: Build the Network and Load Device Configurations

Part 2: Troubleshoot OSPF

Background/Scenario

OSPF is a popular routing protocol used by businesses worldwide. A network administrator should be able to isolate OSPF issues and resolve those issues in a timely manner.

In this lab, you will troubleshoot a single-area OSPFv2 network and resolve all issues that exist.

Note: The routers used with CCNA hands-on labs are Cisco 1941 Integrated Services Routers (ISRs) with Cisco IOS Release 15.2(4)M3 (universalk9 image). Other routers and Cisco IOS versions can be used. Depending on the model and Cisco IOS version, the commands available and output produced might vary from what is shown in the labs. Refer to the Router Interface Summary Table at the end of this lab for the correct interface identifiers.

Note: Make sure that the routers have been erased and have no startup configurations. If you are unsure, contact your instructor.

Required Resources

- 3 Routers (Cisco 1941 with Cisco IOS Release 15.2(4)M3 universal image or comparable)
- 3 PCs (Windows with terminal emulation program, such as Tera Term)
- Console cables to configure the Cisco IOS devices via the console ports
- Ethernet and serial cables, as shown in the topology

Part 1: Build the Network and Load Device Configurations

In Part 1, you will set up the network topology and configure basic settings on the PC hosts and routers.

Step 1. Cable the network as shown in the topology.

Step 2. Configure PC hosts.

Step 3. Load router configurations.

Load the following configurations into the appropriate router. All routers have the same passwords. The privileged EXEC password is **class**. The password for console and vty lines is **cisco**.

Router R1 Configuration:

```
conf t
hostname R1
enable secret class
no ip domain lookup
interface GigabitEthernet0/0
 ip address 192.168.1.1 255.255.255.0
 duplex auto
 speed auto
 no shut
interface Serial0/0/0
 bandwidth 128
 ip address 192.168.12.1 255.255.255.252
 clock rate 128000
```

```
 no shut
interface Serial0/0/1
 bandwidth 64
ip address 192.168.13.1 255.255.255.252
 no shut
router ospf 1
 auto-cost reference-bandwidth 1000
 passive-interface g0/0
 network 192.168.1.0 0.0.0.255 area 0
 network 192.168.12.0 0.0.0.3 area 0
 network 192.168.13.0 0.0.0.3 area 0
banner motd ^
  Unauthorized Access is Prohibited!
^

line con 0
 password cisco
 logging synchronous
 login
line vty 0 4
 password cisco
 login
 transport input all
end
```

Router R2 Configuration:

```
conf t
hostname R2
enable secret class
no ip domain lookup
interface Loopback0
 ip address 209.165.200.225 255.255.255.252
interface Serial0/0/0
 bandwidth 182
ip address 192.168.12.2 255.255.255.252
 no shut
interface Serial0/0/1
 bandwidth 128
 ip address 192.168.23.1 255.255.255.252
 clock rate 128000
 no shut
router ospf 1
 router-id 2.2.2.2
 auto-cost reference-bandwidth 1000
passive-interface g0/0
 network 192.168.12.0 0.0.0.3 area 0
 network 192.168.23.0 0.0.0.3 area 0
ip route 0.0.0.0 0.0.0.0 Loopback0
banner motd ^
  Unauthorized Access is Prohibited!
^

line con 0
```

```
 password cisco
 logging synchronous
 login
line vty 0 4
 password cisco
 login
 transport input all
end
```

Router R3 Configuration:

```
conf t
hostname R3
enable secret class
no ip domain lookup
interface GigabitEthernet0/0
 ip address 192.168.3.1 255.255.255.0
 duplex auto
 speed auto
 no shut
interface Serial0/0/0
 bandwidth 128
 ip address 192.168.13.2 255.255.255.252
 clock rate 128000
 no shut
interface Serial0/0/1
 bandwidth 128
 ip address 192.168.23.2 255.255.255.252
no shut
router ospf 1
 router-id 3.3.3.3
 area 0 authentication message-digest
 passive-interface g0/0
 network 192.168.3.0 0.0.0.255 area 0
 network 192.168.13.0 0.0.0.3 area 0
 network 192.168.23.0 0.0.0.3 area 0
banner motd ^
  Unauthorized Access is Prohibited!
^
line con 0
 password cisco
 logging synchronous
 login
line vty 0 4
 password cisco
 login
 transport input all
end
```

Step 4.   Test end-to-end connectivity.

All interfaces should be up and the PCs should be able to ping the default gateway.

Part 2: Troubleshoot OSPF

In Part 2, verify that all routers have established neighbor adjacencies, and that all network routes are available.

Additional OSPF Requirements:

- Each router should have the following router ID assignments:

    - R1 Router ID: **1.1.1.1**

    - R2 Router ID: **2.2.2.2**

    - R3 Router ID: **3.3.3.3**

- All serial interface clocking rates should be set at 128 Kb/s and a matching bandwidth setting should be available to allow OSPF cost metrics to be calculated correctly.

- The 1941 routers have Gigabit interfaces, so the default OSPF reference bandwidth should be adjusted to allow cost metrics to reflect appropriate costs for all interfaces.

- OSPF should propagate a default route to the Internet. This is simulated by using loopback interface 0 on R2.

List the commands used during your OSPF troubleshooting process:

_____

_____

_____

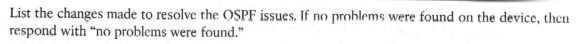

List the changes made to resolve the OSPF issues. If no problems were found on the device, then respond with "no problems were found."

R1 Router:

_____

_____

_____

_____

R2 Router:

_____

_____

_____

_____

R3 Router:

_____

_____

_____

_____

Reflection

How would you change the network in this lab so that all LAN traffic was routed through R2?

_____

_____

_____

_____

Router Interface Summary Table

Router Interface Summary				
Router Model	Ethernet Interface #1	Ethernet Interface #2	Serial Interface #1	Serial Interface #2
1800	Fast Ethernet 0/0 (F0/0)	Fast Ethernet 0/1 (F0/1)	Serial 0/0/0 (S0/0/0)	Serial 0/0/1 (S0/0/1)
1900	Gigabit Ethernet 0/0 (G0/0)	Gigabit Ethernet 0/1 (G0/1)	Serial 0/0/0 (S0/0/0)	Serial 0/0/1 (S0/0/1)
2801	Fast Ethernet 0/0 (F0/0)	Fast Ethernet 0/1 (F0/1)	Serial 0/1/0 (S0/1/0)	Serial 0/1/1 (S0/1/1)
2811	Fast Ethernet 0/0 (F0/0)	Fast Ethernet 0/1 (F0/1)	Serial 0/0/0 (S0/0/0)	Serial 0/0/1 (S0/0/1)
2900	Gigabit Ethernet 0/0 (G0/0)	Gigabit Ethernet 0/1 (G0/1)	Serial 0/0/0 (S0/0/0)	Serial 0/0/1 (S0/0/1)

Note: To find out how the router is configured, look at the interfaces to identify the type of router and how many interfaces the router has. There is no way to effectively list all the combinations of configurations for each router class. This table includes identifiers for the possible combinations of Ethernet and Serial interfaces in the device. The table does not include any other type of interface, even though a specific router may contain one. An example of this might be an ISDN BRI interface. The string in parentheses is the legal abbreviation that can be used in Cisco IOS commands to represent the interface.

10.2.4.3 Packet Tracer–Troubleshooting Multiarea OSPFv2

Packet Tracer
☐ Activity

Topology

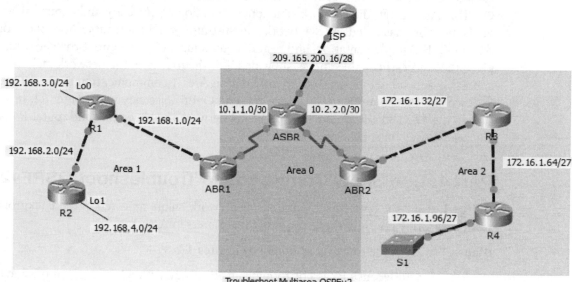

Troubleshoot Multiarea OSPFv2

Addressing Table

Device	Interface	IP Address	Subnet Mask	Default Gateway
ISP	GigabitEthernet0/0	209.165.200.17	255.255.255.240	N/A
ASBR	GigabitEthernet0/0	209.165.200.18	255.255.255.240	N/A
	Serial0/0/0	10.1.1.2	255.255.255.252	N/A
	Serial0/0/1	10.2.2.2	255.255.255.252	N/A
ABR1	Serial0/0/0	10.1.1.1	255.255.255.252	N/A
	GigabitEthernet0/1	192.168.1.1	255.255.255.0	N/A
ABR2	Serial0/0/1	10.2.2.1	255.255.255.252	N/A
	GigabitEthernet0/1	172.16.1.33	255.255.255.224	N/A
R1	GigabitEthernet0/1	192.168.1.2	255.255.255.0	N/A
	GigabitEthernet0/0	192.168.2.1	255.255.255.0	N/A
	Loopback0	192.168.3.1	255.255.255.0	N/A
R2	GigabitEthernet0/0	192.168.2.2	255.255.255.0	N/A
	Loopback1	192.168.4.1	255.255.255.0	N/A
R3	GigabitEthernet0/1	172.16.1.62	255.255.255.224	N/A
	GigabitEthernet0/0	172.16.1.65	255.255.255.224	N/A
R4	GigabitEthernet0/0	172.16.1.94	255.255.255.224	N/A
	GigabitEthernet0/1	172.16.1.97	255.255.255.224	N/A

Objectives

Troubleshoot a multiarea OSPFv2 network.

Background/Scenario

A large organization has recently decided to change the network from single-area OSPFv2 to multiarea OSPFv2. As a result, the network is no longer functioning correctly and communication through much of the network has failed. As a network administrator you must troubleshoot the problem, fix the multiarea OSPFv2 implementation, and restore communication throughout the network. To do this, you are given the Addressing Table above, showing all of the routers in the network including their interface IP addresses and subnet masks. You are told that in Area 1 communication to the 192.168.4.0/24 network is down and that router R2 is unable to form an OSPF adjacency with router R1. In Area 2, communication to the 172.16.1.64/27 and 172.16.1.96/24 networks has been lost and router R4 is unable to form an adjacency. Area 0 is behaving as expected.

Part 1: Use Show Commands to Troubleshoot OSPFv2 Area 1

In Part 1, using the particular symptoms of network failure reported in the Background/Scenario, begin troubleshooting configuration settings at the routers in Area 1.

Step 1. Check the router configurations in Area 1.

a. Because R2 is not forming an adjacency with R1, console into R2 and check its interface IP address configuration and its multiarea OSPFv2 configuration. Use the **show running-config** command to view the configuration.

Is R2's OSPF router process configuration present and correct? Are the network statements, including subnets, wildcard bits, and area numbers correct?

---

b. On R2, issue a **show ip ospf interface** command to check the hello timer interval configuration and to verify that hello messages are being sent.

Is R2's hello timer interval configuration set to the default setting? Is the dead time interval 4 x the hello time interval? Are hellos being sent?

---

c. If R2's configurations and settings are correct then the problem of not forming an adjacency must be with R1. Console into R1 and check the network interface and OSPFv2 configurations in the running-configuration.

Are the R1 network interfaces configured correctly? Is there a problem in the R1 OSPFv2 routing process configuration that would cause an adjacency failure?

---

d. Correct the configuration error on R1.

```
R1# configure terminal
R1(config)# router ospf 1
R1(config-router)# no passive-interface G0/0
```

e. If the problem has been corrected, R1 should receive a syslog message to the console showing an OSPF adjacency change from loading to full.

Did a syslog message appear in the R1 console reporting an OSPF adjacency change?

Step 2.   Check the router configurations in Area 2.

   a.   Because it was reported that the network has lost contact with the Area 2 subnets 172.16.1.64/24 and 172.16.1.96/24, verify this at the Area 2 Border Router (ABR2) using the **show ip route** command.

Does the ABR2 routing table show the presence of the 172.16.1.64/24 and 172.16.1.96/24 networks?

   b.   Check to see if ABR2 has established an OSPFv2 neighbor adjacency with R3.

Does ABR2 show two OSPF neighbors? Which neighbor ID signifies R3 and how do you know this?

   c.   Because ABR2 has formed a neighbor relationship with R3, the problem may be with the OSPFv2 configurations on either R3 or R4. Console into R3 and check the OSPFv2 configurations in the running-configuration.

Are there any problems with the R3 OSPFv2 routing process configurations?

   d.   To correct the problem, replace the OSPF routing process network statement that places the 172.16.1.64/24 subnet in Area 0 and change it to Area 2.

```
R3# configure terminal
R3(config)# router ospf 1
R3(config-router)# no network 172.16.1.64 0.0.0.31 area 0
R3(config-router)# network 172.16.1.64 0.0.0.31 area 2
```

Did a syslog message appear in the R3 console reporting an OSPF adjacency change? What does this signify?

   e.   Verify that the R3 routing table has routes to all of the networks in all of the OSPF areas.

Are any routes missing? If so, which ones?

   f.   It appears that R3 is missing the OSPFv2 interarea 192.168.0.0/21 summary route. To solve this problem, completely remove the OSPFv2 routing process from router R3 and then re-add it.

```
R3# configure terminal
R3(config)# no router ospf 1
R3(config)# router ospf 1
R3(config-router)# router-id 3.3.3.3
R3(config-router)# network 172.16.1.32 0.0.0.31 area 2
R3(config-router)# network 172.16.1.64 0.0.0.31 area 2
```

g. Now verify that the R3 routing table has learned the OSPF interarea summary route to the 192.168.0.0/21 subnet.

Is the OSPF interarea route to the 192.168.0.0/21 subnet in the routing table?

_____

10.2.4.4 Packet Tracer–Troubleshooting Multiarea OSPFv3

Packet Tracer
☐ Activity

Topology

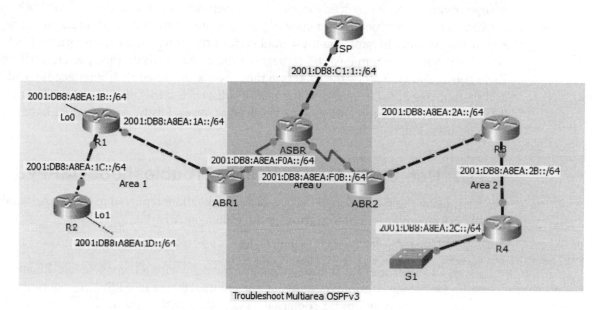

Troubleshoot Multiarea OSPFv3

Addressing Table

Device	Interface	IPv6 Global Unicast Address	IPv6 Link-local Address	Default Gateway
ISP	GigabitEthernet0/0	2001:DB8:C1:1::1/64	FE80::C1	N/A
ASBR	GigabitEthernet0/0	2001:DB8:C1:1::2/64	FE80::7	N/A
	Serial0/0/0	2001:DB8:A8EA:F0A::1	FE80::7	N/A
	Serial0/0/1	2001:DB8:A8EA:F0B::1	FE80::7	N/A
ABR1	Serial0/0/0	2001:DB8:A8EA:F0A::2	FE80::5	N/A
	GigabitEthernet0/1	2001:DB8:A8EA:1A::1	FE80::5	N/A
ABR2	Serial0/0/1	2001:DB8:A8EA:F0B::2	FE80::6	N/A
	GigabitEthernet0/1	2001:DB8:A8EA:2A::1	FE80::6	N/A
R1	GigabitEthernet0/1	2001:DB8:A8EA:1A::2	FE80::1	N/A
	GigabitEthernet0/0	2001:DB8:A8EA:1C::1	FE80::1	N/A
	Loopback0	2001:DB8:A8EA:1B::1	FE80::1	N/A
R2	GigabitEthernet0/0	2001:DB8:A8EA:1C::2	FE80::2	N/A
	Loopback1	2001:DB8:A8EA:1D::1	FE80::2	N/A
R3	GigabitEthernet0/1	2001:DB8:A8EA:2A::2	FE80::3	N/A
	GigabitEthernet0/0	2001:DB8:A8EA:2B::1	FE80::3	N/A
R4	GigabitEthernet0/0	2001:DB8:A8EA:2B::2	FE80::4	N/A
	GigabitEthernet0/1	2001:DB8:A8EA:2C::1	FE80::4	N/A

Objectives

Troubleshoot a multiarea OSPFv3 network.

Background/Scenario

A large organization has recently decided to implement a multiarea OSPFv3 network. As a result, the network is no longer functioning correctly and communication through much of the network has failed. As a network administrator you must troubleshoot the problem, fix the multiarea OSPFv3 implementation, and restore communication throughout the network. To do this, you are given the Addressing Table above, showing all of the routers in the network including their interface IPv6 addresses. You are told that in Area 1, R2 is unable to form OSPF adjacencies. In Area 0 and Area 2, three routers ABR2, R3, and R4 have not been able to form OSPF adjacencies. Lastly, ABR1 and R1 have not received default route information.

Part 1: Use Show Commands to Troubleshoot OSPFv3 Area 1

In Part 1, using the particular symptoms of network failure reported in the Background/Scenario begin troubleshooting configuration settings at the routers in Area 1.

Step 1.   Check the R2 configuration in Area 1.

   a.   Because R2 is not forming an adjacency with R1, console into R2 and check its interface IP address configuration and its multiarea OSPFv2 configuration. Use the **show running-config** command to view the configuration.

Is R2's OSPFv3 routing process configuration present and correct? Has OSPFv3 been activated on the g0/0 and Loopback 1 interfaces and have they been set to the correct area?

---

   b.   If R2's OSPFv3 configurations are correct, it is possible that OSPFv3 has not been configured on the R1 G0/0 interface. Console into R1 and issue a **show running-config** command to check the G0/0 interface for the **ipv6 ospf 10 area 1** configuration.

Is R1's OSPFv3 routing process configuration present and correct? Has OSPFv3 been activated on the g0/0 interface and set to Area1?

---

   c.   It is possible that the hello-interval and dead-interval timers have been altered from their default values of 10 seconds and 40 seconds respectively. A timer mismatch can cause the routers to not form adjacencies. If the dead-interval timer is not four times the value of the hello-interval timer, that could also cause the routers to not form adjacencies. Check the hello-interval and dead-interval timer values on R1 and R2.

```
R1# show ipv6 ospf interface g0/0
R2# show ipv6 ospf interface g0/0
```

Is there a mismatch or incorrect configuration on either the R1 or R2 hello-interval or dead-interval timers?

---

   d. Correct the hello-interval and dead-interval timer configuration errors on R2.

```
R2# configure terminal
R2(config)# interface g0/0
R2(config-router)# ipv6 ospf hello-interval 10
R2(config-router)# ipv6 ospf dead-interval 40
```

If the problem has been corrected a syslog message should appear in the R2 console showing an OSPF adjacency change from LOADING to FULL. State if the problem has been corrected, and if so, what is the Nbr address?

Step 2. Check the router configurations in Area 2 starting with ABR2.

   a. Because it was reported that routers ABR2, R3, and R4 were all unable to form OSPFv3 adjacencies, console into the ABR2 border router to see why it is unable to form an adjacency with ASBR router.

     Is ABR2's OSPFv3 routing process configuration present and correct? Has OSPFv3 been activated on the s0/0/1 and g0/1 interfaces and have they been set to Area2?

   b. OSPFv3 requires the presence of a 32bit dotted decimal router-id. Because ABR2 has no IPv4 addresses assigned to any of its interfaces, a router-id needs to be manually configured. Configure ABR2 with a 6.6.6.6 router-id.

```
ABR2# configure terminal
ABR2(config)# ipv6 router ospf 10
ABR2(config router)# router-id 6.6.6.6
```

If the problem has been corrected, syslog messages should appear in the console showing OSPF adjacency changes from LOADING to FULL. State if this is the case, and what neighbor Nbr addresses appear?

   c. On ABR2, a syslog message showing an adjacency change from LOADING to FULL with Nbr 3.3.3.3 means that R3 is now participating in the OSPFv3 Area 2 process. Check that R4 has provided route information for its connected networks to the OSPFv3 topology database.

```
ABR2# show ipv6 ospf database
```

Looking at the output of the **show ipv6 ospf database** command, what information would signal the presence of R4?

Step 3. Check ASBR for OSPFv3 default route distribution.

   a. Because ASBR is the edge router, it should have a static IPv6 default route configured. If so, it can distribute that route using OSPFv3 and a **default-information originate** command.

     Is there an IPv6 default route configured on ASBR? Does the OSPFv3 routing process configuration have a **default-information originate** line present?

b. On ASBR, add a **default-information originate** command to the OSPFv3 routing process.

```
ASBR# configure terminal
ASBR2(config)# ipv6 router ospf 10
ABR2(config-router)# default-information originate
```

c. Check the IPv6 routing tables of ABR1 and ABR2 to see if the default route was discovered through OSPFv3.

Looking at the output of the **show ipv6 route**, did the router learn of the default route from OSPFv3? If so, list the line or lines that signify this.

_____

10.2.4.5 Lab–Troubleshooting Multiarea OSPFv2 and OSPFv3

Topology

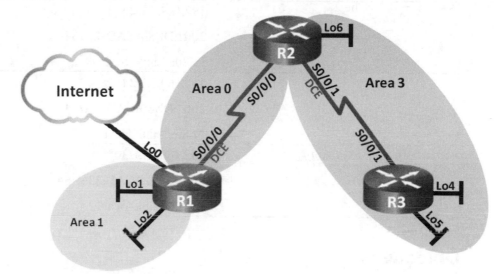

Addressing Table

Device	Interface	IP Address
R1	Lo0	209.165.200.225/30
	Lo1	192.168.1.1/24
		2001:DB8:ACAD:1::1/64
		FE80::1 link-local
	Lo2	192.168.2.1/24
		2001:DB8:ACAD:2::1/64
		FE80::1 link-local
	S0/0/0 (DCE)	192.168.12.1/30
		2001:DB8:ACAD:12::1/64
		FE80::1 link-local
R2	S0/0/0	192.168.12.2/30
		2001:DB8:ACAD:12::2/64
		FE80::2 link-local
	S0/0/1 (DCE)	192.168.23.2/30
		2001:DB8:ACAD:23::2/64
		FE80::2 link-local

Device	Interface	IP Address
	Lo6	192.168.6.1/24
		2001:DB8:ACAD:6::1/64
		FE80::2 link-local
R3	Lo4	192.168.4.1/24
		2001:DB8:ACAD:4::1/64
		FE80::3 link-local
	Lo5	192.168.5.1/24
		2001:DB8:ACAD:5::1/64
		FE80::3 link-local
	S0/0/1	192.168.23.1/30
		2001:DB8:ACAD:23::1/64
		FE80::3 link-local

Objectives

Part 1: Build the Network and Load Device Configurations

Part 2: Troubleshoot Layer 3 Connectivity

Part 3: Troubleshoot OSPFv2

Part 4: Troubleshoot OSPFv3

Background/Scenario

Open Shortest Path First (OSPF) is an open-standard link-state routing protocol for IP networks. OSPFv2 is defined for IPv4 networks, while OSPFv3 is defined for IPv6 networks. OSPFv2 and OSPFv3 are completely isolated routing protocols, meaning changes in OSPFv2 do not affect OSPFv3 routing, and vice versa.

In this lab, a multiarea OSPF network running OSPFv2 and OSPFv3 is experiencing problems. You have been assigned to find the problems with the network and correct them.

Note: The routers used with CCNA hands-on labs are Cisco 1941 Integrated Services Routers (ISRs) with Cisco IOS Release 15.2(4)M3 (universalk9 image). Other routers and Cisco IOS versions can be used. Depending on the model and Cisco IOS version, the commands available and output produced might vary from what is shown in the labs. Refer to the Router Interface Summary Table at the end of this lab for the correct interface identifiers.

Note: Make sure that the routers have been erased and have no startup configurations. If you are unsure, contact your instructor.

Required Resources

- 3 Routers (Cisco 1941 with Cisco IOS Release 15.2(4)M3 universal image or comparable)
- Console cables to configure the Cisco IOS devices via the console ports
- Serial cables as shown in the topology

Part 1: Build the Network and Load Device Configurations

Step 1. Cable the network as shown in the topology.

Step 2. Load router configuration files.

Load the following configurations into the appropriate router. All routers have the same passwords. The enable password is **class**, and the line password is **cisco**.

Router R1 Configuration:

```
enable
conf t
hostname R1
enable secret class
ipv6 unicast-routing
no ip domain lookup
interface Loopback0
 ip address 209.165.200.225 255.255.255.252
interface Loopback1
 ip address 192.168.1.1 255.255.255.0
 ipv6 address 2001:DB80:ACAD:1::1/64
 ipv6 ospf network point-to-point
interface Loopback2
 ip address 192.168.2.1 255.255.255.0
 ipv6 address 2001:DB8:ACAD:2::1/64
 ipv6 ospf 1 area 1
 ipv6 ospf network point-to-point
interface Serial0/0/0
 ip address 192.168.21.1 255.255.255.252
 ipv6 address FE80::1 link-local
 ipv6 address 2001:DB8:ACAD:12::1/64
 ipv6 ospf 1 area 0
 clock rate 128000
 shutdown
router ospf 1
 router-id 1.1.1.1
 passive-interface Loopback1
 passive-interface Loopback2
 network 192.168.2.0 0.0.0.255 area 1
 network 192.168.12.0 0.0.0.3 area 0
 default-information originate
ipv6 router ospf 1
 area 1 range 2001:DB8:ACAD::/61
```

```
ip route 0.0.0.0 0.0.0.0 Loopback0
banner motd @
  Unauthorized Access is Prohibited! @
line con 0
 password cisco
 logging synchronous
 login
line vty 0 4
 password cisco
 logging synchronous
 login
 transport input all
end
```

Router R2 Configuration:

```
enable
conf t
hostname R2
ipv6 unicast-routing
no ip domain lookup
enable secret class
interface Loopback6
 ip address 192.168.6.1 255.255.255.0
 ipv6 address 2001:DB8:CAD:6::1/64
interface Serial0/0/0
 ip address 192.168.12.2 255.255.255.252
 ipv6 address FE80::2 link-local
 ipv6 address 2001:DB8:ACAD:12::2/64
 ipv6 ospf 1 area 0
 no shutdown
interface Serial0/0/1
 ip address 192.168.23.2 255.255.255.252
 ipv6 address FE80::2 link-local
 ipv6 address 2001:DB8:ACAD:23::2/64
 ipv6 ospf 1 area 3
 clock rate 128000
 no shutdown
router ospf 1
 router-id 2.2.2.2
 passive-interface Loopback6
 network 192.168.6.0 0.0.0.255 area 3
 network 192.168.12.0 0.0.0.3 area 0
 network 192.168.23.0 0.0.0.3 area 3
ipv6 router ospf 1
 router-id 2.2.2.2
banner motd @
  Unauthorized Access is Prohibited! @
line con 0
 password cisco
 logging synchronous
 login
```

```
line vty 0 4
 password cisco
 logging synchronous
 login
 transport input all
end
```

Router R3 Configuration:

```
enable
conf t
hostname R3
no ip domain lookup
ipv6 unicast-routing
enable secret class
interface Loopback4
 ip address 192.168.4.1 255.255.255.0
 ipv6 address 2001:DB8:ACAD:4::1/64
 ipv6 ospf 1 area 3
interface Loopback5
 ip address 192.168.5.1 255.255.255.0
 ipv6 address 2001:DB8:ACAD:5::1/64
 ipv6 ospf 1 area 3
interface Serial0/0/1
 ip address 192.168.23.1 255.255.255.252
 ipv6 address FE80::3 link-local
 ipv6 address 2001:DB8:ACAD:23::1/64
 ipv6 ospf 1 area 3
 no shutdown
router ospf 1
 router-id 3.3.3.3
 passive-interface Loopback4
 passive-interface Loopback5
 network 192.168.4.0 0.0.0.255 area 3
 network 192.168.5.0 0.0.0.255 area 3
ipv6 router ospf 1
 router-id 3.3.3.3
banner motd @
  Unauthorized Access is Prohibited! @
line con 0
 password cisco
 logging synchronous
 login
line vty 0 4
 password cisco
 logging synchronous
 login
 transport input all
end
```

Step 3.   Save your configuration.

Part 2: Troubleshoot Layer 3 Connectivity

In Part 2, you will verify that Layer 3 connectivity is established on all interfaces. You will need to test both IPv4 and IPv6 connectivity for all device interfaces.

Step 1. Verify the interfaces listed in the Addressing Table are active and configured with correct IP address information.

    a. Issue the **show ip interface brief** command on all three routers to verify that the interfaces are in an up/up state.

    b. Issue the **show run | section interface** command to view all the commands related to interfaces.

    c. Resolve all problems found. Record the commands used to correct the configuration.

    _____

    _____

    _____

    _____

    _____

    _____

    d. Using the **ping** command, verify that IPv4 and IPv6 connectivity has been established on all directly connected router interfaces. If problems still exist, continue troubleshooting Layer 3 issues.

Part 3: Troubleshoot OSPFv2

Note: LAN (loopback) interfaces should not advertise OSPF routing information, but routes to these networks should be contained in the routing tables.

Step 1. Test IPv4 end-to-end connectivity.

    From each router, ping all interfaces on the other routers. Record your results below as IPv4 OSPFv2 connectivity problems do exist.

    _____

    _____

    _____

Step 2. Verify that all interfaces are assigned to the proper OSPFv2 areas on R1.

    a. Issue the **show ip protocols** command to verify that OSPF is running and that all networks are being advertised in the correct areas. Verify that the router ID is set correctly, as well for OSPF.

b. If required, make the necessary changes needed to the configuration on R1 based on the output from the **show ip protocols** command. Record the commands used to correct the configuration.

_____

_____

_____

c. If required, re-issue the **show ip protocols** command to verify that your changes had the desired effect.

d. Issue the **show ip ospf interface brief** command to verify that the serial interface and loopback interfaces 1 and 2 are listed as OSPF networks assigned to their respective areas.

e. Resolve any problems discovered on R1 for OSPFv2.

Step 3.   Verify that all interfaces are assigned to the proper OSPFv2 areas on R2.

a. Issue the **show ip protocols** command to verify that OSPF is running and that all networks are being advertised in their proper respective areas. Verify that the router ID is also set correctly.

b. If required, make any necessary changes to the configuration on R2 based on the output from the **show ip protocols** command. Record the commands used to correct the configuration.

_____

_____

_____

c. If required, re-issue the **show ip protocols** command to verify that your changes had the desired effect.

d. Issue the **show ip ospf interface brief** command to verify that all interfaces are listed as OSPF networks assigned to their proper respective areas.

e. Resolve any problems discovered on R2 for OSPFv2.

Step 4.   Verify that all interfaces are assigned to the proper OSPFv2 areas on R3.

a. Issue the **show ip protocols** command to verify that OSPF is running and that all networks are being advertised in their respective areas. Verify that the router ID is also set correctly.

b. If required, make the necessary changes to the configuration on R3 based on the output from the **show ip protocols** command. Record the commands used to correct the configuration.

_____

_____

_____

c. If required, re-issue the **show ip protocols** command to verify that your changes had the desired effect.

d. Issue the **show ip ospf interface brief** command to verify that all interfaces are listed as OSPF networks assigned to their proper areas.

e. Resolve any problems discovered on R3 for OSPFv2.

Step 5. Verify OSPFv2 neighbor information.

Issue the **show ip ospf neighbor** command to verify that each router has all OSPFv2 neighbors listed.

Step 6. Verify OSPFv2 routing information.

a. Issue the **show ip route ospf** command to verify that each router has all OSPFv2 routes in their respective routing tables.

b. If any OSPFv2 routes are missing, troubleshoot and resolve the problems.

Step 7. Verify IPv4 end-to-end connectivity.

From each router, ping all interfaces on other routers. If IPv4 end-to-end connectivity does not exist, then continue troubleshooting to resolve any remaining issues.

Part 4: Troubleshoot OSPFv3

Note: LAN (loopback) interfaces should not advertise OSPFv3 routing information, but routes to these networks should be contained in the routing tables.

Step 1. Test IPv6 end-to-end connectivity.

From each router, ping all interfaces on the other routers. Record your results as IPv6 connectivity problems do exist.

_____

_____

_____

_____

Step 2. Verify that IPv6 unicast routing has been enabled on all routers.

a. An easy way to verify that IPv6 routing has been enabled on a router is to use the **show run | section ipv6 unicast** command. By adding the pipe section to the **show run** command, the **ipv6 unicast-routing** command is displayed if IPv6 routing has been enabled.

b. If IPv6 unicast routing is not enabled on one or more routers, enable it now. If required, record the commands used to correct the configuration.

_____

_____

Step 3. Verify that all interfaces are assigned to the proper OSPFv3 areas on R1.

a. Issue the **show ipv6 protocols** command to verify that the router ID is correct and the expected interfaces display in their proper areas.

b. If required, make any necessary changes to the configuration on R1 based on the output from the **show ipv6 protocols** command. Record the commands used to correct the configuration. It may be necessary to reset OSPF process by issuing the **clear ipv6 ospf process** command.

_____

_____

_____

c. Re-issue the **show ipv6 protocols** command on R1 to make sure changes took effect.

d. Enter the **show ipv6 route ospf** command on R1 to verify that the interarea route summarization is configured correctly.

```
R1# show ipv6 route ospf
IPv6 Routing Table - default - 12 entries
Codes: C - Connected, L - Local, S - Static, U - Per-user Static route
       B - BGP, R - RIP, I1 - ISIS L1, I2 - ISIS L2
       IA - ISIS interarea, IS - ISIS summary, D - EIGRP, EX - EIGRP external
       ND - ND Default, NDp - ND Prefix, DCE - Destination, NDr - Redirect
       O - OSPF Intra, OI - OSPF Inter, OE1 - OSPF ext 1, OE2 - OSPF ext 2
       ON1 - OSPF NSSA ext 1, ON2 - OSPF NSSA ext 2
O   2001:DB8:ACAD::/61 [110/1]
     via Null0, directly connected
OI  2001:DB8:ACAD:4::/64 [110/129]
     via FE80::2, Serial0/0/0
OI  2001:DB8:ACAD:5::/64 [110/129]
     via FE80::2, Serial0/0/0
OI  2001:DB8:ACAD:23::/64 [110/128]
     via FE80::2, Serial0/0/0
```

e. Which IPv6 networks are included in the interarea route summarization shown in the routing table?

_____

_____

f. If required, make the necessary configuration changes on R1. Record the commands used to correct the configuration.

_____

_____

g. If required, re-issue the **show ipv6 route ospf** command on R1 to verify the changes.

```
R1# show ipv6 route ospf
IPv6 Routing Table - default - 11 entries
Codes: C - Connected, L - Local, S - Static, U - Per-user Static route
       B - BGP, R - RIP, I1 - ISIS L1, I2 - ISIS L2
       IA - ISIS interarea, IS - ISIS summary, D - EIGRP, EX - EIGRP external
       ND - ND Default, NDp - ND Prefix, DCE - Destination, NDr - Redirect
       O - OSPF Intra, OI - OSPF Inter, OE1 - OSPF ext 1, OE2 - OSPF ext 2
       ON1 - OSPF NSSA ext 1, ON2 - OSPF NSSA ext 2
O   2001:DB8:ACAD::/62 [110/1]
     via Null0, directly connected
```

```
OI  2001:DB8:ACAD:4::1/128 [110/128]
      via FE80::2, Serial0/0/0
OI  2001:DB8:ACAD:5::1/128 [110/128]
      via FE80::2, Serial0/0/0
OI  2001:DB8:ACAD:23::/64 [110/128]
      via FE80::2, Serial0/0/0
```

Step 4.   Verify that all interfaces are assigned to the proper OSPFv3 areas on R2.

    a.   Issue the **show ipv6 protocols** command and verify that the router ID is correct and that the expected interfaces are showing up under their proper areas.

    b.   If required, make any necessary changes to the configuration on R2 based on the output from the **show ipv6 protocols** command. Record the commands used to correct the configuration. It may be necessary to reset OSPF process by issuing the **clear ipv6 ospf process** command.

_____

_____

_____

    c.   Verify that the configuration change has the desired effect.

Step 5.   Verify that all interfaces are assigned to the proper OSPFv3 areas on R3.

    a.   Issue the **show ipv6 protocols** command to verify that the router ID is correct and the expected interfaces display under their respective areas.

    b.   If required, make any necessary changes to the configuration on R3 based on the output from the **show ipv6 protocols** command. Record the commands used to correct the configuration. It may be necessary to reset OSPF process by issuing the **clear ipv6 ospf process** command.

_____

_____

_____

    c.   Verify that the configuration changes have the desired effect.

Step 6.   Verify that all routers have correct neighbor adjacency information.

    a.   Issue the **show ipv6 ospf neighbor** command to verify that adjacencies have formed between neighboring routers.

Step 7.   Verify OSPFv3 routing information.

    a.   Issue the **show ipv6 route ospf** command, and verify that OSPFv3 routes exist to all networks.

    b.   Resolve any routing issues that still exist.

Step 8.   Verify IPv6 end-to-end connectivity.

From each router, ping all of the IPv6 interfaces on the other routers. If IPv6 end-to-end issues still exist, continue troubleshooting to resolve any remaining issues.

Reflection

Why not just use the **show running-config** command to resolve all issues?

Router Interface Summary Table

Router Interface Summary			
Router Model	Ethernet Interface #1	Ethernet Interface #2	Serial Interface #1	Serial Interface #2
1800	Fast Ethernet 0/0 (F0/0)	Fast Ethernet 0/1 (F0/1)	Serial 0/0/0 (S0/0/0)	Serial 0/0/1 (S0/0/1)
1900	Gigabit Ethernet 0/0 (G0/0)	Gigabit Ethernet 0/1 (G0/1)	Serial 0/0/0 (S0/0/0)	Serial 0/0/1 (S0/0/1)
2801	Fast Ethernet 0/0 (F0/0)	Fast Ethernet 0/1 (F0/1)	Serial 0/1/0 (S0/1/0)	Serial 0/1/1 (S0/1/1)
2811	Fast Ethernet 0/0 (F0/0)	Fast Ethernet 0/1 (F0/1)	Serial 0/0/0 (S0/0/0)	Serial 0/0/1 (S0/0/1)
2900	Gigabit Ethernet 0/0 (G0/0)	Gigabit Ethernet 0/1 (G0/1)	Serial 0/0/0 (S0/0/0)	Serial 0/0/1 (S0/0/1)

Note: To find out how the router is configured, look at the interfaces to identify the type of router and how many interfaces the router has. There is no way to effectively list all the combinations of configurations for each router class. This table includes identifiers for the possible combinations of Ethernet and Serial interfaces in the device. The table does not include any other type of interface, even though a specific router may contain one. An example of this might be an ISDN BRI interface. The string in parentheses is the legal abbreviation that can be used in Cisco IOS commands to represent the interface.

10.3.1.1 Class Activity–OSPF Troubleshooting Mastery

Objective

Explain the process and tools used to troubleshoot a single-area OSPF network.

Scenario

You have decided to change your routing protocol from RIPv2 to OSPFv2. Your small- to medium-sized business network topology will not change from its original physical settings. Use the diagram on the PDF for this activity as your company's small- to medium-sized business network design.

Your addressing design is complete and you then configure your routers with IPv4 and VLSM. OSPF has been applied as the routing protocol. However, some routers are sharing routing information with each other and some are not.

Open the PDF file that accompanies this modeling activity and follow the directions to complete the activity.

When the steps in the directions are complete, regroup as a class and compare recorded activity correction times. The group taking the shortest time to find and fix the configuration error will be declared the winner only after successfully explaining how they found the error, fixed it, and proved that the topology is now working.

Required Resources

- Topology diagram
- Packet Tracer software
- Timer

Topology Diagram

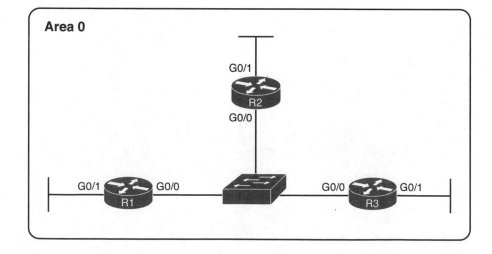

Directions

Choose a partner from the class with whom to work on this activity. Use Packet Tracer to create the topology diagram shown for this activity.

Step 1.   Build the topology based on the modeling activity page for this scenario.

Step 2.   Configure the routers.

    a.   Use IPv4 for all interfaces.

    b.   Incorporate VLSM into the addressing scheme.

    c.   Make one intentional configuration error.

    d.   Verify that the network does not work based upon the intentional error.

    e.   Save your file to be used with Step 3.

Step 3.   Exchange your Packet Tracer file with another group.

    a.   Find the configuration error on the Packet Tracer network file you received from another group.

    b.   Fix the OSPF configuration error so that the network operates fully.

    c.   Record the time it took to find and fix the OSPF network error.

    d.   When complete, meet with your class to determine the Master Troubleshooter for the day.

Packet Tracer
☐ Activity

10.3.1.2 Packet Tracer–Skills Integration Challenge

Topology

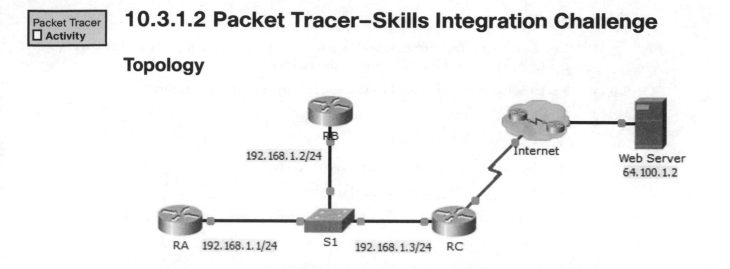

Addressing Table

Device	Interface	IP Address	Subnet Mask
RA	G0/0	192.168.1.1	255.255.255.0
RB	G0/0	192.168.1.2	255.255.255.0
RC	G0/0	192.168.1.3	255.255.255.0
	S0/0/0	209.165.200.225	255.255.255.252

Scenario

In this Skills Integration Challenge, your focus is OSPFv2 advanced configurations. IP addressing has been configured for all devices. You will configure OSPFv2 routing with passive interfaces and default route propagation. You will modify the OSPFv2 configuration by adjusting the OSPF timers. Finally, you will verify your configurations and test connectivity between end devices.

Requirements

- Use the following requirements to configure OSPFv2 routing on **RA** and **RB**:
    - OSPFv2 routing requirements:
        - Process ID 1
        - Network address for each interface
        - Enable authentication for area 0
    - OSPF priority set to 150 on the LAN interface of **RA**
    - OSPF priority set to 100 on the LAN interface of **RB**
    - Set the hello interval to 5
    - Set the dead interval to 20

- Use the following requirements to configure **RC** OSPFv2 routing:
    - OSPFv2 routing requirements:
        - Process ID 1
        - Network address for the LAN interface
        - Set all interfaces to passive by default, but allow OSPF updates on the active LAN interface
        - Set the router to distribute default routes
    - Configure a directly attached default route to the Internet
    - OSPF priority set to 50 on the LAN interface
    - Set the hello interval to 5
    - Set the dead interval to 20

Note: Issue the **clear ip ospf process** command on RC if the default route does not propagate.

- Verify your configurations and test connectivity
    - OSPF neighbors should be established and routing tables should be complete.
    - **RA** should be the DR, **RB** should be the BDR.
    - All three routers should be able to ping the Web Server.